The Early Church

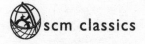

scm classics

The Early Church

From the beginnings to 461

W.H.C. FREND

scm press

A catalogue record for this book is available
from the British Library

978 0 334 02909 0

First published in 1965 by
Hodder and Stoughton
Second edition published in 1982 by
SCM Press
This new edition published in 2003 by
SCM Press
13-17 Long Lane London EC1A 9PN

Second impression 2008

SCM Press is a division of
SCM-Canterbury Press Ltd

Printed in Great Britain by
CPI Bookmarque, Croydon, CR0 4TD

Contents

Preface

This classic work has been in and out of print since it was first published in 1965. When it first appeared it provided for the first time a general, readable and yet scholarly introduction to the early Church in English. Since then it has been invaluable reading for anyone interested in this formative period of the Christian Church, whether student or scholar, lay or ordained.

Professor Frend, who has now devoted more than fifty years to the study of the early Church, has since become one of the foremost Church historians in the English speaking world and has published a series of important books on this period, drawing upon his practical experience and expertise as an archaeologist in field in North Africa, Egypt, Crete, Asia Minor and Britain, as well as his formidable learning and linguistic skills. Hence, any reader who is already familiar with Professor Frend's works will notice that many of the themes, movements and ideas which are presented for the first time in this book (and his earlier book, *The Donatist Church: A Movement of Protest in North Africa* (1952)) have subsequently been taken up and dealt with by him on a larger scale, most notably in his *Martyrdom and Persecution in the Early Church* (1965), *The Rise of the Monophysite Movement* (1972), *Religion Popular and Unpopular in the Early Christian Centuries* (1976), *Archaeology and History in the study of the Early Church* (1988), *The Archaeology of Early Christianity: A History* (1996) and his magisterial *The Rise of Christianity* (1984). The fourth volume of his collected works on the history of the early Church has just been published (2002). But as a concise, accessible, and thorough survey of the entire Patristic period, through to the Council of Chalcedon in 461, this early work remains invaluable.

In this book Professor Frend clearly delineates the geographical, historical, cultural and social context of the early Church as the setting in which the Christian faith emerged and developed to ultimately become the official religion of the Roman Empire. The vicissitudes of the Church as it emerged from Judaism as a distinct sect, its endurance of persecution and conflict, its battle to define and defend its faith, its organization and self-understanding and, in particular, its dogmatic formulation of its beliefs in creeds and councils, are covered with masterly insight and precision.

Professor Frend's approach is distinctive for its real inter-disciplinarity and practical awareness of the contribution of archaeological research and discoveries. The fathers and teachers of the Church – both orthodox and heretical – emerge as real individuals whose identity and thought were defined by the particularities of time, place and circumstance. The resulting picture is a much subtler one than simply a battle of truth against falsehood, but rather appears as the conflict between different traditions and practices. All of the main figures are given a sympathetic hearing and are presented to the reader refreshingly free of hagiography, 'warts and all' (an approach furthered in his subsequent work on *Saints and Sinners in the Early Church* (1985).

Professor Frend also offers the reader a tremendous historical overview of the vast Roman Empire in which the Church evolved. The main sees emerge with all their distinctive characteristics and interests, and the somewhat chequered history of their inter-relations and conflicts is deftly interwoven into the complicated tapestry of the Church's organization and definition of doctrine. Similarly, the perennially ambiguous relations between the Church and secular society, or the Church and 'state', are carefully drawn to the reader's attention, and the uneasy balance between the two made clear.

The study of the early Church has seen a tremendous international revival of interest in the period since this book was first written, and a number of important new discoveries have been made. Professor Frend takes account of these in the useful bibliographies which provide further reading at the end of each chapter and in the extensive notes which accompany the text. His frequent recourse to primary texts, however, make this book a timeless work which scarcely needs such updating. It can stand alone as a work which has shaped the understanding and work of historians of the Church for more than half a century, and, thanks to this new and timely edition, will continue to do so well into the third millennium.

Dr Carol Harrison
Lecturer in the History and Theology of the Latin West
University of Durham
November 2002

Preface by the Author

This book was first published in 1965, and was based on lectures which I gave in Cambridge to students preparing for the Cambridge Certificate of Theology. It was intended primarily as a historical study tracing the rise and development of the Christian Church within the framework of Greco-Roman society down to the period of the Council of Chalcedon in 451 and the pontificate of Pope Leo, 440–461. By this time, the Church's triumph throughout the Roman Empire, with the notable exception of Britain, was complete, and the structure of its doctrine and organization enshrined in four ecumenical councils.

Since 1965 two main developments have taken place. First, an enormous amount of new material relating to the early Church has been discovered. The continuous discovery of early Christian basilicas and other remains have confirmed evidence from literary sources that Christianity had become the predominant religion of the Empire by around 400. The work of the archaeologists has been supported by patristic scholars. The discovery by the Austrian researcher, Johannes Dinjak, of a hitherto unknown group of thirty letters and memoranda, twenty-seven written by Augustine of Hippo himself, has been a major event. Further light has been thrown on the early life of the Persian religious reformer, Mani (Manichaeans), by the decipherment of a minute papyrus in the Cologne collection.

The new Manichaean document points to the second development, namely the expansion of knowledge about the non-orthodox Christian movement. Discoveries now available to students include the publication in English of fifty-two treatises and fragments of the Gnostic Library from Nag-Hammadi in Upper Egypt, by Professor James M. Robinson and his colleagues (*The Nag-Hammadi Library in English*, Harper and Row 1977). In addition, the publication of many of the discoveries, including frescos and manuscripts found during the 'Save Nubia' international archaeological project to salvage as much as possible of Nubian remains in the Nile valley before their destruction by the rising waters of Lake Nasser behind the High Dam at Aswan, have demonstrated the vigour and religious and artistic achievement of the Nubian Monophysite Church. These and other similar discoveries have enabled students to study the relations between orthodox and non-orthodox movements within early Christianity from new angles. These early heresies condemned by the Church can now speak for themselves.

These new perceptions have already been affecting scholarly approaches to some of the more familiar problems in Church history. The Arian controversy, spanning the period between 318 and 381, has undergone a considerable revision through R. P. C. Hanson's magisterial work *The Search for the Christian Doctrine of God*, T.&T.Clark 1988, in which it has been shown that during the fourth century nearly all involved in the dispute were fumbling towards the solution that eventually emerged with the Council and Creed of Constantinople in 381. Athanasius *contra mundum*, against the world, was mainly due to his disciplinary failings rather than his unswerving stand in support of a previously accepted orthodoxy.

Another explosion of research resulted from the spate of international conferences held in 1986–87 to mark the 1300th anniversary of the return to Catholic orthodoxy of Augustine of Hippo. One of the main lines of research that emerged from the enormous quantity of material discussed was a reappraisal of Augustine's ideas in the period 384–386, when he was at Milan with a political career in mind prior to his conversion to orthodoxy in August 386.

Finally, to Roman Britain. The last thirty years have intensified study of the traces of Christianity in Roman Britain and raised anew the question why alone among the western provinces of the Empire, Christianity failed to weather the onset of the Germanic invaders and had to be replanted by St Augustine of Canterbury in 597. Numerous individual finds have been made, the most important being the hoard of Communion silver (?) discovered at Water Newton in Northants in 1975. Evidence suggests that the Church was making steady progress at least until the death of Constantius in 361, but then faltered. The reason awaits the results of further research, though the combination of barbarian invasion and local revolt in 367–69 may have contributed to the destruction of Christian communities at a crucial time of their development.

Little of this will appear in the pages of this book, which I have decided to leave unaltered (except for the correction of mistakes). I have, however, recast and updated the bibliographies at the end of each chapter to include these discoveries, removing work now superseded, and introducing readers to work most accessible to them down to 1990.

I take this opportunity to thank Fortress Press for republishing the book in the United States in 1981 and SCM Press for putting it once more into the hands of English-speaking readers.

W. H. C. Frend
Little Wilbraham, Cambridge
June 1991

Abbreviations

C.I.L.	*Corpus Inscriptionum Latinarum.*
C.S.E.L.	*Corpus Scriptorum ecclesiasticorum latinorum,* Vienna, 1866–
G.C.S.	*Griechische christliche Schriftsteller der ersten drei Jahrhunderten.* Leipzig, 1897–1940; Berlin, 1947–
J.E.H.	*Journal of Ecclesiastical History,* 1950–
J.T.S.	*Journal of Theological Studies,* 1900–
O.G.I.	*Orientis Graecae inscriptiones selectae,* ed. W. Dittenberger Leipzig, 1903.
P.G.	Migne, *Patrologia Greco–Latina.*
P.L.	Migne, *Patrologia Latina.*

Introduction

In Judea, "under Tiberius all quiet."[1] Thus Tacitus, writing about the period of the Crucifixion. Both he and his contemporary Suetonius refer to minor matters, the remission of taxes, the growth of ill-feeling between Jews and Samaritans, and suchlike, but of the events that have made the governorship of Pontius Pilate forever memorable, not one word.

This is the first problem confronting the historian of the early Church. The emergence of the Christian mission took place wholly within the framework of Palestinian Judaism, and though through the Dead Sea Scrolls and the writings of Josephus, we are now relatively well informed about conditions in Palestine in this period, we still lack contemporary views of Christianity other than those provided in the Pauline Epistles, and the traditions that lie behind the Gospels and Acts. The impact of Christianity on the Jewish and Greco–Roman worlds is still not easy to establish.

The change, too, in historical perspectives requires a look beyond the range of Christian orthodoxies. Christianity was a cultural movement as well as a religion. Marcion, Valentinus, or Paul of Samosata were "heretics," but they also represented strong currents of thought in their contemporary society. From the outset also, the Church contained within its own bounds the often contradictory movements prevalent in the Jewish world of the day. It is difficult to point to any time after the Ascension when it was truly one. Differences between Palestinian Christianity and the Christianity of the Greek-speaking proselytes of the Jewish Dispersion were succeeded by contrasting emphases and interpretations of the faith in the Greek and Latin halves of the Roman Empire. After the triumph of Christianity in the fourth century, cultural, social and political influences played their part in hardening intellectual differences. It will be no longer adequate to label the African Donatists "schismatics" and the Egyptian Monophysites "heretics" without further ado. Conflicts over

1

orthodoxy have rarely been simple conflicts over truth and error. Both now and then they have in part been the outcome of clashes of cultures, themselves represented by deep-rooted territorial or social traditions. All this, as well as the story of the great leaders of the Church and their ideas, and the development of Christian life and doctrine, is the task of the historian of the early Church to uncover. If by so doing he can further the cause of human understanding, he is thankful for that too.

PART ONE

1

Rome and the Mediterranean World

Even today the observant traveler in the Mediterranean will find much to remind him of the Greco-Roman past. Whether it is the tradition of the beast-combats and gladiatorial shows of the arena preserved in the bullfights of the Spanish peninsula, whether the survival of Romano-African building technique in the tiled penthouse roofs of the Kabyle homestead, whether the wooden plows and burnooses of the North African peasant, the terraced cultivation of the vine, the ubiquitous olive and, above all, the donkey, there is a living past unchanged since the days of Augustus. The ruins of great cities like Timgad, Leptis Magna and Baalbek speak of an urban life which once had been, but the life of the countryside has remained as it was 2,000 years ago.

It is against the background of the Mediterranean world that we start this brief survey of early Christian history. How did the Church gradually conquer this world, until by the mid fourth century it had become a great popular movement expressing the hopes of earthly prosperity and future salvation of townsman and peasant alike? What were the ideas that inspired this movement? How were they expressed in organization, liturgy and creed? Who were its leaders, and what did they represent? Why did unity, at least in the sense of uniformity, elude the Christian congregation from the very moment that its Lord ascended into the heavens?

The year is 27 B.C., the date which may be taken to mark the transition from Roman Republic to Roman Empire. Roman power had reached its "natural frontiers," the Rhine, the Danube, the Euphrates and the Sahara Desert. What was added by the Empire, namely Britain, Dacia, Arabia and Mauretania, were buttresses to protect what had already been won. Octavian's victory over Mark Antony at Actium in 31 B.C. had been hailed alike in Italy, Asia Minor and even, after the death of Cleopatra, in Egypt as the beginning of a new era. Order would now reign where

4

chaos had prevailed. In the eastern provinces, the victor was proclaimed "bringer of good news" (*evangelion*), "savior," and "manifestation of Zeus." Within a few years temples were being erected in his honor in the provincial capitals, and the calendar of Asia (western Asia Minor) revised so as to begin the year with the birthday "of the god and savior of the whole human race."[1]

In Rome the sequence of events was no less momentous for being clothed in constitutional forms. On 11 January 27 B.C. Octavian had closed the doors of the temple of Janus to mark the return of peace—for the first time in 200 years. Five days later the Senate bestowed on its hero the title of Augustus. The text of the great inscription at the entrance of the temple of Augustus at Ancyra (Ankara), which expresses the ideas of the Emperor's immediate circle, reads:

> In my sixth and seventh consulships (28–7 B.C.), when I had extinguished the fires of civil war after receiving by common consent absolute control of affairs, I handed the commonwealth over from my own control to the free disposal of the Senate and the people of Rome. For this service done by me I received the title of Augustus by decree of the Senate, and the doorposts of my house were officially covered with laurels; a civic crown was put up over my door, and a golden shield was placed in the new Senate-house [built by Julius Caesar]. with an inscription recording that it was a gift to me from the Senate and people of Rome in recognition of my valour, my clemency, my justice, and my fulfilment of duty (*pietas*). After that time I took precedence of others in dignity, but I enjoyed no greater power than those who were my colleagues in any magistracy (tr. Ernest Barker, *From Alexander to Constantine*, p. 229).

In theory, Octavian was only the chief citizen of the Republic; in practice, he was its absolute ruler. First, the term Augustus. Contemporaries, poets such as Ovid, pointed out its connection with the sacred language of worship.[2] Two centuries later, the romanized Bithynian civil servant, Dio Cassius, recorded how the title implied that its bearer was somewhat more than mortal.[3] The appearance of the bay leaves of Apollo on Augustus's head on his coinage suggests that the Emperor believed himself to be under Apollo's special protection. This "special relationship" with the world of the gods was symbolized alike for Roman citizen and subject provincial in the cult of the Emperor's "genius." In veiled form it was the worship of the Emperor himself, for the genius was more than "guardian spirit." It had something in the nature of essence, the energizing and life-giving force of a personality, in this case the divine power assuring the permanence of the imperial house.[4] In the provinces the "genius of Caesar" was a common form of oath in commercial and personal transactions, and to refuse it could be interpreted as disloyalty.

The inscription does not refer to some of the more material props to the Emperor's power. These included command over some thirty legions stationed on the frontiers or in provinces where disturbance was likely. Governors, such as Pontius Pilate, procurator of Judea from A.D. 27 to 36, were his agents subject to his appointment and recall. There were also the imperial freedmen who made up the lower and middle ranks of a considerable civil service, "they of Caesar's household" (Phil. 4:22). There was, finally, the Emperor's personal inviolability through the perpetuation of his power as tribune. He was the center of the system to whom all looked for security and good government, and, as one of the Augustan inscriptions found at Cyrene shows, the Emperor made it plain "to all who inhabit the provinces how much I and the Senate take care that none of our subjects suffer wrong or extortion."[5] The imperial *providentia* watched over the interests of all.

The system brought immense benefits to the inhabitants of the Mediterranean world. Apart from local though severe wars such as the Jewish war of 66–73, the provinces away from the frontiers enjoyed almost unbroken peace between 30 B.C. and A.D. 193, and then from 197 to the death of Alexander Severus in 235. A public orator, Aelius Aristides of Smyrna, could address Antoninus Pius in circa 150, "Wars have so far vanished as to be regarded as legendary events of the past. A man can travel from one country to another as though it were his native land . . . to be a Roman citizen, nay even one of your subjects is sufficient guarantee of personal safety."[6] Thirty years later, Irenaeus, Bishop of Lyons, no friendly critic of the existing world, wrote, "The world has peace thanks to the Romans. Even the Christians can walk without fear on the roads and travel whithersoever they please."[7]

Peace, ease of communications and trade went together. Flavius Zeuxis had to face nothing worse than the storms off Cape Malea on his seventy-two business trips from Hierapolis to Phrygia to Rome. There were Greek-speaking trading colonies in Lyons and Vienne, and at Salona, which were eventually to play a part in bringing Christianity to their fellow provincials.[8] There was trade in pottery, glass and grain between Gaul, the Rhineland and Britain. St. Paul's journeys across what even today is among the roughest country in Asia Minor, including the Taurus passes and the high plateau of Phrygia, show what was possible in the first century A.D. "Perils of robbers" did not deter him from planning voyages to Spain and Illyria; and there were other missionaries almost as adventurous, such as Epaphras who evangelized the towns on the headwaters of the Maeander, and the disciples of John who must have been Palestinians by origin settled in Ephesus. The catalog of peoples and tongues at Pentecost shows something of the cosmopolitan character of the Jerusalem pilgrimages. Whether St. Thomas ever reached south India or not, Roman merchants did.[9]

Language and ideas followed trade. The native languages did not die out. Phrygian, Berber and Celtic continued to be spoken, but one effect of the unification of the Mediterranean under Augustus and his successors was the emergence of two common languages, Latin in the West, and Greek in the East. The language boundary, crossing the Balkans between Skopje and Sofia and the Mediterranean between Malta and Crete, was to be of tremendous significance for the evangelization of the provincials and the development of Christian doctrine and practice.

Provincial administration enhanced the unifying factors within the Empire. In all the provinces there were some cities which possessed full Roman franchise, the *coloniae*, settled originally by Roman citizens, such as retired veterans, and other towns, the *municipia* where citizenship had been conferred on a native community. But below these, the *civitates*, tribal or cantonal capitals, could aspire to rise to the higher status, and members of local native aristocracies could and did acquire Roman citizenship. By the end of the first century, the Emperor was a Spaniard (Trajan) and his best generals an Anatolian (C. Julius Quadratus Bassus) and a Moor (Lusius Quietus). Add to this a uniform system of justice which, while respecting local customs, applied the principles of Roman law, an appellate system which enabled a citizen to take his case to the Emperor himself, and a common currency, and one can visualize a community of life and interest such as the Mediterranean peoples have not enjoyed before or since. Moreover, the prosperity seeped down into the remotest frontier area, giving the peoples of the Roman world wealth and ease of life which was not to be theirs again before the close of the fifteenth century.[10]

There was, however, a price to pay. Despite prevailing security and relative prosperity, the first two centuries A.D. were not among the great progressive ages of humanity, ages in which new technical advances produce new patterns of life. One looks in vain for the development of a scientific outlook or even for the application of what had already been discovered for productive use. There was seemingly no advance in the techniques of agriculture and seafaring. Despite considerable literary output and readership no one thought of the printing press. Despite large and assured markets no serious improvement in spinning and weaving techniques took place, and despite the discovery of the use of steam in Alexandria circa 40 B.C., Hero did not anticipate James Watt. Even Pliny the Elder, one of the very few men in the ancient world who lost his life through a scientific interest in natural phenomena,[11] produced few original ideas of his own. His *Natural History* in thirty books, written circa A.D. 75, was mainly a vast handbook of existing knowledge. With Ptolemy (circa 150) the current idea that the earth was the center of the universe and that the sun and stars revolved around it became received doctrine, with serious results for the development of religion and science in Europe for the next fifteen hundred years.

Ignorance of the physical nature of man and the universe led directly to astrological and metaphysical speculations which colored the religious thought of the time. All classes and, it would appear, all parts of the Mediterranean shared these speculations. The familiar words of St. Paul to his Galatian converts, "How turn ye back to the weak and beggarly rudiments whereunto ye desire to be in bondage again?" (Gal. 4:9), provide an interesting example. The key word is "rudiments," Greek *stoicheia*, meaning demonic beings or forces in the universe to whom Paul believed men and women had been enslaved before their conversion. Equally significant are the words used by Seneca to his friend Marcia in A.D. 60 when in a message of comfort to her after the death of her child, he portrays the journey of the soul through the stars. "You will see," he says, "the five planets pursuing their different courses and sparkling down to earth from opposite directions. On even the slightest motion of these hang the fortunes of nations and the greatest and smallest events are shaped to accord with the progress of a kindly or unkindly star."[12] Horoscopes were avidly compiled and interpreted. The most important deity to the ordinary mortal was not Zeus but Chance (Tyche) or Fate. This was the power who ended life, and from whose thralldom salvation must be sought.

An unprogressive society ruled by impersonal forces whose nature was not understood might also have been morally degenerate. This was not the case. Innumerable grave memorials testify to the affection of family life, as do surviving papyrus letters to its decency and sobriety. But there was also gross impurity unrestrained by effective censorship. Some of the wall paintings and objects from Pompeii or the motifs of lamps from the legionary fortress of Vindonissa on the Danube leave no doubt as to the existence of this aspect of life. "Gather ye rosebuds while ye may" or "Let us eat and drink for tomorrow we die" were not merely Christian and Jewish satire.[13] But the cheery hedonism that inspired many of the grave memorials[14] had its darker side. There was heartlessness too, shown in the exposure of unwanted children and gross exploitation of the underprivileged, the slaves, the conquered peoples who formed the bulk of the peasant population and the urban poor. The life also of an

8

intelligent woman must have been only a degree less boring and frustrating than that of the harem. It is not surprising that Christian apologists wrote of their Faith "changing men's tyrannical dispositions,"[15] and reforming their morals, or of women and slaves hearing the liberating message both of Judaism and Christianity gladly.

How did the cults and philosophies of the ancient world meet the needs of its inhabitants? Let us consider religion under two headings, social and personal. The social aspect was designed to ensure the existing world order, and in particular the eternity and prosperity of the Roman people. The fear of chaos if the Roman Empire fell was shared even by the Jews[16] and Christians.[17] So the Roman public religion was not a creed to which one subscribed so much as a series of cult acts performed by professionals, the priests, designed to win a right relationship between the gods and men. On the resultant *pax deorum* depended the welfare of the State and its inhabitants. The Emperor by his example of *pietas* and *virtus* promoted the safety of his subjects, and acted as intermediary between them and the gods. Roman citizens were expected to revere and serve the Roman gods and not to practice any alien cult. Customarily, however, they might do so as long as the cult did not offend the laws and usages of Roman life, i.e., outrage to the gods through political or social crimes.

Two examples, either side of the beginning of the Christian era, show the store set on conformity to the State cults. First, Polybius, the pro-Roman Greek historian of the Republic writing circa 150 B.C. "But the quality in which the Roman commonwealth is most distinctly superior (over the Greeks) is in my opinion the nature of their religious convictions. I believe that it is the very thing which among other peoples is an object of reproach, I mean superstition, which maintains the cohesion of the Roman State."[18] Secondly, Celsus the pagan apologist writing about A.D. 178 based his final appeal to the Christians to return to the faiths of their ancestors in order to save the Empire from destruction, and as a token of loyalty to the Emperor himself. "Even if someone tells you to take an oath by an emperor among men, that also is nothing dreadful. For earthly things have been given to him, and whatever you receive in life you receive from him."[19] A generation later, in 212, the Emperor Caracalla conferred Roman citizenship on nearly all the free inhabitants of the Roman world with the object as the preamble of the edict stressed, "that the Roman gods shall rejoice in the grateful sacrifice from the multitude of new citizens."[20] Common worship of the gods was both the symbol and the proof of a united Empire. In the provinces any town of importance would have its own capitol modeled on that of Rome and dedicated to the Roman gods, Jupiter, Juno and Minerva. The Christian refusal even to recognize these deities as protectors of the communities in which they dwelt was a standing provocation to the authorities and the ordinary provincials alike.

Roman religion was therefore more a national cult than a personal religion. It concerned the "general order of the State." Intrinsically, when analyzed, it still remained the outlook of a people in an early stage of development, the gods of light, of battle, and of agriculture reflecting the experiences of centuries before the establishment of the Empire. Not even Augustus's restoration of temples and Varro's encyclopedic work of investigation and definition of the roles of the various ancient deities could make Roman animism and pantheism a personal religion. For that, the individual had to turn to the philosophies of the day and above all to the mystery religions.

At Athens Paul encountered Stoics and Epicureans. Of the latter little need be said. Epicurus of Samos (432–370 B.C.) believed that the root of all evil was fear, above all fear of death and the beyond. The gods, he thought, had little if any concern in the lives of men. Death was merely long, untroubled sleep. Take away, therefore, fear of death by suggesting that there was no immortal soul to survive, and what prevented the enjoyment of happiness? This meant to Epicurus above all friendship and just dealing. "Live quietly." Pain could be endured. Ultimately chance ruled everything. The universe was composed of atoms whose random encounters produced life. It was a machine, neutral between right and wrong, without caprice or malevolence. To some Romans this negative view of the universe and man's role in it was attractive. Horace and Lucretius each found the gospel of Epicurus a justification and a relief, but not many followed them. In the provinces some educated men were Epicureans. As late as circa A.D. 200, one of the longest and most elaborate funerary inscriptions, that of Diogenes of Oenoanda in Asia Minor, included the creed "There is nothing to fear in God. There is nothing to feel in death. Evil can be endured, Good can be achieved"— the quintessence of the Epicurean faith.

The Stoics had far greater influence. Theirs became the outlook of the educated provincial in the West in the first two centuries A.D. They played some part in shaping both Jewish and Christian ethics, and they could number among their following the great names of Seneca, Epictetus, Marcus Aurelius and perhaps one might add, Pelagius. Zeno of Cittium in Cyprus (fourth century B.C.) taught that virtue consisted in living according to reason, for the reason within each human being was a part of the divine reason, the fire which underlay all life. The universe was an harmonious whole, not a collection of atoms. "Either an ordered universe," mused Marcus Aurelius, "or a welter of confusion. Assuredly then, a world order. Recall to your mind the alternatives, a foreseeing Providence or blind atoms—and all the abounding proofs that the world is one city."[21] Man could be at home in the universe, for whether he were emperor, soldier, or slave he partook of the same creative power that guided it. He was a tiny fragment of the seminal word or universal reason. To Marcus Aurelius all situations were alike. All were aspects of the divine harmony into which the individual must fit himself. "Whatever is expedient to thee, O World, is expedient to me."[22] "Alexander and his groom were alike. Both passed and perished."[23] "Asia and Europe are but corners of creation; the ocean is but a drop and Athos but a grain in respect of the universe, the whole present but a point in eternity. All is petty, mutable, and transient."[24]

With the sense of grandeur went a sense of resignation. Events moved forward on a predetermined course which no human agency could alter. It gave no hope of immortality beyond the memory of one's virtuous deeds. It was a creed of earthly duty, but not an answer for the religious mind. The criticism made by Justin Martyr circa A.D. 130 was apt. "I put myself," he wrote, "in the hands of a Stoic, and I stayed with him a long time, but when I got no further in the matter of God, for he did not know himself and he used to say that such knowledge was not necessary, I left him."[25]

Justin went on to Platonism before turning finally to Christianity, and in the East, Platonism or its popular derivatives provided the intellectual alternative to fatalism. Plato (429–347 B.C.) had believed that knowledge of the universe was possible, but not through means so variable and unreliable as the human senses. Beyond the visible world existed a transcendent world of forms and ideas which could be apprehended by the mind alone. In other words the human mind was capable of forming a synthesis from the confused mass of impressions which rained in on it through the senses. But Plato went on to assert that justice, beauty, truth, goodness, etc., were not the results of thoughts and actions but had an objective existence in themselves to which the human soul must ultimately conform. Crowning the whole system was the ideal good on which converged all other aspects of reality like the apex of a pyramid. The transition to a theology of God and a creation moved and guided by his providence was easy, and Plato provided also a system for the individual to apply to himself. Man's task was conformity so far as possible with ideal justice and goodness. Through apprehension of the real forms, preexisting and continuing to eternity, a man could distinguish the

11

demands of a debased and transitory life on earth from a real existence beyond which his soul would ultimately enjoy. On earth he must master the irrational element within himself by ascetic practices and thought. He must purify his being and prepare for the soul's liberation. The body was a prison, the mere envelope for the soul. This alone would ascend to reality. These views, ultimately optimistic in their view of human nature, gave hope to many of the provincials of the Greek-speaking world. They provided an antidote to Iranian demonology by their assertion of monotheism and call to philosophic asceticism. They were to have a profound effect on the theology of the Christians in Alexandria.

The philosophies, even in their popular form, were for the few. More people, including many women, looked to the mystery cults for comfort and salvation. Of these, Isis-worship, Orphism, Mithraism, the Bacchics and Pythagoreans were among the most important. The hold which they exercised on their worshipers may be illustrated by a description of Juvenal (circa A.D. 120) of a pious adherent of the cult of Isis. "Three times in the depths of winter the devotee of Isis will dive into the chilly waters of the Tiber, and shivering with cold will drag herself around the temple with bleeding knees; if the goddess commands, she will go to the bounds of Egypt and take water from the Nile and empty it within the sanctuary" (*Satires*, vi, 523 ff.). It was no exaggeration. The story of Lucius in Apuleius' *The Golden Ass* is a tale also of sacrifice and obedience to the goddess who was known as Queen of Heaven.

The mystery cults were all refinements of age-old legends of growth and rebirth shown in the seasons, to which influences from Babylonian religion and Hinduism had been added. In the majority a mother goddess was worshiped with a male deity who was either her consort or her son. He represented the power of vegetation dying in the autumn to be reborn in the following spring. So too, humanity, the victim of the powers of chaos and negation, would rise triumphant through knowledge of and identification with the god. By initiation into these systems the individual gained that identification: he was no longer "a stranger and afraid in a world I never made," but a participant in immortality. "I conquer fate and fate obeys me," read Plutarch's *Praises of Isis and Osiris*. Lucius describes how, on his initiation into the rites of Isis, he "trod Proserpina's threshold. I passed through all the elements and returned. It was midnight, but I saw the sun radiant with bright light. I came into the very presence of the gods below and the gods above, and I adored them face to face."[26] He was saved. He could fathom the secrets of the universe. He was no longer afraid.

These cults spread all over the Mediterranean world, brought by soldiers and travelers and above all accompanying the great waves of Eastern immigrants that invaded the city of Rome from the mid second century B.C. onward. These immigrants confronted the Roman authorities with the major problem of working out a tolerable relationship between the official religion and the cults. Roman religion though nationalistic was not inhospitable to other religions, and, moreover, recognized the right of subject and allied peoples to their own worship. Throughout Roman Republican history there had been a tendency to expand the pantheon. Juno and Mars had originally been the gods of Italic tribes, and Cybele was introduced during the final crisis of the Punic war in 204. The problem was at what stage did "foreign worship" become "evil worship" (*prava religio*) abominable to the Roman gods? For instance, in the Celtic provinces of northwestern Europe it was possible to find Roman equivalents for the Celtic gods Teutates and Tanaris, but what about rites involving human sacrifice practiced by their priests, the Druids? In Rome the cult of Dionysus could in itself be beneficial to the community, but when the worship degenerated into conspiratorial orgy it must be repressed.

One finds the authorities working pragmatically from case to case. If the foreign deities appeared to threaten the prestige of the Roman gods they would be suppressed; if their rites gave rise to scandal their adherents would be punished. If Roman citizens participated in foreign religion to the point which offended either of these canons they also could expect sanctions. This policy was illustrated by the case of the Bacchanals. Though the affair arose in 186 B.C. it was described in detail by Livy in the reign of Augustus.[27] The worship had been introduced into Rome from the Greek cities of south Italy, and had become immensely popular. Then scandals began. There were rumours of people being poisoned and done to death in the rites, and of a conspiracy to fire the city. The Senate acted, and Livy put these words into the mouth of the consul Postumius: "For there is nothing more deceptive in appearance than false religion. Where the power of the gods is put forward as a pretext for crimes fear takes hold of the mind lest in punishing human deceits we may be violating something of the divine law which had been mingled with them. For men who were wisest in divine and human law judged that nothing was more dissolvent to religion than where sacrifice was made to foreign rather than to native deities."[28]

The passage sums up the difficulties the authorities faced. However much they might suspect the mystery cults as insulting to the gods of Rome and a cloak perhaps for black magic and conspiracy against the State, they were reluctant to go to extremes. Individuals would be punished with the utmost harshness, as were the Bacchanals, and practices put under strict supervision, but the worship itself was not proscribed. The worshipers of Isis and purveyors of horoscopes and unlicensed auguries would be similarly dealt with, experiencing in the century either side of the Christian era a bewildering succession of persecution, unofficial tolerance and official favor. Despite all the bans and temporary proscriptions Isis, the Bacchae and the rest reestablished themselves in Rome. The Christians in the time of Nero were another "foreign cult." Their association with Judaism, however, was a vital factor in shaping Roman policy toward them, for the Jews in the first century A.D. were among the most difficult of the legacies which Rome inherited from her conquest of the Hellenistic world.

FURTHER READING

Altheim, F., *A History of Roman Religion*, Methuen 1939

Barker, Sir E., *From Alexander to Constantine*, Oxford University Press 1956

Charlesworth, M.P., *The Roman Empire*, Oxford University Press 1951

Ferguson, J., *The Religion of the Roman Empire*, Thames and Hudson 1970

Fox, R.Lane, *Pagans and Christians*, Viking 1986

Glover, T.R., *The Conflict of Religions in the Early Roman Empire*, Cambridge University Press 1929

Macmullen, Ramsay, *Roman Social Relations 50 BC - AD 284*, Yale University Press 1974

Macmullen, Ramsay, *Paganism in the Roman Empire*, Yale University Press 1981

Millar, F.G.B., *The Roman Empire and its Neighbours*, Duckworth 1981

Nock, A.D., *Conversion*, Oxford University Press 1933

Syme, R., *The Roman Revolution.*, Oxford University Press 1939

Taylor, L.R., *The Divinity of the Roman Emperor*, American Philological Association 1931, reissued Garland, New York 1979

Witt, R.E., *Isis in the Graeco-Roman World*, Thames and Hudson 1971

2

Rome and
First-Century Judaism

In the Jews the Romans encountered a people with the strongest national sentiment, who had adherents and sympathizers throughout the Empire, and who believed that their religion was destined to be the religion of mankind. The successive exiles and returns had divided Judaism into three main groups: those who remained beyond the Euphrates, in Babylon and elsewhere and were now subjects of the Parthian rulers; those who returned to Palestine; and those, probably the most numerous of all, who lived as traders, professional men, and artisans in most of the larger towns of the Greco-Roman world, and in some provinces in the East formed a part of the rural population as well.

The Babylonian group of Jews only affect the situation indirectly. Their existence, however, guaranteed the maintenance of pro-Parthian sentiment among the Jews as a whole. Persia had exercised a strong influence on the religion of Israel, particularly in the development of the hope of bodily resurrection, the form of the Last Judgment, and an understanding of world history in terms of apocalyptic. Moreover, as a glance at Ezra and Nehemiah shows, the Persian rulers were regarded as Israel's benefactors. This favor was not forgotten, and when Rome was involved in war with the Parthian rulers who were the heirs to the former Persian Empire, Jewish sympathies tended to lie with them. The statement attributed to the Rabbi Simeon ben Yohai in the second century A.D.: "If you see the horse of a Persian tied to a post in the land of Israel, expect the footsteps of the Messiah,"[1] sums up these hopes of earthly deliverance at the hands of Persian military power.

Indeed, the Jews in Palestine confronted Rome with the most difficult of political and military problems. The Law of Moses had envisaged a community free from all contaminating influences of neighboring non-Jewish tribes and dedicated to the service of Yahweh. The long history of Israel as preserved in the priestly tradition enshrined in the Old

15

Testament told of the struggle often against overwhelming odds of the Jewish people to live up to this ideal. Since the conquests of Alexander the Great, however, the Jews who had returned to Palestine after the Exile found themselves faced not only by local heathen tribes but by the progressive and all-pervading influence of Hellenism. Quite apart from the Greek cities established within the traditional frontiers of Israel, such as Gadara, Sepphoris, Gerasa (Jerash) or Tiberias, Greek institutions and way of life exercised a considerable attraction for members of the wealthier Jewish families in Jerusalem. As early as 300 B.C. an observer and traveler in Palestine could remark that "the Jews had greatly altered the ordinances of their forefathers" as the result of their contact with Greek civilization.[2]

As on previous occasions, however, when the traditional Jewish way of life appeared to be threatened, a strong movement of opposition arose. The ill-conceived effort of Antiochus IV, the Seleucid ruler of Syria, to absorb Israel into a single uniform Hellenistic State, to downgrade Yahweh into a local Baal, and to forbid the practice of the Law of Moses produced violent opposition. The Maccabean Wars (167–42 B.C.) were in part civil wars, in part wars of liberation, and they ended with the independence of Judea under their own Hasmonaean dynasty. With all their cruelty, corruption and violence, the rulers of the new Jewish State were determined that it should be free from idolatrous influences. To the Aramaic-speaking Palestinian Jew, Greek thought existed only to be controverted, and the Greek language, apart from the Jerusalem schools, was confined to the city territories of the Greek settlers.

Meantime, Rome had come into contact with the Jews as an ally against the reviving power of the Seleucids. In 161 B.C. Judas Maccabaeus had sent an embassy to Rome to form an alliance and this had been accepted.[3] Even though nearly a century later in 63 B.C. Pompey had conquered Palestine and captured Jerusalem, the Jews continued to be treated as an allied nation, free therefore to live by their own religion and laws. Rome continued to ride Israel with a light rein. For the time being the high priests at Jerusalem were treated as an autonomous power, and in 46 B.C. Julius Caesar concluded a further treaty of alliance with John Hyrcanus which assured Judaism complete religious freedom in Palestine and valuable privileges in the Dispersion. Under Herod "the Great" Rome found another reliable friend, who, however much he may have been hated by his own people, kept Judea loyal to Augustus. When he died, 12 March 4 B.C., his kingdom was divided between his three sons. Of these Philip and Antipas kept their territories, but in A.D. 6 aften ten years of cruelty and tyranny the third, Archelaus, was deprived of his and banished to Vienne in Gaul. Only then did Augustus decide to place Judea under the direct rule of a procurator. Between A.D. 27 and 36 the procurator of Judea was Pontius Pilate.

However discreet the Roman "presence" may have been, it was bound to arouse the same intense emotions among the religious-minded and patriotic Jews as the Seleucid government had done before it. The Jewish Sanhedrin was left in charge of local administration and remained the supreme court regarding matters of Jewish law. The death penalty, however, it could not impose. A copper coinage was minted locally without the Emperor's head, and prayers and sacrifices in the Temple were accepted as expressions of loyalty in place of participation in the imperial cult. Yet for all that, apart from the Sadducean aristocracy who controlled the high-priesthood, the Romans were hated both as idolaters and as the occupying power. Like the British in Palestine after the Second World War they served as general scapegoats for the cultural, social and economic ills of the territory. The contrast indeed between friendly relations between individual Jews and Roman officers, and generalized antipathy toward Rome as the representative of idolatry, strikes a relevant chord in the contemporary world.

At the time of Jesus' ministry the evidence of this underlying hostility is to be found in the writings produced by the various sects into which the religious-national tradition of Judaism had divided. In the New Testament, Sadducees, Herodians, and Pharisees are mentioned. The first two represented the ruling Temple hierarchy but the Pharisees were in the same tradition of nationalistic pietism and religious orthodoxy as had inspired many of the Jews who had rejected Hellenization under the Seleucids. Now they were equally opposed to a return of Greek influence through Herod and his Roman masters. Their views are well illustrated by the Psalms of Solomon, Enoch, and the Assumption of Moses, all of which look forward to the coming of a deliverer of Israel, an "anointed one," "the Son of David" who would overthrow the rule of the idolaters and the backsliding Israelites who upheld their power.

More significant even than the Pharisees, however, were the Essenes. These are not mentioned in the Bible, and until the discovery of the Dead Sea Scrolls their existence was known only through the works of Philo, Josephus and Pliny the Elder. At the time of writing, it seems reasonably clear that the Covenanters of the Scrolls were Essenes,[4] and they thus present the historian with the possibility of looking into the minds of a Palestinian group who combined pietism and zeal for the law with an equally intense militancy against idolatry, including that represented by Rome. The sect saw itself as an holy community, "the so·s of Zaddi,"[5] and the elect of Israel. They had retreated into the desert, as they said, "to separate themselves from the abode of perverse men who walk in the way of wickedness."[6] There they would enter into the covenant of the Last Days, which included active preparation for the final cosmic and military conflicts in which Belial and all his hosts would be destroyed.

It seems quite evident that these covenanters were the "bearers and in no small part the producers of the apocalyptic tradition of Judaism."[7] Their library at Qumran contained an extraordinarily rich collection of apocalyptic literature, such as fragments of the Testaments of the patriarchs, Daniel, the cycles of Enoch, and pseudo-Mosaic works.` Moreover, this tradition contributed toward shaping the apocalyptic tradition of the early Church, and in particular, inspired the theology of martyrdom and separation from pagan society which dominated so much of the Church's thought in the first three centuries A.D.

To Rome's difficulties in Judea were added the even more complex problems caused by the Jewish Dispersion in the Mediterranean world. The successive exiles and returns from captivity had resulted in Jews settling outside the borders of Palestine, and this movement received further impetus following the conquests of Alexander the Great. At this period and through the third century B.C. the relations between the Jews and their Greek-speaking neighbors were not on the whole bad. The Jewish religion was regarded as a rather peculiar philosophy, and the Jews themselves were accepted as good colonists, people who would cultivate the land and in general widen the area of civilization for which the Greek settler in Asia Minor and Syria stood. Thus, Antiochus III settled 2000 Jewish families in Phrygia at the turn of the third century B.C. "as well disposed guardians of our possessions." This, though the best known, was probably by no means the only organized settlement.[9] Wherever Greek inscriptions have been found in Asia Minor in any numbers there have been Jewish inscriptions also, and wherever Paul and Barnabas went on their first missionary journey they found a Jewish synagogue with its circles of full-Jews, proselytes and inquirers. In Antioch[10] the synagogue was a flourishing institution and in Alexandria the Jews dominated two of the five quarters of the city.[11] There were Jewish communities in the chief towns along the North African coast and in southern Spain. As the Jewish philosopher Philo described it, the Jews settled in very many of the most prosperous countries in Europe and Asia.[12] No one country could hold them, so populous were they. If one reads through the catalog of nations and territories listed by Luke in Acts 2 one can see what an immense movement the Dispersion was.

In the communities where they had settled, the Jews often formed a wealthy and influential section of the population. Here also, Acts is significant. We see them mainly as an urban influence but as a powerful one. At Pisidian Antioch for instance, they are associated with "the chief people" and with "pious women," presumably wealthy also.[13] At Ephesus, Paul himself numbered members of the governing group of this big city among his friends.[14] In another town of Asia, Akmonia, the Jews had attracted members of the family of Julia Severa, related to the old Phrygian royal house, to their faith.[15] At Laodicea, Apamea, and Adramyttium there were large Jewish communities who sent contributions in gold each year to Jerusalem as temple tax.[16] At Stobi in northern Macedonia we find a certain Tiberius Claudius Polycharmus leaving no less than a quarter of a million sesterces to build a new synagogue and cult center.[17] In the first century A.D. the Jews of the Dispersion were economically among the most prosperous subjects of the Empire.

There in part lay the rub. For all their adoption of the Greek language and residence in the Greek cities they stood ostentatiously outside the life and organization of the communities in which they had settled. Wherever they dwelt, their community life was centered round their synagogues and their social and ethical life developed in organizations suited to enable them to observe the law. They subjected themselves to their own courts, and their rulers even in third-century Alexandria were reputed to have very great powers indeed.[18] Paul himself in 2 Corinthians 11:24 refers to his receiving on five occasions "forty stripes save one" in a synagogue; a century later the beating of Christians in the synagogues of the Jews in Asia was a common occurrence.[19] They kept apart in life and in death from their pagan neighbors, burying their dead in their own cemeteries and looking for the future gathering-in of Israel.

This situation would have caused the Jews to be suspected and disliked but probably not actively hated. The Jew, however, was not content to keep himself to himself. In the towns where he settled there was continuous agitation and proselytization. Moreover, this was fairly successful. Thus circa A.D. 75, Josephus writing of the situation in Antioch and after saying that the Jews enjoyed equal privileges with the Greeks there, went on, "They also made proselytes of a great many of the Greeks continuously and thereby in a sort of way brought them to be a portion of their own body."[20] In Alexandria the Jews there "offered a friendly welcome to all those who were minded to obey their laws."[21] And we know from Acts that many Greeks in the towns of Asia were so minded.

Until the Greeks found a rallying point in allegiance to the imperial cult there was nothing in their outlook strong enough to resist the appeal of monotheism, universality, the philosophy of history, and high ethical code that the Jews offered. The propaganda such as that contained in Psalm 115, directed against idolatry, or in Wisdom against the outward manifestations of Hellenistic culture, reached its mark. The Greeks scattered about the eastern Mediterranean were settlers who possessed a higher material culture and pride of present and past achievement, but were threatened by vigorous alien communities within their walls who possessed a more consistent and more moral religious and social outlook. The result was conflict, sometimes breaking out in massacres such as that which occurred in Alexandria in 38,[22] or in the scenes of murder and pillage that took place in town after town in Syria on the outbreak of the Jewish war of A.D. 66.[23] This was a situation which challenged all Rome's powers of statesmanship in the Hellenistic parts of her dominions.

The Roman position was rather different. In Rome itself the Jews were simply one among many foreign communities with their own religion. Admittedly they were numerous, their numbers having been swelled by the influx of prisoners brought to Rome by Pompey after his capture of Jerusalem in 63 B.C. But apart from a single incident in 139 B.C. when the Praetor in charge of foreigners in Rome (*praetor peregrinus*) Cn. Cornelius Hispanus ordered the expulsion of Jews "who tried to taint Roman manners with the worship of Jupiter Sabazius,"[24] the Jews appear to have enjoyed complete peace and calm in Rome throughout the Republican period.

The reason is not too far to find. Romans and Jews first met as allies, an alliance which embraced the Jews both in Palestine and the Dispersion. The Greek inhabitants of the cities of Asia Minor were distrusted. The fact that they had joined Mithradates and massacred the Roman merchants in their midst was not forgotten, and when in the 50s and 60s the town councils of Ephesus, Parium, Halicarnassos and Delos tried to whittle down the extraordinary status of the Jews among them, the Roman Government stepped in to protect the Jews.[25] Thus a decree of Dolabella, governor of Asia, soon after the death of Julius Caesar reads: "I do therefore grant them [the Jews] freedom from going into the army, as former governors have done, and permit them to use the customs of their forefathers in assembling together for sacred and religious purposes, as their law requires, and for collecting oblations necessary for their sacrifices."[26] In a similar decree sent to the Parians by the praetor Caius Julius [?] on behalf of the Jews in Delos about the same time, the Jews are described as "friends and allies," and while their common meals and festivals were specifically authorized, others held by the Greek inhabitants were not.[27] The Jews repaid these signs of favor with loyal service to Julius Caesar and in Rome they showed an almost ostentatious loyalty to Augustus by naming a synagogue after the imperial house.

The establishment of the imperial cult, however, and its immense popularity among the Greeks brought about a gradual change. The problem of Greek loyalty was largely solved. The world became the Greco-Roman instead of the Roman world. Though individual Romans may have continued to take advantage of their position in the provinces to harass the local Greek inhabitants, as they evidently continued to do in Cyrene in Augustus's reign, there was no genuine sympathy for the Jews either. In the same speech that contained a long tirade against the Greeks in Asia, Cicero pointed out how even before Pompey's capture of Jerusalem the Jewish laws and way of life were incompatible with the Roman.[28] In Augustus's reign the Jews were beginning to attract unfavorable notice in the capital. Horace records contempt for Jewish superstition, and mentions how his friend Aristius Fuscus had told him that he could not discuss some private affairs with him, as it was "the thirtieth Sabbath," and he "did not want to upset the circumcised Jews."[29]

A few years later, in A.D. 19, a trivial incident showed that good feeling between the Jews and Romans in the capital was beginning to wear thin. Josephus records that a noble Roman lady named Fulvia had become a proselyte but then had been tricked by unscrupulous immigrant Jews. Somehow or other the affair got mixed up with some vicious conduct by priests of Isis, and the upshot was that the Jews and worshipers of Isis were treated with impartial justice and ordered out of the city. Some 4,000 Jewish freedmen were drafted to Sardinia to fight bandits in an unhealthy climate.[30]

Meantime, in the East other factors were gradually moving official opinion against the Jews. In Palestine there were vague but none the less real fears of a Jewish national rising. From A.D. 27 the Jews had felt the impact of Pontius Pilate, from contemporary accounts the first really unsympathetic Roman governor of Judea.[31] While the Jewish authorities had protested bitterly against Pilate's intention to march his troops through the city carrying their standards, symbols of "idolatry," Pilate was constantly on the alert for signs of revolt. Barabbas, "guilty of insurrection," and the superscription on the Cross, "Jesus of Nazareth king of the Jews," sum up the situation at this time.

It was in Alexandria, however, that events occurred showing how far Romano-Jewish relations had deteriorated. In the summer of 38 Greek and anti-Jewish extremists had come to power.[32] They took the chance of a visit by King Agrippa on his way to take up his new kingdom in northerٸ Palestine to riot against the Jews. Agrippa was mocked, the Prefect ɔf Egypt, A. Avillius Flaccus, openly took the side of the Greeks and a horrible and destructive pogrom broke out. Though Flaccus was eventually dismissed and judicially murdered when in exile, the Jews were not recompensed.[33] The Emperor Caligula to whom an embassy was sent was unsympathetic. Only his murder on 24 January 41 prevented his megalomaniac tendencies from forcing a crisis on the Jews by insisting that they placed his statue in the temple at Jerusalem and worshiped it.

Subsequently both Jews and Greeks in Alexandria sent embassies to Claudius, nominally to congratulate him on his accession, in fact to attempt to win the Emperor's favor for their respective causes. Claudius's reply has been preserved, characteristically enough on the back of a tax receipt belonging probably to a village secretary in the territory of Philadelphia.[34] It shows the Emperor as rigorously judicial. Both sides had been guilty of riot and feud, and were rebuked. The Jews should enjoy the privileges they possessed in the time of Augustus, but no more, and they were not to behave as though they lived in a city separate from their Alexandrian neighbors. Then the Emperor showed his true feelings. The Jews "are not to introduce or invite other Jews who sail down to Alexandria from Syria or Egypt, thus compelling me to conceive the greater suspicion; otherwise, I will by all means take vengeance on them as fomenting a general plague (i.e. disorder) for the whole world."[35] Claudius realized that although the Greek oligarchies could be a nuisance the Jews might menace the safety of the Roman world. With that realization the Romano-Jewish alliance came to an end. In another quarter of a century the Jewish revolt was to imprint itself on the minds of contemporaries as one of the greatest of all wars. It was no time for giving favor to any offshoot of Judaism. But at this moment the first Christian missionaries were beginning to take the Word beyond the confines of Palestine.

FURTHER READING

Appelbaum, S., *Jews and Greeks in Ancient Cyrene*, E.J.Brill, Leiden 1979

Burrows, M., *The Dead Sea Scrolls*, Secker and Warburg 1956

Burrows, M., *More Light on the Dead Sea Scrolls*, Secker and Warburg 1958

Caird, G.B., *The Apostolic Age*, Duckworth 1955

Cross, F.M., *The Ancient Library of Qumran and Modern Biblical Studies*, Duckworth 1958

Dix, Dom G., *Jew and Greek*, Dacre Press 1953

Grant, F.C., *Roman Hellenism and the New Testament*, Oliver and Boyd 1962

Hardy, E.G., *Christianity and the Roman Government*, Allen and Unwin 1928, chs.1, 2.

Hengel, M., *Judaism and Hellenism*, SCM Press and Fortress Press 1974 (two vols., reissued as one, 1981)

Jeremias, J., *Jerusalem in the Time of Jesus: An Investigation into Economic and Social Conditions during the New Testament Period*, SCM Press and Fortress Press 1969

La Piana, G., 'Foreign Groups in Rome', *Harvard Theological Review* 1925, 183-401

Rajak, T., *Josephus*, Duckworth and Fortress Press 1984

Schürer, E., *The History of the Jewish People in the Age of Jesus Christ (175 BC-AD 135)*, revised and edited by G.Vermes and F.Millar, T.&T.Clark 1973-86

Smallwood, E.M., *Philonis Alexandri. Legatio ad Gaium*, E.J.Brill, Leiden 1961 (Introduction)

Tcherikover, V., *Hellenistic Civilization and the Jews*, Jewish Publication Society of America, Philadelphia 1959

Yadin, Y., *Masada: Herod's Fortress and the Zealots' Last Stand*, Weidenfeld and Nicolson 1973

3

The Primitive Community
41–70

So far we have been discussing the pagan and Jewish background to Christianity. We now turn to study the impact of the new religion on this many-sided ancient world. How did the primitive community appear to contemporaries, and how was it that after a generation of toleration by the Roman authorities, it was overtaken by the catastrophe of the Neronian persecution?

Significant of the Church's slow spread through the Greco-Roman world is the silence of the Classical writers of the first century A.D. concerning it. Tacitus, Pliny the Younger and Suetonius all writing between 110–20 treat Christianity as a new phenomenon which has to be explained to their readers. Of the Jews, Philo does not mention the Crucifixion in his critical analysis of the career of Pontius Pilate which he wrote not much later than 41.[1] Josephus mentions briefly John the Baptist and the martyrdom of James in 62 but about Jesus (except in the Slavonic version) he is silent. Conspiracy or insignificance? We do not know, though one suspects the latter. So, the historian is thrown back on the Christian sources, on the Pauline Epistles written between 49 and 62, on Mark's Gospel, on Luke-Acts written up slightly later, and Matthew as representing the tradition of the Church in Palestine and Syria post 70. In the Gospel of Thomas he may also have an early Aramaic tradition, though much distorted by later Gnostic editing, and he would be wise to accept one of the traditions behind John as Judean and dating back to before the fall of Jerusalem. It is not very much. The Christians hoped that the bridegroom would not tarry. Only when the Parousia was delayed and Christians had lived and died in the Church was the oral tradition of Jesus' life and teaching reduced to writing.

There is, however, one other check on the meager information regarding the life of the primitive Church contained in Acts, namely, the Scrolls. The Dead Sea covenanters were contemporaries with Jesus and

24

his disciples. They too believed themselves to be the elect of Israel, the community of the poor awaiting the arrival of the Messianic kingdom, and from time to time their writings shed a quite unexpected light on otherwise obscure passages in the Christian Scriptures.

Immediately after the Crucifixion, it appears that Peter and the other disciples returned to Galilee (Mk. 14:28 and 16:7). There, however, Peter had a vision of the risen Lord, perhaps that recorded in John 21, and soon after the disciples abandoned their workaday lives to which they seem to have returned and set out for Jerusalem. There they would establish redeemed Israel and await the return of their Lord. The Ascension found them with their hopes restored and the experience of Pentecost confirmed them in their belief that Jesus was indeed the Christ, and that he had risen from the dead and sat at the right hand of God (cf. Acts 2:32 ff.).

The decision to go to Jerusalem had in itself been a momentous one. Not so long before the covenanters had elected to go into the wilderness to await the coming of the Messianic age. "In the wilderness prepare ye the way of the Lord" derived from Isaiah 40:3 was a tradition accepted by them and many of the Christians. But in the wilderness they stayed, to be destroyed probably by Vespasian's forces in 68, and to be dug up by the spade of the archaeologist nearly 1,900 years later. Their influence on the future history of humanity was almost nil. Jerusalem, however, was the center of Jewry, where Jews from all over the Greco-Roman world and beyond its borders gathered for the Passover, and, once gathered, discussed and retailed information. Part of this information could now concern Jesus of Nazareth and the strange reports regarding him.

Back in Jerusalem the Christians now established themselves as an active "sect" among their fellow-Jews. They "continued with one accord daily in the Temple" (Acts 2:46), that is, they were a good deal less "heretical" than the Essenes who refrained from temple worship. Significant parallels exist, however, between the organization of the primitive community and that of their contemporaries at Qumran. As Theodore Gaster points out, the two bodies use the same words in "the same quasi-technical sense as denoting parts of their ecclesiastical organization."[2] Thus the deliberative assembly of both was known as *esah*, and the community itself as *edah*. The three Christian "pillars of the Church" (Gal. 2:9) and twelve disciples (made up to this number by Matthias's election) seem to correspond to the three priests and twelve laymen, "men of special holiness," who administered the affairs of the covenanters. Both claimed to be the Congregation of Israel, they lived and worshiped as a

25

community, and in both societies the penalties for failing to contribute all one's possessions to the common pool were severe. For the covenanter such an act of omission involved exclusion "from the state of purity" entailed by membership and the loss of one quarter of his food ration for a year.[3] The Christians, as Ananias and Sapphira found to their cost, substituted sudden death for slow starvation.[4] The Bridegroom could not be waited upon at his coming by unworthy servants.

The memory of these exclusively Palestinian-Jewish preoccupations may perhaps be preserved in those passages of Matthew's Gospel (10:23, 10:5–6 and 15:24) which indicate a narrow horizon for the mission. But be this as it may, circumstances soon shattered the injunction of "Go ye not into the way of the Gentiles." It was inevitable that sooner or later the Christian message would pass beyond the bounds of Aramaic-speaking Judaism. Soon it was necessary to recognize the existence of Greek-speaking Christians by the appointment of the "deacons" to serve at the communal meal (Acts 6:1–3.). These all had Greek names, and one, Nicholas, was a proselyte. Then, some of the Hellenistic synagogues in Jerusalem were in a state of ferment. The combination of criticism of official Judaism and the belief that Jesus was indeed Messiah roused the authorities, and the ringleader among the Hellenist sympathizers with Christianity, Stephen, was stoned.

Once again, however, Jewish authorities miscalculated. The Greek-speaking Christians were scattered, but they took their message with them. Soon there were Christians in Damascus and Antioch, and Peter after many hesitations at last came to the view that Gentiles must be admitted to salvation. He preached in Caesarea, the Greco-Roman capital of Palestine, Herod's city, where his Master had never trod. But more than that, Stephen's martyrdom gave the signal to men who had gradually and reluctantly come to the conclusion that the law as it stood was not a guide to life. "I was alive without the law once; but when the commandment came, sin revived and I died" (Rom. 7:9). The blinding experience on the road to Damascus revealed to Paul that "they which are in Christ Jesus [who] walk not after the flesh but after the Spirit" (Rom. 8:1) and this new law was the law of liberty. The old wine of Judaism could no longer suffice. St. Paul accepted the implications of his conversion.

A short and sharp persecution ordered by the conservative Herod Agrippa between 41–4 was succeeded by a long period of calm. James the brother of John son of Zebedee was indeed dead, but Peter was released from prison; he was, however, no longer leader of the Christian community. For the next eighteen years, until 62, this office was the prerogative of Jesus' brother, James, and Jerusalem was the center and directing arm of the Christian mission.

Little is known about this remarkable man. After 70 the Jerusalem Christians found themselves a despised, dispersed and persecuted minority among the Jews of Palestine, and only vague traditions concerning James survived. Harnack's view, however, that the Jerusalem Christians intended to form a sort of "Caliphate" led by Jesus' kinsmen, and within the boundaries of Judaism, cannot be wide of the mark.[6] James was regarded by later tradition as a high priest, resplendent in priestly insignia, and accorded the title of "the Just," a term once given to the leader of the covenanters.[7] In Thomas Jesus commits the Church to James as his successor,[8] as in Matthew he commits it to Peter.[9] His allegiance to Judaism is also evident. The Christians paid their Temple tax (Matt. 17: 24), and when in 58 Paul came to Jerusalem with a glowing report on his mission to the Gentiles James received him coolly. He informed him of adverse reports that had been circulating about his activities and urged him to prove his loyalty to Judaism by taking (like him) a Nazarite vow. So long as James lived, Jerusalem was the center of the Church and the Christians there aspired to the role of an holy remnant leavening and guiding the Jewish people in the short intervening period that remained before the end of the age.

Paul, however, emerged from the Arabian desert with different views. He was determined from the first to carry the message beyond the bounds of Palestine to the Gentile world. The time to be "a light for the Gentiles" (Is. 49:6) had come. Jesus had been the second Adam, manifesting to the saints the "mystery that had been hid from all ages and generations" (Col. 1:26), and for the pagans he was the "unknown God" whom they worshiped in ignorance. Him Paul would now explain. At the conclusion of the first missionary journey in 49 the Apostolic Council wisely agreed that there should be two missisions, one for the Jews under Peter, and the other for the Gentiles under Paul.

For the next decade the Church's history is dominated by Paul and his fellow apostles, Barnabas primarily, but there were others such as Apollos, Epaphras, Epaphroditus and Junias. Their activities amounted to a vast proselytizing mission in Gentile country, carried out with the utmost vigor. What the Pharisees had attempted to do—and John the Baptist's followers had shown the way at Ephesus and Alexandria—Paul and his friends set out to achieve. They aimed at preaching the Gospel from one end of the Mediterranean to the other before the Last Day overtook them. There can be no doubt that Paul hoped to reach Spain and

Illyricum, and the determination with which he traversed some of the roughest country in Asia Minor in the face of every type of peril showed the zeal and mettle of the man. It was desperate work, for the Gentile world had somehow or other to be given the chance of repentance while there was yet time.

Overwhelming difficulties, however, stood between the Apostles and the fulfilment of their plans. It is difficult to imagine two more typical Jews than Paul, the trusted agent of the Sanhedrin, and Barnabas, the Levite from Cyprus. Paul's knowledge of the literature of those whom he sought to convert was minimal, derived from anthologies. He had studied in Jerusalem under Gamaliel in preference to his native Tarsus, and he was acutely conscious of his standing as a Pharisee, "For I also am an Israelite, of the seed of Abraham, of the tribe of Benjamin" (Rom. 11:1; cf. Acts 22:3). The reactions of his audience were what one might expect—either ironical or suspicious. "What rubbish are these fellows talking" with their Jesus and Anastasis (Acts 17:18), or the more sinister comment at Thessalonica, "these men being Jews teach customs which are not lawful for us to receive being Romans" (Acts 16:21).

In practice, therefore, the Pauline mission was directed toward Hellenistic Jews and those who had some previous contact with Judaism. Apart from his unsuccessful effort at Athens, the synagogue rather than the agora was the starting point of his work. This impression is strengthened if we note the people mentioned in Acts with whom Paul came into contact. There is Lydia the semiproselyte of Philippi, Aquila and Crispus, prominent Jews at Corinth, and Justus. Apart from Trophimus of Ephesus it is not easy to point to any ex-pagan among Paul's circle, and his chief successes are scored among Greeks who were already "devout" (cf. 17:4, at Thessalonica). Finally, when he declares (18:6) that he would henceforth "go unto the Gentiles," his step was not in practice a very momentous one. He left the synagogue at Corinth for the house of Justus "who worshiped God" (i.e., was a proselyte).

One must not overlook, however, the incidental effect which Paul and his friends had on the pagan population of the cities which he visited. At Lystra this was immediate and profound, "The gods are come down in the form of men." There may also be a grain of truth in the story of Thecla, the young noblewoman of Iconium, who took a vow of chastity after overhearing Paul speaking in a house across the street, and was eventually charged with sacrilege when she struck the crown of bay leaves from the head of her would-be fiancé. She was said to have been eventually saved from death in the amphitheater by the intervention of the aged Queen Trypheneia who was living at Iconium at the time. At least the latter is an historical personage, and the accusation of "sacrilege" and not Christianity suggests verisimilitude.[10] Moreover, Paul in his three years at Ephesus associated with the chief men of the city, who were pagans, and his preaching caused at least some decline in the sales of votive figures to be offered in the temples of Artemis. With the uproar caused by Demetrius the precedent for future anti-Christian pogroms in the cities of Asia was set.

But all the time, the real battle was with the Jews. If Paul's teaching succeeded in detaching the outer circle of interested Greeks from the synagogue, they were lost. God's promises to Abraham regarding the universal character of the Jewish religion could not be fulfilled, and once the local Jews had grasped the implications of Paul's message their hostility knew no bounds. The Apostle's tribulations at Thessalonica, Philippi, Beroea and Corinth stemmed from Jewish hatred. He was the man "who was turning the world upside down," the ringleader of the heretical sect of "Nazarenes," and if they could persuade the Roman authorities that his teaching was also seditious, so much the better. The treatment meted out to the master was reserved for the apostle as well.

Down to 64 danger threatened the Christian Church from the Jews and the Jews alone. Even accepting the apologetic bias in Luke's Gospel and Acts, it is clear that in the generation after the Crucifixion the Roman authorities evinced no hostility toward the new sect. Interference in what appeared to be a quarrel between two groups of Jews over the niceties of the law was something which authorities then (as now) would be glad to avoid; moreover, Paul was a Roman citizen and, we may suspect, except in moments of exaltation an interesting and not unsympathetic personality. Hence, the officials with whom he came into contact were ready to help him so far as they could. The impression he produced on Sergius Paulus, Proconsul of Cyprus in 46, was not isolated. Gallio drove his accusers from his presence at Corinth, and in the long-drawn-out crisis at Jerusalem from 58–60, the successive procurators Felix and Porcius Festus stonewalled his enemies' imprecations that he was worthy of death. Once arrived in Rome, Paul was more or less left to his own devices to preach the Word, with a good deal of success, "no one preventing him."

Thus, while in Palestine the relations between Roman and Jew were moving along a collision course, the Christians were not molested. What caused the sudden change of fortune in 64? If the two Letters to the Thessalonians stood alone we might suspect that the Christians were in fact guilty of harboring disloyal and antisocial thoughts toward their contemporaries. Paul's attack on the watchwords of the time *Pax et Securitas* is bitter; "Sudden destruction" would come on those who preached them, and unrestrained are his hopes that the End would come "with a shout" or as he told the Corinthians (1 Cor. 15:52) "in the twinkling of an eye." The vast mass of humanity would be left to destruction while the Christians were gathered into safety. Romans, however, written some seven years later, in 57, shows a different temper. The "moderate" had now triumphed in Paul. Let every "soul be obedient to the powers, for there is no power except from God." He therefore "that resisteth the power, resisteth the ordinance of God" (Rom. 13:1-2), and as Irenaeus was to point out a century and a half later, Paul meant earthly and not esoteric powers.[11]

Moreover, the Roman community had not called for any specially hostile treatment. How it was founded we do not know. There were proselytes from Rome in Jerusalem at Pentecost (Acts 2:10) and it may be that some of these took the message to Rome. It seems a more likely explanation than the battle of magic between Peter and Simon Magus above the Roman forum recorded in the *Acta Petri* which is supposed to have launched the Christian mission there. It is not easy either to unravel the development which lay behind Suetonius's epigrammatic "Judaeos impulsore Chresto assidue tumultuantes Roma (Claudius) expulit."[12] Chrestus was both the usual name for Christ in the West, and also a common name among slaves and freedmen from Asia, but that there was some sort of disorder involving Jews in 49 (and perhaps in 41 as well) and that some members including Prisca and Aquila found themselves expelled from the city is evident enough. Christianity may have had something to do with it. The cloud soon passed. In 57 Paul could write of the Roman community as one whose "faith is spoken of throughout the whole world" (Rom. 1:8), even though when he arrived there in 60 he found the Jewish leaders ill-acquainted with Christianity except by hearsay. This in itself is difficult to equate with a Petrine mission in the 50s, though Palestinian Jews who would fall into Peter's field were numerous in the city. Between 60 and 64 the progress of the Gospel was the work of Paul.

Such was the position when on 19 July 64 a vast conflagration devastated two entire quarters of the city of Rome, causing considerable loss of life and rendering thousands homeless. Suspicion fell on Nero himself who was believed to want to rid the city of a crowded and unsightly area in order to plan it anew and also to extend his own palace. Then, to quote Tacitus's well-known account of the events:

> Consequently, to get rid of the report, Nero fastened the guilt and inflicted the most exquisite tortures on a class hated for their abominations, called Christians by the populace. Christus, from whom the name had its

origin, suffered the extreme penalty during the reign of Tiberius at the hands of one of our procurators, Pontius Pilatus, and a deadly superstition, thus checked for the moment, again broke out not only in Judea, the first source of the evil, but also in the City, where all things hideous and shameful from every part of the world meet and become popular. Accordingly, an arrest was first made of all who confessed; then, upon their information, an immense multitude was convicted, not so much of the crime of arson, as of hatred of the human race. Mockery of every sort was added to their deaths. Covered with the skins of beasts, they were torn by dogs and perished, or were nailed to crosses, or were doomed to the flames. These served to illuminate the night when daylight failed. Nero had thrown open his gardens for the spectacle, and was exhibiting a show in the circus, while he mingled with the people in the dress of a charioteer or drove about in a chariot. Hence, even for criminals who deserved extreme and exemplary punishment, there arose a feeling of compassion; for it was not, as it seemed, for the public good, but to glut one man's cruelty, that they were being destroyed (tr., J. Steveson).

A possible explanation is that Nero was able to transfer suspicion to the Jews; they in turn pushed the blame on to the hated rival synagogue, and this time it stuck. The idea is not an unlikely one. At this period the Jews were not popular, and they were suspected throughout the Greco-Roman world of incendiarist leanings. Three years later, Antioch was to be the scene of a pogrom caused by a false accusation by a renegade Jew that the Jews of the city had set the town on fire. Many refused to accept a sacrifice test and perished miserably.[13] The Jews, however, were partly to blame for these suspicions. The Jewish Sibylline poems of this period foretold the fiery end of the Greco-Roman world. "God shall burn the whole earth and consume the whole race of man. He shall burn everything up and there will remain sooty dust."[14] These threats were read, and remembered. The earliest commentator on the persecution, the writer of *I Clement* in circa 100, also implies that the Jews were to blame. He was writing from Rome to the Church in Corinth reproaching the community for allowing duly elected presbyters to be ousted by malcontent young men. At the beginning of his letter he points out how envy, jealousy and fratricidal conflict had been the bane of the old Israel, and then he writes:

But, to finish with these ancient examples, let us come to the athletes of the recent past; let us take the noble examples of our own generation. Through jealousy and envy the greatest and most righteous pillars (of the Church) were persecuted, and contended unto death. Let us set before our eyes the good (i.e. heroic) Apostles: Peter, who through unrighteous jealousy endured not one or two but many labors, and so having borne witness proceeded to his due place of glory. Through jealousy and strife Paul displayed the prize of endurance; seven times in bonds, driven into exile, stoned, appearing as a herald in both the East and the West he won noble fame for his faith; he taught righteousness to the whole world, and after reaching the limits of the West bore witness before the rulers. Then he passed from the world and went to the holy place, having shown himself the greatest pattern of endurance[15] (tr. J. Stevenson).

Clearly, he had the fate of Peter and Paul in mind, and he places this in the context of internecine rivalries among God's people, "envy and jealousy" not pagan persecution. The conclusion he would want his readers to draw seems evident.

This granted, some of the obscurities in Tacitus's narrative disappear. The Christians were accused of incendiarism (not of being Christians), and the underlying reproach of "hatred against the human race" (odium generis humani) was the same as that leveled by the populace against the Jews and is to be found elsewhere in Tacitus. These Christians then were a sort of Jewish sect, but Tacitus goes on to describe the affair in language reminiscent of Livy's account of the Bacchanal conspiracy. Here also a "great multitude" was involved, there were nocturnal rites, a plot to burn the city, and in both cases the punishment was lethal, cruel and theatrical. It was designed both to strike terror into the guilty and appease the outraged gods of Rome. In Suetonius's brief reference to the persecution, which he included among Nero's miscellaneous actions of which he approved, the Christians are charged with black magic as well as of introducing a new and dangerous cult.[16]

Thus, fifty years after the event, members of the Roman governing class seem to have regarded the affair as the destruction of a conspiracy fomented by some extremist sect among the Roman Jews, and these were crushed in exactly the same way as the Bacchanals and other purveyors of malevolent rites, such as the Druids, had been. The stroke was directed, however, against guilty individuals, and not against the God of the Christians. A generation later, the Roman community was once more well-established and influential and the Christians were to enjoy another 130 years free from serious molestation. The Neronian persecution was a single catastrophe, but not the beginning of a consistent policy of repression.

What was the ultimate effect of the catastrophe? The question has been a bone of contention for generations of legal historians. Broadly speaking, Sherwin White has been justified in dividing opinion into two main streams roughly corresponding to ecclesiastical persuasions.[17] Thus the majority of the French and Belgian scholars and Roman Catholics generally have tended toward the view that the Neronian persecution was followed by a general law prohibiting Christianity, and that this law was the basis for future persecutions. On the other hand, German and English scholars, and most lay historians have treated the Neronian persecution as a police action directed against an ill-disposed sect. Future persecutions were carried out by the magistrates in various cities where there were sizeable groups of Christians through their powers of coercion (*coercitio*), which could be brought into play against dangerous groups or individuals.

On the whole, a modified version of the second theory fits the facts best. It is just possible that after 64 the Christians were the subject of a *Senatus-consultum* just as the Bacchanals had been in 186 B.C., but no trace of such a decree has been found, and no Christian apologist in the second century mentions its existence. Moreover, Tertullian's famous *institutum neronianum*,[18] on examination would seem to refer to a Neronian "usage" and is part of the African's panoply of argument to show that "only bad emperors persecuted." On the other hand, *coercitio* on its own will not do. The magistrates did not take the initiative against the Christians. They waited until someone denounced an individual as one, and then tried the case. Hence the sporadic nature of the anti-Christian repressions in the second century. Even so, for a denunciation to receive a hearing at all, Christianity must have been illegal. The clue to this curious situation lies in the corporate and Judaistic character of the Christian community. Official Judaism was *religio licita*, its offshoots were not, and as a member of an illegal religious and social community an individual could be denounced and punished.[19]

In any event, the Neronian persecution had no sequel in the provinces, and within two years the tactlessness of the Roman procurator in Palestine, Gessius Florus, had provoked a general revolt among the Jews there. To some contemporaries, such as Josephus, it was the greatest war of all time, and whether it deserved this title or not, it was fought out with a savagery rare even in the ancient world. Soon the Christians in Palestine were faced with the dilemma implicit in their position since Jesus' ministry. Should they throw in their lot with the Jewish nationalists or not? James had already been struck down in 62, the victim of the same combination of conservative nationalism and mob violence that had been fatal to his Brother.[20] Six years later the supreme crisis came. What the anxious debates in 67–8 were we do not know, but a firm tradition describes the Christians leaving Jerusalem while there was yet time and establishing themselves in Pella, a Greek city across the Jordan.[21] It was another momentous step. In 70 Jerusalem fell, the Essenes fighting both there and at Masada for the Lord Yahweh against the Lord Caesar to the last man, and winning the admiration of their enemies by their hopeless valor.[22] The Christians were neutrals. They played no part in the heroic sacrifice of the Jewish nation; and like other "moderates" they were to receive no thanks. Their position in Palestine was damaged beyond repair. There, orthodox Judaism was to be permanently the victor. The work of James perished with him. The Christian hope now lay in the Dispersion. The next fifty years would decide whether the missionary labors of Paul would bear fruit, or whether the Jews and pagans would prove too strong there also.

FURTHER READING

Bammel, E. and Moule, C.F.D. (eds.), *Jesus and the Politics of His Day*, Cambridge University Press 1984

Bruce, F.F., *Paul and Jesus*, Eerdmans 1974

Bultmann, R., *Primitive Christianity in its Contemporary Setting*, Thames and Hudson 1956

Davies, W.D., *Paul and Rabbinic Judaism: Some Rabbinic Elements in Pauline Theology*, SPCK 1948 and Fortress Press [4]1980

Deissmann, A., *Light from the Ancient East*, Hodder 1921

Ehrhardt, A.A.T., *The Apostolic Succession*, Lutterworth Press 1953

Harnack, A.von, *The Mission and Expansion of Christianity*, Williams and Norgate 1904 reissued Harper and Row 1962

Jalland, T.G., *The Origin and Evolution of the Christian Church*, Hutchinson 1948

Judge, E.A., *The Social Pattern of Christian Groups in the First Century: Some Prolegomena to the Study of New Testament Ideas of Stoical Obligation*, Tyndale Press 1960

Knox, W.L., *St Paul and the Church of the Gentiles*, Cambridge University Press 1938

Malherbe, A.J., *Social Aspects of Early Christianity*, Louisiana State University Press 1977

Meeks, W.A., *The First Urban Christians*, Yale University Press 1983

Ste Croix, G.E.M.de, 'Why were the Early Christians Persecuted?', *Past and Present* 26, November 1963, 6-38

Schoeps, H.J., *Paul: The Theology of the Apostle in the Light of Jewish Religious History*, Lutterworth Press and Westminster Press 1961

Sherwin White, A.N., *The New Testament and Roman Law*, Oxford University Press 1963

Simon, M., *Les Premiers Chrétiens*, Presses universitaires de France 1952

Streeter, B.H., *Primitive Christianity*, Macmillan 1929

Turner, C.H., *Studies in Early Church History*, London 1912

4

The Old Israel
and the New
70–135

The years that followed the fall of Jerusalem are among the most obscure in the life of the primitive Church. The Church is still basically a
Jewish body, its organization and worship modeled on that of the synagogue and its relations with the outside world seen principally through
Jewish eyes. In Palestine it fights for survival, while in the Dispersion it
begins gradually to win over the outer circle of synagogue inquirers and
to make headway among the pagan provincials. Despite eschatological
expectations portrayed in the darkest of apocalyptic hues, in which the
pagans are represented as enemies and persecutors doomed to everlasting
destruction, it seldom comes to the notice of the authorities. The repression under Domitian, if such it was, the brief correspondence between
Pliny and Trajan in 112–13, and Hadrian's rescript to Minucius Fundanus,
Proconsul of Asia in circa 125, are isolated events amid decades of silence.

The main problem confronting the Church in the sixty years separating
the two great Jewish wars was its relations with Judaism. The speed and
extent of the Jewish recovery after 70 both in Palestine and the Dispersion
have sometimes been underestimated. In these two generations Judaism
was far from being a spent force politically or culturally. After the surrender of Jerusalem Roman treatment of the Jews had not been vindictive.
They were no longer an "allied people," Jerusalem ceased to exist as the
Jewish capital, the payment of two drachmas previously made to Yahweh
by the Jews was now handed over to his conqueror, Jupiter Capitolinus,
but Judaism remained *religio licita*, and in the Dispersion no serious
brake was put on Jewish proselytism. Soon Palestinian Judaism found
new leaders in Gamaliel ii, who was recognized by the Romans as Nasi
or Prince of Jewry, and his younger contemporary Rabbi Akiba. The
academy at Jamnia (Jabneh) provided the Jews with a new cultural and
theological center. Here, toward A.D. 90 the Jewish canon of the Old
Testament was codified and a special "benediction" added to the Shema,

35

cursing the Christian heretic and excluding him everlastingly from the fellowship of the synagogue. The Church in Palestine sank to the level of a despised minority, known only as Jews who had abandoned inconvenient parts of the law; and in that obscurity it was to remain until the Constantinian epoch.

In the Dispersion, however, the struggle was more even, as Christian and Jew vied with each other in pursuit of Gentile proselytes. It was about A.D. 95 that Josephus wrote his two books of Jewish apologetic against the Egyptian, Apion, in which he sought to present Judaism as the "reasonable man's religion," and recorded the welcome given by Jews to those who accepted their advice and became converts. The intensity of Jewish hostility toward Rome shown in apocalyptic works such as iv Ezra and iii Baruch did not extend to the Greek inhabitants of Asia Minor, and indeed, Judaism made some progress there. In Phrygia there were Jewish commercial guilds,[1] while Jewish inscriptions continue to record the benefactions of wealthy patrons. On the Greek mainland the enormous sum left by Ti. Cl. Polycharmus[2] to the Jews of Stobi was probably not an isolated example of affluence. A wealthy community and synagogue flourished at Ostia also. There was, too, the prestige of leaders such as Josephus, men of worldwide repute and possessed of social status superior to any Christian leader of the day.

Yet with all these advantages Judaism faltered and the victory in the Dispersion went to the Christians. Jewry could never free itself from the shackles of the law. Trypho's advice to Justin circa 137, "If you desire salvation, first be circumcised, and then follow God's new moons,"[3] was repellent absurdity to many admirers of Hebrew monotheism and Hebrew ethics. "The fussiness and stupidity" of the Jews became a byword among these inquirers.[4] Christianity benefited correspondingly and spread. By the turn of the century we hear of communities in the provinces of Asia Minor north of the Taurus, in Bithynia, in Pontus where Marcion's father was Bishop of Sinope, and perhaps before the disaster of 79 at Pompeii and Herculaneum.

At each stage, however, Jewish heresy and Jewish malediction dogged the Christians. In the Pastorals the writer of the letter to Titus denounced "evil teachers" spreading false doctrine "especially from among the circumcised" (Titus 1:10). In 107 or so, in Antioch and the cities of Asia Minor, Ignatius on his way to martyrdom at Rome found himself at grips with some form of Jewish Docetic heresy which was misleading the faithful. His hatred of the Jews burns through his letters. "It is monstrous to talk of Jesus Christ and to practise Judaism,"[5] he cries in his letter to the Christians of Magnesia. Jewish teaching could be dismissed as "strange doctrines and ancient fables,"[6] useless for the Christian to pursue.

The Epistle of Barnabas (probably Alexandrine, 100-30) contains a bitter attack on the Jews and denies them any right to the prophecies of the old dispensation.[7] It is noticeable too, that the apocryphal but non-Gnostic Gospels attributed to the early second century and found in Egypt, paint the Jews in the worst of lights and Jesus' denunciation of them is made correspondingly strong.[8] But it is in the pages of Revelation with their terrible comparison between the "true" and the "false" Jews and the denunciation of the "synagogue of Satan" whose members were enemies and persecutors of the saints that the intensity of ill-feeling between the two groups can most easily be seen.[9] In the province of Asia the struggle between Jew and Christian was bitter and incessant. By the end of the first century it was contributing toward the hostility which the Christian would soon encounter throughout the Greco-Roman world.

All the time, however, the demands of Jesus' message were breaking up the Jewish mold in which the primitive Church had been set. There could not be a Jewish counterpart to the Eucharist, with its solemn memorial and sacrificial elements, because the rite referred only to Jesus. Similarly, water baptism as the sole means of initiation had meaning only in virtue of Christ's baptism. If Judaism generally provided the outward form of the Christian service, it contributed little or nothing to its inner meaning. Moreover, with the fall of Jerusalem the Temple and its ceremonial ceased, and there was no longer anything to tie the growing Christian communities of the Dispersion to the traditional center of Jewry.

Meantime, the Church had been evolving its own organization and liturgy suited to its own needs. In the first generation after the Crucifixion the Christians had seen themselves as the bearers of a unique message of Jesus of the lineage of David who was Messiah, who had wrought mighty works, had given a new and authoritative teaching and law, had died and risen again. Victorious over the evil powers of the universe he would return and judge the living and the dead and establish a kingdom which would have no end. The Christians were living in a brief interim which would precede the Coming, but however brief, some form of organization and outward means of preparing for the events to come must be presupposed.

Like the legal position of the Christians after 64, the question of the ministry has been bedeviled by the demands of various Christian traditions. On the one hand, we are told that "the foundation of the Christian *ecclesia* and the establishment of the germs of a formal ministry go back to Our Lord himself."[10] Moreover, "the Christian society was to be an hierarchical society governed by the Apostles with St. Peter at their head." This view accepted by Roman Catholics is ably set out by A. Fliche and V. Martin in the first volume of their monumental *Histoire de l'Église*.[11] On the other hand, the school of Church historians following Harnack and Lietzmann have considered that the Church gradually evolved its organization, until by A.D. 90 its ministry and some parts of its liturgy corresponded in their outward forms to those of the Hellenistic synagogue.[12]

Both ideas embody elements of truth, though not altogether for the reasons stated by their authors. Apart from A. A. T. Ehrhardt,[13] few critics have taken into account the vital differences between the needs of the ministry in Jerusalem and in the Dispersion, the one Aramaic-speaking, thinking in terms of Jerusalem and Jewish nationalist aspirations in Palestine, the other working in the Greco-Roman world and the intellectual environment of synagogue and Septuagint. In addition, our documents do not tell a consistent or even a coherent story. No amount of ingenuity can fully reconcile the differing accounts of the ministry to be found in *I Clement*, the *Letters* of Ignatius and the *Didache* respectively. Ignatius writes as though the norm of Church government was the bishop, priest and deacon, with absolute power in the hands of the bishop. The *Didache* treats the bishop on a lower level than the prophet and teacher,[14] while *I Clement* though asserting the preeminence of bishops gives no clue whether there was to be one bishop or a college of presbyter-bishops in each See.

The question indeed, whether Jesus sought to found an *ecclesia* is not properly stated. Israel was already an *ecclesia*, a "congregation of the faithful" and "people of God," among whom, however, were individuals set apart to carry out particular functions, such as Levites and rabbis. The decisive step taken by Jesus was to identify his own followers as the true Israel, perhaps in this case taking into account the long tradition of the holy remnant and the vine symbolism of Maccabean nationalism (John 15:1). Jesus' thoughts had their roots in the Palestinian past. Thus, from Pentecost onward each Christian felt himself in a particular way the witness of the truth of Jesus' message and under the guidance of the Holy Spirit. His baptism, that is, reception of the Spirit, had made him "in Christ," just as circumcision had been the guarantee of membership of the old Israel. The Holy Spirit was his leader marking him off from unrepentant Jews and Gentiles alike. "It seemed good to the Holy Spirit and to us . . ." (Acts 15:28) was the way in which the Christian expressed his membership of his community in the first century A.D., regardless of any office he might hold.

Against this background, one sees how a different form of ministry could evolve in Jerusalem and in the Dispersion respectively. The New Israel was pledged to the fulfillment rather than the destruction of the law, and its organization must therefore be recognizably that of the Israel of the law wherever it was planted. So, whether we accept the Peter tradition of leadership of Matthew or the James tradition of Thomas,[15] we find early on at Jerusalem a Christian Sanhedrin presided over by James, assisted by the twelve disciples representing the twelve tribes of Israel. Possibly also, there was an inner council of three, consisting of James, Peter and John the son of Zebedee. And James, as we saw in the last chapter, had monarchical powers. Here, surely, is one of the starting points of the tradition both of monarchical episcopacy and also of the apostolic succession. James was the high priest and head of the Church as his Jewish counterpart was the interpreter of Yahweh to the Jews. In Jerusalem pre-70 the latter was also prophet and priest, the all-powerful guardian of the covenant which he handed unblemished to his successor. It is interesting that the first Christian who seriously concerned himself about episcopal succession lists was the Palestinian Hegesippus circa 170. In the Clementine *Homilies* also (probably of third-century Palestinian Christian origin), the success of the mission would be crowned by the acceptance of a monarchical bishop in the new-formed community.

Meantime, in the Dispersion a much looser organization was emerging. In 45 we find that at Antioch, along with the Apostles, there were "prophets" and "teachers." These are the oldest distinctive offices in the Church and as the *Didache* (chaps. 11-13) shows, they remained the primary offices of the Church in some places until the turn of the second century. When one looks at the well-known Pauline texts (1 Cor. 12:28 and Eph. 4:11), "And God hath set some in the Church, first Apostles, second prophets, thirdly teachers . . ." to various types of assistant, the Apostle was speaking of the internal organization of a community with which his readers would be familiar. These offices could all be paralleled in the Judaism of the time.

The problem is, therefore, how the bishop, priest and deacon came into existence, and what their relation was to the more primitive offices of the Church. In answering these questions, we should not forget the Jewish environment in which Paul and his friends worked. We notice first how the Christians at Antioch commissioned Paul and Barnabas for their first missionary journey. "They laid their hands on them and sent them away" (Acts 13:3). This followed the prescribed method of setting apart an individual who had been selected for the Levitical order. As in Numbers 8:10, "The Children of Israel shall put their hands upon the Levites." In the first congregations they established, the Apostles "laid hands" on those whom they appointed presbyters (Acts 14:23) and these, like the Jewish *zequenim*, acted as administrators, judges and rulers of the Christian synagogues. It was with reference to these functions that Paul was to write to the Corinthian presbyters in 53. In the later missionary journeys, however, we find bishops and deacons, and not presbyters, such as at Philippi and Colossae. Why the change? The deacon was a subordinate, whether he served the saints at table in Jerusalem, or helped the bishop at the cult meal, or, like Phoebe at Cenchraea, kept house for necessitous Christians in a busy port. At this stage he presents no serious difficulty. The problem of Church Order revolves round the office of the bishop.

There is no clear-cut solution.[16] Paul addresses the same people at Ephesus first as "presbyters" and then as "bishops," and whether the Church in Rome was governed by a bishop or a council of presbyters in circa A.D. 100, when Clement wrote to the Corinthians on behalf of the Church there, we may never know. One difficulty is that the term *episcopos* (bishop) had two different meanings. First, there was the literal meaning of "overseer" which included in synagogue parlance overseers of charity, or guardians of the scrolls, but secondly, the term could mean "priest" as it was used regarding Eleazar in Numbers 4:16. Both meanings survived in Christianity. In the *Shepherd of Hermas* (Rome, 100–30) we hear of "bishops" looking after hospitality on behalf of the community and therefore acceptable to the Lord (*Similitudes* 9:27), but there was also the more usual meaning, denoting the head of the community. Just as each synagogue had its ruler, or board of rulers, so each church had its bishop or perhaps board of presbyter-bishops, among whom there must always have been a president (in Rome, circa 160 Justin calls him *prohestos* and not *episcopos*). This development took place not only on administrative grounds but also for more important reasons arising out of the needs of the Eucharist. A bishop must be not only a virtuous man, husband of one wife, etc., but a person fitted to represent Jesus, himself both priest and victim, at the solemn moment of the Eucharist before the sacramental meal eaten by each community before dawn on the "Day of the Lord" (Sunday). Also, he must represent the people should the Lord return as expected on that day. These factors applied only to Christianity, and made for the singling out of one individual resident in the Christian community as its leader, or bishop.

All this did not come about in a day, but looked at closely, our authorities, namely the Pastorals and Johannine letters in the New Testament, *I Clement*, the letters of Ignatius and the *Didache*, give some idea of how this was taking place in the churches of the Dispersion at the turn of the second century. The Pastorals and Johannine letters show that there were still men of high-priestly and apostolic authority responsible for churches within a defined region (such as Titus had been in Crete) and able to call to order resident officials such as Diotrephes "who loveth to have preeminence" must have been (3 John). There were also "prophets and teachers" as *Didache* shows, and in certain circumstances these could take precedence over the bishop in the administration of the Eucharist (*Didache* 10:7). But the regional leaders with apostolic authority were dying out and the power of the prophets was already on the wane. They had been itinerant officials whose message or prophecy would be directly connected with the Coming. It would generally be apocalyptic in content, intelligible only in the context of the Last Days when "the Spirit would be poured out." The future lay with the resident clergy, and by A.D. 100 in Antioch and among many of the communities in Asia Minor and on the Greek mainland the bishop with his priests and deacons was in control. Ignatius, traveling through the cities of western Asia Minor on his way to martyrdom, shows that Polycarp had already begun his long reign in Smyrna, and that bishops were in authority in the other towns which he visited. His own clamant emphasis on episcopacy could not have been wholly unrepresentative of the Christian scene.[17] With the recession of the Second Coming into the distant future (see 2 Peter 3:3-4) the way was open for the bishop, assisted by his presbyters and deacons, to become the norm of Christian government throughout the Greco-Roman world.

Two other documents of this period tell us something about the internal life of the primitive Church, namely the First Epistle of Clement (*I Clement*) and the letter of Polycarp to the Philippians. *I Clement* is at first reading a very dull work, but as one considers it further it becomes extremely significant. We do not know its exact date. The "calamities" or "critical circumstances" of which the writer speaks at the beginning of his letter need have no connection with persecution, but could refer simply to time-consuming difficulties which had prevented him from replying to the letter of the Church of Corinth before. Even so, a date about A.D. 100 seems indicated, and Clement himself was probably a presbyter at Rome charged with liaison with other Christian communities. The problem he faced was the irregular deposition of some presbyters at

Corinth by the "young men" of the community. It was a matter of discipline. No question of belief was involved, and this alone makes Clement's assumptions about what a Christian held very interesting. Clement shows that the concept of God was Trinitarian, "Have we not one God, and one 'Christ and one Spirit of Grace poured out upon us?" he asks (chap. 46:6). God was creator and ruler of the universe "all-merciful and beneficent Father." There was no trace of the Gnostic dualism of the next century. The universe was an ordered and harmonious whole, controlled by God, in which each grade and individual had its part to play. Jesus was both His servant (*pais*) and Son, and as in Hebrews, represented as the "High Priest of our offerings and guardian of our souls." He preexisted before the Incarnation and was associated with the Father and Holy Spirit as both savior and redeemer. The Christian who became "in Christ" through baptism was a member of a fellowship which was both a new creation and a continuation of the old Israel.

Clement was steeped in the Septuagint and the moral and ethical law of Judaism. To him it was Scripture and he quotes it more than a hundred times. It is evident that he sees the Christian order as a natural progression from the Jewish order. "Of our father Jacob came the priests and Levites who serve the altar of God. From him comes Jesus Christ according to the flesh" (chap. 32:2), and so too, in the well-known passages in chapters 42 and 44 he regards the Christian priesthood as the lineal descendant of that of Israel. The organization of his community also was a matter of course and tradition, not something that had come into being recently or which would end soon, and his distress at the behavior of the Church of Corinth toward their presbyters is obvious. Yet it was not his duty to chide and rebuke. He contented himself with reminding the Corinthians of past examples of fortitude and humility, not least, those of Jesus himself and the Apostles. The Roman representatives despatched to Corinth were simple messengers. As in Paul's time, it is evident that in both secular and religious matters the two cities were linked by the closest ties.

Clement does not tell us much about his Church's use of the New Testament nor of the details of its organization. He assumes rather than expounds. Polycarp of Smyrna's letter to the Church of Philippi written circa 108 fills a gap.[18] Where Clement is still thinking in terms of Logia (it seems evident that his Gospel like that of Thomas contained no Passion Narrative), Polycarp shows that the four Gospels, 1 Peter, the Pastorals, Hebrews and some at any rate of the Pauline Epistles were being read in church. He also shows us a neat concentrated little community, with its separate divisions of presbyters, deacons, widows and

42

the mysterious "young men" as we find them in *I Clement*, each occupying its appointed function. It was a Christian synagogue, concerned with its own life and purity of doctrine, determined to be "blameless before the Gentiles"[19] but utterly unconcerned in their affairs.

It is difficult to think of this letter having been written in the reign of Trajan. At this time the Church was more interested in the Coming and in stamping out false Judaistic teaching than in the state of the world in whose material prosperity it was sharing. The Roman Empire was scarcely more interested in the Church. Only at rare intervals did their paths cross.

For Rome, Judaism both as a political force and as an erosive propaganda was still the main preoccupation. *Exuere patriam*[20]—to desert (the law of) the country and one's ancestors, and to spurn the accepted ethic and religion was the reproach against the convert to Judaism. As Juvenal shows in a satire written circa 125, the process of conversion was often subtle, lengthy, but in the end complete.[21] It was probably through Judaism that Domitian's "persecution" of the Christians arose.

At least this is a possible explanation for the events in Rome in 95, at the end of Domitian's reign. Then, we hear from Dio Cassius that the Emperor had his cousin and heir presumptive Flavius Clemens and his wife Flavia Domitilla arrested, together with the consul for the year 95, Acilius Glabrio.[22] Clemens and Domitilla were charged with "atheism" in that they had "slipped into Jewish customs," and they were condemned, Clemens and Glabrio to death, Domitilla to exile on the island of Pantellaria. There is the usual difficulty over the evidence. Dio does not say that any of these nobles were Christians, but, though he was writing in 225 in Bithynia, one of the most Christianized provinces of the Empire, he never mentions Christianity! Even so, when Domitian was assassinated in September 96, and his successor Nerva recalled the exiles, the coin which commemorated these events spoke of "abuses of the Jewish tax" being abolished.[23] Moreover, while the catacomb of Domitilla was Christian by the mid-second century or a little later, it was not so originally, when Domitilla granted the land for the benefit of her freedmen. All one can say is that perhaps Christianity had something to do with the "Jewish customs" into which Clemens and Domitilla fell. Even so, a lawyer named Pliny had been in Rome at the time, and could write to Trajan seventeen years later that "he had never been at a trial of Christians."[24]

In Asia, however, where Christianity was strongest, various developments were increasing the chances of outright persecution. Here, from the middle of the second century (Melito of Sardis), Domitian was regarded as the second persecutor of the Church, and perhaps with good reason.[25] For the policy which in Britain had led to deliberate efforts at romanization by building towns and markets, led in Asia to an alliance between the Roman authorities and the local priesthoods and between the cult of Caesar and the national cults of Asia and Phrygia. Moreover, Domitian, unlike his predecessors Vespasian and Titus, was interested in propagating his own cult. His great statue at Pergamum and his temple at Laodicea warned Christians that the Lord Caesar expected to be worshiped as well as obeyed. At the same time, the Christians shared to the full the tensions and expectations of their Jewish rivals. For those like Polycarp[26] who agreed with the writer of 1 Peter "Fear God. Honour the King" (1 Pet. 2:17), there were many more who shared the hopes of Revelation, of the Four Horsemen, of fire and brimstone, and vengeance on the persecutors of the saints, and of the thousand years rule of the just. In the 90s, there were famines in Asia Minor such as Revelation describes, and it is more than idle speculation to associate the martyrdom of Antipas and the harrying of those who refused to wear the mark of the beast (an imperial stamp on purchases) to these years. Revelation is probably the reality behind Domitian's reputation as a persecutor.

The provinces of Asia Minor also provide the only other evidence of interest by the authorities in the affairs of the Christians. The province of Pontus–Bithynia on the Black Sea coast had been the scene of shameful mismanagement. The cities had been corruptly governed, vast sums of public money had been squandered, incompetent administrators had tried to erect public buildings on swamp-ground where they collapsed. Faction and discontent were rife. Early in 112 Trajan (98–117) sent his friend and experienced lawyer Pliny as his special representative to the province to attempt to put matters right, and Pliny's tenth book of letters shows how he attempted to deal with the situation. Of this collection, two letters in volume ten deal with the Christians. It seems that Pliny only came on them late in his mission, probably at the end of 112 when he had reached the town of Amastris in the eastern part of the province. He appears to have been told that the local temples were in a bad way, and that a sect called Christians were to blame. Some Christians were brought before him. They made a bad impression. Pliny asked them in the customary way three times whether they accepted the accusation, and when they refused to deny it sent them off for execution, for he adds in his report "whatever they were guilty of, their very obstinacy deserves to be punished."[27]

Then complications began to arise. Individuals recanted, and someone produced a list with a large number of names on it, many of whom were innocent, and others though they had once been Christians had ceased to be so three, five or even twenty years previously. For this group Pliny applied a sacrifice test to which he added the demand of "cursing Christ," i.e., abjuring a demonic name. Thoroughly interested, he investigated further, tried to get more information from two deaconesses, and came to the conclusion that he was dealing with simply an extravagant superstition. Meantime, his remedial measures had had their effect. Animals were being brought for sacrifice and the temples were being frequented again. Pliny could send a satisfactory report to his master.[28]

Trajan's reply was as short as Pliny's report had been prolix. To quote it:

> You have adopted the proper course, my dear Secundus, in your examination of the cases of those who were accused to you as Christians, for indeed nothing can be laid down as a general ruling involving something like a set form of procedure. They are not to be sought out; but if they are accused and convicted, they must be punished—yet on this condition, that whoso denies himself to be a Christian, and makes the fact plain by his action, that is, by worshiping our gods, shall obtain pardon on his repentance, however suspicious his past conduct may be. Papers, however, which are presented unsigned ought not to be admitted in any charge, for they are a very bad example and unworthy of our time (tr., J. Stevenson).

Pliny had in fact done very well and the Emperor could afford a word of praise to a conscientious civil servant.

Once again, we have to try to avoid the legal tangle which generations of historians and lawyers have built up around this incident. To take the facts as they are revealed by the exchange of letters, Christianity for some reason was an offense and Polycarp seems to confirm that the Christians were liable to persecution,[29] and yet Christians are rare enough for Pliny to refer the whole affair to his master. They had evidently not been the subject of a *lex* proscribing them. Indeed, Pliny had tried and punished them by virtue of his magisterial powers, acting on information received from accusers. He was struck by the defiance of the first batch of the accused, and concluded that this was precisely the sort of behavior he had been sent to Bithynia to quell. Trajan's answer allowed him discretion within the limits of the general instructions issued to Proconsuls, namely to set the province free from evil men whom they should seek out; but Christians were not to be sought out, and if they recanted, and worshiped the Roman gods, they were to be freed.

As neither "treason" (*maiestas*) nor atheism are specifically mentioned the alternative remains that as in Rome in 64, the Bithynian Christians were regarded as members of some form of illegal Judaistic association, which was perverting the worship of the gods in the province. It is clear that Pliny was pleased when he found that Christians ate ordinary food and even more pleased that they had given up their *agape*, the common meal, the hallmark of a society. The latter, whether public or secret, were the curse of the province, and only a short time before Trajan had forbidden the 150 firemen in the city of Nicomedia to form one.[30] He was not now going to legalize that of the Christians. The wind, however, was to be tempered for the shorn lamb, and repentant Christians were to be dealt with according to the "liberality" and "humanity" of the times.

Finally, the *collegium* (association) theory fits what is known of the views of provincials in the Greek east about the Christians later in the century. In 165 the satirist Lucian of Samosata on the Euphrates describes a dissolute Cynic, Peregrinus, during a brief but intense flirtation with Syrian Christianity as a Christian *thiasarches* (i.e., leader of an association)[31] and a decade or so later the anti-Christian apologist, Celsus, opens his *True Doctrine* with the sentence "There are some public societies that are legal, but secret societies are not"[32]—and the Christians belonged among the latter. Perhaps Ignatius of Antioch had been arrested a few years before as leader of the Christian *collegium* there, and as a Roman citizen sent to Rome to be tried and punished.

Trajan had good cause to avoid exacerbating religious dissensions especially where Judaism or its offshoots were concerned. In 115 when away on his great campaign against Parthia, the Jews of the Dispersion rose.[33] In Cyrenaica they proclaimed a certain Lukuas or Andreas as king, and wreaked havoc in the province. Nothing of the hated Gentiles must remain. The temple of Zeus at Cyrene was undermined and its huge columns allowed to come crashing to the ground. There they stayed, until raised by British Army engineers after the Second World War. The provincial highways were hacked up in an excess of fanaticism against the works of idolatry. Thousands of Greeks were killed. In Alexandria and Cyprus there were also terrible risings. The Jewish revolt perhaps saved Parthia. It spelled doom for the Dispersion Jews as both a political and religious threat. Reprisals were grim and calculated, and in some areas such as Cyprus, Jews were treated as open enemies and banned entry. The Christians had stood aside, and they now benefited.

Trajan died in August 117, and it seems that his successor, Hadrian, may have aimed at drawing a distinction between Jews and Christians in favor of the latter. We find that in a letter to the Proconsul of Asia, Minucius Fundanus in 124–5, replying to a question by his predecessor, Hadrian ordered that a Christian must be accused of definite crimes under due process of law before he could be condemned, and if the charge failed he had the right of cross-charging his accuser under the *calumnia* procedure.[34] To modern ears this was no great concession. The courts were still open to hear charges against Christians, and Christianity was not legalized. But few would risk the penalties of *calumnia* for the sake of bringing a charge, and there were still fewer Roman officials empowered to decide capital charges. It would need a grave situation in the community or a bitter enemy to denounce a Christian. No wonder then, that Justin Martyr included a copy of the text of the rescript at the end of his *I Apology* written in 155.

The Jews were not so lucky: Hadrian was in Palestine in 129 on his way to Egypt, and seems to have given the Jewish leaders a half-promise that they would be allowed to return to Jerusalem. For some reason which we can only guess at (perhaps in an obscure way connected with the drowning of his favorite Antinous in the Nile in 130) Hadrian took a bitter dislike to the Jews. He equated circumcision with castration, i.e., made it a criminal offence, and instead of fulfilling the hopes of Palestinian Jews, ordered the restoration of Jerusalem, but as an wholly pagan city *Aelia Capitolina*. For two years discontent simmered, to flare up in 132 in a series of guerrilla actions directed against the Roman garrisons and traders. Once again, the initial successes went to the Jews. Their leader, Bar Kochba, declared his independence of Rome by minting his own coins and instituting his own era. Akiba and his friends rallied to his cause. They accepted him as son of the star and as messiah. They were soon undeceived. Rome gradually gained the upper hand. Recently, discoveries in the caves overlooking the Dead Sea have revealed evidence for the last desperate stands of the Jewish nationalists.[35] By 135, 985 villages had been devastated, and Hadrian had himself proclaimed Imperator for the second time.[36] Akiba suffered martyrdom. The hopes of apocalyptic Judaism died with him.

The Christians had not supported Bar Kochba. Indeed, they had been persecuted by him. But in some ways they were affected by his defeat. The blighting of Jewish apocalyptic hopes entailed a blighting of their own. As the writer of 2 Peter shows, doubts were already being raised as to the reality of the Coming. These doubts were not to be stilled.[37] From now on, in the settled Christian communities apocalyptic was on the wane, its place being taken by speculation about the nature of Jesus' promise, his ministry and his revelation of the world beyond. With the emergence of Gnosticism in the person of Basilides at Alexandria circa 132 the history of Christian doctrinal controversy begins.

FURTHER READING

Bauer, W., *Orthodoxy and Heresy in Earliest Christianity*, Fortress Press and SCM Press 1972

Brandon, S.G.F., *The Fall of Jerusalem and the Christian Church*, SPCK 1957

Campenhausen, H.von, *History of the New Testament Canon*, A.& C.Black 1972

Campenhausen, H.von, *Tradition and Life in the Church: Essays and Lectures in Church History*, Fortress Press and Collins 1968

Charles, R.H., *Studies in the Apocalypse*, Schweich Lectures 1919, Oxford University Press 1922

Daniélou, J., *The History of Early Christian Doctrine before the Council of Nicaea*, Vol.1, *The Theology of Jewish Christianity*, Darton, Longman and Todd 1964 (a very important work)

Ehrhardt, A.A.T., *The Apostolic Succession*, Lutterworth Press 1953

Frend, W.H.C., 'The Persecutions: Some Links between Judaism and the Early Church', *Journal of Ecclesiastical History* 9, 1958, 2

Hardy, E.G., *Christianity and the Roman Government*, Allen and Unwin 1925 (the later chapters are very useful for the period 70-130)

Jalland, T.G., *The Origin and Evolution of the Christian Church*, Hutchinson 1948

Kirk, W.E. (ed.), *The Apostolic Church and the Ministry*, Hodder 1946 (especially the essay by Dom Gregory Dix)

Koester, H., 'GNOMAI DIAPHORAI: The Origin and Nature of Diversification in the History of Early Christianity', in *Trajectories Through Early Christianity*, ed. J.M.Robinson and H.Koester, Fortress Press 1971

Lampe, G.W.H., 'Grievous Wolves', in *Christ and Spirit in the New Testament*, ed. B.Lindars and S.S.Smalley, Cambridge University Press 1973

Merrill, E.T., *Essays in Early Christian History*, Macmillan 1924 (useful on the Pliny-Trajan corrspondence)

Sherwin White, A.N., *The Letters of Pliny: A Historical and Social Commentary*, Oxford University Press 1966, 691-712 (the Pliny-Trajan correspondence and Christian liturgy in the early second century)

Simon, M., *Verus Israel*, Paris 1948

Swete, H.B. (ed.), *Essays on the Early History of the Church and the Ministry*, Macmillan 1918

Telfer, W., *The Office of a Bishop*, Darton, Longman and Todd 1962

5

The Gnostics. Marcion
130–80

With the second capture of Jerusalem we reach the end of the Judeo-Christian period of the Church's history. As we have seen, up to now much of its outward form and many of its aspirations had been Jewish, Jewish in the dominance of apocalyptic, Jewish in its defensive arrogance toward the pagan world, Jewish in its tight set little communities with their strict internal discipline, their hierarchical structure, and also their social conscience. In 130 a traveler through the cities of Asia Minor might be excused if he failed to differentiate adequately between the old and the new Israel, for amid all their mutual execrations, was it not merely a question of one group fasting on Mondays and Thursdays and the other on Wednesdays and Fridays?[1] If the Christians were harmless it was only because there were not many of them. Had not the Jewish-Christian prophet Elchesai foretold a colossal apocalyptic war on the Romano-Parthian frontier; and had not this been fulfilled in 115? Yet, of those who had been attracted by the confident prophecies of the end of the world many had fallen away.

But some pagans had inquired further, and by 130 there were men, such as Justin of Neapolis (Nablus in Samaria), who having tried every philosophy from Stoicism, through the Peripatetics to Platonism, finally turned to Christianity. Christian teaching and Christian bravery in face of death had converted him, and he was not alone. The influx of Greeks into the Church, however, was bringing its own problems. A century later, Origen had a pertinent remark to make on the effect of the Christian message on thinking Greeks of Alexandria.

> So then, since Christianity appeared to men as something worthy of serious attention, not only to people of the lower classes as Celsus thinks, but also to many scholars among the Greeks, sects inevitably came to exist, not at all on account of factions and love of strife, but because several learned men made a serious attempt to understand the doctrines of Christianity.

The result of this was that they interpreted differently the scriptures universally believed to be divine, and sects arose named after those who, although they admired the origin of the word, were impelled by certain reasons which convinced them to disagree with one another.[2]

If in addition we concede with R. M. Grant that by 135 apocalypticism was no longer a tenable outlook, then a reaction was to be expected in both the Jewish and Christian worlds.[3] It took the form of Gnosticism.

Gnosis means simply knowledge. For the orthodox Jew and Christian alike it was one of the gifts of the Spirit. In Christian terms it meant knowledge of God and of his work gained through faith in Jesus Christ, study of Scripture and obedience to divine precepts. The new man, Paul declared, who puts away the vices of the heathen was renewed into knowledge (Col. 3:10). Clement of Rome also wrote, "Let a man be faithful, let him have power to utter knowledge, let him be wise in the discernment of arguments" (*1 Clement* 48:3). It had some association, derived from Daniel, with apocalyptic and in such concepts as "knowledge unto salvation" was connected with an understanding of the world beyond. Even so it remained only one aspect of a Christian's armory, as Paul in a famous passage points out, something that would pass away, leaving love as the Christian's supreme attribute (1 Cor. 13:13).

But in a hostile universe believed to be governed by Chance (Tyché) and by demonic forces, salvation obtained through the steady accumulation of virtue during a long life seemed pedestrian and inadequate. People wanted to know that they were saved, and this is what the Gnostic claimed to be able to tell them. Valentinus, the most famous of the Alexandrian Gnostics (*flor.* circa 160), in his *Letter to Rheginos* speaks of redemption as "the spiritual resurrection which devours the psychical and fleshly resurrection," i.e., incomplete systems in which Jews and Greeks put their trust.[4] His followers justified their position vis-à-vis other Christians by claiming,[5] "it is not only baptism that frees (from the power of fate) but Gnosis—knowledge of what we were, why we have come into being, where we are and at what point we have been placed (in the cosmos), whither we are hastening, from what we have been redeemed, and what is birth and rebirth." A similar claim was made by the Ophite sect of Gnostics about the same time. "We alone know the necessity of birth and the ways by which man enters the world. And so, being fully instructed, we alone are able to pass through and beyond decay."[6] These quotations represent the Gnostic viewpoint. Gnosis was knowledge of the mysteries of the universe and through that knowledge, power to overcome the demons that guided the universe. By acquiring Gnosis the individual won salvation and union with God for his soul and also the answer to all the great questions of this life, "whence is evil," and "whence is man."[7] He was the illuminated one, and to the Christian Gnostic, the source of illumination was Christ.

In the second century Gnosticism was a worldwide movement. There were Gnostics in southern Gaul, in Rome, Carthage, Asia Minor, Syria and Egypt, but the real centers of inspiration were Alexandria and Syria, and the great leaders of the movement, Basilides, Valentinus, Heracleon, Menander and Satornilus, were Egyptians or Syrians. It had, however, been preached in the first century by the Docetic heretics referred to in the Pastoral and Catholic Epistles and in the *Letters of Ignatius*. There were also obscure movements associated with Simon Magus and Cerinthus. Simon was the reputed founder of Gnosticism and had been encountered by St. Paul during his mission through Samaria; Cerinthus was a Jewish-Gnostic prominent in Asia Minor about A.D. 100.[8]

Articulate Gnosticism was therefore emerging contemporary with the first Christian missions. That, however, does not tell us very much. The questions the Gnostics were asking, and their solutions, were also the themes of the great mystery religions throughout the Mediterranean area at this period. How did Gnosticism differ from these? Until the discovery of the library of fifty-two Gnostic books found at Nag Hammadi north of Luxor in Upper Egypt, in 1945, it was almost impossible to discover what the Gnostics believed, and hence the measure of their threat to the Church. Why should Irenaeus of Lyons have spent a large part of his episcopate in attempting to refute them, and how was it that they provided the spur to the formulation of Clement's and Origen's theology in Alexandria, and inspired so much of the angry sarcasm of Tertullian in Carthage?

Research into Gnosticism has been helped by two of the Nag Hammadi works which have now been translated, namely *The Gospel of Truth* and the *Secret Teaching of John*. The *Gospel of Truth* may have been written by Valentinus himself. It is a summons to self-knowledge and life, to turn oneself to God through Gnosis, and by self-mastery to win the means of return to God. It is couched in phrasing not dissimilar to some forms of Existentialism. Natural man was represented as stumbling about in a state of ignorance, beset by fears and phantoms. "Sometimes one is in a battle, one gives blows and one receives blows. Or one falls from a great height . . . at other times it is as if one met death at the hands of an invisible murderer"—a dream life full of terrors, the reflections of the terrors the unenlightened soul would meet in the beyond. The Gnostic elect, however, received self-knowledge through the Gospel of Truth which Christ brought and was able to turn to God and be saved, "as one who makes himself free and awakes from the drunkenness wherein he lived, and returns to himself."[9]

One can understand how this message, with its reminiscences of Homer and Plato, could appeal to the Greek-speaking provincial. But the Gnostics did not regard themselves as allies of the current Greek philosophic systems. In another of the Nag Hammadi works, *The Treatise of the Three Natures*, the author writes scathingly about philosophers. "They did not possess the possibility of knowing the cause of existing things, because this was not communicated to them."[10] Greek philosophy was the epitome of demonic confusion. The ladder of truth lay through emancipation from current philosophies and mysteries to a right understanding of the Christian and Jewish writings, and above all, to an understanding of the relationship of the New to the Old Testament. On the definition of that understanding orthodox and Gnostic clashed.

The *Secret Teaching of John* was one of the works most read by the Nag Hammadi Gnostic and is typical of second-century Gnosticism. It illustrates the mixture of Jewish and non-Jewish elements in Christian sectarian beliefs. The writer sets the scene of the Gnostic revelation in Jerusalem shortly after the Crucifixion. John, the brother of James, was going up to the temple when he was met by a Pharisee named Ananias. The latter upbraids him, "Where is your Master, whose follower you were?" When John replied "He has gone to the place whence he came," the Pharisee countered, "This Nazarene deceived you with deception, and hardened your hearts and estranged you from the tradition of your fathers." The reproach of being a renegade Jew struck home, and, deeply perturbed, John went out to a desert place, and while in great grief and despondency had a vision of the risen Christ who revealed the secret of salvation in Gnostic terms.[11]

God is unknowable, the beginning, the end, immeasurable light, the giver of eternity, ultimate mercy, above and beyond this world. But out of this transcendent God came spirit, "the fount of the Spirit flowed out of the living water of Light" (cf. John 7:38). Spirit became operative in the primary seed, the first thought, and from her originated the heavenly order. The five first eons included primal man, equipped with perfect reason, willpower and intellect, and light "which is Christ." Then there were other heavenly beings in descending order, making twenty-nine in all,[12] until the creation of Sophia (wisdom). But Sophia was not content with her station. Desire (sexual desire) within her drove her into reproduction, and from the result came the creator of the visible universe, "the First Archon of Darkness," Ialdabaoth or Yahweh, the jealous god of the Old Testament. Ialdabaoth, we are told, "joined himself with the Unreason that was within him, and called the Powers into existence." These powers belonged to the world of Jewish angelology, and they in turn created the planets and their rulers. Finally, Adam was brought into being, an imitation of primal man who existed from the beginning, in fulfillment of the words of Genesis 1:26 paraphrased by the author as "Let us make a man after the image and after the appearance of God." In Adam was concentrated the light which Ialdabaoth had received from Sophia, but in order to control him Ialdabaoth fettered him to a body made out of the elements of the universe, earth, water, fire and wind, representing "matter, darkness, desire and the Opposed Spirit." The last named was Ialdabaoth's agent who directed man toward his lower desires, including a desire to procreate. Thus, in each man was both a godly spark derived from the world of light and also the temptations to wickedness implanted by Ialdabaoth and his archons. These were destined to struggle for possession of the soul. Finally, Christ was sent by God, the Father of all, to acquaint mankind of its true nature and enable its soul to free itself from the Opposed Spirit and to return to the realms of light.

This was the "mystery" revealed to John in reply to the Pharisee's challenge. This strange system, largely Jewish in inspiration, but clothed in myth and allegory like the current Hellenistic mystery religions, can be found in one Gnostic system after another. Understandably, those current in first-century Syria, such as Simon Magus's or Menander's, are more overtly Jewish than the later traditions but all had important features in common. First, God was existence without qualities except those of ultimate being, and was separated from creation by a vast complex of heavenly powers. It was due to some catastrophic action by the lowest of these powers that the universe came into existence. Secondly, the ruler of the universe, defined as Yahweh Ialdabaoth (child of Chaos) or even a pagan high-god such as Saturn, was not the true god, and did not even know of his existence. Hence, his laws, such as the various covenants between Yahweh and the Jewish people, were not divine laws but merely temporary expedients of varying validity. Man was in ignorance of God until the coming of a being from the world of light, defined by Christians as Christ or in some pagan mysteries as Heracles, awoke him to his true self. But Christ as a heavenly being could not make contact with the matter out of which the universe was created without defilement. Hence, there was neither Incarnation, nor Passion, nor Resurrection; and the Gospels told simply a story of the temporary union of a Heavenly being and a man, Jesus of Nazareth. Mankind was divided into three categories, the elect or illumined who were predestined to salvation, the "psychics," men and women who were capable of salvation, and the vast majority of humanity, who ate, drank and married—and died eternally.

The danger with which the teaching of Valentinus and Basilides confronted orthodox Christianity needs no emphasis. The Old Testament was rejected after detailed examination in learned commentaries and well-written treatises such as the *Letter* of Ptolemy to Flora. The denial of the human element in the Savior and his suffering, death and resurrection struck at the heart of Christianity. There was no place for a doctrine of the Trinity, for there was no place for the Holy Spirit. As one critic of the early Gnostic systems pointed out, "strange opinions concerning the grace of Jesus Christ" led to the rejection of Christian morality, "For love they have no care, none for the widow, none for the orphan, none for the distressed, none for the afflicted." How could those who did not believe in the reality of Christ's body offer a valid Eucharist?[13]

Moreover, the dualistic approach to the universe, inevitable if the universe was controlled by beings not "of God," induced fatalism in the individual's moral outlook. Predestination of humanity into its three watertight categories made nonsense of a loving God active throughout the universe, and of man's own responsibility for accepting or rejecting his law. Here was a Christianity without an ethical impulse and pessimistic in its view of the world. It could hardly have become a major religion of mankind. Finally, Gnosis was a secret teaching imparted to the believer alone. It was not to be proclaimed nor for that matter confessed before pagan magistrates. As another Nag Hammadi document asserted, "These revelations are not to be disclosed to anyone in the flesh and are only to be communicated to the brethren who belong to the generation of life."[14] There was to be no "witness against the world," and no acceptance of the inspiration of the Holy Spirit dependent on such witness. The Gnostic was not a man of martyrdom. Indeed, he deliberately rejected its necessity, and as one who was saved he saw no reason against giving formal acknowledgment of the gods of his city or eating meats sacrificed to idols.[15] The body which enjoyed the sacrificial meats was doomed to destruction anyhow. Its abuse, or alternatively its destruction by rigorous fasts and privations, merely speeded the liberation of the spark of light within it. Nirvana replaced Heaven and Hell.

Yet the Gnostics were not only proclaiming ideas which corresponded with much current educated thought, but bequeathed a considerable legacy to Christian doctrine. They had raised questions which the Church has been hard pressed to answer. The docetic Christ (i.e., the Christ who only appeared to have human form) has exercised his hold on religious minds from that day to this. This view of Christ requires human intermediaries, such as Mary Magdalene or the Virgin Mary, to communicate his message and experiences to mankind. It is no accident that the earliest accounts of the Assumption of the Virgin appear to be Egyptian Gnostic legends.[16] Then, the Church could never cease to concern itself with the problem of evil. Augustine and Luther, like Valentinus and Basilides, wrestled with the same issue "Whence came evil?" and "Why?", and Augustine was for nine years satisfied with the answer given by the Manichees, who in Africa had accepted a great deal of the Gnostic heritage. Then again, the Gnostics forced their orthodox opponents to define their terms and look more closely at their doctrine. They provoked the first great essay at a Catholic theology, Irenaeus of Lyons's *Against the Heresies*, circa 180–5. Gnostic commentaries on Scripture provoked orthodox replies. The Gnostic organization on the lines of philosophic schools accelerated Christianity organized round a centralized hierarchical government. Finally, their emphasis on the harmony of true religion and reason and their equation of the instructed Christian with a status approaching that of Plato's Guardians had a profound effect on the development of Christian thought in Alexandria. Neither Clement nor Origen was to reject the Gnostic ideal of the truly rational soul moving irrevocably toward ultimate harmony with God. They merely claimed that Gnostic methods did not further that ideal.

The Gnostic leaders were not the only threat to the cohesion of the Church in the second century. Marcion may not have been a sort of forerunner of Luther as some German admirers have implied, but he was an outstanding individual. He justly deserved the awe-inspired opposition of orthodox tradition of the second and third centuries as the arch-heretic of their day. Alone among Christian thinkers of his time he saw the Old Testament for what it was, namely the religious history of the Jewish people. It had nothing to do with Christianity. God's supreme gift to mankind, the teaching and revelation of Christ, needed no argument from Old Testament prophecy to support it, and no allegorical interpretations to iron out uncomfortable pieces of Scripture. God through Christ had made all things new in one supreme act of love for creation.

Marcion was born about A.D. 85, the son of the Christian "bishop" of Sinope on the Black Sea.[17] He was a wealthy man, a shipowner and merchant whose business took him about the Mediterranean and to Rome. Early in his career, however, he fell foul of the churches in Asia Minor, was denounced by Polycarp of Smyrna with characteristic vigor as "firstborn of Satan," and left his native province for Rome. Here he was at first accepted, and he donated the large sum of 200,000 sesterces (50,000 silver denarii) to the community there. He wrote a work known as the

Antitheses, fragments only of which have survived, was excommunicated circa 144, and spent the remaining fifteen to twenty years of his life founding communities in opposition to the great Church which had cast him out.

What was his message? Like his Gnostic contemporaries whom he resembled in many ways, Marcion rejected Yahweh's identification with God. God was the unknown God of Acts 17:23, characterized by love, boundless peace and serenity. This God was Father of Jesus Christ, but had no tie with creation: rather, his object in sending Jesus Christ to the world was to free mankind from the power of Yahweh. But Marcion did not regard Yahweh as evil, merely that his law represented bare natural justice, the eye for an eye, the justice which the new covenant was designed to supersede. Rigorously criticizing the Old Testament, Marcion pointed to the text of Isaiah 45:7, "I make peace and it is I who send evil, I, the Lord do these things." He contrasted this with Jesus' saying that a tree was known by its fruit, a good tree cannot bring forth evil fruit, and then pointed to the series of injunctions and lessons in the Old Testament which are contradicted in the New. Elisha had children eaten by bears. Christ commanded, "little children come unto me." Joshua had the sun stopped in its path in order to prolong a slaughter. Christ, through St. Paul, said, "Let not the sun go down on your wrath." In the Old Testament divorce was permitted; in the New Testament it was not, except for adultery. Thus the Old Testament could not be the word of God, but at best that of an inferior being; and Marcion found the clue to God's redemption of mankind in Luke's account of Christ's appearance in Capernaum "in the fifteenth year of Tiberius Caesar." The abrupt start of the ministry signified God's sudden intervention in the affairs of the world.

Marcion found what he needed in Luke's Gospel, and in the ten Pauline Epistles. This was the word of God. Acts which told the deeds of the disciples who had failed to understand Jesus' message and the Apocalypse which depicted God's vengeance on persecutors and unbelievers, he rejected as the work of Judaizers. He aimed instead at providing the Church with its own canon of Scripture independent of the Septuagint, independent of Judeo-Christian writings, a Scripture worthy of a loving God and the saving purpose of his Son. For the believer himself, seized with love and compassion, trust in God's goodness sufficed for salvation.

Unfortunately, like the Gnostic, the Marcionite appeal was to a perfectionism impossible for the ordinary individual to attain. The Marcionite Christian was an ascetic who rejected marriage, and though organized as a church with a hierarchy and creed its appeal was toward individual purity rather than universal salvation. It prospered in Syria and on the Mesopotamian frontier area where one of the earliest Christian inscriptions found, dated 318/19, comes from a Marcionite community,[18] but elsewhere Marcion's missionaries had less success.

Marcion's religion was in reality a religion of personal feeling. As his disciple Apelles said in a debate in Rome with a Catholic opponent, one felt rather than could prove that the Old and New Testaments belonged to different worlds. The prophecies were not consistent. Moses was no guide to the Christian. Rhodon, Appeles' opponent, laughed. A philosopher who could not prove his case by logic was not worth hearing.[19] It might be that the laugh was on Rhodon, because what religion is capable of human "proof"?

FURTHER READING

Blackman, E.C., *Marcion and his Influence*, SPCK 1948

Casey, R.P., 'The Study of Gnosticism', *Journal of Theological Studies* 36, 1935, 45-60

Cross, F.L., *The Jung Codex*, Mowbrays 1955

Dart, J., *The Laughing Savior: The Discovery and Significance of the Nag Hammadi Gnostic Library*, Harper and Row 1976

Foerster, W., and Wilson, R.M., *Gnosis. A Selection of Gnostic Texts*, Oxford University Press 1972 (two vols.)

Grant, R.M., *Second Century Christianity*, SPCK 1957

Jonas, Hans, *The Gnostic Religion*, Beacon Press, Boston [2]1970

Logan, A.H.N., and Wedderburn, A.J.M., *The New Testament and Gnosis*, T.&T.Clark 1983

Pagels, E., *The Gnostic Gospels*, Random House 1979 and Weidenfeld and Nicholson 1980

Robinson, J.M. (ed.), *The Nag Hammadi Library*, Harper and Row 1977

Rudolph, K., *Gnosis*, T.& T.Clark 1983

Turner, H.E.W., *The Pattern of Christian Truth*, Mowbrays 1954

Wilson, R.McL, *The Gnostic Problem*, Mowbrays 1958

Wilson, R.McL, *Studies in the Gospel of Thomas*, Mowbrays 1960

6

A Generation of Crisis
160–85

Most Gnostics, though not the Marcionites, had been willing to give a formal acknowledgment to the Greco-Roman deities. They did not court persecution, and they had abandoned the apocalyptic view of the Church's mission which had been one of the main sources of inspiration for its hostility against the authorities. It might appear therefore that their comparative strength in Egypt, eastern Syria, Rome and the province of Asia would guarantee Christians peaceful relations with the Empire.

During the reigns of Hadrian (117–38) and Antoninus Pius (138–61) this was broadly speaking true. The Church, though far more in the world than during the previous generation, enjoyed a considerable degree of toleration. There was, however, no change in its legal status. Christians were simply not "sought out." There were public debates between Jews and Christians, such as that held between Justin and Trypho at Ephesus circa 137,[1] or between Jason and Papiscus in Alexandria.[2] High officials in the service of the Proconsul of Asia, such as Florinus, were Christians,[3] Christian leaders, whether Gnostic or orthodox, moved freely about the Mediterranean; Polycarp, Bishop of Smyrna, one of the largest towns in the province of Asia, could assert at his trial that he had been "86 years in the service of Christ,"[4] and up to that moment no one had molested him. As Eusebius wrote (*Hist. Eccl.* iv. 7:1), "the Churches like brilliant lamps were shining throughout the world and the faith in our Savior the Lord Jesus Christ was flourishing among all mankind." The several new centers of Christianity in Asia Minor and the Aegean Islands which he mentions in this period support his claim.

Yet while official policy remained tolerant, and persecution and mob violence against the Christians were restrained, popular opinion in the Greek-speaking world was gradually becoming more hostile. The Christian *Letter to Diognetus*, perhaps circa 150, speaks about Christians being "condemned and persecuted by all men," and Justin in both his *Apologies*

58

written in 150 and 155 tells of the hounding and harrying of individual Christians. In the decade 150–60 the provincials seem to have made up their minds that orthodox Christians, by refusing worship to the gods, were responsible for all manner of ills, such as famine, plague and earthquake, that could befall a community; and in addition, were guilty of cannibalism, incest and black magic, evils liable to bring down divine wrath on communities which permitted them. To quote the well-known passage from Tertullian, though written in Carthage thirty years later: "If the Tiber reaches the walls, if the Nile does not rise to the fields, if the sky doesn't move or the earth does, if there is famine, if there is plague, the cry is at once, "Christians to the lion." What, all of them to one lion?" (*Apol.* 40:2, tr. T. R. Glover).

Under Marcus Aurelius (161–80) the administrative procedures by which a Christian could be accused were apparently eased sufficiently to make it worthwhile for informers to denounce them,[5] while popular fury was fanned by agitators including Jews. The Christians had finally taken over from the Jews the unenviable role of public enemies of the city state.

From the Acts of the martyrs to which he had access, Eusebius records details of two terrible instances of violence against the Christians in this period. In circa 165–8 there had been a local persecution in Symrna and twelve Christians had been condemned to the beasts.[6] But the beasts proved reluctant, and in one case the confessor had to drag an animal toward him in order to be eaten, "the sooner," as he claimed, "to be freed from an unjust and wicked life."[7] This enraged the crowd, and the cry went up, "Kill the atheists. Let Polycarp be fetched." Polycarp, Bishop of Smyrna, was found, arrested, and eventually brought before the Proconsul. The following memorable scene took place, recorded by a Christian at the time.

When he approached the proconsul asked him if he were Polycarp, and when he admitted it he tried to persuade him to deny, saying: "Respect your age," and so forth, as they are accustomed to say: "Swear by the genius of Caesar, repent, say: "Away with the Atheists"; but Polycarp, with a stern countenance looked on all the crowd in the arena, and waving his hand at them, he groaned and looked up to the heaven and said: "Away with the Atheists." But when the Governor pressed him and said: "Take the oath and I will let you go, revile Christ," Polycarp said: "For eighty and six years have I been his servant, and he has done me no wrong, and how can I blaspheme my King who saved me?" But when he persisted again, and said: "Swear by the genius of Caesar," he said: "If you vainly suppose that I will swear by the genius of Caesar, as you say, and pretend that you are ignorant who I am, listen plainly: I am a Christian. And if you

59

wish to learn the doctrine of Christianity fix a day and listen." The pro-consul said: "Persuade the people." And Polycarp said: "You I should have held worthy of discussion, for we have been taught to render honour, as is meet, if it hurt us not, to princes and authorities appointed by God; but as for those, I do not count them worthy that a defence should be made to them." And the proconsul said: "I have wild beasts, I will deliver you to them, unless you change your mind." And he said: "Call for them, for change of mind from better to worse is a change we may not make; but it is good to change from evil to righteousness." And he said again to him: "I will cause you to be consumed by fire, if you despise the beasts, unless you repent." But Polycarp said: "You threaten with the fire that burns for a time, and is quickly quenched, for you do not know the fire which awaits the wicked in the judgement to come and in everlasting punishment. But why are you waiting? Come, do what you will.'" (Eusebius, *H.E.* iv. 15. 18 Tr. Kirsopp Lake.)

Polycarp was burnt, the Jews "who were extremely zealous, as is their custom," assisting in this.[8] The scene shows clearly how little room there was for compromise between the Christian and the authorities once the issue had been joined. Polycarp was a well-respected member of the community. He had servants, and friends among the city aristocracy who tried in vain to help him; he refused all offers of escape and when the formal question had been put, was he a Christian, he accepted the full consequences of avowal, trusting in future divine vengeance on his persecutors.

So too, in 165 did Justin Martyr in Rome. He had been the victim of a private grudge by a member of the rival radical teachers, the Cynics. The case was heard before the Prefect of Rome, Junius Rusticus, an aged offi-cial who had been a friend of both Antoninus Pius and his son Marcus. He too attempted to dissuade Justin and failed. The latter believed that on death he would go straight to Paradise, and on admitting that he had a meeting place where he taught, and that he taught Christianity, was condemned to be scourged and beheaded. For Eastern and Western Christians alike he was "philosopher" and "martyr."

Most horrible of all, however, was Eusebius's record of the events at Lyons in 177, citing copiously from a contemporary document.[9] Here it is not merely the brutality of the mob and the weakness of the authorities that appalls. There is a strong suspicion that the ultimate cause of the persecution was a desire by the Gallic nobility, who were responsible for providing gladiators for the annual Games at Lyons, to save money by taking advantage of a decision by Marcus that criminals might be substituted at one tenth of the cost.[10] What better criminals were there than the Christians? In any event, the outbreak began with scenes of mob violence leading to a wholesale arrest of the Christians in the city. These were very largely immigrants from Asia Minor, and the Church there, as in other parts of the Celtic provinces, could be represented as an exclusive foreign cult with secret rites brought in by immigrant traders from the East.[11] No love was lost between these Christians and their Gallic neighbors, who had received classical civilization in its material and intellectual forms with enthusiasm. The provincial governor took the line of least resistance. A public trial of the Christians was held and under torture some of their slaves confessed that their owners had been guilty of incest and cannibalism, just as the mob had suspected.[12] After this there was no scope for mercy; those who did not recant were committed to inhuman conditions in prison, and substituted for gladiators as the showpiece for the Games at the annual feast of the Three Gauls on 1 August. The last to perish was the heroic slave Blandina.

One point of constitutional interest arises from the Eusebian narrative. Early in the proceedings the governor had written to Marcus Aurelius informing him of what was happening and probably asking what was to be done about the Roman citizens among the accused. The Emperor replied that those who recanted were to be freed unless they were accused of other crimes in addition. Apparently, it was no longer necessary to send Roman citizens to Rome for punishment as it had been in Pliny's time.[13] The governor could punish them on the spot. The regulations concerning Christians, however, had not changed. Recantation still brought freedom, though now the informer looking for scandal could count on a sympathetic hearing. The persecution also was directed against individuals. The corporate property of the Church was not disturbed, and in a year or two the Christians were able to elect a new bishop to replace the martyr, Pothinus, namely the presbyter Irenaeus.

The reign of Marcus Aurelius marked the climax of popular anger against the Christians. It was accompanied by serious attacks on the intellectual position of the Church. About 165 the satirical writer Lucian of Samosata on the Euphrates wrote an account of a Cynic called Proteus Peregrinus. Lucian hated the Cynics as quacks and exhibitionists, and it served his purpose to tell the story of a phase in Peregrinus's life when the latter became a Christian. Peregrinus, suspected of parricide, had fled from his native Prusa in northwestern Asia Minor to Syria; there he met the Christians, and they welcomed him with open arms. He soon became a "prophet, cult leader, and community chief," and he even started writing commentaries on Scripture. Then he was put in prison, and Christians for miles around clubbed together to alleviate his lot. "They show," Lucian wrote, "incredible speed whenever public action is taken [i.e., against one of them] for in no time they lavish their all [on

61

the victim]." Eventually he was let out by a mildly sympathetic governor, and after he had offended against Christian dietary regulations he resumed his career as a Cynic. Lucian's view of the Christians was that they were credulous, fanatic, and bound together by the fact that they had "rejected the Greek gods," simpletons perhaps, but none the less dangerous.[14]

Thirteen years later another educated provincial, probably also from Syria, wrote a thoughtful and thoroughgoing attack against Christianity. Celsus was not a satirist, and he had taken the trouble to read many of the books of the Christians. He knew something about Judaism and the relations between Jews and Christians as well.[15] He shows us the Church as it appeared to an outsider, still Jewish in outlook, divided among a number of warring sects, an organization that rejected reason among human virtues, that looked forward to the end of the world in great blaze, an illegal society which proselytized, and preached disloyalty to its converts.

Celsus began with the assertion that "public associations are legal but secret societies are not" and that the Christians were among the latter.[16] The climax of his work was that the duty of a good citizen was loyalty to the common beliefs, deviation from which would impair the safety of the civilized world. Polytheism reflected nature, each deity having his special function as the expression of God, and consequently special duties in Creation. The emperor was the representative of deity on earth. "To the emperor," Celsus wrote, "all on earth is given and whatever you receive in life you receive from him."[17] Therefore Christians should "help the emperor with all your might and labor with him as right requires, and if he calls on you take the field with him and share the command of legions, and be magistrates, and to do all this for the salvation of laws and religion."[18] To Celsus, the real charge against the Christians was their lack of civic sense and disloyalty to an empire the benefits of whose rule they were enjoying. When one reads Tertullian's famous "Nothing is more foreign to us than the State" (*Apol.* 39), and his statement that the duty of a Christian soldier was desertion (*De Corona Militis* 11), one can appreciate Celsus's problem.

But Celsus was not content with assertion alone. He indicated the weaknesses in Christian theology which led to these antisocial views. The radical error of both Judaism and Christianity was that they separated man from the rest of creation. "They say that God made all things for man,"[19] a claim which was simply not true. Plants grew for the sake of animals as well as for man. Before he came to live in cities man did not have unquestioned supremacy over animals. In no way was man better in

God's sight than ants and bees.[20] God's care was for the whole universe and not only for one of his creatures.

This error Celsus traced back to a false idea of God. As a Platonist he conceived of God as the first cause, the good and the beautiful, but only dimly intelligible to the human mind. He could not descend in the form of a man, for that would bring him into contact with mortality and change.[21] Here Celsus was trying to solve the problem the Gnostics had posed. How can a perfect being have contact with an imperfect creation without losing his perfection? And Jesus Christ with his vacillations and weakness on the Cross was no advertisement for the Godhead. "If Jesus really wished to display his divine power, he should have appeared to the actual men who had reviled him."[22] But the God of Christians behaved like an angry old man, taking vengeance on his enemies, roasting people alive,[23] and the Christians themselves were a miserable but arrogant collection of nonentities, "frogs holding a symposium round a swamp or worms a conventicle in a corner of the mud, debating which of them was the most sinful, and saying, 'God reveals all things to us beforehand and gives us warning. He forsakes the whole universe and the course of the heavenly sphere to dwell with us alone.' "[24]

But all the time the Christians were active. Celsus gives a firsthand account of the other side of the Christian mission. For him it was not a matter of souls being saved from burning or worse, but an attempt to subvert society, to destroy family life, to sow disaffection among the subjects of the Empire. He does not bother with the cruder charges against the Christians. Christians were revolutionaries and amply deserved punishment when caught. Thus, in a well-known passage he describes the missionary at work. "We see them in our own homes, wool dressers, cobblers, and fullers, the most uneducated and common individuals, not daring to say a word in the presence of their masters who are older and wiser. But, when they get hold of the children in private, and silly women with them, they are wonderfully eloquent, to the effect that the children must not listen to their father, but believe them, and be taught by them."[25]

There was more than an element of truth in Celsus's remarks. Proselytism was one of the causes of Christian unpopularity as it had been of Jewish. In times of stress, families were riven apart, and the women members who were Christian sometimes found their worst enemies in husbands, fathers, and brothers who had been shamed by their action.

The orthodox Christians of the latter half of the second century had therefore to fight on two fronts. They had to try to convince middle-class provincial opinion that the charges of atheism, cannibalism, etc., leveled against them were untrue, and they had to disprove Gnostic claims that Christian perfection had no need of an exclusive attitude toward the world, or a Church organization. It was partly these needs and partly doubts concerning the exclusive relevance of apocalyptic that brought into being the Christian apologetic movement of the second century. There is no need here to go through the arguments of all the Apologists in turn. It suffices to say that the earliest recorded Christian Apology was written by Quadratus reputedly in Athens in Hadrian's reign. This was followed by a curious work by a writer called Aristides, probably circa 145, the most pro-Jewish of the Apologists, and that after Justin a veritable cascade of apologetic writing issued from Christians in the last years of the reign of Marcus Aurelius. These writings paved the way for those who tried to combine apologetics with systematic theology: Irenaeus, Clement, and Tertullian.

Against the pagans, the Apologists first denied the truth of the scandalous accusations against the Christians and then moved over to an attack on paganism itself. They drew their ammunition from two main sources. The first was the long tradition of Hellenistic–Jewish criticism of paganism which can be traced back to the second century B.C. and beyond, and is well represented by Psalm 115, the Book of Wisdom and Isaiah 44. Pagans were accused of worshiping God's creation rather than God himself. Their idols were dumb and lifeless; they were made of rotten wood or rusty metal.[26] Pagan ethics were an accurate reflection of the immoral legends concerning the gods of Olympus, and any truth in pagan philosophy was a crude plagiarism of Scripture. Added to this assault were arguments derived from current popular forms of rationalism which were being propagated by the Stoics and Cynics. Christians were fond of using argument attributed to the philosopher Euhemeros, who claimed that the gods were really human beings who had been declared gods on account of services rendered to mankind. Osiris, for instance, was the discoverer of grain, Prometheus of the use of fire. It is interesting to find the same "letter" from Alexander the Great to his mother, relating how he had frightened Egyptian priests into confessing that their gods were only deified men, in the Greek Apology of Athenagoras[27] and the Latin of Minucius Felix (Rome, circa 210). It may have formed part of a Christian anthology on anti-pagan texts.

On the positive side, the Apologists stressed the truth of monotheism and claimed that only the Christian appreciation and worship of God was valid. The universe had been created by the word of God, was governed by his laws, but these were apprehensible by human reason. Only the demons, argued Justin, the forces of chaos and unreason represented by idolatry, held mankind in bondage. There was no excuse for this now that the way of escape had been shown by Jesus Christ, and the means of redemption by baptism and repentance of sin. Far from the Christians being outcasts, theirs was a special position in humanity. "To put it shortly," as the Christian writer of the *Letter to Diognetus* (circa 150) claimed, "what the soul is in the body that the Christians are in the world."[28] And, being opposed to disharmony and unreason themselves they were automatically good citizens, loyal to the Emperor and willing to carry out his commands, so far as service to God allowed.

The arguments which the Apologists used led them logically to oppose the Gnostics. Granted that both in their own way looked to the harmony of Christianity and the State, the Apologists stressed the intimate connection between the truth of the Christian religion and the soundness of Christian ethics. Thus Justin asserted as one of the proofs of Christianity that its converts were transformed from wanton and dissolute to temperate living,[29] and Athenagoras could write (circa 177) that "With us you will find unlettered people, tradesmen and old women, who though they are unable to express in words the advantages of our teaching demonstrate by acts the value of their principles."[30] The Gnostic had no such guiding light, nor the same ethical principles that led the Apologist unhesitatingly to witness and to the martyr's death, and he forfeited thereby one of the strongest arguments in Christianity's favor.

Moreover, in the debate with the educated pagan, the Apologist insisted both on the antiquity and the coherence of Christian teaching. It was not new, and therefore revolutionary. Hence his insistence on the unity of the two Testaments, and the argument from prophecy, namely that Christ indeed fulfilled the Hebrew prophets' statements concerning man's redemption. Thus Justin, "I will present the evidence that the things we say as disciples of Christ and of the prophets who came before him are the only truths and older than all the writers who have lived."[31] Even the greatest of the Greek philosophers partook of this truth only in part. Plato, to Celsus the spiritual guide, was merely an ally to Justin, pointing toward the true philosophy of Christ.[32]

It is very doubtful whether the Apologists had any serious effect on the policy of the Roman authorities. One cannot imagine any but a convinced Christian reading the long, involved *First Apology* of Justin with its heavy reliance on Scriptural quotation and forced and irrelevant allegories. But they did serve notice that Christianity was now an intellectual force to be reckoned with, and they contributed to the Church's ability to survive the crisis of Marcus Aurelius's reign.

Meanwhile, the struggle with the Gnostics was continuing. Apart from the arguments of Justin and his friends, the Church called on its armory of superior organization backed by a longstanding if somewhat one-sided teaching tradition. The man who welded these various factors into a truly formidable weapon against nonorthodoxy was Irenaeus of Lyons.

Irenaeus had been one of the few survivors from the holocaust of 177. An immigrant from Smyrna, he had known Polycarp as a young man and carried a lifelong impression of him as a bishop and a man of apostolic authority. It is also possible that before settling in Lyons, he had spent time in Rome and had known Justin. However, by 180 he was Bishop of the Church in Gaul, and turned his efforts to smiting the Gnostics whom he found making inroads into his congregation. The five books *Against the Heresies*, written circa 185, both expose Gnostic theories to detailed and devastating criticism, and contain a good many of the seeds of western Catholicism.[33] So does his later work, *The Demonstration of Apostolic Preaching*, designed as a handbook of Christian apologetic against Judaism and heresy.

First and foremost, Irenaeus defined the Apostolic Faith as that which was held universally by all Christian communities irrespective of the believer's race or level of intelligence. Thus he claims, "this faith, as I have said, the Church though scattered in the whole world carefully preserves, as if living in one house . . . For the languages of the world are different but the meaning of the [Christian] tradition is the same."[34]

The same tradition was taught among churches of Germany and the Celtic lands as in those of Egypt and Libya. This of course was not strictly true for the Rule of Faith in Egypt differed considerably from that expounded by Irenaeus, but in fairness it must be conceded that other orthodox travelers of Irenaeus's period such as the Palestinian Hegesippus[35] or the Phrygian merchant Avircius Marcellus (circa 210) had been impressed by the fact that everywhere Christians had the same organization and rites.[36] From the Rhone to the Euphrates the Faith ostensibly was one.

Once more against the Gnostics, Irenaeus defined the bases of the Christian Faith. God was one. The same God who created the universe was the God of Israel in the Old Testament. With him, Jesus Christ was united as his word and Son, and his coming had been predicted through the Holy Spirit by the Hebrew prophets. Moreover, Christ truly ministered, suffered and died and was received into Heaven, whence he would also return. All mankind would rise at the Last Day and be judged.

This was the deposit of Faith transmitted by Christ's Apostles to the Church for the redemption of believers, and it had been passed on by their successors the bishops. To them and them only had the government of the Church been entrusted. "Therefore," claims Irenaeus, "obedience is due to those presbyters who, as we have shown, are in the succession after the Apostles, and who with their episcopal succession have received according to the will of the Father the *charisma* of truth."[37] To Irenaeus, Polycarp was the type of "blessed presbyter" who taught what he himself had learned from the Apostles.

So the idea of apostolic succession was to be linked with that of episcopal authority. Others, such as Ignatius, had stressed the fact of the bishop's authority against the claims of heretical teachers. Hegesippus had sought to confirm (circa 175) that the chief Christian churches did have Apostles as their founders. Irenaeus, however, linked the two ideas, and in his hands the bishop becomes the supreme arbiter of the Church's doctrine and discipline. Rome, founded by the two Apostles Peter and Paul, Irenaeus cites as a model See, and in a famous but ambiguous sentence affirms that "every church must assemble at (or "be in harmony with") this church because of its outstanding preeminence, that is, the faithful from everywhere, since the apostolic tradition is preserved in it by those from everywhere."[38] Naturally this sentence has been a source of inter-Christian strife. The real problem seems to be to interpret what Irenaeus meant by *convenire ad*. Was it the literal meaning of "assemblage," or the metaphorical "to be in agreement with"? We do not know what the original Greek text stated. Eusebius, however, had read the sentence but did not attribute great significance to it, for in the *Ecclesiastical History* he cited only the passage which immediately followed it.[39] In Irenaeus's time, Rome was a microcosm of the Roman world, and Irenaeus saw it as a microcosm of the Church, including, as he himself had probably experienced, Christians from all over the Roman world. It was, as he states, "the greatest and best-known See."

Having established a Rule of Faith and its dispensation by episcopal authority as the means of a Christian's redemption, Irenaeus attacked other important Gnostic arguments. If creation with its glaring evils and contradictions was not the result of an imperfect combination of opposites, what was the cause? If God and matter were not eternally contrasted, how were the imperfections of the universe to be explained? Irenaeus took his stand on Hebrew monotheism and the real harmony of the Old and New Testaments. The essential community of God and creation had been destroyed by Adam's sin, a sin due to his own free will and not to the action of evil archons. But from that disobedience resulted the whole long course of human estrangement from God, and human redemption involved a dramatic reversal of this process. Irenaeus's concept of the "summing up" of all things in Christ (*anakephalaiosis*) was not original. Justin had worked out the parallel between Eve and Mary,[40] Paul had already spoken of Christ as the second Adam, and in St. Luke's account of Pentecost at which men speaking different tongues could none the less understand one another, it is possible to see a dramatic reversal of the situation at Babel. But Irenaeus's detailed application of the idea to human redemption was new. Thus Jesus' obedience by his crucifixion on a tree renewed and reversed what had been done by Adam's disobedience in connection with a tree, and Eve's seductions were concealed by the faithfulness of the Virgin Mary. "As the human race," Irenaeus stated, "was subjected to death through [the act of] a virgin, so was it saved by a virgin, and thus the disobedience of one virgin was precisely balanced by the obedience of another."[41]

Here was a great panorama of religious history in which mankind, struck down by the disaster of the Fall, gradually moved forward toward reconciliation with God. "What we lost in Adam, we might regain in Christ, namely the image and likeness of God."[42] Even so, the advance had been slow. Not everything had been revealed at once. Irenaeus set human progress in the framework of four successive covenants, that from Adam to Noah, then from Noah to Moses, from Moses to the coming of Christ, and finally the new covenant of Jesus Christ.[43] Each had been valid for its own time, and now, the Holy Spirit was continually renewing the Church.[44] These arguments enabled him to explain the reason for the obviously lower standards of conduct portrayed in patriarchal times compared with the demands of Christian life. Gnostic and Marcionite dualism found itself confronted by an orthodox theory of progressive revelation based on traditional Hellenistic-Jewish and Christian arguments. Instead of Christ "suddenly appearing," his ministry was the climax of a long process of human development stretching back to the beginning of time. Moreover, Jesus' ministry had been a real ministry, for to redeem all conditions of man Jesus himself must experience those same conditions. "If he did not truly suffer, no thanks to him."[45] Finally, by the Church's sacraments Christ's divine life was imparted to humanity, and by sharing it, man himself would become divine.

It was a noble and a decisive answer to Gnosticism. Irenaeus showed that an orthodox understanding of the Bible could make as good sense as a Gnostic one. He was the first to set out the canon of the four Gospels together with other apostolic writings alongside the Old Testament. His development of allegory as an aid to the interpretation of the latter was also in the full tradition of both Jewish and Pauline thought. We see a powerful mind at work inspired by a conviction that Christianity was relevant for mankind as a whole. At the very moment when the old

Israel was turning in upon itself and reducing religious study to an ever more minute examination of sacred texts, Irenaeus was developing new ways of Scriptural interpretation in a wider perspective. In so doing he was laying out the boundaries of human speculation which were to hold good until the mid-nineteenth century, and was preparing the ground for Biblical Christianity to become the religion of a large portion of the civilized world.

One deviation significantly escaped the lash of Irenaeus's criticism. While they were in prison, the confessors of Lyons had been pressed for their opinion on a new, prophetic movement which had been sweeping the Churches in Asia.[46] In view of Eusebius's text we can probably date the emergence of Montanism in Phrygia to circa 172, and associate it with a reaction against the pogroms and persecutions which were being inflicted there on the Christians. At this time, Christians in Phrygia were startled by the appearance of Montanus, perhaps a one-time priest of Cybele, accompanied by two companions, Priscilla and Maximilla, who claimed to be prophets inspired by the Paraclete. Their message was uncompromisingly apocalyptic. They announced that the Parousia would take place near the villages of Tymion and Pepuza some fifteen miles from the city of Philadelphia. It was a revival of the wilderness theory of the Coming, and it was heard gladly. People summoned by the prophets to attend the inauguration of the Millennium abandoned homes, families and work to stream into the countryside. Wars and rumors of wars were freely prophesied, and death by martyrdom prepared for by continence and fasting was enjoined as the command of the Holy Spirit.

The Montanist movement had been long in preparation. Partly, it was the reaction to Christianity of a native population living in contact with Judaism, and the enthusiasm with which the prophetic message was heard anticipated a similar reaction among the North African provincials in the next century. Partly also, it was the outcome of a tradition of Christian prophecy which had survived alongside the episcopal tradition. The church of Philadelphia had been singled out by the Seer in Revelation on account of its zeal (Rev. 3:7 ff.). The daughters of the evangelist Philip were all reputed to be prophetesses and had been laid to rest in the Phrygian town of Hierapolis. Later, in the second century, prophets such as Quadratus and Ammia (a good Phrygian name) had flourished in the same area. Montanism blended the prophetic and orgiastic native Phrygian religion with exalted preaching about the approaching End. The orthodox clergy took fright.

Montanus's message was difficult to refute. Apocalyptic was the contrary of Gnosticism and was not unorthodox. No one wished to become a "slayer of prophets." The bishops whose positions as leaders of the churches were threatened could, however, assert that the prophecy was inspired by the devil and moreover that the prophets "should not speak in ecstasy," which they did.[47] The case could be argued both ways. The prophets of Israel had spoken with their own voice, but on the other hand, Adam had been put into a "deep sleep," and the Holy Spirit could hardly share possession of the prophet with the latter's own spirit. The man was as Montanus claimed "a lyre" and the spirit "the plectrum." There were attempts to exorcise the two women prophetesses,[48] and bishops met in council to excommunicate Montanus and his following. Gradually, the forces of ecclesiastical law and order gained the upper hand. Before she died circa 179, Maximilla complained, "I am driven as a wolf from the sheep. I am not a wolf, I am the word, and spirit and power."[49] Worse still, the end of all things, so confidently prophesied, did not occur. But if beaten in the cities, Montanism took root in rural Phrygia. It became the religion of a Christian peasantry. With its own organization, led by *koinonoi* (i.e., Participants in the sufferings of Christ), and a cult which demanded an ascetic way of life, rejection of the secular world, and open proclamation of the Christian name, it produced the first social and religious schism of the Christian East. The Montanist, like the Donatist in Africa, was a "soldier of Christ."[50]

Meantime, Montanus's message had spread westward to Rome, perhaps as early as 175, and to Gaul by the time the pogrom broke out in 177. The Lyons Christians were by no means unsympathetic. They too believed that the approach of antichrist and the end of all things was near and that their own sufferings were an indication of this. Theirs also was a religion of the Paraclete "witnessing against the world," but they stopped short of schism, and Eusebius records that the answer which they gave the Roman community on the subject was orthodox enough. Irenaeus was the bearer of that reply. One can detect a strange ambivalence in his theology. Alongside of episcopacy as the guiding force in the Church, he placed the representatives of the work of the Spirit, the visionaries and the martyrs. Every just man was of the priestly order, he declared (iv. 17:1). False prophecy he condemned,[51] but no believer in Montanus's message would call his prophecy false. The approach of the End he accepted as a fact, and the climax of his great requisitory against the heretics was the victory of the saints and martyrs in the thousand years rule of the just and their triumph at the final judgment.[52] Indeed, the heart of his theology lay in its eschatology. The progressive development of man's religious conscience had a place too for experience more recent than the ministry of Jesus. If uncanonical works could be accepted for Christian reading, such as the prophetic *Shepherd of Hermas*, why not the utterances of Montanus's "new prophets"? Irenaeus would not have pushed his conclusions so far. But on the other side of the Mediterranean Christianity had at last begun to take root in a Latin-speaking environment. Thanks to the genius of one born rebel, Tertullian, it was the sectarian charm of Montanism that was to inspire the outlook of the new Latin Church. The Gospel message had sufficed for Christianity's youth. The New Prophecy spoke for an age that awaited the end of the age.[53] The consequences of this conviction for the future unity of the Church were to be incalculable.

FURTHER READING

Calder, W.M., 'Philadelphia and Montanism', *Bulletin of the John Rylands Library* 7, 1923, 309-46

Campenhausen, H.von, *The Fathers of the Greek Church*, Random House 1959 and A.&C.Black 1963 (useful essays on Justin and Irenaeus)

Carrington, P., *The Early Christian Church*, Vol.2, Cambridge University Press 1957 (this book is useful for the second century but suffers from a lack of references)

Chadwick, H., *Early Christian Thought and the Classical Tradition: Studies in Justin, Clement and Origen*, Oxford University Press 1966

Dodds, E.R., *Pagan and Christian in an Age of Anxiety: Some Aspects of Religious Experience from Marcus Aurelius to Constantine*, Cambridge University Press 1965

Frend, W.H.C., *Martyrdom and Persecution in the Early Church*, Blackwell 1965 (ch.10)

Grant, R.M., *Greek Apologists of the Second Century*, SCM Press 1988

Hanson, R.P.C., *Allegory and Event*, SCM Press 1961 (a rather argumentative work but very useful on the historical background to the allegorical interpretation of scripture)

Labriolle, P.de, *La réaction paienne*, Paris 1924

Labriolle, P.de, *La crise montaniste*, Paris 1913

Lawson, J., *The Biblical Theology of St Irenaeus*, Epworth Press 1948

Origen, *Contra Celsum*, edited and translated by Henry Chadwick, Cambridge University Press 1953

Ste Croix, G.E.M. de, 'Why were the Early Christians Persecuted?', *Past and Present* 26, November 1963, 6-38 (a very important statement)

Whittaker, M., *Tatian: Oratio ad Graecos and Fragments*, Introduction, texts and translations, Oxford University Press 1982

Wingren, G., *Man and Incarnation*, Oliver and Boyd 1958 (a useful study of Irenaeus)

7

Three Cities: Rome, Carthage and Alexandria 185-235

The crisis of the reign of Marcus Aurelius had been overcome. The Church had survived, and with the exception of a brief but violent interlude in 202-3, was to suffer no organized persecution for half a century. As a result it gathered strength, and when in 235 the long period of peace was broken it had ceased to be a sect and become one of the main religions of the Roman Empire.

The earlier part of this period had witnessed the climax of the achievement of the primitive Greek-speaking Church. A firmly based episcopal organization able to communicate easily throughout the Mediterranean world, a Canon of Scripture, a Rule of Faith and a lucid and well-argued defense against Gnosticism ensured a uniformity of belief and practice such as Christendom has never achieved before or since. The destruction of this unity was not due either to heresy or persecution but to the comparatively sudden emergence of a Latin-speaking Church in Carthage in the last decade of the second century. The North African interpretation of Christianity differed radically from that of the now predominant Hellenistic churches of Alexandria and Antioch and was also at variance with Rome.

Before this took place, however, the Church had secured two permanent gains; firstly, the Canon of Scripture, which gave it an authoritative sacred book independent both of the Septuagint and Gnostic works, had for practical purposes become fixed, and secondly, the various Rules of Faith which had been emerging in different Churches in the second half of the century were becoming consolidated into set creeds.

The Canon had been developing slowly and unevenly through the second century. Polycarp cites a number of New Testament books which obviously were being read in the Church at Smyrna in 107-8, but when circa 160 Justin set down his account of *The Dialogue with Trypho* he could not point to any single document as the Christian New Covenant.

It is against this background of uncertainty that Marcion's effort to give the Christians an unmistakably Christian book must be judged. In the 170s even, the Canon was still fairly open. The Montanists could claim canonical authority for the "new prophecy," while their extreme opponents the *Alogi* of Asia Minor could reject St. John's Gospel, and start the long tradition of criticism which has ascribed the Fourth Gospel to the Judeo-Christian Gnostic, Cerinthus. All the time, the Gnostics were turning out their own versions of Gospels and Epistles which have formed the basis for popular legend about Christ's childhood from that day to this. The work of fixing what was Scripture and what was not had become urgent, and the final decisions may well have been due to agreement between the Roman and Asian Churches between 180 and 200.

The Roman version of a Canon accepted about 200 has survived in a Latin document named after Muratori, its publisher. It shows that while the four Gospels, Acts and Pauline Epistles were not open to challenge, some of the lesser books were still under scrutiny. An interesting process of selection and rejection had been going on. Thus the Apocalypses both of John and Peter were accepted, the latter a lurid and horrible document, as well as the Wisdom of Solomon, but the allegedly Marcionite "Pauline" Epistles to the Laodiceans and to the Alexandrians were rejected. The *Shepherd of Hermas* might be read, but not read in church, and curiously enough, there is no mention of Hebrews or 1 and 2 Peter. This may be an accident for of the lesser Epistles only 3 St. John is omitted.[1]

The Canon of Scripture was one weapon against deviation; the creeds were another. Here too one finds evidence for a slow emergence of set beliefs until the last years of the second century. Canon Kelly has demonstrated[2] how the creeds gradually developed from two quite different sources, namely affirmations about the nature of Christ on the one hand and baptismal interrogations on the other. The former have their roots in Christian apologetic and witness. Thus in 1 Cor. 8:6 Paul contrasts Christianity with polytheism in the words "We, however, have one God the Father, from whom are all things, and we to him, and one Lord, Jesus Christ, through whom are all things, and we through him." In the next decade or so, Timothy was solemnly adjured, "I charge you in the sight of God and of Jesus Christ who shall judge the quick and the dead and by his appearing and his kingdom" (1 Tim. 2:4). These statements have nothing to do with baptism, nor has the most striking of all, the affirmation found in Ignatius's letter to the Christians of Tralles: "Be deaf when anyone speaks to you apart from Jesus Christ who was of the stock of David, who was from Mary, who was truly born, ate, drank,

THE EARLY CHURCH

was truly persecuted under Pontius Pilate, was truly crucified and died in the sight of beings earthly, heavenly and under the earth, who was also truly raised from the dead, his Father raising him" (*To the Trallians*, 9:4). Yet we can hardly speak of a "creed of St. Ignatius," despite the fact that nearly all the affirmations concerning Christ found in later creeds are found there also. Ignatius may perhaps have been reminiscing from a Eucharistic sequence, but his object was apologetic, to point to the facts of Christ's earthly life in order to confute his Jewish-Docetic opponents.

It is noticeable that these affirmations concern Christ alone. They assume the Father, but make no mention of the Holy Spirit. The theology they express is more Binitarian, that is God-Logos or Father-Son, than Trinitarian. For the emergence of the latter one has to look to the formal questions which were put to a convert before his baptism. In these questions, Christianity was continuing the tradition of Judaism, and as in the Old Israel initiation involved the washing away of sin and regeneration so too it did in the New. In the New as in the Old a long preparation, probably as much as three years, had to be undergone before the candidate made his declaration of Faith. From Justin Martyr we learn that the Christian was baptized in the name first of the Father, then of the Son, and then of the Holy Spirit (cf. Mt. 28:19), and at each stage in the ceremony would reply to a formal question regarding his belief.[3] By the end of the second century, the greater Churches were standardizing their statements of belief in set terms which were to become the creeds. Two of these early statements have survived, one associated with Rome and the other with Asia Minor. That taken from a document known as the Epistle of the Apostles and dated to Asia Minor circa 180 reads: "[I believe] in [the Father] the ruler of the universe, and in Jesus Christ [our Redeemer] and in the Holy Spirit [the Paraclete], and in the holy Church, and in the forgiveness of sins."[4]

Individual clauses might differ from Church to Church (for instance, an early creed of Alexandria refers to Christ as "Only begotten Son," while the Asian creed cited above adds "the forgiveness of sins"). Their arrangement, however, and main clauses were the same. There remained the problem of enforcement. Uniformity of language, namely Greek, was a help, but it can hardly be an accident that in the last quarter of the second century a number of powerful episcopal figures emerge, all endowed with a sense of disciplinary purpose. In the two years 189–90, we are confronted by Victor of Rome, 189–99, the first Latin-speaking bishop, Demetrius of Alexandria 189–232, and Serapion of Antioch 190–209. Carthage, a few years later, was to elect another powerful cleric, Agrippinus. These men were concerned above all with enforcing discipline and uniformity in their Churches, and from Serapion's dealings with his subordinate bishop at Rhossos (on the gulf of Issus) it is evident that deviations from the set canon of Scripture brought condign censure with them.[5]

Even so, relative security and the expansion of the Church into Latin-speaking areas were facing the Christians with new situations and new tests. From now on, the dominance of Asia in the affairs of the Church was to be shared not only with Rome, but with Carthage and Alexandria as well. To understand the separate theological outlooks that developed in these three great cities, we must turn to the situation in each.

Rome, despite Irenaeus's praises, was a wealthy, influential, but none the less a curiously obscure Church. With the exception of the Adoptionists[6] it never produced a theological school of its own, and down to the time of Leo, elected no bishop who could claim world authority through his own personality. This could be due both to a change of language from Greek to Latin which took place in the period 230–50, and hampered the emergence of a distinctive Roman theology, and a long residual Hebraism which showed itself in the overwhelming choice of Old Testament motifs in catacomb paintings and predominantly Jewish nomenclature among the Roman Christians in the first three centuries. By the end of the second century however, Rome had three main attributes which marked it off from other Churches. First, it could claim foundation by two Apostles, and, moreover, that these Apostles had been martyred there. "The most great and universally known church founded and established at Rome by the glorious Apostles Peter and Paul," so Irenaeus could write.[7] From the excavations beneath the Vatican carried out between 1939 and 1949, it is evident that the tradition by which St. Peter had been martyred in Rome in 64 had been accepted and a shrine was erected over his supposed place of burial by about 160.[8] The cult of the martyr-Apostles had begun. Secondly, because of its apostolic authority and its position in the capital of the Empire, members of the various rival schools of thought in the middle and late second century were glad to have the support of Rome, and like Marcion, Valentinus and Polycarp were prepared to come to Rome and argue their views there. Thirdly, its wealth was already proverbial. There is an interesting fragment of a letter from Dionysius of Corinth to Bishop Soter of Rome circa 170, which reads (Eusebius, *H.E.* iv. 23), "This has been your custom since the beginning to do good in manifold ways to all Christians, and to send contributions to the many churches in every city, in some places relieving the poverty of the needy, and ministering to Christians in the mines by the contribution you have sent from the beginning, preserving the ancestral custom of the Romans."

In 189 Pope Victor entered on an already considerable heritage. In the previous few years the Christians in Rome had had friends at court in the person of Marcia, mistress to the Emperor Commodus, and Eusebius claims that in this period some noble Roman families, in reality probably some of the women members, were converted.[9] The Roman Church began to take on a more Latin air, and the controversies which were to rage within it over the next thirty years diminished further the predominance of the Asian element.

The first of these controversies concerned the date of Easter. This was not a triviality, for like the Jews of the world revealed by the *Book of Jubilees* and the Dead Sea Scrolls, the Christians attached immense importance to calendrical details, and the precision of the Fourth Gospel may be due as much to this fact as to the writer's sense of historical accuracy. In this case the issue was between the custom of the churches in Asia of keeping Easter in 14 Nisan (the day on which the Passover lamb was slain) regardless of the day of the week on which it fell, and that observed in Rome and elsewhere, where the Easter fast was maintained from the Friday until the Sunday following 14 Nisan, when it was succeeded by a joyful Eucharist. Difference of custom would not have mattered in churches nearly a thousand miles apart, but when once in every seven years the large Christian community in Rome from Asia would be celebrating the death of Christ, while the rest of the Roman Christians were celebrating his resurrection the situation was clearly inconvenient. In 155 Polycarp and Pope Anicetus had argued the question without result. The Asians kept to their Johannine calendar, the Romans to that of the Synoptics. But Victor, nettled perhaps by a pro-Montanist leadership among the Roman Asians, determined to enforce the Roman view on the rest of Christendom. He ordered conferences of bishops to be held from "Rome to Osrhoene" with the result that he got his way everywhere except in the all-important provinces of Asia Minor. In a moment of arrogance he excommunicated the recalcitrant Churches. He was met by a dignified letter of protest from the senior bishop, Polycrates of Ephesus, who quoted Apostolic authority for the Asian rite, and more effectively, perhaps, by an offer of mediation by Irenaeus.[10] The crisis blew over; Victor probably withdrew his excommunication. For the next half-century the compilation of Easter Calendars designed to fix an Easter period independent of Jewish (and Johannine) calculations was a frequent task among Western theologians. It was not until the Council of Nicaea in 325 that Asia finally abandoned 14 Nisan.[11]

The other controversies concerned doctrine and discipline. The Monarchian Controversies between 200 and 230 in Rome are important not because of the clownish individuals who were involved on both sides, but because they raised questions which foreshadowed the great Trinitarian controversies of the next century. Broadly speaking, if the Parousia was to be delayed indefinitely and if the Gnostic account of the divine Savior was unacceptable, how was Jesus Christ to be worshiped in relation to his Father? Moreover, how was the Trinity in whose name the convert was baptized to be explained to inquirers? How could the inherited Hebrew belief in one God be reconciled with the Christian belief in Father, Son (or Word) and Holy Spirit? In the ensuing controversies the Asian element in Rome again found itself on the wrong side of orthodoxy. In Pliny's time, the Bithynian Christians had worshiped Christ "as God," and a good many Asians were prepared to agree with a certain Noetus of Smyrna when, circa 200, he claimed that "Christ was the Father Himself, and that the Father Himself was born, suffered and died."[12] They would probably have agreed too with his expostulation to the presbyters of Smyrna who were preparing to expel him from the Church. "What evil then am I doing in glorifying Christ?" Noetus came to Rome, and for two decades found support for his views, through Polemon (flor. 210), Praxeas (flor. 210-20) and most important of all, Sabellius (flor. circa 220). Much will be heard of "Sabellius the Libyan" during the Arian controversy. He appears to have claimed that though the Trinity consisted simply of modes (hence the term Modalist) or aspects of the Father, God acted as Father in the creation, the Son in redemption and Holy Spirit in prophecy and sanctification.[13] There was one substance but three activities—loaded terms when it came to defining belief. Moreover, Victor's successors, Zephyrinus, 199-217, and Callistus, 217-22, were not unfavorable to this type of theology.

The other type of Monarchians were less well received at Rome. They too believed in a single undifferentiated God, but arrived at this view by reducing the role of the Son and Holy Spirit. According to the followers of the two Theodoti, the one a leather merchant from Byzantium and the other a banker (flor. 200), and to Artemas (flor. 230), God sent his Spirit on to the man Jesus at his baptism and gave him the power to work miracles. The perfect cooperation between the human and divine in Christ led to his adoption into the Godhead after the resurrection.[14] This view embodied an element of primitive Christology. Christ was the last and greatest of the prophets, perfectly inspired by the Holy Spirit, the "high priest after the order of Melchisedek." It was not entirely a travesty to claim that it had been held by the Church in Rome, for half a century before the prophet Hermas had represented very similar views of the Godhead. We shall be finding these ideas predominant in the Syrian Church later in the century.

The danger of both these viewpoints was that they led back to Judaism, for to the Modalist there could be little difference between Jesus' ministry and the theophanies of the Old Testament, while the Hebrew prophetic lineage of Adoptianism is evident. The bishops of Rome, however, either veered to the Modalist standpoint or were, like Zephyrinus, incapable of formulating an acceptable alternative.

This task devolved on one of the most obscure, enigmatic, but also prolific of the early Christian writers, Hippolytus (circa 155–236). We do not even know whether all the chronicles, commentaries, antiheretical diatribes and calendrical works ascribed to him were written by one man. It has been claimed that some of Hippolytus's works were written by a Roman presbyter and antipope of that name, but that some are the work of a Palestinian bishop who lived at the same period.[15] Hippolytus tried to solve the problems raised by the Monarchians by admitting that God was God from eternity. He could not, however, be without reason, wisdom and power, and therefore created his Word who became Christ, part of the Godhead, yet distinct from the Father. He divided the Trinity according to function, which allowed a distinction of persons: "The Father commands, the Son obeys, the Holy Spirit gives understanding" (*Against Noetus*, 14). But in practice the Holy Spirit had little place in his system, and Jesus Christ was simply a created being to whom divinity had been assigned. When Callistus whom he attacked charged him with being a "ditheist" there was little which he could reply.[16] His work shows the complexities into which Christian doctrine was already moving.

Hippolytus and Callistus had, however, quarreled before. The latter was a sordid character with an unenviable past, but when in 217 he was elected Bishop in opposition to Hippolytus he had a clear idea of the practical needs of the Church. Christianity was now rapidly expanding. Standards required in Apostolic times were no longer possible to maintain. Was the Church to remain a company of the elect on earth, hedged around with the taboos of purity derived from Leviticus, or was it to be a school for sinners bound together by a sacramental life administered by an ordered hierarchy? Callistus favored the second view, Hippolytus, championing apostolic tradition, supported the first. He claimed that Callistus "connived at the sensual pleasures of men by saying that sins were forgiven to everyone by himself." Worse still, he allowed twice-married bishops, priests and deacons to continue in clerical office. He also broke with secular Roman legal practice by recognizing unions of aristocratic Christian women with slaves and freedmen, and he allowed himself the prerogative of forgiving clergy who had committed adultery or homicide, i.e., two of the three "sins unto death," which with apostasy were recognized as such by both Jews and Christians. Hippolytus wrote a bitter personal tirade against his adversary.[17] More important, these actions attracted the ire of the great Carthaginian theologian, Tertullian. His attack on Callistus entitled "On Chastity" though full of invective, also elaborated an alternative theory of Church government. The first round of a century-long duel between Rome and Carthage had begun.

Momentous things had been happening in North Africa in the previous twenty years. What caused the rapid expansion of Christianity in Carthage and its surroundings in the last years of the second century it is impossible to say. Perhaps anger at the well-meaning attempt of the Roman authorities to tame and standardize the traditional cults of Carthage may have had something to do with it. The first Christian document from North Africa, the Acts of the Scillitan martyrs (July 180), breathes protest against Roman religion and Roman *mores*. The martyrs gave thanks for the death sentence as a passport to Paradise, and when the new religion burst on the scene with Tertullian's challenging *Apology* in 197 it was already the religion of an opposition. African Christians had been gaining notoriety as "faggot-fellows" and "half-axle men"[18] through their spirit of desperation and contempt of death. Even at this early stage the African Church was a Church of the martyrs. Moreover, the Church regarded itself as an exclusive body of the elect in constant expectation of the Last Days. "We are a society," wrote Tertullian, "with a common religious feeling, a unity of discipline and a common bond of hope."[19] "In prayer we await the trumpet of the angel,"[20] he says elsewhere. It was a society fed by "the books of God," with a profound belief in the necessity of a pure membership, in the reality of God's judgment and in the ever-present guidance of the Spirit. Of compromise with the world and the affairs of the world, there was none.

The persecution launched by Septimius Severus against converts both to Judaism and Christianity in 202-3 provides firsthand evidence of the temper of the Church at Carthage at this time. Among those arrested was the daughter of a well-to-do provincial named Vibia Perpetua, along with her slave Felicitas and their catechist, the presbyter Saturus.[21] Perpetua left a diary of her life in prison. Behind the natural exaltation of a young confessor can be discerned principles which were to be permanent in the African Church. From the moment she entered prison, Perpetua felt herself to be under the direction of the Holy Spirit. Her baptism was a baptism into the death of Christ. She was to request nothing, it is stated, from the baptismal waters except the sufferings of the flesh. She was filled with the Spirit, she could demand visions of Paradise and she conversed with the Lord.[22] She and her companions were inspired by apocalyptic hopes and they hastened to their deaths in the amphitheater at Carthage in the conviction that very soon they would be turning the tables on their persecutors.[22]

It was also a convert and at this time a Carthaginian presbyter, Tertullian, who gave these aspirations a lasting place in Western theology. Tertullian was one of the born rebels of history, a man in revolt successively against the army mess life of his father's household, against the purposelessness of Roman provincial culture, then as a Christian against the laxness and complacency of the Church in Rome and Carthage, and finally even against the sect-life of the Montanists. Paradoxically, he died not in the arena but of extreme old age (circa 240).

It is almost impossible to do justice to him in this sketch. He was a man in love with truth which he identified with a puritanical and martyr-directed Christianity. Today he would have been a political journalist turning out the weekly 4,000-word article, topical to the day, and profoundly sensitive to wrong and injustice. He was a born debater with a superb command of language. It is impossible to read him and avoid the intensity of his feelings, and the sincerity of his views. There is a vein of splendid sarcasm in his style when, for instance, he pictures the Lord as saying on judgment day that while he had entrusted the Gospel once and for all to the Apostles he had thought better of it now and made some changes to suit the heretics,[24] or his description of the Christian engaged in pious meditation while drinking in the bestialities of the arena.[25] But all the time his wit, his exaggeration and malice were turned to one end, the vindication of Christianity against the Greco-Roman world in preparation for the millennium of the saints.

His earlier works show clearly the principles that were to govern his life and thought. Christianity was the religion of Christ crucified, set out in the Bible which was inspired by the Holy Spirit. He had no sympathy with the Monarchians or the Gnostics who sought to diminish the reality of Christ and his ministry. Christ did love men, and for men he humiliated himself to die on the cross. "It is incredible because it is foolish. He was buried and rose again. It is certain because it is impossible."[26] "You bisect Christ with a lie. The whole of him was Truth."[27] Service to Christ, however, demanded rejection of the world which belonged to Satan. "We turn our back on the institutions of our ancestors,"[28] he wrote early in 197, and his denial of any role to pagan philosophy in molding Christian thought was as prompt. "What indeed has Athens to do with Jerusalem?

What has the Academy to do with the Church? What have heretics to do with Christians? . . . Away with all attempts to produce a Stoic, Platonic or dialectic Christianity. We want no curious disputation after possessing Christ Jesus, no inquisition after receiving the gospel."[29] Though not openly disloyal to the Empire, and regarding it as a guardian against forces of chaos,[30] he had little use for its institutions. "What is more foreign to us than the state?" was one of his more challenging utterances.[31] The Christian's destiny was to be a martyr. Thus he would win forgiveness for his own sins, thus spread the kingdom of Christ. "The blood of martyrs is seed."[32]

His reaction to opposition among clergy at Rome and Carthage to his views was characteristic. He shook the dust of orthodoxy off his feet and joined the Montanists. It was thus in Africa that the New Prophecy gained its greatest success. Tertullian's conversion did not mean his abandonment of previously held convictions. Granted however, that the Holy Spirit was perpetually active in the Church, its most recent manifestation through the Phrygian prophets was a valid witness and indeed further evidence that the End was near. From 207 onward references to the New Prophecy begin to find their way into Tertullian's work, but they never predominate. Their role is to corroborate and to sustain the opinions of the author. The prophets inculcated a stern moral creed and an even sterner morality for the priesthood. This Tertullian accepted. Whereas previously he had allowed flight in time of persecution, in his Montanist De Fuga in Persecutione, he did not; in earlier days he had conceded a widow the right of remarriage, in De Monogamia he refused it; in his De Paenitentia he allowed the possibility of an act of repentance to a deadly sinner, as a Montanist he would not. There were matters of degree befitting the Last Days.

All the time, however, it was the Holy Spirit who inspired the Church and its members. In his tract on baptism he urged that the waters were the abode of the Spirit and that by definition the rite could not be administered by one in a state of sin.[33] The Church must be "without spot or wrinkle"[34]—prophetic words, for Tertullian was affirming a doctrine of the Church which Cyprian and Donatus would in turn sustain. Naturally, Tertullian had no use for Callistus's ideas on the restoration of adulterous clergy. But the vital difference between his attack and that of Hippolytus was that Tertullian's was founded on a doctrine of the Holy Spirit worked out over the previous twenty years. Against Callistus's identification of Church with numerus episcoporum (the company of bishops) Tertullian asserted an ecclesia spiritus per spiritalem hominem (a Church of the spirit through [membership of] spiritual individuals) whose second baptism, to wash away sins committed after the first, was martyrdom. This is what made the African opposition to Rome in the third and fourth centuries formidable. Principles as well as personalities were at stake.

The uncompromising assertion of the work of the Holy Spirit would have sounded strange in the third great Christian center which was emerging at this period, Alexandria. Here African theology, as defined by Tertullian in his attack on the Monarchian Praxeas by the neat formula of God as "one substance" though of "three persons"[35] would have encountered opposition. In 200 Alexandria was probably the wealthiest (Rome not excluded) and most theologically active See in the Mediterranean. It had also been the city of Philo, and the work of harmonizing Greek philosophy and culture with Hebraic faith was to continue when that faith was represented by Christianity. How Christianity reached there we do not know. But during the first half of the second century it developed from a strongly Judeo-Christian outlook to a strongly Gnostic one. We do not know for certain the names of the early bishops, but Basilides, Valentinus and Heracleon represented between them a succession of Gnostic teachers in Alexandria extending for half a century between 130 and 180. Then orthodoxy began to come into its own. The year 189 saw the election of Bishop Demetrius who was to govern the See for no less than forty-three years, while a few years earlier, about 180, a converted Stoic, Pantaenus, set up in Alexandria what came to be known as the Catechetical School. At this stage it was a small establishment at which the children of Christians were taught the rudiments of the Faith and new converts were instructed. When Pantaenus left to carry the Christian message to India, his pupil Clement became its head and gave it a far greater importance.

Clement (circa 150–circa 215) was a Greek, perhaps from Athens. Like Justin he had wandered about the world and even after he became a Christian journeyed through most of the Greek-speaking parts of the Empire. His Christian teachers included an astonishing variety of schools. "One was in Greece—the Ionian," he writes, "the next in Magna Graecia . . . others in the East and in this region one was an Assyrian, and the other a Palestinian, a Hebrew by descent. The last of all (in power he was the first) I met and found my rest in him, when I had caught him, hidden away in Egypt." This was probably Pantaenus, and Clement continued his master's work attempting not without success to evangelize members of the Alexandrian-Greek aristocracy and to substitute an orthodox, or better, an ecclesiastical Gnosticism in place of the Gnosticism of the Egyptian teachers.

His method and his convictions were the precise opposite of those of his contemporary in Carthage. In the three works in which he described the Christian's advance toward perfection, the *Protreptikos* (Exhortation), *Paidagogos* (Tutor), and *Stromata* (Miscellanies) he elaborated a theology which in effect substituted the logos of the Alexandrian Jewish philosopher Philo for the Holy Spirit, and provided Greek philosophy with an assured place in the divine pattern. His doctrine of God forbade a purely negative view of philosophy, for Clement's God was the God of the Platonists, existence, intelligible only through his Word and consciousness. This Word was always with God but distinct from him, just as human thought is distinct from the thinker. The individual illumined by baptism was open to the guiding influence of the Word, and by accepting that guidance could move toward communion with God.

In this dispensation, naturally, philosophy had a part to play. If the Word was the source of all things it was also the source of the world and its philosophies. These might miss the finer chords of the "true music of Amphion" as Clement describes Christianity.[36] They might contain "weeds"[37] and add nothing to divine truth, but they enabled the Greek to cooperate in the work of God as the law had done for the Jews. They provided an essential preparatory phase for the understanding of the truth and reception of baptism. "There is but one river of truth," wrote Clement, "but many streams pour into it from this side and from that." He goes on: "The law is for the Jew what philosophy is for the Greek, a schoolmaster to bring them to Christ."[38] While Faith remained the foundation of Christianity, the enlightened Christian advanced from Faith toward knowledge, the deeper understanding and imitation of the Word, not arrived at through any single act, but by a daily obedience to the divine command. Like his Gnostic opponents, Clement saw spiritual perfection in intellectual terms attainable by an *élite*, though he stressed the need for a visible Church and rejected the determinism which characterized the Gnostics. Even so, while Tertullian's ideal for the Christian was martyrdom, Clement's was that of the Gnostic ascetic. For him the joys of Paradise lay in no material benefits but in "becoming like God," enjoying a freedom from all passions which might hinder the soul from attaining this end.[39]

Alexandrian Christian thought had moved far from Palestine. It must be admitted that Clement's Christ was an abstraction, and no more than his Gnostic opponents could he conceive of a wholly human Savior. "He himself," he writes of Jesus, "was wholly without passion and into him there entered no emotional movement, neither pleasure nor pain."[40] Also, the primacy was given to reason rather than Faith. But it was a noble and optimistic creed. It laid the way open for the harmony between Christianity and the best of this world's thought, and between the Christian Church and the Roman Empire. The end of man was spiritual refinement by divine education, not judgment and Hellfire. By 200 two theologies based on different eschatologies, different understandings of the Trinity, and even different ethics were characterizing East and West respectively. Had Irenaeus returned to Smyrna, it might have enabled Polycarp's See to act as mediator between the ideas of Carthage and those of Alexandria. For a century more the fact of the illegality of Christianity kept the Eastern and Western Churches together and prevented schism. The die, however, was cast. When Clement passed from the scene, probably in Cappadocia circa 215, after leaving Alexandria at the time of the Severan persecution twelve years before, his mantle had already fallen on a young man whose lifework was to systematize and refine the Christian Platonism of Alexandria. The influence of Origen was to be incalculable in molding the life and thought of the Greek-speaking Church.

FURTHER READING

Bigg, C., *The Christian Platonists of Alexandria*, Oxford University Press 1913

Bray, G.L., *Holiness and the Will of God: Perspectives on the Theology of Tertullian*, Marshall, Morgan and Scott 1979

Chadwick, H., *Early Christian Thought and the Classical Tradition: Studies in Justin, Clement and Origen*, Oxford University Press 1966

Evans, R.F., *One and Holy*, SPCK 1972

Frend, W.H.C., *Martyrdom and Persecution in the Early Church*, Blackwell 1965 (chapter on Rome, Carthage and Alexandria)

Glover, T.R., *The Conflict of Religions in the Early Roman Empire*, Methuen 1932 (chs. 9 and 10 give useful studies of Clement and Tertullian)

Jaeger, W., *Early Christianity and Greek Paideia*, Harvard University Press 1962

Jalland, T.G., *The Church and the Papacy*, SPCK 1944 (ch.2)

Labriolle, P.de, *Latin Christianity*, London 1924

La Piana, G., 'The Roman Church at the End of the Second Century', *Harvard Theological Review* 18, 1925, 210-77

E.G.Osborn, *The Philosophy of Clement of Alexandria*, Cambridge University Press 1957

Ottley, R.L., *The Doctrine of the Incarnation*, Methuen 1949 (contains a good sketch on Monarchianism)

Prestige, G.L., *Fathers and Heretics*, SPCK 1954

Wolfson, H.A., *The Philosophy of the Church Fathers*, Vol.1, *Faith, Trinity, Incarnation*, Harvard University Press 1956 (esp.ch.15)

8

Origen

Compared with Origen, Clement's work was that of an amateur, for not unjustifiably Origen has been regarded as the greatest figure in the Christian Church between Paul and Augustine. He was a great teacher, a great exegete, a great philosopher, a brave man, and a man of action. For a century after his death all the leading ecclesiastics in the Greek-speaking world were to some extent his disciples. Both sides in the Arian controversy could claim him as their master.

Some idea of his career can be gained from his admirer, Eusebius of Caesarea, who devoted nearly the whole of the Sixth Book of the *Ecclesiastical History* to Origen and could draw on his extensive library at Caesarea. He was born in Alexandria about A.D. 185, the son of Leonides, a Greek convert to Christianity, while his mother may have been an Egyptian-Jewess.[1] He was, as Eusebius claims, "noteworthy from his cradle" (*H.E.* vi. 2:2); a sort of infant prodigy who showed enormous interest in the Bible. He became a pupil of Clement, but in 202–3 Christian converts were bitterly persecuted in Alexandria. Clement seems to have fled, many of his pupils were martyred, and Origen's own father arrested and imprisoned. While in prison Origen wrote encouraging him to stand firm, and he himself was only restrained from provoking martyrdom through his mother hiding his clothes so that he could not go out. In the same year, however, Bishop Demetrius appointed him to head the Catechetical School and give regular instruction to catechumens. He had outstanding success. It was the first step on a great career. His father dead and his property confiscated, Origen came under the influence of a rich Gnostic lady who held a sort of salon to which Gnostics and orthodox flocked. As we have seen in sketching Clement's theology, the division between the two groups in Alexandria was largely a matter of sentiment. Was one for the Gnostic teacher, or for the Church? Origen was emphatically for the Church. He refused to pray with Paul the

Gnostic chaplain, and his dislike of Gnosticism remained throughout his life. Meantime he sold his father's library of secular books so as to be able to give his instruction without fee, contenting himself with a small annuity. He showed too, his ascetic and extreme temperament, by taking Matt. 19:12 literally, an act not altogether unusual even among the orthodox of the time,[2] but in Origen's case, fatal to his career (Eusebius, *H.E.*, vi. 8).

Up to now the streak of fanaticism in his character had predominated, but at this time he took another step which was to have an equal influence on his outlook. He attended lectures on pagan philsophy, and it seems that Ammonius Saccas, the master of the great Plotinus, was Origen's master also. Here he met another Alexandrian, Heraclas, who was to succeed Demetrius as Bishop of Alexandria. Soon Origen was able to leave the first stages of instruction in the school to him, while he devoted himself to giving more capable pupils a thorough grounding in philosophy and theology (Eusebius, *H.E.*, vi. 15).

It was in this period of his life, probably extending to 219, that Origen began to achieve the astonishing integration of the Biblical and philosophical elements in his thought that was to be his greatest contribution to the Church. He was familiar with the works of the school of Middle Platonists, and it was from them that he derived his concept of God and of knowledge. More than a generation later the anti-Christian writer, Porphyry (232–305), summed Origen up by saying that though he "professed the teaching of the barbarians (Jews) and lived as a Christian contrary to the laws, his views of God and of the world were those of an Hellene," though unfortunately "he introduced Greek ideas into foreign myths."[3] There is an element of truth in this, for as Werner Jaeger has pointed out, Origen's theology "was based on the Greek idea of *paideia* (culture) in its highest philosophical form."[4] He lived in both worlds.

At the end of this period, however, after he had even visited Rome and listened to Hippolytus, his first love remained the Bible. He quite rightly considered that if anyone desired to study the Bible he must learn Hebrew and have an accurate text, and he set out to do both. He accepted the help of a Jewish tutor and then, off and on for the next twenty years, he worked at a massive critical edition of the Septuagint. It was arranged in six columns, whence it derived its title of *Hexapla*. The first column contained the Hebrew text of the Old Testament, the second a transliteration of that text in Greek characters, and in the remaining four columns Greek versions which were in circulation at the time, namely those of the two second-century Jewish proselytes, Aquila and Theodotion, the Septuagint, and that of the Jewish-Christian, Symmachus. For some parts of the Old Testament Origen added other versions, and for the Psalms one which he claimed to have found in a jar near Jericho.[5] The texts were minutely compared one with another, and the Septuagint was marked with asterisks and other symbols drawing attention to its variations when compared with the original Hebrew. It was a work of enormous industry, and also something completely new. Christianity had at last produced a great Biblical and literary critic.

Origen, however, was this and something more. His works of systematic theology and exegesis which he began to write from about 220 onward were compiled in response to intellectual challenges of the day. He was no theorist. As he says in his *Commentary on St. John* (5:8): "Today, under pretext of Gnosis, heretics rise against the Church of Christ. They pile on their books of commentaries. They claim to interpret the Gospel and Apostolic texts. If we are silent and do not oppose them with true teaching famished souls will be fed with their abominations." Strong words, but his hatred of Gnosticism provided the spur to some of his immensely long works. So too, his abhorrence of Monarchianism led him at some unspecified date to address an assembly of bishops and put one of their number, Heracleides, through a searching and uncomplimentary examination. It is important to realize that his own theology of the Logos (Word) was evolved in answer to practical issues of the day. As he said, it was necessary to make a distinction between God the Father and God the Son, for, "in this way we avoid falling into the opinion of those who have been separated from the Church and turned to the illusory notion of monarchy, who abolish the Son as distinct from the Father, and virtually abolish the Father also. Nor do we fall into the other blasphemous doctrine which denies the deity of Christ."[6] From this plain statement we see that the Monarchian controversies were no schoolroom debate, but were playing a vital part in the formulation of the doctrine of the Trinity in the Greek-speaking Church.

Origen's most characteristic work, the *Peri Archon* (Latin, *De Principiis*), a work of systematic theology about "main" and "original things," was also directed primarily against the Gnostics. From his initial assertion that he did not intend to deviate from the teaching of the Church, Origen was at pains to show that the Gnostic doctrine of God and Gnostic dualism were inadequate as a view of the world and guide to conduct.

This part of Origen's life shows him at his most serene. Already in 214 he had become known outside Egypt, and had been consulted on some unspecified topic by the governor of Arabia. Next year, however, the calculated vengeance of the Emperor Caracalla against the Alexandrians who had satirized him for the murder of his brother, Geta, in 212, drove him into exile. The bishops of Jerusalem and Caesarea in Palestine were his friends and though Origen was still only a layman they allowed him to preach in church. Demetrius was annoyed and in 219 recalled him to Alexandria,[7] but the estrangement between the two men eased, and for the next nine years Origen was at Alexandria writing and teaching. At this time, he was helped by a wealthy patron, Ambrosius, whom he had converted from Gnosticism and who had supplied him with all the secretarial aid which even he needed.

Probably in 229, however, Origen was invited to the province of Achaea (that part of Greece which included Athens and Corinth) to settle a dispute between the churches there. He went without Demetrius's permission, and now at last agreed to be ordained as presbyter at the hands of his friends of Jerusalem and Caesarea.[8] On hearing this Demetrius was furious. He claimed that he alone had the right of ordaining Origen and pointed out as Origen was a eunuch his ordination was illegal. A synod of clergy in Alexandria declared Origen banished, and soon after, just before Demetrius died in 232 after an episcopate of forty-three years, another synod deposed him from the priesthood.[9]

The cause of this quarrel seems to have been largely personal, though perhaps behind it one may also see a clash between the ambitious hierarch and a teacher whose scholarship he could not match, but whom none the less he wanted to control administratively. While at this stage there was no question of Origen's doctrinal unorthodoxy, it is interesting that Heraclas, Demetrius's successor (232–47), did not recall him from exile.

Origen therefore was to spend the last twenty-two years of his life in Caesarea. He endured Demetrius's malice stoically, regretting only his inability to get on with his *Commentary on John*.[10] He must, however, have been saddened at receiving no recall from his old associate Heraclas. But these were not years of decline. He reestablished his school in Caesarea, and perhaps almost at once, in 232, he received an invitation from the Empress Julia Mammaea to come to Antioch, where he discussed "divine things" with her, and formed the highest opinion of her religious sense. In Origen's view, she was "the wonder of all."[11] Later, he was to receive letters from the Emperor Philip (244–9) and his wife,[12] both of whom were favorably disposed toward the Christians.

Before this latter occasion, however, the Church had faced renewed persecution. Christianity was now one of the great internal problems facing the Roman Empire. Under the Severan dynasty, represented by the Emperor Alexander Severus and his mother Julia Mammaea, Christianity had been tolerated, and Christian buildings such as the church at Dura-Europos were being erected. At the court there had been a tremendous interest in religious questions. It was there that the *Life* of the Stoic hero, Apollonius of Tyana, had been written up by Philostratus, and Apollonius was represented as a demigod and savior undergoing experiences and working miracles very similar to those of Jesus. Moreover, Origen was not the only Christian with whom the court had contact, for in 227 Alexander Severus had appointed a prominent Palestinian Christian writer, Julius Africanus, as architect of the new imperial library in the Roman pantheon. In March 235, however, the Severan dynasty fell victim to a revolution. The rough, but efficient soldier, Maximin, who assumed the power, regarded Christianity as an hostile influence associated with an effete court, and took immediate steps to curb the power of the Christian leaders.[13] In Rome, Bishop Pontian and his now aged rival, Hippolytus, were deported to an unhealthy area in Sardinia where they died. The threat of active measures reached Caesarea. Origen's reaction was typical. For his patron Ambrosius and the Caesarean presbyter, Protoctetus, he wrote the *Exhortation to Martyrdom*. We cannot linger over this work, except to point out that in its reminder to Christians of his own day of the example of the Maccabees and its emphasis on the superiority of Christian over Greco-Roman examples of bravery, Origen showed that he remained a man of martyrdom, capable of the strongest opposition to the assumptions on which the Empire was based.

The danger, however, soon passed. Maximin was busier fighting on the frontiers than warring on the Christians. In about 237 Origen formed a relationship which was to ensure his fame as a teacher and inspirer of men. The story of how Gregory Thaumaturgus (The Wonderworker) came to discover Origen is one of the few human stories that have come down to us from that period.[14] Gregory and his brother originated from an aristocratic family in Cappadocia and were studying Roman law at Berytus (Beirut). Their sister had married a senior civil servant on the staff of the governor of Coele-Syria whose capital was Caesarea. One day Gregory was asked to escort his sister from Antioch to Caesarea. He left Berytus accompanied by a military escort, and once in Caesarea he came into contact with Origen. He had always been attracted by Christianity, and had considered conversion as a boy of fourteen; now he accepted it gladly, and the pen-portrait he left of Origen, when he at length returned to Cappadocia circa 243, is one of the classics of Christian antiquity.

Gregory shows Origen as his friend and tutor as well as his catechist and teacher. He was the only man "who understands the divine utterances purely and clearly, and knows how to interpret them to others."[15] Nothing remained "hidden and inaccessible," and Origen himself, "when he saw that his efforts were not without reward, went back, dug over again, watered and in general used all his art and care to make us bear fruit."[16] His course embraced the whole field of Greek and Biblical learning, but always in the last resort, loyalty must be given to the Bible. "He did not advise one to attach oneself to any particular philosopher, however great his reputation might be among men, but to God and His prophets."[17] He showed his pupil that Christianity was the religion of a rational being, and conversion the step from ignorance (not sin) to enlightenment.

The association lasted four to five years, when Gregory returned to Cappadocia to spend another thirty years as a missionary bishop there. Meantime, during the next five years Origen traveled and preached from his base in Caesarea. He went into Palestine "to investigate the footsteps of Jesus," further east to Bostra to controvert Monarchianism,[18] then back to Caesarea to write his last two great works, his *Commentary on Matthew* and *Contra Celsum*. In the latter he again presents Christianity as a reasonable faith, one, however, which through its power of survival and moral demands was superior in every way to paganism.

In the *Commentary on Matthew* he already foresaw the possibility of renewed persecution, but this time on a world scale. He was not far wrong. Decius succeeded Philip in 249. In 250 Origen found himself in prison in Tyre and though it is an exaggeration to call him a martyr of the Decian persecution, his death in 253 or 254 may have been hastened by the ill-treatment he received.[19] When he died, Christianity was no longer on the defensive. He had shown it to be both an intellectual and an inspiring faith, the only one for which intelligent and unlettered alike could die. On the one hand, he prepared the way over the next century for the conversion of the Greek-speaking provincial aristocracy who were fundamentally Platonist in outlook, and on the other he provided an intellectual basis for the Egyptian monastic movement. As a speaker he was not impressive, the fine passages in his sermons being too intermingled with verbiage and irrelevancies. Nor was he patient with his audience. Momentary inattention by assembled bishops to an involved argument on whether the soul had or had not blood set off a flood of invective and abuse.[20] But he was a tremendous worker, keeping his team of stenographers perpetually busy with a card-index memory, and a conviction that Christianity was *the* Faith for mankind. For a century Greek theologians were to be for or against him; and his truest disciplès were to be the Cappadocian Fathers, the spiritual heirs of Gregory Thaumaturgus.

What was his distinctive contribution to Greek theology? The great mass of Origen's works were exegetical. He commented on the text of nearly every book in the Bible, and as Lietzmann has said, he lived in the Bible to an extent which no one else rivaled before Luther.[21] In some ways he showed a critical faculty far in advance of his time, not only in the whole concept of the *Hexapla* but in his treatment of specific problems like the authorship of the Letter to the Hebrews. He points out that the Letter "has not the apostle's rudeness in speech" and "that it is better Greek in the framing of its diction, will be admitted by everyone who is able to discern differences of style." At the same time, "the thoughts of the epistle are admirable and not inferior to the acknowledged writings of the apostle."[22] This was a fair judgement, and that it was not an isolated tour de force in the Christian school of Alexandria is indicated by his pupil and future bishop (247–64) Dionysius's equally exact and penetrating analysis of the Apocalypse.[23]

Literary criticism, however, and the establishment of a text were only the first stage in Origen's exegesis. He disliked the pettifogging literalism of the rabbis of the day who claimed that Jesus could not be Messiah because in his time lions and lambs had not lain down together and he had not preached deliverance to captives,[24] and he revolted from the abandonment of the Old Testament by Marcionites and Gnostics on the strength of this or that text. He saw the Bible as a single whole, the inspired word of God, His saving and educating message to humanity, perfectly self-consistent with itself. And, just as the human frame consisted of the trinity of body, soul, and spirit, so interpretation of Scripture was to be understood under three headings, the literal, moral and spiritual.[25] The moral meant the drawing out of some lesson from a text quite intelligible to the ordinary Christian, but the spiritual meaning was of a higher and different order.

Origen's comparative study of the Bible and his familiarity with the methods of literary criticism of his day had shown him, as it had shown the Valentinians and Marcionites, that some texts just could not be accepted as they stood. "Greet no man in the way" (Lk. 10:4) or "Let the dead bury the dead" (Lk. 9:60) were absurd as they stood, Christ could not have seen "all the kingdoms of the world," while the account of his cleansing the Temple by violent means seemed to be "uncharacteristic" of the Son of God.[26] But God cannot be the contriver of evil. "If God does what is evil, he is no longer God," he replied to Celsus.[27] Somehow or other the true, inspired meaning must be created from an obdurate text. Origen's method was based on allegory. To the agreed tradition among orthodox exegetes that incidents in the Old Testament directly prefigured the promises of the New, Origen added a new factor derived from his Platonist studies. All things, even the simplest, in the Bible reflected the real and spiritual order beyond the visible world. It was the duty of the exegete to find the clue to this spiritual truth in a given text, and by analogy and comparison with other texts to work out the message. Thus, Jerusalem, Zion, Carmel, Beersheba and hundreds of other places ceased to be geographical expressions, but under Origen's imaginative erudition became the mirrors of heavenly truth. Every word of Scripture meant something, otherwise it would not have been written, he argued. Today much of this can be dismissed as irrelevant, but for the time, it established the Bible as a consistent whole, all equally important to the Christian as the word of God.

Emerging from his study of Scripture was the first systematic attempt to establish a doctrine of the Trinity, proof against the Gnostics and Monarchians on the one hand, and the Adoptionists on the other. While Origen accepted the tradition of the Church, he claimed even as he recapitulated it in the beginning of *De Principiis*, that the instructed Christian had the right and duty of considering its implications in the light of philosophy.[28] His God, therefore, was the absolute being of Plato, but in place of the passive qualities of beauty and goodness, Origen asserted the divine quality of love. Love was active, and it must be manifested through an object, and that object was God's Word or Son, ever-begotten, continuing with God through all ages. "Our Savior is the effulgence of (the Father's) glory," and the "exact image of the Father,"[29] words which inspired the Fathers at Antioch at the Dedication Council of 341. Although an exact image of God, and coeternal with him, He was different from God, for God alone was immutable, but the Son was being eternally generated and linking God with creation. As Origen told the somewhat puzzled and shocked Heracleides in the *Dialogue*, "We confess two Gods," though one in unity.[30] The Holy Spirit was the first of the beings created by the Word, and so logically was a creature and not God. Later, this was to become the stumbling block of all the Greek Logos-theologians. No more than in Valentinus's system did Origen have a distinctive place for the Holy Spirit, nor indeed for the doctrines which depended on him. His Trinity was of three graded beings united in a single substance but possessed of individualities, of which, however, two only, God and his Word, were relevant to mankind.

Such was Origen's view of the divine world, outlined in *On First Principles* and elsewhere. Below this was the world of inferior spirits.

Originally, as he says, "before the ages minds were all pure, both demons and souls and angels offering service to God, and keeping his commandments."[31] But these beings also had free will. They became bored, and when the devil led a revolt of the powers, God drove them out, imprisoning them in bodies which became more heavy and opaque in proportion to their fault. But even so, as all possessed free will all had the power to return to God. Man too belonged to this order of creation. Origen insists time and again that he possessed the means of willing his salvation. We mount step by step in our knowledge of God, but each step is Christ. In a striking passage at the end of the *Dialogue with Heracleides*, he exclaims, "Let us therefore take up eternal life. Let us take up that which depends upon our decision. God does not give it us, he sets it before us." "Behold I have set life before thy face" (Deut. 30:15).[32] That life was Christ, who by uniting human and divine nature enabled the former to rise toward its ultimate glorification. For Origen, therefore, Christ was the guide, educator and leader of mankind, revealing the whole essence of God so that man might rise toward God and be united with him.[33]

It was an optimistic theology in which there was neither Heaven nor Hell, but only the gradual education and purification of the universe and its beings until once more God was all in all. The perfect status of God's creation would be restored. Applied to history, Origen noted the coincidence of Christ's coming in the reign of Augustus, and pointed to the fact that thanks to the peace and unity brought about by the latter, the Christian message had been able to spread.[34] He looked forward beyond city and national boundaries until all spoke a common language through the acceptance of Christ.[35] His was the gospel of universal hope.

In the next century this aspect of his thought earned him condemnation. Even so, his implicit denial of resurrection of the body, and his acceptance of a soul's successive reincarnation in the process of purification would have been open to criticism. Valid today is the charge that he had no idea of Christianity as an historical religion. The Jesus of Luke's Gospel, growing up and increasing in knowledge (Lk. 1:80) would have had little meaning to him. And what of the reality of a human soul in Jesus? But in Syria it was precisely this aspect of Jesus' life and ministry that was being pondered. Within a decade of Origen's death two systems of theology were confronting each other: one based in Alexandria and expressing Origenist ideas of God-Logos, the other in Antioch stressing the work of Christ under the inspiration of the Holy Spirit. The condemnation of Antiochene theology in the person of Paul of Samosata in 268 by the Origenists foreshadowed the tragedy of Nestorius a century and a half later.

FURTHER READING

Cadiou, R., *Origen, His Life at Alexandria*, Herder, St Louis and London 1944

Daniélou, J., *Origen*, Sheed and Ward 1955 (this is the key work on Origen)

Faye, E.de, *Origen and his Work*, Columbia University Press, New York 1929

Grant, R.M., *The Earliest Lives of Jesus*, Harper Bros and A.& C.Black 1961

Kelly, J.N.D., *Early Christian Doctrines*, Longmans [5]1978

Koch, H., *Pronoia and Paideusis*, De Gruyter, Berlin 1931

Labriolle, P.de, *La réaction paienne*, Paris [10]1948 (useful for the religious outlook of the Severan dynasty)

Prestige, G.L., *God in Patristic Thought*, SPCK 1952

Trigg, J.W., *Origen*, John Knox Press and SCM Press 1985

Westcott, B.F., 'Origen', *Dictionary of Christian Biography*
(see also the chapters on Origen in Bigg, *Christian Platonists* [p.84 above], von Campenhausen, *Fathers of the Greek Church* [p.71 above], and Prestige, *Fathers and Heretics* [p.84 above]. Origen's *De Principiis* has been translated by G.W.Butterworth)

9

Decius–Valerian:
A Decade of Persecution
249–59

The Decian persecution of 250–1 was the first general persecution of the Church throughout the Roman Empire, and it was the severest test which Christianity was called upon to face. At this stage, while Judaism had faded as a political force Christianity and paganism were roughly in equilibrium. Origen had shown that Christianity and the philosophy of the Greco-Roman world could be harmonized, though in that harmonization Christianity would be the predominant partner. The Church was no longer on the defensive, searching to justify its existence by far-fetched interpretations of prophecies found in barbarian writings. It could claim the ear of the educated Greco-Roman world. Christianity was advancing during these years in both the Greek and Latin halves of the Empire. Origen describes how Church office was becoming sought after, that the harvest of souls being gathered in was enormous, and he beseeches his hearers not to despise the convert from heathen parents.[1]

In the West, Tertullian for all his exaggeration paints a similar picture of the "world passing from you (the pagans) to us,"[2] and of the impossibility of rooting the Christians out by force. Eusebius's comment on the reign of Philip is significant. It was a time "when the faith was increasing and our doctrine was boldly proclaimed in the ears of all."[3] Origen felt secure enough to allow his sermons to be recorded by shorthand writers. The Millennium of the city of Rome celebrated in 247 might have appeared to usher in a new and Christian era. Outside the frontiers of the Empire the founder of Manichaeism watched the situation in circa 243, and commented that Christianity had become as much the religion of "the West" (i.e., the eastern frontier provinces of the Empire) as Buddhism was of India, and he intended to combine both in a true religion for the whole world.[4]

Success, however, had brought its own problems. Both Origen[5] and Cyprian of Carthage[6] comment on the numbers of nominal Christians, of their lack of enthusiasm for martyrdom, of the enervating effect of wealth and position, and of clergy and even bishops taking on profitable secular tasks, such as being bailiffs to great landowners. Moreover, despite its gains, the Church was still mainly an urban organization. Except in parts of Asia Minor the countryside was barely touched. The Christians were sufficiently well-known to be immediate targets in the event of repression but not sufficiently popular to be able, like Athanasius a century later, to escape.

Paganism too, in all its bright, contrasting forms, was far from a dead, or even declining force. The excavation of Dura-Europos in the inter-war years provides an insight into the religious and intellectual life of a Greco-Roman town in the mid-third century. Dura was captured by the Persians in 255–6 and thereafter the site was abandoned until rediscovered by Breasted just after the First World War. Nearly every block had its temple and nearly every community its shrine. Palmyrenes, Syrians, the descendants of the old Macedonian settlers, and "foreigners" from farther down the river have all left their mark in the religious architecture of the town. So to a lesser extent did Mithraism. Among the inhabitants belief in astrology seems to have been universal. The Jews had their richly decorated synagogue, and interestingly enough, the Christian church was in the same quarter, one but only one among the many religions represented in the town.[7] It was the same in other provinces, not least in North Africa where the great age of temple building is 170–235, and over all the religious and secular life of the people brooded the gods of Rome and the cult of the Emperor.

The early part of the third century had seen an intensification of the imperial cult. The Emperors were regarded as earthly representatives of an all-beneficent creator, who was coming more and more to be expressed through a universal sun-god. Caracalla's title of "master of the world" and "lover of Serapis" typified the mood of the time, and the Emperor's divine role was gladly accepted by his subjects. Thus in 183 the aggrieved peasants on the Saltus Burunitanus in Proconsular Africa turned to the providence of the Emperor Commodus for redress.[8] As Celsus had pointed out a few years before, whatever the provincial received on earth he received by way of the divine benefaction of the Emperor (*Contra Celsum* viii. 67). It is indeed astonishing how loyalty even to obscure Italic gods of the Roman people seems to have extended in these years to the garrisons of the frontier provinces. These soldier-citizens felt Roman. So it appears did most of the ordinary provincials on whom Caracalla's *Constitutio Antoniniana* of 212 had conferred citizenship. If ever the Roman gods had to be appeased in time of peril through a general call to sacrifice, they would obey. And, what of the Christians?

This question was soon to be asked and answered. The reign of Alexander Severus (222–35) had witnessed a gradual increase in the numbers and efficiency of Rome's external enemies. In 226 the friendly Parthian ruling dynasty had been overthrown in a revolution and replaced by the Sassanids, whose avowed object was to reconquer for Parthia all the territory which Darius I had once ruled. That meant the expulsion of Rome from Syria, Asia Minor and Egypt. A few years later, the Franks and Alemanni on the Rhine frontier began to move, and it was in protest against the Emperor's military incompetence that Maximin had seized power in March 235. Under his rule 235–8, and that of the Gordians who followed, 238–44, the situation was stabilized temporarily, but in 248 the Roman frontier was again threatened, this time by the Goths from across the Danube. The Emperor Philip was unable to deal with the situation, and after a brief struggle gave way to an able but conservative commander C. Quintus Messius Decius, who was proclaimed Emperor in the autumn of 249.

Opinions differ as to whether Decius's measures had the negative aim of crushing the Christians or the positive one of reawakening loyalty to the gods of the Empire through a universal act of sacrifice, from which the Christians by excluding themselves became outlaws. The positive element in Decius's policy is evident. His adoption of the name Trajan after the greatest of the emperors, his coinage honoring the imperial heroes of the past, his appointment of a senatorial deputy-emperor with the Republican title of Censor, and indeed, the order of a general sacrifice, all point to the conservative radicalism which was to typify the new breed of Illyrian soldier-emperors. They stood for Rome and her traditional values, and they suspected that the Christians did not. Moreover, Christianity had been associated with the disastrous policies of Philip. Also, as we know from Origen, it was sounding defiance to the Roman laws and boasting its power of survival in the face of all that the pagans could do.[9] In the larger towns it had become unpopular. Even before Philip fell Alexandria had been the scene of a gruesome pogrom.[10]

The measures against the Christians seem to have been divided into two phases. In the first, lasting from December 249 to February 250, punitive measures were taken against Christian leaders. Fabian, Bishop of Rome, was arrested, tried apparently before Decius himself, and executed on 20 January 250. The Emperor's comment was that he would rather face a rival for the throne than a successor to the Bishop.[11] Babyllas of Antioch and the old campaigner Alexander of Jerusalem suffered the same fate, Dionysius of Alexandria barely escaped, and

Cyprian of Carthage went into hiding. So far, action against Christian leaders could be construed as the purge of elements supporting the previous regime, much as Maximin's measures in 235 had been directed against his predecessor's adherents.

The second phase opened in June and lasted into the autumn of 250. Decius ordered a general sacrifice and supplication to the gods seemingly to be undertaken by all the citizens of the Empire, but probably with a bias toward forcing the Christians either to comply or to declare themselves. From surviving contemporary accounts from Carthage, Alexandria, Ephesus and Rome, it is clear that the authorities scored tremendous initial success. Commissions were appointed to supervise the sacrifice in each locality, and in the Fayoum in Egypt no less than forty-three certificates (*Libelli*) given to those who sacrificed have survived, and these show us what happened.[12]

A typical example may be quoted: "To the commission chosen to superintend the sacrifices at the village of Alexander's Isle. From Aurelius Diogenes, son of Satobous of the village of Alexander's Isle, aged 72 years, with a scar on the right eyebrow. I have always sacrificed to the gods, and now in your presence in accordance with the edict I have made sacrifice, and poured a libation . . ." It is a solemn legal document, and the formal language coupled with the emphasis on Decius's full imperial title indicates the extraordinary nature of the occasion.

Meantime in Alexandria Christian morale had broken. A contemporary account of events has been left in a letter which Bishop Dionysius wrote to his colleague Fabius of Antioch. On the arrival of the edict (probably ordering a General Sacrifice)

> . . . all cowered with fear: and of the more eminent persons, some came forward immediately through fear, others in public positions were compelled to do so by their business, and others were dragged by those around them. Called by name, they approached the impure and unholy sacrifices, some pale and trembling, as if they were not sacrificing but rather to be themselves the sacrifices and victims to the idols, so that the large crowd that stood around heaped mockery upon them, and it was evident that they were by nature cowards in everything, cowards both to die and to sacrifice. But others ran eagerly towards the altars . . .[13]

Similar scenes took place in Carthage, where the proceedings were in the hands of a commission of five leading citizens. The altars in the temples were overwhelmed by the eager crowd of Christians coming forward to sacrifice, and the magistrates begged many to return the next day.[14] Outside Carthage entire congregations, in one case led by their bishop, apostatized.[15] Thousands of other Christians contrived one way or another to possess themselves of certificates of sacrifice. In Rome also, crowds besieged the Capitol in their readiness to conform, and at Smyrna the State gained its greatest triumph of all, through the open apostasy of Euctemon the Bishop.[16] Polycarp's trust had been betrayed. All over the Mediterranean Christianity lay seemingly in ruins.

Unfortunately for the State, there was no effective means of following up this victory. Christians had only to lie low, avoid being too obvious on the day appointed for sacrifice and then resume membership of the Church. Only prominent Christians were pursued, but there was no effective prison service where they could be detained for long periods. For the rest, the authorities, overwhelmed by their apparent success, were content to let matters be. In both Carthage and Alexandria there is evidence that about a score of confessors were imprisoned for obduracy, and there were some executions. But on the whole surprisingly little force had to be used. Meantime, the Gothic peril remained. Decius found the Gothic king Kniva a wily and dangerous opponent. His campaign in 250 had cleared the barbarians from along the Moesian (modern Bulgaria) Danube, but in June 251 he was lured into the marshes near Abrittus in the Dobrudja. There he was defeated and killed. Though his successor Gallus attempted to continue the persecution in 252 it never regained momentum. It remained for the Christians to lick their wounds and pick up the broken pieces of their organization.

For Carthage, we are well informed about events in the next few years. Cyprian's eighty-one letters and dozen treatises provide a remarkably clear picture of Christian life and thought in Africa between 248–58. Cyprian himself, we learn from Jerome,[17] had been a lawyer, who had gradually been won over to Christianity by the arguments and example of Christians. His conversion, however, had brought him to a very different frame of mind to that of his contemporary, Gregory the Wonder-worker. While the latter had seen in the new Faith one that filled his mind "with a rational instead of an irrational admiration of the divine ordering of the world," Cyprian saw it as a command to reject the world. Christianity meant liberation from vice, darkness and insecurity, not the perfection of the hitherto incomplete yearning after the divine. Redemption from sin rather than enlightenment through the guidance of the divine Word was his expectation from his new Faith.[18] In the two converts we see Eastern and Western theology drifting inexorably apart.

No compromise with the world! Cyprian found the works of Tertullian a perfect teacher. He became prominent in the Church of Carthage, and in circa 248 despite his comparatively junior status as a Christian was elected Bishop against the wishes, however, of five of the leading Carthaginian presbyters. Within a year, his Church faced persecution, Cyprian withdrew into hiding, and not surprisingly disaster overtook the leaderless community. As he admits, the great majority of the Christians in Carthage lapsed.[19]

The complicated and even bewildering detail of the years 250–1 cannot be told here.[20] Cyprian's correspondence emphasizes three main points. First, events in Carthage and Rome were closely interrelated. Secondly, an interregnum ensued in both centers following Fabian's execution and Cyprian's flight. While in Rome the presbyters were willing and able to maintain the cohesion of the community, in Carthage power fell into the hands of inexperienced but vainglorious confessors. Thirdly, the persecution revived the generation-old antagonism between the rigorists and laxists, the Church of the Spirit against the Church of the Sacrament.

Cyprian's conduct had not escaped the censure either of the Roman presbyters or the confessors in Carthage. The latter, however, overplayed their hand, for when toward the end of 250 penitent lapsed began to clamor once more for readmission to the Church they told Cyprian to "have peace with the holy martyrs"[21] and handed out "letters of peace" (*libelli pacis*) wholesale.[22] Cyprian was able to return to Carthage early in 251 and set about putting an end to the disorder.

His central idea was the unity and oneness of the Church; for just as God was one so must his people on earth be one, and to divide that people on any pretext was the worst of sins. Unity was expressed through a federation of episcopally governed communities, each bishop being autonomous, in the sense that he was possessed by and guided by the Holy Spirit and was answerable to God for his acts and those of his flock.[23] The Apostles had been bishops, and therefore their successors were rulers of the Church. Grace was confined to an exclusive, visible Church, outside whose bounds no salvation was possible. "He cannot have God for his father who has not the Church for his mother. If he who was outside the ark could escape, he too who was an alien and outside the Church could also escape."[24] These theories so akin to the Judeo-Christianity of the Clementine *Recognitions* had become the tradition of North Africa where the Church of the Holy Spirit had now merged with the Church of the bishops. The combination of powers gave Cyprian his unique authority. Between 251–6 he showed how this was to be used.

First, the rebellious confessors must be dealt with. Cyprian had already urged that the "glory of a confession of faith belonged to the Church as a whole" whose representative was, of course, the bishop.

Soon after Easter 251 he held a council of bishops at Carthage. There the claims of the confessors to remit penances by the lapsed were rejected. The *libellatici* (i.e., those Christians who had accepted a *libellus* or certificate of sacrifice but had not actually sacrificed) were to be subjected to vigorous inquiry and awarded penances according to the gravity of their offence. The *sacrificati* (those who had sacrificed) were only to be readmitted on their death beds.[25] Secondly, Cyprian lent his aid to crush intrigue and rigorist schism in Rome. His enemies of 248 had foregathered there, and with splendid inconsistency had turned from upbraiding Cyprian's severity toward the confessors to supporting the party of narrow-minded fanatics round the theologian Novatian. When Cornelius was canonically elected Bishop on 5 March 251, the latter allowed himself to be acclaimed Bishop also. In a brisk campaign-tract written in the autumn of 251 entitled "On the Unity (or "Oneness") of the Catholic Church," Cyprian applied the principle of one bishop one See to the benefit of Cornelius.[26] Thus far Rome and Africa were at one.

So long as Cornelius lived, this situation lasted. In July 252, however, he died a prisoner at Centumcellae whither he had been deported under a brief recrudescence of persecution under the Emperor Gallus. His successor Lucius left no particular mark on history, but on 12 May 254 he was replaced by a vigorous personality, Stephen.

Meantime, the repercussions of the Decian persecution were continuing. Novatian's support among the major bishoprics of Christendom was not negligible. In the West, the bishop of the major Gallic See, Arles, declared for him, and in Antioch, Bishop Fabius was only narrowly dissuaded from the same course. Novatian's emissaries continued to plague Cyprian. On the other hand, the problem of restoring clergy who had lapsed during the persecution was proving intractable. In the autumn of 254 the congregations of the Spanish churches of *Emerita* (Merida) and *Legio* (Leon) appealed to Cyprian for advice as to whether sacraments given by their lapsed bishops were valid. Stephen had been persuaded to restore these men to their offices, and the affronted Spaniards had appealed over his head to Cyprian.[27]

The letter written by Cyprian on behalf of the council summoned to consider the question throws a good deal of light on North African sacramental theology. There was no doubt that the Spanish bishops had accepted testimonials as to their orthodoxy as pagans. In the African view, they were apostates, in a state of ritual impurity, and by the test of an appeal to passages in the Old Testament, such as Exodus 19:22, 28:43, and Leviticus 21:17 dealing with prescriptions for the order of Levite, incapable of administering a valid sacrament. Worse than this, a

101

congregation which clove to such ministers was itself in danger of sharing their damnation. "Nor let the people flatter themselves as if they can be free from the contagion of the offense, when communicating with a priest who is a sinner," wrote Cyprian, and their plain duty was "to separate themselves from a prelate who is a sinner, and not to mingle themselves with the sacrifices of an unrighteous priest."[25] This was a development of a standpoint already expressed by Tertullian. The Church's sacrament, the vehicle of the Holy Spirit, could not be administered by those from whom the Holy Spirit had departed. There might be some "tares" and backsliders among the people of God, but none among his ministers.

How this particular issue ended we do not know, but a year later a new difficulty arose which was to throw still further into relief the contrasting views as to the nature of the Church now emerging in Rome and Carthage. It was four years since the end of the persecution, and the Church had regained all the ground it had lost. The example of Cyprian's clergy during the plague in 252 and the war against the Kabylie tribes which broke out the following year had caught popular imagination. But among the new converts some had been those baptized by Novatianist ministers, and when these rallied to Cyprian's Church the question arose whether they needed a further baptism or not.

The African Church had so far spoken with one voice. Tertullian had declared that baptism given outside the Church was invalid, and this view had been upheld by a council held by Agrippinus, Bishop of Carthage, in circa 220. For the African Christian the baptismal rite summed up his view of the Church. It was at this point that the convert renounced the world and literally took on the Holy Spirit and became a member of the people of God. It stood to reason that a minister who was himself outside the Church could not convey the Spirit in baptism, and thus an ex-heretic or schismatic would have to be baptized anew when he came into the Church. On the whole, this view was accepted in Asia Minor, and it typified the outlook of a small, gathered community for whom baptism often preceded the second baptism of martyrdom.

In Rome, however, another tradition had grown up. Confirmation, the laying on of hands, was coming to share with baptism an equal importance in a Christian's life. In this extremely numerous community, baptism signified the formal entry into Church membership, but reception of the Spirit was delayed until confirmation. Hence, Stephen concluded that provided baptism had been performed in the name of the Trinity it was valid regardless of the status of the minister. He could even be a

Marcionite, for "whether in pretense or in truth Christ is preached" (Phil. 1:18).[29]

The Africans were themselves not entirely united, and three councils had to be held between autumn 255 and autumn 256 before they spoke unanimously.[30] Meantime, the quarrel with Stephen grew worse. Cyprian was threatened with excommunication as a "false Christ" and "deceitful worker."[31] He replied by holding a full council at Carthage on 1 September 256 which eighty-seven bishops attended, and after he had briefly stated his case, and declared that no one should set himself up "as bishop of bishops or by tyrannical terror force obedience on his colleagues," man after man rose to support him. Not for the last time was a North African council to put a Roman bishop in his place. "Heretics can either do nothing or they can do all. If they can baptize, they can also bestow the Holy Spirit. But if they cannot give the Holy Spirit because they have not got it themselves, neither can they spiritually baptize. Therefore we judge that heretics must be baptized."[32]

It was a simple statement of the purity of the visible Church, and it was to be reiterated by the African Donatists in the fourth century. We do not know how Stephen reacted to it. According to Cyprian's supporter in Asia Minor, Firmilian of Cappadocia, it was with that same insolence that a century later St. Basil was to find intolerable in Pope Damasus. "A deputation of bishops from Carthage," Firmilian wrote, "he received with patience enough and gentleness for he even refused ordinary conversation with them, and he cared so much about love and charity that he forbade the brotherhood receive them in their houses" (*Letter* 75:25). In Alexandria, however, Dionysius, untroubled by a doctrine of the Church dependent on a doctrine of the Holy Spirit, was able to take up a mediating position. For the East, the question was that of *heretical* baptism, not *schismatic* baptism. Dionysius urged forbearance on Stephen. He should not disturb the customs of the African and Asian Churches, and when Stephen died on 2 August 257 he pressed the same advice on his successor Xystus (Eusebius, *H.E.*, vii. 7:5).

The year 257, however, was no time for inter-Church feuds. Valerian, Decius's censor, had been called to the purple in October 253, and the next four years saw the Empire face the full force of combined barbarian and Persian attack. While the Franks and Alemannen threatened the Rhine frontier, the Goths overran the buttress-province of Dacia, and in the East, Dura-Europos fell after an heroic defense revealed by the archaeologist's spade, and even Antioch was lost for a short time. Moreover, despite the warnings of Bishop Gregory many of the Christians along the Black Sea coast made common cause with barbarian invaders. Militarily and economically the Empire seemed on the verge of ruin.

In contrast, the Christian Church was gaining in numbers and wealth. Cyprian's letters show that the Church had come to be regarded as a safe trustee and was able to pay out large sums for charitable purposes.[33] Its ministry was paid and permanent.[34] These factors repeated in Alexandria may have influenced Valerian's chief financial officer, Macrianus, to heed the advice of Egyptian priests and recommend a renewal of pressure on the Christians. Valerian had hitherto been favorable to them, remarkably so if we can believe Dionysius of Alexandria, but evidently allowed himself to be persuaded.[35] However, the first edict, probably in the summer of 257, did not aim at the suppression of Christianity, but merely insisted that the Christian leaders should perform some act of acknowledgment to the traditional Roman ceremonies. This is made quite clear from the following dialogue between the deputy prefect of Egypt, Aemilianus, and Bishop Dionysius who appeared before him:

Aemilianus: . . . (words not quoted by Dionysius) And verbally I spoke with you about the kindness that our lords have displayed on your behalf. For they gave you the opportunity of safety if you were willing to turn to that which is in accordance with nature and worship the gods which preserve their Empire, and forget those gods which are contrary to nature. What therefore do you say to these things? For I do not expect that you will be ungrateful for their kindness, in as much as they are urging you on to a better course.

Dionysius: Not all men worship all gods, but each are certain whom he regards as such. We therefore both worship and adore the one God and Maker of all things, who also committed the Empire to the Augusti, most highly favored of God, Valerian and Gallienus; and to him we unceasingly pray for their Empire, that it may remain unshaken.

Aemilianus, the deputy-prefect, said to them: And who prevents you from worshiping this god also, if he be a god, along with the natural gods? For you were bidden to worship the gods, and the gods whom all know.

Dionysius: We worship no other God.
(tr. Lawlor and Oulton, slightly altered).[36]

That was the end. Dionysius was deported to the oasis of Kufra where he began to evangelize the Libyans. In Carthage, Cyprian maintained a similar stand, but only suffered removal from the capital to the pleasant surroundings of Curubis (Kurba) on the Gulf of Hammamet. In Numidia, however, the order was carried out more severely and some of the Numidian bishops were remitted in horrible conditions to the mines of Sigus.

The first edict had forbidden the Christians to hold services or enter their cemeteries; otherwise they were not to be molested. Next year, however, Valerian decided for reasons which are not explained on more severe measures. Early in August 258 a rescript reached Rome ordering that bishops, presbyters and deacons should be punished by summary execution. Senators, lesser nobles (*egregii viri*) and Roman knights (mainly senior civil servants) should forfeit their property, and if they persisted in their Christianity should suffer execution. Lower civil servants (*caesariani*) should be reduced to slavery, and *matronae* deprived of their property and banished.[37] Its object was to deprive the Church of upper-class support and property, and perhaps even use confiscated property to swell the imperial war chest. It was carried out ruthlessly. In Rome, Xystus and four of his deacons were arrested in the catacombs and executed. In Africa, Cyprian was brought back to Carthage, and told that for a long time he had "lived an irreligious life, drawn together a number of men bound by an unlawful association and professed himself an open enemy to the gods and the religion of Rome"—a single sentence summarizing the real charges of the Roman authorities against the Christians—and was given one final chance of recantation. He refused, and on 14 September 258 became the first bishop-martyr of Africa.[38]

The persecution continued for another year, and in Africa was probably more destructive of human lives than the Great Persecution forty years later. The populace was still against the Christians, and the Acts of the Martyrs of the period tell of Christian clergy being hounded before the magistrates. But these measures did not appease the gods. Valerian rightly assumed that the real peril to the Empire came from Sapor's armies in the East. The campaign of 259 was indecisive. In June 260, however, he found himself confronted with superior numbers of Persians near Edessa (east of the upper Euphrates); he was lured into a parley and taken prisoner. The Roman military position in the East disintegrated.

His son and colleague, Gallienus, now bade for public opinion. This time, however, he recognized the strength of the Christians in the eastern provinces. The policy of persecution was rapidly dismantled and in a rescript addressed to Dionysius and his colleagues in Egypt in 261 he restored to them the property of the Church and assured them of freedom from molestation.[39] Persecution and repression had proved in vain. Christianity was now a decisive force in the Eastern provinces of the Empire, and its loyalty was a necessity in face of the external threat. The next forty years were to prove the truth of this. The Great Persecution when it came in 303 was foredoomed to failure.

FURTHER READING

The Decian and Valerianic persecutions are discussed in the *Cambridge Ancient History*, Vol.12 (chapters by A.Alföldi, H.Lietzmann and N.H.Baynes). See also H.M.Gwatkin, *Early Church History to 313*, Vol.7, Macmillan 1912, ch.23.

For Cyprian, E.W.Benson, *Cyprian, His Life, His Times, His Work*, Macmillan 1897, remains a standard work. See also G.G.Willis, *Saint Augustine and the Donatist Controversy*, SPCK 1950, ch.4; also my *The Donatist Church*, Oxford University Press ²1971, ch.10. On the problem of the Cyprianic work *On the Unity of the Church* see M.Bévenot, SJ, 'St Cyprian's *De Unitate*, Ch.iv in the Light of the Manuscripts', *Gregoriana*, Rome 1938, and subsequent articles. An excellent translation of Cyprian's letters with an introduction has been made by G.W.Clarke, *The Letters of St Cyprian* (4 vols.), Ancient Christian Writers 43-47, Newman Press, New York 1984-89.

G.W.H.Lampe, *The Seal of the Spirit*, Longmans 1951 (for the rival doctrines of the church held by Rome and Carthage).

The best edition of the Acts of the Martyrs is R.Knopf and G.Krüger, *Ausgewählte Märtyrerakten*, Tübingen 1929, in which the Acts of Pionius and others cited in this book will be found. See also, for texts with English translation, *The Acts of the Christian Martyrs*, edited and translated by H.Musurillo, Clarendon Press 1972.

10

The Dawn of the New Era
260–303

The rescript of Gallienus opened a new era for the Church. Not that the Empire had capitulated. Refusal to sacrifice on public occasions on the grounds of Christianity could still be death,[1] but the Church had now established itself as a political and religious force to be reckoned with. Though the evidence is obscure, one can detect how the bishops of the great Sees were becoming public men pronouncing in their sermons and festal letters on public affairs. Dionysius of Alexandria and his opponent Paul of Samosata begin the line of ecclesiastical statesmen. Christianity was no longer a bar to advancement in the imperial service, and by 300 we hear of senior Christian officers and influential Christians at the Emperor's court.[2] In some cities, such as Aquileia and Nicomedia (on the gulf of Iznik in Asia Minor), the churches were conspicuous public buildings, while converts such as the Africans, Arnobius and Lactantius show that at last Christianity was continuing to attract able minds from the provincial upper classes.

The successive emperors who followed Valerian were in no position to renew the policy of repression. Gallienus favored the Christians for political ends—his personal views seem to have inclined him toward the Neo-Platonists. Throughout his short reign his successor Claudius II (268–70) was engaged in defeating the Goths who had swarmed into the Balkan provinces. His victory at Naissus (Nis) in 269 was a milestone in the military recovery of the Empire, but he had little time for internal policies before he died of the plague. Under the great soldier-Emperor Aurelian (270–5) the barbarians were driven back everywhere and the frontiers established on the Danube and the Rhine. The Gallic provinces which had seceded in 259 were restored to the central authority. In the East, the powerful Palmyrene kingdom of Zenobia which had succeeded Roman authority in Syria and Northern Mesopotamia was overthrown. These successes Aurelian attributed to the favor of the sun-god, and in

274 he erected a magnificent temple in Rome to him. Sol shared with Jupiter the role of protector of the Empire. Next year the Emperor may have considered taking action against the Christians[3] but he was struck down by mutinous officers (April or August 275) before he could put his plan into effect. Probus (276–82), Carus (282–3), Carinus (283–5) were too engaged in further fighting or in frustrating military conspiracies to revive this policy, and for the first nineteen years of his reign, Diocletian (284–305) left the Christians to their own devices.

Thanks to these Balkan soldiers, the Roman Empire had been saved from collapse. For another century and a half the Mediterranean world was to remain under its authority, but at appalling cost. Armies had had to be raised, paid and supplied. Fortifications and roads had to be repaired, and many of the cities, especially in the West, transformed from prosperous open towns into fortified enclosures. A horde of administrators and inspectors descended on the provinces. The burden fell severely on the provincial city aristocracies, people who had hitherto been most loyal to the Roman Empire and its gods; for in addition to the responsibility for finding the money, labor and supplies required, they were confronted with an unprecedented collapse of the currency. By 260 the silver content of the chief denomination in use (the *antoninianus*) had fallen from around forty per cent at the time of its origin circa 212, to fifteen per cent under Decius to two percent in the second half of Gallienus' reign (260–8).[4] The last decade had witnessed a veritable crash. Economic insecurity bred by these conditions is expressed in the vast coin hoards hidden in the middle years of the third century in practically every province of the Empire. Deep pessimism and belief that catastrophe was near pervaded the literature of the period. Thus in 252 Cyprian's erstwhile friend the Carthaginian magistrate, Demetrianus, wrote, "the mines are nearly exhausted, there is nothing in the fields, no sailor on the seas, no soldier in the camp, there is no honesty in the marketplace, justice in the courts, trust in friendship, skill in the arts, discipline in morals."[5] The world was at its last gasp. Were the Christians to blame, or were the old gods failing?

Among the great mass of the inhabitants of the Empire, the countryfolk, the results of the economic crisis were more complex. They had less to lose, and land usually recovers quickly even from the devastation of war. In some parts of the Empire, such as North Africa, the villages were increasing in number and size as the third century wore on. But though their inhabitants' crops or their holdings may have been relatively rich, there was no escaping the tax collector and the soldier. In Asia Minor and Egypt holdings were abandoned and peasants fled either to the desert or to the protection of powerful landowners. "Am I to take flight?" or "Am I to become a beggar?" were among the stock questions put by the peasants in the Fayoum to their oracle.[6] In Gaul they revolted. People began to revert to systems and ideas that had prevailed before the coming of Greece and Rome. Coptic, linguistically the direct descendant of ancient Egyptian, and Syrian emerged as regional languages and literatures. The villa and the dependent village replaced the city state as the predominant unit of society. Above all, the Church was superseding the pagan temple as a refuge for the oppressed and as the symbol of the new era.

An obscure but lasting revolution was taking place in the religious loyalties of the rural population in some of the great provinces of the Empire. The great rivals of Christianity, Mithraism, the worship of Isis, and even the imperial cult still attracted their adherents, and in the 270s, Christianity was coming face to face with a still more serious threat through the dualistic religion of Mani from beyond the Persian frontier.[7] But even so, the influence of this religion was mainly confined to the towns or to groups of individuals. Of more profound significance was the apparent loss of favor of the great national deities who had held sway in their respective territories for millennia. In one North African township the last of a long series of dated dedications to Saturn-Baal Hammon is A.D. 272,[8] and the next dated inscriptions there are Christian,[9] or that in another town dedications to Saturn were being used in the fourth century to pave the streets. In the same period, however, the number of Christian bishoprics doubled, and there were probably as many as 250 by the time of the Great Persecution. Many of these new bishoprics were in rural areas. As the records of that time show, the country population of Numidia had become violently pro-Christian though the depleted city oligarchies remained loyal to the old cults. By 300 North Africa was largely lost to paganism.

Much the same story can be repeated in Asia Minor. In Cappadocia the missionary work of Gregory the Wonderworker was extremely successful. Though the statement of his biographer, Gregory of Nyssa, that when he arrived at Neo-Caesarea in 243 there were seventeen Christians and when he died nearly thirty years later there were only seventeen pagans, may be an exaggeration, it is obvious that he caused an appreciable movement toward Christianity in the province.[10] In many Phrygian towns also, the patient study of funerary inscriptions reveals a steady conversion to formulas which may be recognized as Christian. In the countryside no disguises were practiced. Numerous tombstones, dated between 248–79, proclaim a ringing image "from Christians to Christians," and emphasize the Christian qualities of the deceased such as his benevolence, his asceticism, and his life as "a soldier of Christ."[11] When in 325 the small town of Orcistus petitioned to be granted municipal status, one of the arguments the inhabitants used was that "they were all Christians."[12] It was no doubt calculated to please the Emperor, but was probably true of them and of other centers of the Anatolian plateau.

In Egypt and probably also in Syria these same developments were taking place. Egyptian hieroglyphic inscriptions cease after 251 and inscriptions referring to sacrifices in honor of the emperors after 295. We have on the other hand the eyewitness account of Eusebius of the conversion of the Copts to Christianity when he was in Egypt in 311–12 during the final stages of the Great Persecution. He stresses that Christians formed the majority of the population, that while the spirit of idolatry was striving to keep the Egyptians in a ferment, "thousands of the inhabitants were deserting paganism—and anyone not wholly lacking in vision could see this" (*Demonstratio Evangelica*, ix. 2). In contrast to the situation described by Dionysius of Alexandria fifty years before, when not even parts of the outskirts of Alexandria had heard of Christ, his altars were now in every town and village (*ibid.*, viii. 5). Families were racked by religious strife. In all this, the beginnings of the monastic movement were being born. Antony's flight from even the primitive surroundings of his village took place about 270. Egyptian monasticism was to be a Coptic movement. Its emergence at this time shows how seriously the predominance of Greco-Roman culture was being challenged.

Similar processes were therefore going on in widely separated parts of the Mediterranean world—though not in the Celtic provinces of the northwest of the Empire. Africa and Egypt were the granaries of the Eastern and Western halves of the Empire respectively, and no Emperor could afford widespread disaffection there. The victory of the Church in these provinces would have been decisive whether Constantine had seen a vision or not. Why this movement took place it is virtually impossible to say. One observer, the Neo-Platonist Alexander of Lycopolis in Upper Egypt, stresses the attraction of Christianity for the crowds owing to its simplicity,[13] but nothing tells us why those crowds should so suddenly have abandoned worship that had satisfied their ancestors for countless generations. Increasing Romanization that divorced the gods from the people they were supposed to protect, a syncretism which robbed them of their majesty, and the universal onset of hard times—all these may have played their part. The Church also gave to the countryfolk two ideas to which their old religion could not aspire, social justice and freedom from an oppressive world on the one hand, and the assurance of victory over the demonic power wielded by the former gods, on the other. In Africa certainly Christianity came to reflect deep-felt social grievances. In Egypt also, flight from the world to religion was also flight from the tax collector.[14] The same term "anchoresis" soon came to describe both. Finally, rural Christianity shared one other factor in common. It was a religion of the elect. It was Biblical in its inspiration and Old Testament in its outlook. Every word of the Bible was regarded as sacred. Its adherents saw themselves as the chosen of God, separated in every respect from the heathen. They believed in the rapid approach of the second Advent. Their fanaticism was to give the edge to every religious controversy whether in East or West, and to add to intellectual differences the antagonisms of social and cultural strife.

The recrudescence of a fanatical and apocalyptic form of Christianity among native converts came just when in other ways the gap between the Church and the Empire was narrowing. Not only were Christians holding important offices of State, but in some of the provincial centers it was even possible for formal pagan offices to be performed by Christian city councilors.[15] The growing standardization of Christian worship and hierarchy was also working in the same direction. The ceremonial in the Eucharist remained simple, prayers being said standing or kneeling, the palms outstretched or folded upon the breast. There was, however, little scope for any out-of-the-ordinary administration of the Cup by a "prophet" or for extempore prayers and singing by laymen such as is referred to by Tertullian.[16] Everything was being done in accordance with tradition. The clerical order had been elaborated to include teachers who read the lections and various grades of deacon who read the Gospel, presented the elements at the Offertory and kept discipline in the Church. The clergy had become a caste apart, and like most closed corporations were not interested in stirring up trouble with the powers that be.

The Church was now part of the everyday scene in most of the cities of the Mediterranean. Its government was in the hands of the bishop of a *civitas* or town, assisted by presbyters and deacons. Very occasionally there were *Chorepiscopi* (country bishops) responsible for a group of rural communities. The bishops in the provincial capitals were claiming rights, or at least precedence over their colleagues, and this became more pronounced as ecclesiastical boundaries tended to coincide with civil ones. In Egypt the "pope" of Alexandria possessed undisputed primacy over the other bishops including these of Cyrenaica who ranked merely as his suffragans. By 314 Rome had acquired rights of jurisdiction over the churches of "suburbicarian Italy," roughly corresponding to Italy south of the Po. Antioch ruled the churches of Syria and as far east as the Euphrates. The official designation of the patriarchal rights of Rome, Antioch, Alexandria and Jerusalem set the seal on a system which had been coming into being in the latter half of the previous century.[17]

Under the immediate control of the bishop in the larger cities there had been growing up a comprehensive system of parishes run by presbyters. The early years of the fourth century saw the "title" churches (i.e., parochial churches directly controlled by the bishop) established in the ecclesiastical regions into which the city had been divided. The mainstay, however, of late third-century ecclesiastical administration was the diaconate. Cyprian had used his subdeacons as messengers and liaison officers to keep him in touch with colleagues overseas. By 300 the chief of the deacons had graduated into a special office of *archidiaconus* (archdeacon) ousting the presbyters as the bishop's right-hand man and heir presumptive.[18] The administrative staff of a great See is set out in indignant terms by Cornelius to his colleague Fabius of Antioch protesting against his pro-Novatianist learnings. "This vindicator of the Gospel" [i.e., Novatian], he writes, "did not know that there should be one bishop in a catholic church . . . that there are forty-six presbyters, seven deacons, forty-two acolytes, fifty-two exorcists, readers and doorkeepers and upward of fifteen hundred widows and persons in distress," who had to be supported by the Church.[19]

No wonder this powerful ecclesiastical machine was opposed to enthusiasm. We see the latent tensions developing in Egypt in the 260s when Bishop Dionysius savagely rebuked his colleague Nepos of Arsinoe for teaching that the Millennium as described in the Apocalypse was not allegorical but would be actual fact.[20] Nepos was, however, speaking for rural Christianity against the Christian philosophy of Alexandria. In Africa the Carthaginian clergy were evidently bent on controlling the cult of martyrs and their relics. Alleged martyrs had to be carefully "screened" and only if successful were permitted veneration.[21] The Church was fast becoming a "mixed body" despite itself, and there is little doubt that by the end of the century there were many clergy who were prepared to accept the Roman view of baptism and the doctrine of the Church associated with it. The idealism, however, of the new Christians both in Egypt and Africa retained its appeal. Should crisis arise, would the Church of the Holy Spirit follow the lead of the Church of the bishops, or would it go its own way? The Great Persecution was to show.

Schism was not the only danger that threatened. The same problems concerning the nature of the Trinity that had beset Origen now beset his successors. Even before Bishop Dionysius went into exile in 257 he was involved in a wrangle with his suffragans in Cyrenaica. These had accepted the Modalist or Sabellian view of the Trinity, and were teaching that the Word or Son was to be identified with the Father. They had invented the technical term of *uiopator* (ὑιοπάτωρ) to make their point, but Dionysius needed no such precision of heresy. He was furious, refused to hear the Cyrenaicans and in a letter to Xystus II warned him of their error.[22] There the matter rested until after the Valerianic persecution. Then the Cyrenaicans turned the tables. In one of his letters to a colleague explaining his views Dionysius himself had pressed his original reasoning too far. The Son was described as a "creature" and the three essences of Father, Son and Holy Ghost were so separated as to be capable of being understood as three gods.[23] The Cyrenaicans complained to Dionysius of Rome, and he showed that in any dispute between the Origenist theories of the Trinity and Modalism Rome would incline to the latter. Dionysius of Rome's letter to the bishop of Alexandria demonstrated also the razor's edge on which orthodoxy was resting. A new word was making its appearance in the theological vocabulary of the East. *Homoousios* (consubstantial) had been rejected by Dionysius of Alexandria, but not by his colleague of Rome.

The fact was, that the metaphysical terminology between the Greek and Latin Churches was hopelessly confused, the Latin term *substantia* (substance) serving to translate both the Greek term *ousia* (essence) and *hypostasis* (individuality). Thus, when Dionysius of Alexandria asserted God in three *hypostaseis* his colleague in Rome thought he meant three "substances," i.e., three different natures. Later when the Latins asserted God in one *hypostasis* and three "persons" (*personae*), the Greeks thought that they were talking about *personae—prosopae*, which had the meaning of purely outward characterization such as provided by an actor's mask. They believed that the West was Modalist in its theology. This was indeed true up to a point, but the difficulties of language exaggerated the differences between the two branches of Christian thought.[24]

In the last year of his life, 264, Dionysius of Alexandria was involved in a still more serious affair. In Antioch, the new Bishop, Paul of Samosata, 261-72, was a flamboyant character.[25] He was also procurator of the city in the name of Queen Zenobia of Palmyra. But his crime in the eyes of Dionysius was ecclesiastical. He asserted among other things that the Virgin Mary gave birth to a man, and that the Spirit who anointed him was the same Spirit that had inspired the prophets. But in Jesus' case the inspiration was complete. The spirit took up his abode in him as in a temple.[26] Moreover, Paul also used the term *Homoousios* to

113

describe the relationship between Word and Father, but in a sense that seems to have suggested the evidence of some quality prior to both.[27]

All this was abhorrent to the school of Alexandria. Paul was concerned with the humanity and historical existence of Jesus, and the Syrian Church as a whole looked to the regeneration of humanity through baptism on the model of Jesus' own acceptance of the Spirit in the waters of Jordan. The preexistence of Christ and the economy of the Trinity left them cold. The Origenists scented Adoptianism. Three councils were held, and finally Paul was exposed by the arguments of an Origenist priest in Antioch and declared deposed in 268. For the first time a council had imposed a test of orthodoxy. The problem of the contrast between a Christ descended from on high and displaying before man the perfection of the divine nature, and a Christ "sprung from beneath" sharing our humanity and raising it by moral activity toward God, had been decided in favor of the former. The first round in the battle between the Alexandrian and Antiochene schools had been won by the Alexandrians.

As the third century drew to a close, the tensions within the Church were becoming more explosive. Eusebius looking back on the situation as he had seen it as a young man could write, "But when as the result of greater freedom a change to pride and sloth came over our affairs, we fell to envy and fierce railing one against the other, warring upon ourselves so to speak as occasion offered with weapons and spears formed of words, and ruler attacked ruler and laity formed factions against laity, while unspeakable hypocrisy and pretense pursued their evil course to the furthest end."[28] It was a grim picture of ecclesiastical strife at the moment of Christianity's triumph. Paganism had indeed been defeated. The world was ripe for religious change, but not for religious peace.

FURTHER READING

Armstrong, A.H., 'Plotinus', *Cambridge History of Later Greek and Early Mediaeval Philosophy*, Cambridge University Press 1967, 195-268

Bethune-Baker, J.F., *Introduction to the Early History of Christian Doctrine*, Methuen 1952, ch.8 (on the correspondence between the two Dionysii)

Calder, W.M., 'Christian Inscriptions in Phrygia', *Anatolian Studies*, 1955 (third-century Christianity in Phrygia)

Frend, W.H.C., 'The Failure of the Persecutions in the Roman Empire', *Past and Present* 16, 1959, 10-30

Gregoire, H. *Les Persécutions dans l'Empire romain*, Brussels 1955

Maxwell, W.D., *The Outline of Christian Worship - Its Development and Forms*, Oxford University Press 1963

Stevenson, J., *The Catacombs*, Thames and Hudson 1978

11

The Great Persecution
303-12

One final trial awaited the Christians. Exactly why the Great Persecution broke out when it did, on 23 February 303, is uncertain. Its sudden and unexpected character is revealed in the writings of the time, especially by the Christians Eusebius and Lactantius, who were both eyewitnesses of the events they describe. For nineteen years Diocletian had been Emperor and the Christians had been left in peace. As we have seen, high positions in the Emperor's court were occupied by them, and his own family seems to have favored them. Up to 303 the keynote of the reign had been reconstruction. Soon after assuming power in November 284 the Emperor had divided his responsibilities with a colleague, Maximian, who was to govern the Western provinces (early 285) and was promoted Augustus March 286. Later, in 293 each Emperor appointed a deputy, or Caesar, to assist him. Diocletian chose Galerius, and Maximian, Constantius. Successively the army, provincial administration and currency were overhauled, and new life was put into the cities of the Empire. This involved the rebuilding of temples and the revival of pagan cults. Indeed, the whole spirit of the Diocletianic reform was religious-conservative, harking back to the traditional virtues of Rome. The inscription on the obverse of the new "people's" coinage read, "To the Genius of the Roman People." The Empire was placed under the patronage of the old Roman gods, Jupiter and Hercuies.

Conservative religious values and a desire to secure a minimum of conformity from the "whole race of the Romans" were clearly among the reasons that led Diocletian and his colleagues to try conclusions with the Christians. The fear of foreign-inspired religious innovations sapping the "immemorial customs" was real enough and was shown by Diocletian's rescript to Julian, Proconsul of Carthage, proscribing the Manichees for doing this very thing. It laid down a whole series of penalties for those found guilty of belonging to the sect and ordered their books to be handed over and burnt.[1]

115

Six years later it was to be the Christians' turn. The latter, to judge from Eusebius, were still being taxed with disloyalty and atheism, while in the previous decade paganism had at last produced an able defender in the person of Porphyry of Gaza (232–305?).

Porphyry belonged to the Neo-Platonist school, an enemy of Christianity.[2] He knew of Celsus's work a century before, but he was far better equipped for his task than Celsus had ever been. He held Jesus himself in sincere respect, but then applied the same skillful methods of literary criticism to the Bible that Origen had used, but without Origen's premise that the Bible was the word of God. As a result, the inconsistencies of the Gospel narrative of incidents in Jesus' life were exposed, as were the less attractive aspects of the characters of Peter and Paul, while a brilliant piece of literary acumen showed the Book of Daniel to have been written during the Jewish revolt against Antiochus IV, and therefore of no relevance for Christian prophecy. Had the Empire been in an intellectually and socially more healthy state, this work might have put the Christians back on the defensive. As it was, its conclusions were not lost on some of Diocletian's ablest administrators, including Hierocles, governor of the Black Sea province of Bithynia.

The actual break with the Christians came slowly. Diocletian, ever cautious, refused to be rushed by the arguments of his more vigorous Caesar, Galerius. However, in 298 Galerius became the hero of Rome's great recovery against Persia, and between 298–302 a series of incidents in the army of Syria and North Africa sowed fears in Diocletian's mind that the Christians might not be reliable. He ordered his commander-in-chief, Veturius, to purge the army of them. Then in the winter of 302–3, he and his Caesar consulted the famous oracle of Apollo at Didyma in the Maeander Valley in Asia Minor. They received the cryptic reply "that the just upon the earth hindered him from declaring the truth and that this was the cause of false oracles issuing from the tripods."[3] Diocletian yielded, but on the understanding that there should be no bloodshed.

On 23 February 303 there was posted an edict in Nicomedia ordering all copies of the Scriptures to be surrendered and burned, all churches to be dismantled, and no meetings for Christian worship to be held. Next day a supplementary edict deprived Christians of all honors and dignities, making them all liable to torture and debarring them from being plaintiffs in any legal action. The great church of Nicomedia which stood in full view of the imperial palace was destroyed.[4] A Christian tore down a copy of the edicts with the comment, "More victories over the Goths and Sarmatians." He was caught and roasted alive.

In some of the Eastern provinces the news was received badly. Revolts were reported in Syria and Melitene, the province on the headwaters of the Tigris. Both were sensitive areas in the Roman defense against Persia. Fires broke out in the Emperor's palace, and as a reprisal a second edict went out ordering the arrest of all bishops and clergy. At this stage the authorities ran into the same difficulties as had confronted their predecessors fifty years before, for prisons were designed only to hold malefactors awaiting trial, not to incarcerate large numbers of long-term prisoners. In the summer of 303 Diocletian left for the West to celebrate the twentieth anniversary of his rule, and before leaving he issued a third edict ordering that the clergy should be constrained to sacrifice and then be freed. No effort was spared to compel them to do so. Indeed, all over the Empire magistrates took delight in the recantation of Christians. This was becoming a matter of life and death for the Empire. Lactantius describes the pleasure of Hierocles, Governor of Bithynia, at the recantation of a Christian worn down after two years' interrogations and tortures (*Divine Institutes*, v. 11). Gradually, the prisons emptied. A few recusants who resisted to the last were executed.

Then, a new development took place. In the winter of 303–4, Diocletian became ill on his way back from Rome. Effective government passed to Galerius and in the spring of 304 he ordered a day of general sacrifice throughout the Empire. The penalty for disobedience was death or the mines. This particular order probably went beyond Diocletian's intentions. The latter had been at pains to ensure that Christians shared the burdens of the Empire fairly with other citizens and did not act as silent saboteurs of his reforms. Up to now, as Eusebius points out (*Martyrs of Palestine* 3. i.), "the presidents of the Church alone had been menaced." Now, all Christians were involved; Galerius knew no moderation.

He saw, too, that the stronger policy would need new men to carry it out. Diocletian had begun to train Constantine, the son of Constantius the Caesar of the West, as successor to his father. The young man, now aged about twenty-three, was at court in Nicomedia, and Galerius intended that he should stay there—but under surveillance. Diocletian recovered at length from his illness but allowed himself to be persuaded to 'retire from the government. On 1 May 305 he made a solemn act of abdication before a great parade of troops at Nicomedia, and Maximian less willingly abdicated at Milan. Diocletian was to live on another eleven years in his magnificent palace at Spalato. The new Augusti were Constantius in the West and Galerius in the East, but the natural claimants to the office of Caesar, Constantine and Maximian's son, Maxentius, were passed over.[5] Diocletian sacrificed the hereditary principle in favor of what he believed to be military and administrative efficiency, but the disinherited had no interest in accepting religious policies whose success would perpetuate their own exclusion.

Meantime, what success had the persecution gained? Later generations have filled the Church calendars with the legendary accounts of martyrs in the Great Persecution. In some provinces, however, notably North Africa, Palestine and Egypt, contemporary records survive to tell us what actually took place. To start with the far northwest of the Empire, in the Prefecture of the Gauls, comprising Britain, Gaul, Germany west of the Rhine, Spain (except the southeast) and the opposite coast of Morocco, Christianity was hardly a problem. There were churches in some of the large towns and some of these Constantius demolished. Evidently he did not insist on the surrender of the Scriptures, for ten years later the Donatist schismatics in Africa were to ask that their cause should be judged by bishops from Gaul as Constantine's father "unlike the other Emperors had never persecuted, and Gaul remained free of that crime."[6]

In Africa itself, which was directly under the government of Maximian, the measures were far more thorough. It was in the last fortnight in May that the first edict arrived in both Proconsular Africa (roughly, modern Tunisia) and Numidia (roughly, east and central Algeria). It was acted upon by the city magistrates without any hesitation. The fact that the Christian bishop may have been a well-known figure did not save him from a summons to surrender the Scriptures. At Cirta, the capital of Numidia, the immediate reaction of the Christians was either flight to the hills south of the town or apostasy. The curator (mayor) came to the "house where the Christians used to meet," and the following scene took place:

> *The Mayor to Paul the Bishop*: Bring out the writings of the law and anything else that you have here, according to the order, so that you may obey the command.
> *The Bishop*: The readers have the Scriptures, but we will give what we have here.
> *The Mayor*: Point out the readers or send for them.
> *The Bishop*: You all know them.
> *The Mayor*: We do not know them.
> *The Bishop*: The municipal office know them, that is, the clerks Edusius and Junius.
> *The Mayor*: Leaving over the matter of the readers, whom the office will point out, produce what you have.
> *(Gesta apud Zenophilum, C.S.E.L., xxvi, pp. 186–7,*
> Eng. tr. J. Stevenson, *A New Eusebius,* pp. 287–8.)

The Bishop complied and there was brought out church plate and other property including a large amount of men's and women's clothes and shoes. All this was produced in front of the clergy who included three priests, two deacons, and four subdeacons, and a number of "diggers." The Mayor then continued his examination in order to obtain the copies of the Scriptures. Successively the subdeacons and readers were questioned. There was a certain amount of argument and prevarication, as each tried to shield the other, but in the end the Mayor got his way. The copies of the Scriptures were quietly given up and so, too, was the movable wealth of the church at Cirta. Among those who took part was the subdeacon Silvanus, and he was not allowed to forget his share in the surrender.

Nothing further seems to have befallen the Bishop who died soon afterward. His case was not exceptional. At a synod of twelve Numidian bishops who met on 5 March 305 to elect his successor, no less than four admitted to having handed over the Scriptures to the authorities and a fifth only escaped doing so by feigning blindness. In the proconsular province it was the same. Even the Primate of Africa, Mensurius, only salved his conscience by handing over heretical (probably Manichaean) books to the waiting magistrates. When in December 304 the Proconsul Anulinus interrogated the confessor Crispina at Theveste (Tébessa), he could say with some justification, "All Africa had sacrificed, so should not she?"[7]

This cowardly conduct, however, was not universally accepted. Another contemporary document tells how, toward the end of 303, the congregation of the small settlement of Abitina in the Upper Valley of the Mejerda River (in Tunisia) continued to meet after the apostasy of their bishop. One day they were surprised, and forty-seven of them, including their leader Saturninus and his four sons, were taken away to Carthage. In February 304 they were brought to trial and stoutly maintained their stand before the authorities; then, on their return to prison they made a solemn declaration that no one who maintained communion with betrayers (i.e., those who had surrendered the Scriptures) would participate with them in the joys of Paradise.[8] The confessors were following the tradition of the martyrs in the African Church who, both in Tertullian's and Cyprian's time, were believed to have the right of binding and loosing on earth. Theirs were the keys of St. Peter, as Tertullian (Scorpiace, 10) had claimed a century before. But the assertion of this principle was now a challenge to the Carthaginian hierarchy. Besides, too many of the African clergy had been found wanting.

In Rome, also, the authorities had some initial success. A strong contemporary tradition indicates that Church property was surrendered to the authorities, and that the Bishop, Marcellinus, sacrificed on the Capitol.

The story had sufficient currency to influence events for a considerable time.

In the Western provinces, the persecution came to an end with the abdication of Maximian, and all over the Empire a confused period of semitoleration followed. In the East there was a respite of about nine months lasting until Easter 306, before another general order to sacrifice was promulgated. This called upon all the provincial governors to force every man, woman and child to sacrifice. Army officers called out names from a list. At Caesarea, the capital of the province of Palestine, a youth rushed forward to prevent the Governor from sacrificing. He was executed on 2 April 306.

Syria, Palestine and Egypt were included in the territories governed by the new Caesar, Maximin. He was the most intelligent of the persecuting Emperors, combining ruthless zeal and energy in the cause of paganism with a streak of idealism. Realizing that repression was not enough, he set about systematically reorganizing paganism and turning the weapon of propaganda against the Church. Priests were appointed in every city and those who had served the State well were created "high-priests." "These persons brought great zeal to bear on the worship of the gods whom they served," admitted Eusebius (*H.E.*, ix. 4:2). To discredit the Christians, forged Acts of Pilate, purporting to prove the justice of Christ's crucifixion, were circulated. "Children in the schools," says Eusebius, "had every day the names of Jesus and Pilate on their lips" (*H.E.*, ix. 5:1). The measures had some success. Eusebius records crowds of renegades in Palestine. Indeed, in that province only forty-four executions are recorded between 303 and 313, and forty-six other victims who were deported died. Most of those who died deliberately provoked the authorities. Public opinion was still not committed. But Maximin's effort was fifty years too late, and between 311 and 313 a series of events made the Christians' victory certain.

To understand this we must turn to developments in the West. Throughout 305, Constantine remained at Galerius's capital Nicomedia, but early in the next year he secured Galerius's permission to visit his father who was ill. He set out. Galerius changed his mind, tried to stop him but failed, and he arrived in Britain to be with his father when he died at York on 25 July 306. On the same day the army there acclaimed him Augustus. This was the first dramatic step on Constantine's road to power. The next years were to make his character clear: a lust for power, a strong element of cruelty, a capacity for quick thinking and acting, and a religious sense which allowed him to attribute his success to the intervention of higher powers.[9]

The next years must be passed over rapidly. It suffices to say that after each successive crisis Constantine emerged stronger, until by the end of 310 he had been recognized as "the son of an Augustus" (something between Caesar and Augustus) and controlled all the territory which his father had ruled as Augustus. But he was already thinking of a further advance to the detriment of his reluctant colleagues in the Tetrarchy. Through the mouth of his court panegyrist he was claiming to be descended from the Emperor Claudius Gothicus (268-70), and therefore reasserting the hereditary principle against the military rule of Galerius and his colleagues. The appeal of Monarchy and One Religion against Anarchy and Polytheism was beginning to take shape. In the same year, he had his first vision of power, but the promiser of victory and long life was the shrine of Apollo at Autun.[10] The sun-god now becomes his patron. His coins—the only means open to a Government to proclaim its policy to the mass of the population—bear the device *Soli invicto comiti* (To the unconquered sun my companion) instead of the Tetrarchy's "To the Genius of the Roman People."

He did not have to wait long. In April 311 Galerius was struck down by a mysterious malady, probably cancer of the bowels, and just as illness had forced Diocletian to change his religious policy, so now, he found himself compelled to do likewise. As he lay at Sardica (Sofia) Licinius, whom as a trusted companion in arms Galerius had had appointed Augustus in November 308, visited him and wrung from him an edict of toleration. This is the famous Palinode of Galerius whose text Lactantius has preserved. The edict is in the form of an amnesty. The Christians are berated with the bitterest contempt for their desertion of the customs of their ancestors. Their "ill will," "folly" and cosmopolitanism were condemned, but the fact that they had neither returned to the ways of their forefathers (i.e., paganism) nor worshiped their own god, was equally deplorable. Therefore, Galerius went on "in consideration of our most mild clemency, and of the unbroken custom whereby we are used to grant pardon to all men, we have thought it right in this case also, to offer our speediest indulgence. Christians may exist again, and may establish their meeting houses provided that they do nothing contrary to good order." At the same time, it was "their duty to pray their god for our good estate, and their own, that the commonwealth may endure on every side unharmed, and they may be able to live securely in the inhabitations" (Lactantius, *On the Death of the Persecutors,* 34, Stevenson, 296). Atheism was the worst state. Better the Christian God than this. Toleration was therefore offered in exchange for prayer. The privilege which had been accorded to the old Israel by Rome since the first century B.C. was now formally granted to the new. For Galerius the edict availed nothing. He died a week later on 5 May 311, having commended his wife and family to Licinius.

The part played by Licinius is interesting. For the previous seventy years, since the fall of the Severan dynasty in 235, rival claimants to the imperial power had bid for support either by favoring or persecuting the Christians. We have followed this underlying tendency behind the policies of Maximin Thrax, Philip, Decius, and Galerius. Now Licinius did the same, hoping to secure thereby Galerius's provinces in Asia Minor, which were the best recruiting grounds for the army in the whole Empire, and where Christianity was at its strongest. The bid for Christian support anticipated Constantine's by eighteen months, and the latter's policy can be seen less as an extraordinary action, than as a logical step by someone whose success depended on the overthrow of the remains of the Tetrarchy. Constantine merely carried to its conclusion a development which had been taking shape with increasing speed since the abdication of Diocletian. For the time it was Licinius, however, who demonstrated the full value of a pro-Christian policy.

His bid, however, for supreme power miscarried. Maximin was too quick. The Asian provinces declared for him, and Licinius had to be content with the Balkans (the Prefecture of Illyricum). The Thracian frontier marked the boundary between the two realms.

In his new dominions Maximin at first accepted the policy of religious toleration, but by the autumn of 311 he was already circumventing it. Cities were induced to petition for the removal of Christians beyond their borders, and like everything else that Maximin did this plan was executed thoroughly. A remarkable inscription from the country town of Aricanda in Lycia, addressed to Maximin, Constantine and Licinius, asks that "the detestable practices of the atheists be forbidden and prevented."[11]

In Egypt there was a last, terrible paroxysm of persecution, described by Eusebius in unforgettable terms.[12] In addition, judicial murder or private vengeance deprived the Christians of two of their foremost leaders. Peter, Bishop of Alexandria, was executed on 25 November 311, and Lucian, presbyter and teacher of Antioch, was killed in Maximin's capital, Nicomedia, on 7 January 312. In fact, it was in those few months that the Christian leaders in the East suffered most losses. In a ringing reply to the petition by the citizens of this city against the Christians, Maximin pointed to the material benefits in the form of bumper harvests, which adherence to paganism and recovery of pagan faith brought (Eusebius, *H.E.*, ix. 7:1). It was the pagan version of Constantine's view that the security of the Empire rested on the right worship of the Divinity.

The gods proved fickle. In the winter of 311–12 Maximin led an expedition against the Christian kingdom of Armenia. Why, we do not know. Armenia, however, occupied a key position protecting the northeast frontier of the Empire against an attack from the Persians. The kingdom had had a Christian ruler since Tiradates I had been converted toward A.D. 270. Maybe Maximin wished to restore paganism. In any case he failed, and the blow to his prestige was severe. The gods of Rome could no longer guarantee success, at least beyond the borders of the Empire.

Meantime, all was going well for Constantine. In 311 he had defeated the Frankish tribes on the Rhine frontier. Their kings were thrown to the beasts in the amphitheater at Trier. In the spring of 312 he was ready to bid for Rome. Maxentius had ensconced himself there in October 306, and though his position, unlike that of Constantine, had never been regularized, he had remained unassailable. If he lost Spain to Constantine in 310, he suppressed a formidable revolt in Africa the next year and so secured his corn supplies. Though he deified his father, Maximian, murdered by Constantine in 310, he had shown extreme tolerance toward the quarreling factions of Roman Christians, and had restored liberty to the Church both in Rome and Africa. He had, however, realized the gravity of the threat from Constantine and entered into correspondence with Maximin. Constantine turned to Licinius. His sister, Constantia, was betrothed to him. He could be relied on to hold Maximin while Constantine advanced against Maxentius. In the spring of 312 he crossed the Alps with rather less than 40,000 troops. Through the spring and summer Maxentius's troops, loyal to the memory of his father, fought hard but unsuccessfully. Constantine advanced on Rome. He feared that Maxentius would force him to lay siege to the city throughout the winter. The guardians of the Sibylline books persuaded Maxentius to meet him in pitched battle. The omens were favorable. 26 October was the anniversary of his accession. That evening he advanced along the Via Flaminia and his outposts clashed with those of Constantine five miles north of the city. The rest can be told by Lactantius (*On the Deaths of the Persecutors* 44, 5–6). "Constantine was directed in a dream to mark the Heavenly sign of God on the shields of his soldiers and thus to join battle. He did as he was ordered and with the cross-shaped letter X with its top bent over he marked Christ on the shields." Armed with this sign he engaged the enemy. By the evening of 28 October Maxentius's army was routed, and their leader drowned in the waters of the Tiber. Next day Constantine entered Rome. In February 313 he met Licinius in Milan. Licinius married Constantine's sister, and whether there was a formal "edict of Milan" or no, a policy of benevolence toward the Christians was agreed. The sun, however, as is clear from the coins struck to mark the occasion and the symbols on the Arch of Constantine in Rome, remained the patron divinity of the Empire.

There still remained Maximin. The latter had sought to help Maxentius. His forces had invaded Licinius's dominions. Byzantium had fallen and he was pressing into Thrace. Constantine ordered him to withdraw. Licinius marched eastward. The two armies met north of Heraclea (Erigli) on the Sea of Marmara 30 April 313. Like Constantine, Licinius had a vision. He told his officers that he had been visited nightly by an angel who had dictated to him a prayer to the *Summus Deus*.[13] The words were passed on from man to man and victory went with them. Licinius crossed the Bosphorus and entered Nicomedia. There in June 313 the text of what we know as the Edict of Milan was published in the joint names of Constantine and Licinius. Maximin abandoned Asia Minor north of the Taurus to die at Tarsus in August.

Thus, eleven years of persecution came to an end. With the Edict of Milan the scales tipped insensibly toward Christianity.[14] The two Emperors' purpose was indeed to grant both to Christians and to all others full authority "to follow whatever worship each man desired, whereby whatsoever Divinity dwells in heaven may be benevolent and propitious to us and all who are placed under our authority." But it is noticeable that the Christians are regarded as a positive force. Their opponents are "the others." And to the Christians restitution was to be made in full, their right of worship was assured and their property handed back to them. The thought behind the provisions is contained in the last sentence. "So far we will ensure that, as has already been stated, the Divine favor toward us which we have experienced in so many affairs shall continue for all time to give us prosperity and success, together with the happiness of the State." Both men were in the position of suppliants who had prayed to the Christians' God—and their prayer had been heard.

Why, after all, had the Christians triumphed? Apart from the superior generalship of Constantine and Licinius, there are the factors we have noted in the previous chapter. There was first, the vast ramification of Christian organization extending from Armenia to York, an organization which dwarfed that of the Jewish Dispersion, its only rival, and to which the ancient world could boast nothing similar. Its adherents, too, were drawn from town and countryside alike, and it was the countryside that provided its staunchest exponents. In its high ethical appeal, its banishment of the blood and sacrifice from worship, and adherence to a god at once transcendent and active in the universe Christianity presented in a coherent form ideas to which the pagan world was groping.[15] Among intellectual circles there was the feeling that the national cults were becoming increasingly anachronistic. Statesmen like Aurelian and thinkers like Dio of Prusa and Aelius Aristides had for long conceived the Empire as ruled by a monarch under the patronage of the single Supreme Being. Aurelian's ideal was to be accomplished by Constantine. Meantime, Christians in the Hellenistic East had pointed to the coincidence of the federation of the Empire under Augustus with the coming of Christ. Eusebius writing at this time used his deep knowledge of history to point out that "there was a multitude of rulers before the coming of Christ. All nations were governed by different tyrannies and democracies and men had no intercourse with each other . . . nation rose against nation and city against city, thousands of men were made captives . . ." (*Demonstratio Evangelica* vii. 2). This had gone on until the coming of Christ and Augustus, bringers both of peace and order. Polyarchy and polytheism were thus equated as part of "the bad old days." Mankind was moving forward toward universal monarchy under one Church, and Constantine was God's chosen instrument, the reflection of his divine power. Such were the high hopes of many thinking men of the time. The reality was to bring disillusion.

FURTHER READING

Baynes, N.H., 'The Great Persecution', *Cambridge Ancient History* 12, ch.19

Frend, W.H.C., *Martyrdom in the Early Church*, Blackwell 1965, ch.15

Frend, W.H.C., 'Prelude to the Great Persecution: The Propaganda War', *Journal of Ecclesiastical History* 38, 1987, 1-18

Jones, A.H.M., *Constantine and the Conversion of Europe*, English Universities Press (Hodder) 1949, ch.4

Moreau, J (ed.), *Lactantius, De Mortibus Persecutorum*, Sources chrétiennes 39, Paris 1954 (a very important work)

12

East and West
to Nicaea

The Origin of Donatism

The wreckage of the persecutions remained. The resultant problems
were to influence the development of the Church in East and West for a
long time to come. Both the Meletian and thence the Arian controversies,
and the Donatist schism originated in the events of 304–5. Their contrasting destinies, however, emphasize again the difference of outlook between Christians in the Latin- and Greek-speaking parts of the Empire
which had been developing in the previous century. The Meletians were
never to be more important than a background influence in the first
stages of the Arian controversy and a nuisance to Athanasius. The
Donatists came to dominate North Africa, and their views effected the
formulation of the Western doctrine of the Church and of Church-State
relations.

It was the situation in Africa that first forced itself on Constantine's
attention. There, his victory over Maxentius had been popular, and
guaranteed a ready supply of corn and olive oil without which famine
and disorder would threaten Rome. Constantine too, was eager to show
his gratitude to the God of the Christians to whom he owed his victory.
So, in the winter of 312–13 he instructed the chief official in charge of
the imperial estates in Africa to put a sum of 3000 *folles* at the disposal
of Caecilian, Bishop of Carthage. At the same time he ordered the un-
conditional restoration of lands and property to the Church. Then, in a
letter which was sent to the chief civil administrator in Roman Africa he
mentions that he had heard of the attempts of "some irresponsible individuals to corrupt the congregation of the holy and Catholic Church
with vain and base falsifications." He orders that "any found suffering
under this vain and bastard delusion should be haled before the magistrates." The texts of these letters are preserved in Eusebius (*Hist. Eccles.*,
x. 5:13–17 and x. 6).

Who were these "irresponsibles," and what was the delusion under which they were suffering? If we cast our minds back to the year 304 and the council held by the Abitinian confessors in their prison, and to the implication of their threat against the betrayers of the Word (the *Traditores*), it will become clear: for during the months when they lay in prison, the archdeacon Caecilian had been making himself unpopular with the more enthusiastic of the Carthaginian Christians. He had been accused of actively preventing food from reaching the prisoners,[1] while his superior, Bishop Mensurius of Carthage, had sharply discouraged those who wished voluntarily to die the death of martyrs.[2]

Meantime, events had taken place in the capital of Numidia which were to have some bearing on Constantine's attitude. Since the death of Bishop Paul during 304, the fanatic party among the Christians had gained the upper hand, and were determined to go through with an election of a successor whatever the authorities might say. Probably in the winter of 304–5 their choice fell on the subdeacon Silvanus, who barely eighteen months before had handed over the property of his church to the authorities. But, for some reason or other he was popular with the lower classes and country folk, and when the citizens among the Christians wanted a man of better character as bishop the mob would have none of it. An eyewitness describes how they shut the citizens in the cemetery of the martyrs for two days, and then hoisting Silvanus on to the shoulders of Mutus the quarry-worker acclaimed him bishop. He immediately accepted the bribe of twenty *folles* for making one of his supporters, Victor the fuller, a presbyter. He was to be second to none in denouncing "Carthaginian traitors" a few years later.[3]

We have also a full record of the synod which met in a private house in Cirta on 5 March 305 to consecrate Silvanus as bishop. By African tradition twelve bishops had to be present to make valid an episcopal consecration, and they had to be in a state of grace. They were asked by the Primate of Numidia whether or not they had handed over the Scriptures during the persecution. Four at least of them had done so. None the less, the Primate was forced by his colleagues to "leave them to God" and allow the consecration of Silvanus to proceed. These disclosures were made in private. Publicly, however, the Numidian Primate proclaimed his zeal during the persecution and chided his Carthaginian colleague for laxity.[4]

In the next five or six years the seeds of permanent schism began to germinate. Something like the anger of the "men of the resistance" against the "collaborators" which characterized ex-German-occupied Europe after the end of the Second World War took hold of North

Africa. This time "traitors" (i.e., those who surrendered the Scriptures) replaced "collaborators." We hear of the deposition of bishops and the rebaptizing of clergy who had lapsed. Foremost in this move was a priest from the southern edge of the great plains of Numidia, Donatus of Casae Nigrae.

Formal peace was maintained until 311 when Mensurius, Bishop of Carthage, died while returning from Rome. He had been pleading the cause of one of his clergy whom Maxentius suspected of being an agent of his enemies in Africa. The question was, who was to be his successor? The Carthaginian presbyterate tried to elect a candidate of their own before anyone else, especially the Numidians, could interfere. They failed. They could not agree on a choice, and they themselves were guilty of embezzlement.[5] In the end the lot fell on Mensurius's archdeacon, Caecilian.[6] He was the candidate of the citizen body, but their choice could hardly have been worse. Exception was taken to his consecration and it was rumored that one of his consecrators, Felix, Bishop of Aptunga, was a *traditor*.

The Numidians now arrived on the scene. It seems that the Primate of Numidia had established some sort of right of consecrating the Bishop of Carthage, and Secundus was determined to enforce it. The seventy bishops who came to Carthage with him were a formidable and violent crew. They soon made common cause with the discontented presbyters, and between them declared Caecilian deposed by a council of the same seventy bishops. One of the servants of a rich dame called Lucilla who had fallen foul of Caecilian years before was elected in his place. In the background of this Majorinus was the more formidable Donatus, now in Carthage and acting as liaison between the various groups of dissidents. Thus, by the middle of 312 there were two Bishops of Carthage, Caecilian and Majorinus. Each represented rival forces in the African Church, and the Numidians had thrown their weight against Caecilian. Such was the situation which confronted Constantine on the morrow of the Milvian Bridge.

One may ask why Constantine supported Caecilian from the first. A possible clue is that even at this time he was under the influence of Hosius, Bishop of Cordoba, and the Donatists later came to blame this man for their difficulties. A more powerful motive, however, was Constantine's own outlook. His aim was always the religious unity of the Empire, unity through "the right worship of the Supreme God," and he was against extremists who aimed at forcing their views on the majority. His policy toward Donatus and ultimately toward Athanasius was similar, but in both cases, having decided that right lay with their opponents, he could not press his ideas to their conclusion. Africa and Egypt were too valuable from every point of view to be alienated.

In the spring of 313 he took a further step in the African quarrel which was to render it difficult for him to assume the role of arbiter later on. In a letter addressed to the Proconsul of Africa, Anulinus, he showed that he not only recognized Caecilian as Bishop of Carthage, but was prepared to exempt all clergy in communion with him from the burden of municipal levies. This put a financial premium on orthodoxy, and the anti-Caecilianists protested. On 15 April 313 the Proconsul was confronted by a crowd of Caecilian's opponents, whose leaders handed him two packages. One contained a list of charges against Caecilian, the second, an appeal to the Emperor to appoint judges from Gaul, where there had been no persecution, to arbitrate in the dispute.[7] Constantine decided to grant the petitioners' request at least in part. The Proconsul was required to send Caecilian with ten bishops together with an equal number of his opponents to Rome. There the dispute was to be judged by the Bishop Miltiades, himself an African, and three Gallic bishops. The tribunal was convoked by the Emperor and thus may be seen as a precedent for his action in calling the councils of Arles and Nicaea. At this stage Constantine seems to have regarded the bishops as civil servants whose special function, however, was to intercede with the *Summus Deus* for the safety of the Empire.

Miltiades used the opportunity to transform the ecclesiastical tribunal into a council by summoning fifteen Italian bishops to it. Constantine placed the house of his wife Fausta on the Lateran at Miltiades's disposal and it was there that the sessions opened on 30 September 313.

Meantime, the opposition's first choice as bishop, Majorinus, evidently had died, and they now elected Donatus of Casae Nigrae as his successor. Very little has survived about Donatus. His writings have perished, and we know of him only from the statements of his opponents. But the impression he made on friends and enemies alike was remarkable. He was a great orator and leader of men. He was remembered as a reformer of venerable memory "who purged the Church of Carthage from error."[8] Men swore by his "white hairs," as North Africans today swear by "the beard of the prophet."[9] He was known not even as "bishop" but simply as "Donatus of Carthage," and he ruled his Church for forty-two years. "If they honor Christ with their lips," commented Augustine, "the Donatists honour Donatus in their heart."[10] Like his great predecessor, Cyprian, he combined the prophetic gift with episcopal power. "Wiser than Daniel," he also behaved with the authority of a Jewish high-priest, celebrating the mysteries alone, secluded even from his colleagues as the high-priest had once done in the Temple of Jerusalem, an interesting fact when one remembers how much of Judaism seems to have been embedded in North African Christianity. In face of this formidable man Caecilian might win legal battles but he could never assert his right to the primacy of Africa.

On 5 October 313 Miltiades declared Caecilian vindicated, and condemned Donatus for disturbing discipline, rebaptizing clergy, and causing a schism. As a concession, ordinations performed by Caecilian's opponents might stand, providing that where there were rival appointments the junior should stand down.[11] This judgment was received with little enthusiasm in Africa. It was alleged that Miltiades himself was not free from the taint of *traditio* having been associated with Bishop Marcellinus's sacrifice to the gods in 304. The Donatists (as they now came to be called) protested that the judgment of the council of seventy bishops who had condemned Caecilian in the previous year should not have been set aside, and in any case, little had been heard of the charges against Felix of Aptunga now defined as "the source of all the mischief."

Constantine kept both Caecilian and Donatus in Italy, and reluctantly agreed to a new hearing. His feelings may well be indicated by a passage in a letter to Chrestus, Bishop of Syracuse, written probably early in January 314. He expresses astonishment "that even those very persons who ought to be of one mind in brotherly love are separate from each other in a disgraceful nay, rather, in an abominable manner, and give to those men whose souls are strangers to this most holy religion to scoff"[12]— again the stress on the need of unity within the Church. The bishops must sink their differences.

The Council was to meet at Arles, the capital of the Prefecture of the Gauls on 1 August. Meantime, an inquiry was to be held on the spot in Africa to decide whether or not Felix of Aptunga had been a *traditor*. The assembly which opened under the presidency of Marinus, Bishop of Arles, was by far the most impressive body of clergy that had ever met in the Western provinces of the Empire. Thirty-three bishops, including three from Britain, were there, accompanied by other clergy. The Donatists and Caecilianists were represented by ten bishops each. Again the Caecilianists won and the council went on to condemn the African use of insisting on the rebaptism of reconciled heretics.[13] The old puritanical system was to give way to more liberal notions. Constantine accepted the decision, but the Donatists did not. They appealed once more, this time to the Emperor himself.

It may be that the angry epistle which reached the assembled bishops from the court was written by Constantine and "reveals how he was progressing in the faith." The present writer prefers to be more cautious. Nowhere else in these early years does Constantine speak of himself as "awaiting the judgment of Christ." Nor did he regard the bishops as exclusive judges in ecclesiastical disputes. None the less his anger against the Donatists may have been real enough, and so too his order that their recalcitrant leaders be sent to his court. One suspects, however, that the religious ideas expressed in the letter were more those of Hosius than his own.[14]

For the next twelve months the dispute hung fire. Donatus and his colleagues together with Caecilian remained in North Italy. In Africa two hearings of the case against Felix of Aptunga at Carthage showed that the latter had been the victim of an unscrupulous fraud, and that he was no *traditor*.[15] By this time the verdict was no comfort to Caecilian. The people believed bazaar-rumors and pamphlets which raged against the "pseudobishop" (Caecilian). Constantine returned to Rome on 21 July 315 to celebrate his tenth anniversary as Emperor, and decided to give the Donatists yet another hearing. If they could prove anything against Caecilian, he said, he would consider they had gained their cause.[16] What happened then is rather obscure. For some reason, Caecilian did not attend in Rome at the date fixed for the hearing. Some of the Donatists claiming that the case had gone against him by default tried to return to Africa. Constantine had them arrested and sent on to Milan whither he went himself early in October. Apparently he decided that no good would come from another meeting between the parties, so he sent a commission of two bishops to Africa to investigate and report. Meantime, Caecilian was held at Brescia. The commission spent six fruitless weeks in Carthage. There were anti-Caecilian riots, and the bishops returned after declaring the legitimacy of Caecilian's position. Donatus now asked to be allowed to return to Africa, and when this was refused escaped and made his way back to Carthage. Caecilian followed him, and in February 316 Constantine finally agreed that the remaining Donatist bishops should be allowed to go home.[17]

The firebrands were back in Africa. The situation had become dangerous. There were disorders, and the victims of the Government's countermeasures were being hailed by the Donatists as martyrs. The letter which Constantine now sent to his deputy prefect in Africa throws much light on his views concerning the Church and his own role in it. It is one of the key documents in assessing his religious outlook. He announced that "with the favor of the divine piety I shall come to Africa and shall most fully demonstrate with an unequivocal verdict as much to Caecilian as to those who seem to be against him just how the Supreme Deity should be worshiped. . . ." There was no mention of Miltiades' council, nor of Arles, nor of Felix of Aptunga. Constantine as Emperor would judge the case on its merits. "What more," he goes on, "can be done, more in accord with my constant practice and the very office of a prince, than after expelling error and destroying rash opinions to cause all men to agree together to follow true religion and simplicity of life, and to render to Almighty God the worship which is his due."[18] This letter shows that Constantine was thinking and acting as though he himself were God's own vicar. His orders were to be obeyed by priests and laity alike. Eighteen years later he showed the same attitude in his dealings with Athanasius. It had much in common with that of his predecessors, only Sol-Christus had displaced Jupiter as the divine power under whose providence the Roman Empire prospered.

Constantine never reached Africa. Eventually in the autumn of 316 he reviewed the whole case once more, and on 10 November pronounced Caecilian innocent.[19] What was to happen now? How was the theory of religious toleration proclaimed at Milan and Nicomedia only three years before to be applied? The test was to show that Constantine's basic ideas were no more enlightened than those of Diocletian. Like the latter he was not prepared to tolerate religious dissent, only now, dissent was within the Christian body. Thus early in 317 a "most severe" law was dispatched to Africa, ordering the confiscation of Donatist Church property and the exile of the Donatist leaders.[20] It was in vain. Nothing could make Caecilian acceptable. His use of troops against his opponents in Carthage merely confirmed the view of the majority of African Christians that the Emperor's friendship toward the Church was one of the Devil's tricks.[21] The society of Christ and the society of the world would always be at enmity. When open persecution failed, the Devil fell back on guile; the fundamental hostility of the State toward the Church was not altered. In the West this attitude went deep. We shall see that it was not confined to Africa. It marks one of the great divides between the Eastern and Western doctrines of the Church foreshadowing the theory of the two cities or societies represented by Ambrose, Augustine and their successors.

By 320 the Donatist position was so secure that not even a major scandal could shake it. This took place in December of that year and in the Donatist stronghold of southern Numidia. Silvanus, Bishop of Cirta, quarreled with one of his deacons called Nundinarius. A man of violence, he had him stoned and finally excommunicated him. Nundinarius did not accept this treatment, and unfortunately for Silvanus had kept detailed dossiers which contained all his opponents' weak points. In vain Silvanus's colleagues pleaded with him to come to terms with Nundinarius. He remained adamant and the latter took his case to the civil governor of Numidia, the *Consularis* Zenophilus. The record of the trial has survived, and is thoroughly discreditable to Silvanus.[22] He and other Numidian leaders are shown to have been *traditores* and even murderers. They were also guilty of simony, theft and embezzlement. But even so they remained the popular heroes, and Silvanus on being sent into exile established himself as a "martyr." Within six months, Constantine gave up the idea of coercion and grudgingly gave the Donatists toleration on 5 May 321. At least he had learned his lesson. Never again was he to take active measures against a Christian movement of dissent, though troublesome individuals would still feel the weight of his anger.

For the rest of the reign we learn little about the Donatists. From now on Constantine was to be engaged first in the crusade against Licinius and then with the Arian controversy. From time to time he tried to help the African Catholics, but not effectively. The Donatists went from strength to strength. The Catholic clergy were forced to undertake the onerous municipal duties from which Constantine had specifically freed them. Their churches were seized by their opponents. Their leader Caecilian, after being summoned by the Emperor to the Council of Nicaea, faded out of the picture. We do not know what became of him. Toward the end of Constantine's reign Donatus asserted his power against another feeble effort to remove him, this time by the Emperor's chief minister (*praefectus praetorio*) in the West. Soon after he summoned the greatest of all Church councils to date, 270 bishops answered his call—as many as the total present at the ecumenical council of Nicaea. They deliberated for seventy-five days.[23] By this time Roman Africa was Christian but it was the Christianity of Donatus.

The effect of this on the subsequent history of the Church in the West was momentous. What had hitherto been the most powerful and well-organized Church had broken from the Christians in the other provinces. Schism indeed was far from Donatus's mind. He appointed a Bishop of Rome and he found some support in Spain and Gaul. But the majority of churches maintained that Caecilian was rightful Bishop, and now the See of Rome, so long overshadowed by African influence, had no rival in the West. Caecilian and the African Catholics depended on its support for their survival. When the Roman See emerged from the long obscurity which marks the pontificates of Silvester and Marcus (314–37), it was to represent the views of the West as a whole except for the Donatists. In the East the primacy lay between Alexandria, Antioch and now, Constantinople.

Meletianism and the Beginnings of the
Arian Controversy

While the majority of African Christians were following the rigorism and independence of Donatus, an even more serious situation was taking shape in Egypt. Like the Donatist controversy, the story of Arianism begins with events during the Great Persecution. Probably during 304 a number of Egyptian bishops, including Peter of Alexandria and Meletius of Lycopolis in Upper Egypt, were in prison together at Alexandria. A dispute arose among them on how the lapsed were to be treated after the end of the persecution. Meletius stood for a rigorous policy, Peter for a milder one. The quarrel grew bitter, until Peter stretched a curtain across the middle of the room so that he would not have to see Meletius. The majority of the bishops and the monks, however, went to Meletius's end of the prison, and the two parties ceased to be on speaking terms.[24]

A brief respite followed the abdication of Diocletian and Maximian in May 305. The imprisoned bishops were released, and before Maximin promulgated the fifth edict of persecution Peter had just enough time at Easter 306 to issue a series of rulings governing the treatment of the lapsed. On the whole these were mild. Those who had given way under torture were to be readmitted to the Church after a fast of forty days. Those who had bribed officials or pagans to impersonate them were subjected to penances. Spontaneous martyrs were deprecated and a liberal interpretation placed on the definition of "lapsed" clergy.[25]

One sees an almost exact parallel between the attitude of the bishops of Alexandria and Carthage. Both condemned voluntary martyrs, and both feared their own more violent supporters as much as they did the authorities. Meletius too, like Donatus, defied his chief, imposed penances on his own authority and ordained his own supporters to the priesthood.[26] He too had support in the capital, and one of his friends was a learned and ascetic layman called Arius.

Meantime, the persecution continued and lasted with brief intervals for the next six years. On 25 November 311 Peter himself was martyred, but this did not heal the schism. The Bishop's sufferings, however, seem to have made some difference to Arius's views, for before he was executed he had made his peace with him.[27] For this Meletius regarded him as a traitor, and seven years later his followers were to bring him down on a charge of heresy.

How were they able to do this? We have already seen how the controversy concerning the nature of the Trinity had been developing during the third century. While neither the Adoptionist tendencies of Antioch nor the Sabellian views held in Asia Minor and Cyrenaica were satisfactory, the alternative propounded by Origen and his successors at Alexandria also had its weakness. The tendency in Alexandria was to identify Christ with the divine Logos, as the term was understood by Plato and his Neo-Platonic successors, that is as the link between God and creation. Technically, he was therefore a "creature," yet not created at any point in time. Origen's insight, however, that the Son was subject to an eternal process of creation and while different from the Father in some way was both co-eternal and consubstantial with him, had not been lost. These shades of meaning, though discussed by the Greek-speaking clerics of the capital, were not intelligible to the multitude.[28] Though they provided a theory of creation they did not satisfy the Egyptian Christian's craving for physical salvation and redemption from sin.

Unfortunately, under the pressure both of popular Sabellianism, and also perhaps of Manichaean propaganda,[29] which emphasized the consubstantiality of Christ and God, the Alexandrine school had tended to stress the subordination of the Son to the Father rather than his consubstantiality. Arius, it seems, however, introduced a further element, though in the light of recent research this is not absolutely sure.[30] Before the persecution he had been a pupil of Lucian, the learned presbyter of Antioch. From him he had accepted the idea of Christ's ethical development. At the same time, like his colleagues at Alexandria, he was determined to maintain the oneness and absolute transcendence of God. We acknowledge, he wrote to Alexander, "One God who is alone unbegotten, alone eternal, alone without beginning."[31] Therefore while he held the current subordinationist view of Christ, he seems to have united this with the entirely different teaching of Antioch. For him it was not Jesus who grew in stature and resisted temptation but the incarnate Logos. The latter was therefore neither fully God nor fully man. Since he was not God he could not redeem, and as he was not man he could not provide a pattern of a perfect human life. He was a minister of creation brought into being because the created order could not bear direct relationship with God. The Arian Christ could never be conqueror of sin and death.

This was the weakness of the system, and indeed, ultimately of the whole Logos-Christology from which it was derived. It was however Arius's pedantry and tactlessness which brought the controversy into the open. In unguarded moments he would be prepared to deny that the Word was immutable. According to Athanasius he wrote in a piece of popular verse known as the *Thalia* or *Banquet*, "The Logos is capable of change, as are we all, but of his own free will He continues good so long as he wishes. He is capable of change even as we are, but God, foreknowing that he would remain good, gave him in anticipation the glory which as man and in consequence of his virtue he afterward possessed. God from foreknowledge of his works made him become what he afterward was."[32] This was a highly suspect statement to make in Alexandria.

It is significant perhaps that this curious blend of Neo-Platonism, Origenism and Adoptianism could have been canvassed for so long before trouble broke out. But there was one member of the clergy at Alexandria who was already thinking on radically opposed lines. In the *De Incarnatione* the young deacon Athanasius had emphasized circa 317 the love of God manifested in Christ's supreme sacrifice. The fact that the Word had taken on flesh and sacrificed his mortal body for humanity meant that death was henceforth no more than the passage to joyful resurrection, for Christ had overthrown sin and death once and for all. If the Son was merely a creature he would have needed redemption himself, and man would have remained as he was before, subject to death. Origen himself would have agreed. But the theology that flowed from this statement required community of being between God the Father and God the Son, for only thus could man also attain to divine status and so to immortality. Arius's philosophical abstraction was unacceptable, not least to the Coptic Christians whose aspirations Athanasius was to represent.

But for his quarrel with the Meletians, however, Arius might have remained unscathed. The Meletians had not succeeded as well as the Donatists, but their claim to be "the church of the Martyrs" had a good deal of popular Egyptian backing. Their theology tended toward Sabellianism, and it seems that either they tipped off Bishop Alexander of Alexandria about Arius's teaching, or they may even have threatened the Bishop with a charge of heresy if he failed to act.

Meantime Arius had prospered. Bishop Peter's short-lived successor Achillas (311–12) had appointed him presbyter of the fashionable parish of Boucolis in Alexandria, and in 317 he was second senior presbyter with a reputation for sanctity and learning. Then in the words of the historian Socrates writing about a century later,

> On one occasion at a gathering of his presbyters and the rest of the clergy he (Bishop Alexander) essayed a rather ambitious theological discussion on the Holy Trinity. But one of the presbyters, Arius by name, a man not lacking in dialectic, thinking that the bishop was expounding the doctrine of Sabellius the Libyan, from love of controversy espoused a view diametrically opposed to the teaching of the Libyan and attacked the statements of the bishop with energy. "If," said he, "the Father begat the Son, he that was begotten had a beginning of existence: hence it is clear that

there was when the Son was not ($\tilde{\eta}\nu$ $\delta\tau\iota$ $o\dot{\upsilon}\kappa$ $\tilde{\eta}\nu$). It follows of necessity that he had his existence from the nonexistent" (*Ecclesiast. Hist.*, 1. 5).

Alexander was himself an Origenist, and although he held to the divinity of the Word, eternally generated by the Father, he regarded him as a distinct person. He seemed to think of God as two hypostases or persons, but sharing the same nature. Probably, he would like to have let matters be, but in view of rising controversies and perhaps Meletian threats, in 318-9, he convoked a council of one hundred Egyptian bishops. Arius was condemned and went into exile. From Caesarea he wrote to Eusebius, an old friend and fellow pupil of Lucian of Antioch, who was now Bishop of Nicomedia the procapital of the East. He found encouragement and migrated thither. Eusebius reproached Alexander for his conduct and the latter wrote a rather fumbling circular letter to the Eastern bishops accusing Eusebius of apostasy. The latter retaliated, and a synod which he summoned urged Alexander to take Arius back. Arius was also supported by the influential historian Eusebius who was now Bishop of Caesarea, and he returned to Alexandria.

The chronology of these events is difficult because between 321-4 Licinius finally convinced himself that Christianity was a danger to the Empire, and imposed a series of vexatious restrictions on the Christians. Bishops were not to hold councils, Christians were dismissed from the imperial service, and forbidden to hold services within the walls of cities. Men and women were to worship separately. In the province of Pontus there was open persecution.[33] It is hard to imagine the controversy between Eusebius and Alexander continuing at full blast in these conditions, and yet the historians at no time suggest any significant pause in events.

Licinius's days as co-Emperor with Constantine were numbered. In 313 he had been equally pro-Christian, and like Constantine could claim Christian divine aid in his victory over his enemies. But from now on the paths of the two Emperors diverged. Constantine never wavered from his view that Christianity was the means of worshiping the *Summus Deus*, and that Christian clergy were his ministers. So much is clear from his correspondence in the Donatist dispute. It is less clear that he regarded Christianity as the *sole* means of worshiping God. His retention of the inscription *Soli Invicto Comiti* on the coinage in general circulation in the West, and his choice of the *Dies Solis* (Sunday) as a rest-day throughout his dominions point in the opposite direction.[34] The fact that some Western Christians equated Christ and the sun, as is shown on an early fourth-century mosaic found in the Roman cemetery beneath St. Peter's, Rome, hardly affects this issue.[35] Constantine's first religious conversion had been to the worship of the sun-god Apollo, and though the latter was given a cross on an imperial column at Constantinople he was not entirely superseded.

Licinius, however, had been moving in the opposite direction. In 314–15 he had the worst of a conflict with Constantine and had to concede his old province of Pannonia. Gradually, he came to realize that in the event of another war Constantine would bid for the support of the Christian inhabitants of his dominions; his repression must be seen as a forestalling action. In vain. In the spring of 324 Constantine had his hands free to make his supreme bid. Licinius marshaled 150,000 infantry and 15,000 cavalry, together with a powerful fleet to guard the Bosphorus. It was not enough. Beaten near Hadrianople on 3 July he was forced back on Byzantium, but his admiral allowed himself to be outmaneuvered by Constantine's fleet under the command of his son Crispus. There was nothing for it but to retire across the Bosphorus. Once again Constantine followed up rapidly. On 18 September, he stormed Licinius's defensive position on the heights of Chrysopolis opposite Byzantium. By evening Licinius was his prisoner and Constantine was sole ruler of the Roman world.

One of his first acts was to issue a turgidly worded edict to his new subjects pointing the moral of his victory. "Who could obtain any good who neither recognizes God the author of good things, nor will pay him proper reverence?" His own great success, "starting from the sea that laps distant Britain," had been due to the guidance of the supreme power. "Never can I ungratefully forget the gratitude that I owe, believing this to be the noblest service, this the gift granted to me as I advanced to the regions of the East, which, consumed by more grievous ills, called aloud for the greater healing care at my hand."[36] Then in detail, the Christians were liberated from the annoyances and restrictions which Licinius had imposed on them but even so, contemptuous toleration, freedom to worship in "the temples of lies" was granted to the pagans. It was the logical consequence of the edict of Milan.

This done, Constantine found himself once more confronted by a religious dispute which was threatening the security of important provinces. This time, however, he made no immediate decision to support one party against the other. Indeed, he wrote the sort of rambling but conciliatory letter to Arius and Alexander which might have proved useful at the beginning of the Donatist controversy. Now, it merely underlined the Emperor's ignorance of the underlying problems of Eastern theology. Both Arius and Alexander were told that the questions they were raising were frivolous and that instead of indulging in philosophic bickerings they should live in harmony with each other.[37] The letter was entrusted to Hosius of Cordoba and he did not take long to decide whom to support.

Meanwhile the scene was shifting to Antioch, where on 20 December 324 Bishop Philogonius died. He had been one of Alexander's supporters and this policy was to be continued by his successor Eustathius. The council which met under Hosius's presidency on the occasion of Eustathius's election in January 325 was severely anti-Arian. Though we know little about its results it seems evident that Arius was condemned, Eusebius of Caesarea severely censured and a confessional formula drawn up which conformed to Alexander's views. The son was not *homoousios* but the very image, not of the will or of anything else, but of his Father's very substance (*hypostasis*).[38] The parties in the Church in the East were falling rapidly asunder.

Hosius now reported on the situation to Constantine, and the Emperor decided to call a universal council of the Church. Ancyra (Ankara), the capital of Galatia, was selected first as meeting place, but soon, perhaps because of the climate, as Constantine himself explained, the site was moved to Nicaea, about thirty miles from his capital of Nicomedia. An immense organization was set to work. The imperial postal service was placed at the disposal of the bishops and their staffs. Probably between 250 and 300 arrived. There were only a few delegates from the West but these included the luckless Caecilian. Two deacons represented Pope Silvester. On the other hand, the easterners arrived from the furthest corners of Christendom, from Armenia, Mesopotamia and Persia. Christianity revealed itself as a new missionary force. Many former confessors were there also, some still bearing the marks of persecution. Those present felt that a new era was beginning, and it was in this spirit that Constantine opened the proceedings on 20 May 325.

Unfortunately, unlike the Councils of Ephesus and Chalcedon, no full record of events has come down to us. Eusebius of Caesarea provides some information, especially when it concerns himself, but since the criticism he incurred at Antioch earlier in the year he was an interested party. Much may be gleaned from the two fifth-century historians, Sozomen and Socrates, but they are not impartial witnesses. There exists the statement of faith or creed, which the bishops drew up, and we have the twenty canons on Church law and discipline which the Council agreed. Finally, there are two letters by Constantine, the first to the churches at large informing them of the Council's decision regarding the date of Easter, and the second, addressed particularly to the Church of Alexandria, urging a unanimous ungrudging acceptance of the Council's Creed.

Though the exact course of events is uncertain, it seems that the bishops soon found themselves divided into three main groups. There was Arius and his immediate supporters, perhaps numbering about twenty in all. At the other extreme, and of about the same strength, were the anti-Origenist clerics who found a spokesman in Marcellus of Ancyra and included Athanasius who came as Alexander's attendant. The great majority of the Eastern clergy were ultimately disciples of Origen. Future generations have tended to dub them "Semi-Arian." In fact they were simply concerned with maintaining the traditional Logos-theology of the Greek-speaking Church, and they mistrusted the fanatical anti-Arianism of Marcellus of Ancyra and Eustathius of Antioch.

The situation was very confused. The debates, it was said a century later, resembled a battle in the dark, no one knowing whether he was striking at friend or foe.[39] But quite early on, the Council decided that Arius's theology was unacceptable. Then, Eusebius of Caesarea, probably with the idea of clearing himself of the charges of heresy which he had faced earlier in the year at Antioch, brought to Constantine's notice the baptismal creed of his own Church. This was accepted as *an* orthodox statement, but recent research suggests that it was not in fact used as the basis of the eventual creed of Nicaea.[40]

The real problem which faced the drafting committee—for such indeed they were—was to exclude Arius's ideas. Unfortunately, there were many statements defining the nature of the Son with which Arius could agree. He could accept that Christ "was before all ages" (i.e., a purely temporal concept) and even that he was God from God or the power and image of the Father (i.e., divinity derived from God) but not that he was "truly God from God."

It was at this stage that Constantine made his momentous suggestion. Might not the relationship of Son to Father be expressed by the term *homoousios* ("of the same substance").[41] Its use, however, by the Sabellian bishops of Libya had been condemned by Dionysius of Alexandria in the 260s, and, in a different sense, its use by Paul of Samosata had been condemned by the Council of Antioch in 268. It was thus a "loaded" word as well as being unscriptural. Why Constantine put it forward we do not know. The possibility is that once again he was prompted by Hosius, and he may have been using it as a "translation" of the traditional view held in the West, that the Trinity was composed of "Three Persons in one substance," without inquiring further into the meaning of these terms.

The Emperor had spoken, and no one dared touch the creed during his lifetime. The great majority of the Eastern bishops found themselves in a false position. Their embarrassment is shown by the letter which Eusebius of Caesarea wrote to his flock, explaining why he had agreed. They could see to it that extreme supporters of the Nicene formulas were removed from authority but the text was sacrosanct. It read:

> We believe in one God, the Father All-sovereign, maker of all things visible and invisible. And in one Lord Jesus Christ, the Son of God, begotten of the Father, only begotten, that is from the substance of the Father (ἐκ τῆς οὐσίας τοῦ πατρός). God of God, Light of Light, true God of true God, begotten, not made, of one substance with the Father, through whom all things were made, things in heaven and things on earth: who for us men and for our salvation, came down and was made flesh, and became man, suffered, and rose on the third day, ascended into the heavens; is coming to judge the living and dead. And in the Holy Spirit. And those who say, "There was when he was not," and "Before he was begotten he was not," and that "He came into being from what is not (ἐξ οὐκ ὄντων ἐγένετο)" (i.e., "nothingness"), or those that allege, that the son of God is "of another substance or essence," or "created," or "changeable," or "alterable," these the Catholic and Apostolic Church anathematizes.

The Emperor exerted all his influence toward securing unanimity; and at length only two bishops stood out. These were old friends of Arius, and they were excommunicated. But two other senior bishops, Eusebius of Nicomedia and Theognis of Nicaea, refused to sign the sentences directed against Arius and they too fell under imperial displeasure. Their opposition showed, however, that Nicene theology would not be completely acceptable to the East.

The Council then turned to a number of other problems with the aim of uniting the Church completely.[42] Constantine himself contributed to a compromise over the Meletians. Meletius was to retain his title of bishop, and his ordinations were to be accepted as valid, but his bishops were to rank junior to Alexander's. They might, however, only replace their Catholic opposite numbers with Alexander's consent. It was a common-sense decision, and with good will could have succeeded. But in Egypt as in North Africa good will was lacking.

Other topics included the date of Easter, which was now to be calculated independently of any Jewish calculation of 14 Nisan, the Novatianists, and the organization of the Church. Constantine tried to apply the "Meletian formula" to these old quarrels which followed the Decian persecution, but without success. Novatianism was to continue in Asia Minor for another three centuries. The canons on the organization of the Church confirmed the special status of Rome in Italy, Alexandria in Egypt, and Antioch in Syria. The See of Aelia (Jerusalem) was recognized as possessing special honor, without however prejudicing the metropolitan status of Caesarea. A precedent for the future status of Constantinople which then lay in the archdiocese of Heraclea was thus established. Other canons forbade translations from See to See, thus maintaining the principle of the equality of the episcopate, and the traditional view of each bishop being wedded to his See as the Church was wedded to Christ. It also laid down that a valid consecration must be by at least three bishops of the province supported by the written consent of others and confirmation by the metropolitan.

The Council had met for just one month. It was of great importance in Christian and even in world history. Even today its decisions have some relevance. Was it, or was it not in accord with the witness of the New Testament that Jesus Christ was eternal God, or was he a being who belonged as we ourselves belong to the created world? Despite the *Homoousios* formula, and despite the personal failings of the great champion of Nicaea, Athanasius, it would be difficult not to agree with John Burnaby (*Christian Words and Christian Meanings*, p. 43), "The Church stood upon the Lord's answer, 'Have I been so long time with you, and yet hast thou not known me, Philip? He that hath seen me hath seen the Father,'" (John 14:9).

Apart from this fundamental issue, the Council confirmed the precedents already established in the previous century, that the Holy Spirit would guide and direct the Church best through a council of bishops each of whom was individually a partaker of that Spirit. Even so, the price was a heavy one. The Council had been summoned by the Emperor and the organization, the meetings and even the doctrinal decisions had been in his hands. The problems of Church and State had come to a turning point. What was to be the role of the Christian Emperor? At Nicaea the interests of Church and Emperor coincided, but within two decades the bases of that cooperation were to be challenged, and East and West were to give their different answers.

FURTHER READING

Alföldi, A., *Constantine and the Conversion of Pagan Rome*, Oxford University Press [2]1969
Barnes, T.D., 'Lactantius and Constantine', *Journal of Roman Studies* 63, 1973, 27-46
Barnes, T.D., *Constantine and Eusebius*, Harvard University Press 1981
Baynes, N.H., *Constantine the Great and the Christian Church* (1929), Oxford University Press [2]1972
Cochrane, C.N., *Christianity and Classical Culture*, Oxford University Press 1940
Frend, W.H.C., *The Donatist Church*, Oxford University Press [3]1985
Grant, R.M., 'Religion and Politics at the Council at Nicaea', *Journal of Religion* 55, 1975, 1-12

Greenslade, S.L., *Schism in the Early Church*, SCM Press 1952

Jones, A.H.M., *Constantine and the Conversion of Europe*, English Universities Press (Hodder) 1948

Kelly, J.N.D., *Early Christian Creeds*, Longmans 1950

Moreau, J. (ed.), *Lactantius, De Mortibus Persecutorum*, Sources chrétiennes 39, Paris 1954 (introduction)

Schwartz, E., *Kaiser Constantin und die christliche Kirche*, Stuttgart 1936

Stead, G.C., 'Eusebius at the Council of Nicaea', *Journal of Roman Studies* 24, 1974, 85-101

Stevenson, J., *A New Eusebius*, revised by W.H.C.Frend, SPCK [2]1986 (an essential handbook for the study of this period)

For Donatist documents, see J.L. Maier, *Le Dossier de Donatisme* (2 vols.), Berlin 1987

PART TWO

13

The Arian Controversy
325–60

The thirty-five years that separate the Council of Nicaea from the revolution that acclaimed Julian as Emperor in Paris in May 360 are dominated by a single personality. It is difficult to be neutral about Athanasius. He was a great Bishop of Alexandria, one of the outstanding molders of Christian thought, and a decisive influence in keeping Egyptian monasticism within the Church. But his gifts were those of a politician. He was wily, brutal and unscrupulous, and he was harsh and unforgiving to his opponents. He could see little beyond the righteousness of his own immediate cause. Only in the last decade of his life (362–73) does he show innate qualities of statesmanship and a mellowness of character. His strength lay in his single-minded attachment to the creed of Nicaea, and his perception that the Christian doctrine of redemption required the sharing of the same substance by Father, Son and Spirit. In this he was supported by the great majority of the Western bishops, while in his native Egypt he was all-powerful.

Against the devotion of Athanasius one must balance the statesmanship of successive Roman emperors, and the equally strongly held beliefs of the majority of the bishops in the East. Constantine, Constantius II (337–61), and Valens (364–78) believed that religious unity was essential to the survival of the Empire. Constantine sought to found that unity on broad agreement and to exclude troublemakers.

His policy was followed by his son, Constantius. Moreover, the renewed threat from Persia, which developed soon after his death, compelled his successors to lean heavily on the episcopate in Syria and Asia Minor. Without their support the Eastern provinces would have been irrevocably lost and the Roman Empire would have ceased to exist eleven centuries before the fall of Constantinople. Their theology, however, represented a different tradition from that of Athanasius. They continued to oppose the *Homoousios* formula adopted at Nicaea as being susceptible to heretical interpretation. They strove desperately for definitions which could be claimed as scriptural throughout. In the end, if the alternative description of the Son as "of like essence" to the Father, or *Homoiousios*, was found to be even less satisfactory, it was their interpretation of *Homoousios* that prevailed. Athanasius won his battle over the verbal definition of the Sonship, but it was the theology of Origen that ultimately triumphed.

We may divide the post-Nicene era into four main periods:

(*a*) From the Council of Nicaea to the death of Constantine, 325-37.

(*b*) From the death of Constantine to the end of Athanasius's second exile, 337-46.

(*c*) The climax of Anthanasius's influence, 346-56.

(*d*) The Semi-Arian ascendancy, 356-60.

We may also define the main parties. Outside Egypt the great majority of the Eastern bishops were Origenists. They believed in the Deity of the Son, but they were not prepared to accept its definition by the term *Homoousios* in the sense that this was understood by Athanasius and his friends. They feared that these would reduce the "persons" of the Trinity to mere "energies" or "activities" of the Father, and thus reduce Christianity to Judaism in a new form. They associated these ideas with the name of Sabellius and they dreaded Sabellianism even more than Arianism. Their leaders were Eusebius of Caesarea, St. Cyril of Jerusalem, and Basil of Ancyra. In the reign of Constantius they allied themselves with others, who were prepared to go further along the road of separation between God and Christ and substitute the term "of like essence" (*Homoiousios*) instead of "of the same essence" (*Homoousios*). Leaders of this group included the court bishops who advised successively Constantine and Constantius, such as Eusebius of Nicomedia, and later Acacius of Caesarea (Eusebius the historian's successor), George of Cappadocia who supplanted Athanasius between 356-61, and with leanings further toward the frankly Arianizing party, Valens of Mursa (Essek on the River Danube). On the "left wing" were the disciples of Arius himself, who were to continue to maintain that the Son though he had a moral resemblance to the Father was "unlike Him in essence" (*Anhomoios*), and hence were known as *Anomoeans*. Their representatives included the able Eudoxius, successively Bishop of Germanicia (near Aleppo) 341-58, Antioch (358-60) and Constantinople (360-70), Eunomius, Bishop of Cyzicus 360-64 (d. 393), and the "godless" deacon Aetius. They came into prominence after the council of Sirmium in 357.

147

From the Council of Nicaea to the
Death of Constantine, 325–37

"For the decision of three hundred bishops must be considered no other than the judgment of God." So wrote Constantine to the Church of Alexandria soon after the Council.[1] For him the Creed of Nicaea was divinely inspired truth allowing no alteration. But, if the wording was sacrosanct, its interpretation was not. The Eastern bishops were determined to forbid Sabellian to replace Arian error.

At first all went well. Eusebius of Nicomedia and Theognis of Nicaea soon found themselves back in favor. Perhaps as early as December 326 Eustathius of Antioch was trapped on a number of ethical and doctrinal charges, including that of making insulting remarks about the Empress Helena, and was removed from his bishopric. Next year, Arius himself was prevailed upon to make an acceptable statement of faith and petitioned for readmission to the Church. No mention was made of *Homoousios,* but he accepted that "Christ was born of God before all ages." A reassembled council at Nicaea readmitted him to communion (autumn 327). Then, just as Constantine's policy of unification seemed to command general acceptance, and even the Meletians were being reconciled to Alexander, the latter died on 17 April 328.

His successor was the deacon Athanasius, enthroned 8 June and hailed by his supporters as "an upright man, and a virtuous, a good Christian, an ascetic."[2] The last term was to make him in the eyes of his people "a real bishop" and a national hero. One of Athanasius's first actions was to tour his patriarchate. This took him to the new monastic settlements established by Packhôm (Pachomius) in Upper Egypt. It was well to have gained the good will of these monks, for his immediate problems were less with Arius and his supporters than with the formidable rival ascetics, the Meletians. These had established an extensive and relatively highly organized system of monastic houses, and were strong precisely in the purely Coptic lands of Middle and Upper Egypt. There in 327 they had one bishop in every second or third city, compared with one in every six or seven in the Delta.[3] Athanasius, moreover, was not prepared to follow his predecessor's policy of conciliation, while the Meletians themselves were irked, as they seem to have been led to believe that they would share in the election of Alexander's successor. By 330–1 the feud had come into the open, and Athanasius was summoned to Constantine's court to answer complaints against him.

This time he succeeded. The years 332 and 333 were spent in further visitations of Cyrenaica and the Delta. In 334, however, the storm broke.

His enemies now included both the Arians and Meletians who had joined forces against him, and their charges were serious. He had attempted to levy a tax on Egypt to provide his clergy with linen vestments. He had sent a purse of gold to a powerful official who was in disgrace. He had maltreated a pro-Meletian priest, named Ischyras, and defiled his church by breaking the Eucharistic chalice and throwing down the altar. Finally, he had murdered a Meletian bishop, Arsenius, and used the dead man's hand for magic.

There was substance in all these charges, and together they add up to a picture of tyranny and lack of charity. Arsenius indeed was not dead. He had only been beaten and spirited away by Athanasius's agents.[4] Still, Athanasius hesitated to face the fact-finding commission which Constantine had convoked at Caesarea. He warded off his immediate peril by producing Arsenius alive, but the Emperor was not satisfied, and he called upon Athanasius to face a full ecclesiastical council at Tyre in August 335.

Constantine was aging. He still hoped to see all ecclesiastical disputes settled before he celebrated his thirtieth anniversary as Emperor by consecrating the Church of the Holy Sepulcher at Jerusalem. In the West, Donatus would have to be left to divine judgment, but the problem of Athanasius and his opponents brooked no delay. The Origenists were now in the ascendant in the East. They had followed up their success against Eustathius by securing in circa 330 the removal of Marcellus of Ancyra for heresy. They knew it was the Emperor's wish for Arius to be restored to office. They were in no mood to spare Athanasius. A partisan mission among whom was the young Bishop of Mursa, Valens, was sent to Egypt. They reported against Athanasius. He was therefore declared deposed on the grounds of sacrilege and irregularity of election. Ischyras was made a bishop, and the council moved on for a great assembly on Calvary, 13 September 335.

Athanasius, however, was not yet beaten. He sailed at once for Constantinople. On 30 October he met the Emperor when he was out riding in the city, and would have secured a reversal of the Council's decision, unless his enemies had played a trump card. They accused him of preventing the Egyptian corn fleet from sailing to the new capital. Constantine flew into a rage, and on 7 November 335 Athanasius was banished to Trier on the Rhine frontier. The See of Alexandria was left vacant. The new Meletian leader, John Arcaph, was foiled in his hope of succeeding Athanasius, and he too tasted a spell of exile.

At last it was Arius's turn. In the spring of 336 he was in Constantinople. A great ceremony was prepared to mark his full restoration to office, but he did not live to see it. On the day before, he was struck down, possibly by poison. Next year, on 22 May, Constantine, after receiving baptism at the hands of Eusebius of Nicomedia, passed from the scene.

Constantine is not a man to be summed up in a few words. Since Nicaea his religious views had developed exclusively in a Christian direction. The horrible household tragedy which resulted in the successive executions of his son Crispus and wife Fausta during 326 was believed to have hastened this movement, and so too may his dislike for Rome with its aristocracy and temples.[5] From the skeptical amateur of 325, he becomes the ardent and even penetrating theologian of the 330s. Everything was subordinated to the unity and perhaps even the universality of the Church. In 326 he reputedly wrote to the Persian King, Sapor, proclaiming himself the protector of Christians in the latter's dominions.[6] Christianity was to be the religion of the Roman Empire and thence of the world. The new capital established in 330 on the site of Byzantium on the European side of the Bosphorus was to be a Christian city. And, Constantine himself was to be looked upon by the Greek Christian world as "the equal of the Apostles." The union of religion and State which imperial paganism had sought in vain, was achieved by the first Christian Emperor. To his sons he bequeathed no mean legacy.

From the Death of Constantine to the End of Athanasius's Second Exile, 337–46

In the last years of his reign Constantine had looked beyond the sons of his disgraced and murdered wife Fausta for the future government of the Empire. His nephew Delmatius had presided at the inquiry at Caesarea in 334 and had been declared Caesar in the following year. Other nephews were given responsible posts, and the Emperor's last testament sought to perpetuate the arrangement. But the army would have none of it, and on 9 September 337 a military coup resulted in the three sons of Constantine, Constantine II, Constans, and Constantius II, assuming the title of Augustus, and nearly all his other surviving relatives and close advisers being massacred. Of the three brothers, Constantine II and Constans were already baptized and were Nicene in outlook. Constantius II, on the other hand, leaned toward Arianism. He was the ablest of the three. He had inherited something of his father's character. He was not incapable as a soldier, especially in defense as his successive Persian campaigns were to show. But he was mean, suspicious and petty-minded, and he was a prey to informers and flatterers. He was generally suspected of conniving in the massacre of his relatives in 337. His desire to maintain

religious unity degenerated into a pedantic search for minute formula-
tions which could be imposed on East and West alike. As a well-informed
and fair-minded pagan contemporary observed, "He confused the Christian religion which is plain and simple with old wives' fables" (Ammianus
Marcellinus, xxi. 16:18). He fogged issues which were perplexing enough
in themselves, and the fourteen major councils which met in his reign
solved little. The Church grew into a privileged body, immune from
many of the burdens borne by the rest of the community.[7] The pagan
reaction under Julian (361–3) was not wholly unwelcome even in Christian Asia Minor.

In the division of the Empire Constantius took the East, which he was
to rule for the next quarter of a century, Constans received the Balkan
provinces, and Constantine II the Prefecture of the Gauls, Italy and
Africa. As senior Augustus he announced within a month of his father's
death his intention to restore Athanasius, 17 June 337.[8]

Thus, once more Athanasius became a center of controversy. His return to Alexandria on 25 November 337 did not last long. His enemies
pointed out that he had been condemned by a council. Hence, his return
was uncanonical, and the See was vacant. They elected an Anatolian
named Gregory, from Cappadocia, and supported by the Prefect of
Egypt he entered Alexandria on 22 March 339. After three weeks in
hiding Athanasius gave up the struggle, and withdrew, this time to Rome.

The See of Rome under its able Bishop Julius, 337–52, now comes suddenly into the fore. The obscurity of the most important See in the West
up to this moment is something extraordinary. Constantine had endowed
it magnificently, and had built a great church in honor of St. Peter on
the spot dedicated for the previous two centuries to the memory of the
Apostle. Eusebius tells of thousands of pilgrims visiting the "glorious
tomb of Peter."[9] But apart from representation at the Council of Nicaea,
Rome's share in the defining of the Faith, and indeed in the whole aftermath of the victory of the Church, had been small. Now, with Carthage in
the hands of Donatus, Julius knew how to make his influence felt.

The letter which he sent after a council held in Rome in the autumn
of 340 was a masterly document. Point by point the unfairness of the
Council of Tyre was unmasked. Athanasius was declared innocent,[10] but
so too was Marcellus of Ancyra.[11] Rome never quite deserted the Sabellian
tradition of the third century popes, and hence was led inevitably into
conflict with the majority of the bishops in the East.

In the summer of 341 Eusebius of Nicomedia held a council at Antioch.
The occasion was the dedication of Constantine's Golden Church, and
Constantius himself was present. The upshot was the first batch of the

eighteen Creeds which the Origenists, and indeed all anti-Nicene parties, put out with the aim of ridding the Church of the *Homoousios* formula. Here, only the briefest of sketches of these events can be attempted. What is known as the Second Antiochene Creed, which was adopted by the council, went very near to the Nicene position without admitting the actual consubstantiality of Father and Son. Arianism was repudiated. The Son was the "true light, the way, the truth . . . the perfect image of the Divine Essence, the Power, the Will and the Glory of the Father and firstborn of all Creation." The Trinity existed in "three hypostases, but one will," and these statements were amplified by references to Scripture. The result was a remarkable blend of Platonism and Scriptural definitions of the Divine Wisdom and Word drawn from Proverbs, the Gospels, and above all from the first verses of Hebrews. It was a fair statement of the beliefs of the Eastern bishops as a whole and they were to fall back on it in the future. The findings of the synod of Tyre were upheld. Athanasius remained condemned.[12]

There was thus deadlock between East and West. For the moment, however, the West was in the stronger position. In the spring of 340 Constantine II had attacked his brother, but had been defeated and slain, and Constans was now ruler of roughly two-thirds of the Roman world. He prevailed upon Constantius to accept the summons of a new council to meet at Serdica (Sofia), the last town within the borders of the Western Empire in Thrace. The meeting took place, probably in the autumn of 342. On the one side were some ninety bishops from the West, grouped round Hosius of Cordoba. The former adviser of Constantine had now become the consultant of Constans and an ardent Nicene supporter. Julius was represented by two priests and a deacon. Their object was to secure the vindication of Athanasius, Marcellus, and of Nicaea. Against them were some eighty Origenist bishops from Asia Minor and Syria, prompted by Constantius's officials who accompanied them. Not unnaturally, the meetings ended in deadlock. On the pretext of celebrating a victory of Constantius over the Persians, the Origenists withdrew across the frontier to Philippopolis, and there excommunicated Athanasius and Marcellus once more. For good measure they added Julius of Rome, and Athanasius's host while he was in exile, Maximus of Trier. Finally they sent a copy of their encyclical to known opponents of the rulers of the Western Church, such as Donatus at Carthage.[13]

The Westerners replied in kind. Gregory of Alexandria and Basil of Ancyra were excommunicated and the Creed of Nicaea reemphasized, even to the extent of identifying the Person (*hypostasis*) of the Son with the Father. Instead of the Emperor, the Bishop of Rome was to be regarded as the court of appeal in ecclesiastical causes. Both in theology and discipline a rift had opened between East and West—never to be properly healed. There were too deep divergences of religious history, culture and background.[14]

For the moment, however, a compromise was reached. By 345 Athanasius had been prevailed upon at last to disavow Marcellus of Ancyra, and therefore, the suspicion of Sabellianism. In fact, Marcellus's disciple and former deacon, Photinus, Bishop of Sirmium, had been indiscreet in his doctrinal statements,[15] and his condemnation could be accepted in the West and taken in the East as tacit condemnation of his master. Gregory of Alexandria died in the same year, and Constantius was fully occupied by a war with Sapor on the Eastern frontier. The chance was taken of letting Athanasius return, and this he did, in triumph on 21 October 346.

The Climax of Athanasius's Influence 346–56

The decade 346–56 brings Athanasius to the climax of his power in Egypt. He was now a mature theologian and a great personality where personality counted. Meletianism gradually died down and Arianism was reduced to a minority in Alexandria. His power was firmly based on the monastic movement, and in Egypt that meant the ablest of his suffragans, such as Serapion, Bishop of Thmuis, were chosen from the monks, and these were united behind the Alexandrian Pope. To be Bishop of Alexandria, said a contemporary, Gregory of Nazianze, was to be ruler of the Christian world. The Church was now spreading south beyond the borders of the Roman provinces of Egypt, and we hear of one of Athanasius's disciples, Frumentius, as Bishop of Axum in northern Ethiopia.

Meantime, the stormy petrel of the West, Donatus, had not fared so successfully. Perhaps emboldened by the developments of 345–6, he had approached the Emperor Constans for recognition as sole Bishop of Carthage. Constans temporized. A commission under two officials named Paul and Macarius had gone to Africa to decide between his claims and those of Caecilian's successor, Gratus. Apparently, they tried to bribe Donatus's adherents into supporting Gratus, and not unnaturally Donatus rejected them. It was on this occasion that he asked the famous question, "What has the Emperor to do with the Church?" (Optatus, *On the Donatist Schism*, iii. 3), a question which was to be put by every leader of the Church in the West from Ambrose to Hildebrand. Tales of what was happening in Carthage spread to Numidia, and in this province the commission ran into the full fury of the agrarian discontent of which Donatism was a formidable expression. There was fighting between imperial troops and Donatist fanatics known as Circumcellions. The Bishop of Bagai was killed and another Donatist bishop, Marculus, flogged and finally in November 347 executed. Meantime, on 15 August 347 the Proconsul of Africa proclaimed the unity of the African Church under Donatus's rival Gratus. There was nothing left for Donatus but to follow the example of Athanasius and go into exile, and he died in Gaul in 355. For the moment the Catholics were in the ascendant, but their hold of Carthage was almost as precarious as the Arian hold of Alexandria. On the accession of Julian in 361 the Donatist leaders returned on a tidal wave of popular feeling.

Events in the West ultimately brought Athanasius's "Golden Age" to an end. In January 350 there had been a successful revolution in Gaul against Constans. His supplanter, Magnentius (350–3), quickly gained control of the whole of the Western Empire, but Constantius's reaction was vigorous. He had defended the Persian frontier with dour obstinacy. Now making use of a respite he turned West, and on 28 September 351 won a desperate battle against Magnentius at Mursa. It was the See of the semi-Arian, Valens, and at this crisis of Constantius's life, Valens gave him courage and hope of victory. This he did not forget, and so long as he lived the semi-Arian position was sure of imperial favor.

It took two more years before Magnentius was beaten, but by the autumn of 353 Constantius, now sole Emperor, was ready to settle ecclesiastical problems in the West. Councils were held at Arles in the winter of 353 and at Milan early in 355. At both, Constantius and the indefatigable Valens tried to prevail on the Western bishops to disown Athanasius. There were dramatic scenes. The latent antiimperial theory of the Church in the West came to the surface. "I am the accuser of Athanasius . . . Let my will serve as a canon as it does with the Syrian bishops," thus spake Constantius. At the end of the year, Hosius of Cordoba, though now nearly 100 years old, sent his famous reply to these claims. "God has put into your hand the kingdom. To us [bishops] He has entrusted the affairs of his Church: and, as he who would steal the empire from you would resist the ordinance of God, so likewise fear on your part lest by taking upon yourself the government of the Church, you become guilty of a great offense. It is written, Render unto Caesar the things that are Caesar's and unto God the things that are God's . . ."[16] It was the first statement of the Western theory of the Two Swords. At this stage he was supported by Julius's successor as Bishop of Rome,

Liberius (352-66), and both were exiled. A rival bishop (Felix) was established in Rome.

Only in Gaul, where Christianity itself was weak, and Julian was the Emperor's representative, was there effective resistance. Here the lead in defense of the Creed of Nicaea was taken by Hilary, Bishop of Poitiers. Even so, in the spring of 356 the Emperor's supporters had him deposed by a council held at Beziers and he too was exiled to the other end of the Mediterranean world, to the plains of Phrygian Anatolia. Constantius was now ready for a reckoning with Athanasius. Apart from all else he suspected him of having supported Magnentius five years before. On 8 February 356 the military commander in Egypt, the *dux* Syrianus, surrounded Athanasius's church in Alexander. The troops stormed in to seize the bishop, but Athanasius's friends were too quick for them. The Pope of Alexandria was spirited away to spend six years among the hermits and monks in the cells of Mount Nitria, southwest of Alexandria. The field, however, was left to his enemies. In his own See, George, a Cappadocian, and one-time teacher of the future Emperor Julian, became bishop.

The Semi-Arian Ascendancy 356-60

The opponents of Nicaea and of Athanasius had apparently gained a complete triumph. In the next year, 357, they sought to consolidate their success. In August 357 a small but important synod of Western prelates met at Sirmium under the leadership of Valens of Mursa and his lifelong associate Ursacius of Singidunum (Belgrade). The creed that emerged condemned the use of the term *ousia* in any form as being un-Scriptural—the real purpose, however, of the compilers was to reduce the Son to the position of a second god. "And no one is ignorant that it is Catholic doctrine," they stated, "that there are two Persons of the Father and the Son, the Father greater and the Son subordinated to Him."[17] The Church was back once more to Arian angel-Christology. The description given by Hilary to this declaration as "the blasphemy of Sirmium"[18] has remained.

The creed of Sirmium split the anti-Nicene movement. It may be regarded as the decisive moment in the long Arian controversy. The opponents of Nicaea could agree in their fear of Sabellianism and their dislike of Athanasius, but when it came to formulating an alternative creed which used only the terminology of Scripture they failed. Ten months later, in April 358, Basil of Ancyra summoned a synod in his episcopal See which condemned impartially the tenets of the Anomoeans (as the supporters of Sirmium were called) and Nicenes alike. To them the term

Homoiousios represented the best definition of the relationship between Father and Son, and the Second Creed of Antioch in 341 remained their standpoint.

Meantime, the Anomoeans in the West had gained two signal successes. Hosius was prepared to sign the "Blasphemy" of Sirmium, though he refused to condemn Athanasius. He died shortly afterward at the age of 101. About the same time, Liberius, Bishop of Rome, gave in, excommunicated Athanasius and signed a creed which Hilary describes as "an Arian perfidy" (*Fragments*, vi. 6), and Jerome a generation later calls "heretical."[19] It looks as though this was the "Blasphemy of Sirmium," but it may have been only the Second Creed of Antioch. We do not know for certain. His lapse was regarded as serious, and Athanasius stigmatizes his "lack of firmness of character."[20] But it enabled him to return to his See (August 358) to combat his rival Felix to the delight of the Roman matrons among whom he was popular.

Constantius was now hard pressed with yet another war on the Persian frontier. It was not until the spring of 359 that he could turn his attention to the task of reconciling the differences between his anti-Nicene supporters. Two synods met, one at Ariminum attended by Western bishops and presided over by Restitutus, Catholic Bishop of Carthage, the other at Seleucia, the capital of Isauria, attended by the Easterners. The division between East and West was intentional,[21] and Constantius told the Westerners not to attempt to make any decision touching on their Eastern colleagues.

These twin councils were impressive affairs, the greatest Christian assemblies ever held to date. Some 400 bishops gathered at Ariminum, including three from Britain, while 160 met at Seleucia. Their aim was to give the Church a definitive Statement of Faith. In both assemblies the Semi-Arians were in a commanding position, in influence if not in numbers. At Ariminum Valens and Ursacius and their supporters were well organized. On 22 May 359 they had met and drafted a document, known as the "Dated" Creed from the elaborate method of dating used in the preamble, and this they attempted to force on the council.[22] Moreover, Count Taurus, the imperial commissioner who represented the Emperor at the debates, had orders not to let the council disperse until an agreement had been reached. It was a test of endurance throughout the heat of the Italian summer. In vain, the Gallic bishops and their supporters anathematized Arianism and demanded the deposition of Valens and Ursacius. They were gradually worn down. On 10 October 359, an orthodox deputation to the Emperor was induced to sign a modified version of the Dated Creed in the presence of Valens and Urasacius in the township of Nicé in Thrace. The new *Nicene* formulary of Nicé rejected the controversial terms *ousia* and *hypostasis*. It defined the Son as like (*Homoios*) the Father, but did not add the Origenist "in all things." It did, however, as a concession omit the date and any references to the eternal character of the Emperor.

In Seleucia, where the proceedings had opened on 27 September, matters also went well for the Semi-Arians. Here, Acacius of Caesarea, Primate of Palestine, took the lead. It was argued that though both *Homoousios* and *Homoiousios* were un-Scriptural the term *Homoios* had Scriptural authority and meant the same as *Homoiousios*. The argument was swallowed by the reluctant majority. Opposition both at Ariminum and Seleucia collapsed. By New Year's Day 360 the bishops in East and West had signed away the Creed of Nicaea for that of Nicé. It was not wholly an exaggeration when Jerome wrote, "the whole world groaned in astonishment to find itself Arian" (*Dialogue Against the Luciferians*, 19).

FURTHER READING

Gregg, R.C. and Groh, D.E., *Early Arianism - A View of Salvation*, Fortress Press and SCM Press 1981

Greenslade, S.L., *Church and State from Constantine to Theodosius*, SCM Press 1954

Gwatkin, J.H.M., *Studies of Arianism*, Macmillan [2]1900

Hanson, R.P.C., *The Search for the Christian Doctrine of God*, T.& T.Clark 1988 (a long but masterly study covering the period 318-81)

Kelly, J.N.D., *Early Christian Doctrines*, Longmans [5]1978, chs. 9 and 10

Kelly, J.N.D., *Early Christian Creeds*, Longmans 1950, 254ff.

Lietzmann, H., *From Constantine to Julian*, Lutterworth Press 1950

Stead, G.C., *Divine Substance*, Oxford University Press 1977

Various authors, *L'Eglise et l'Empire au IVe Siècle*, Geneva 1989 (this concentrates on the policy of Constantius II)

Translations of Athanasius's works quoted in this chapter are to be found in the *Nicene and Post-Nicene Fathers*, Oxford and New York 1892, Vol.4

14

Julian the Apostate
361-3

The twin synods of Ariminum and Seleucia are the high-water mark of Arianism. But within three years the situation had been totally changed. Arianism in any shape or form was discredited, and within the boundaries of the Empire was doomed to a slow but irrevocable decline. The prime cause of this debacle was the meteor-like career of the Emperor Julian (361-3), who for seven years amazed the Roman world before he died of wounds received on an ill-fated expedition against the Persians at the age of thirty-two. Two things about this extraordinary man impressed contemporaries and still fascinate the historian. First, here was an eccentric scholar who had seldom moved far from his books and philosophic discussions, and yet proved himself almost overnight a brave soldier, skillful administrator, and born leader of men. Secondly, that as a baptized Christian, in the flood tide of Christianity, who had received the appointment of *lector,* he dropped his Faith like a mask, and spent the twenty months when he was sole ruler of the Roman world in a feverish attempt to restore a dying paganism.

Julian was born at Constantinople on 6 November 331. His mother died the next year, and among his earliest recollections were the horrible murders of his relatives with the suspected connivance of his cousin Constantius on 9 September 337. His father, uncle, eldest brother and three of his cousins all fell. Only his second brother Gallus and he escaped, Gallus because he was ill, and Julian because of his youth. He was placed under the guardianship of the unreliable but extremely able Bishop Eusebius of Nicomedia and his education was entrusted to the Christian eunuch Mardonius. It was he who introduced Julian to the works of Homer and Hesiod and "of all men was the most responsible"[1] for his love of the Classics and his austere morals.

Then, probably in 341 came a six-year period of removal from court to the imperial estate of Macellum in the heart of Asia Minor. This was a pleasant enough place in itself, but it meant that Julian and his brother were away from friends of their own age and from life in the capital. They were given a grounding in the literary and physical education of the day, which included in their case a severe drilling in Christianity with an Arian bent. Among their instuctors was George, Athanasius's ill-fated rival in Alexandria (356-61), whose fine library of Christian and pagan works Julian learned to value.[2]

Toward the end of 347 the two princes were recalled to the capital, and Julian was free to study. As he says of himself (*Letter* 23), "while some men had a passion for horses or wild beasts he from childhood had possessed a longing to acquire books." He met one of the few outstanding pagan teachers of the day, Libanius, who fired him with a love for classical Greece. Though he was not allowed to attend his lectures, he obtained copies of them. From thenceforth he was lost to Christianity. He himself dates his conversion to paganism to this period.[3]

Other influences began to mold his ideas. In March 351 his brother Gallus was created Caesar, and he was able to lead a less restricted life. He studied first at Pergamum and then at Ephesus and at both these centers made contact with pagan philosophers and mystics.

He had been converted to a mystical form of Neo-Platonism. He believed that from a single unknowable supreme being emanated a creator-god, whom the various races of the world had identified as Zeus, Helios, Mithras or Serapis. He was the giver of life, creator and governor of the visible universe and lord of the beyond, whose nature was intelligible to the believer only in rare moments of contemplation. He represented the divine harmony of the universe. Beneath him were ranged the various national deities, such as Jehovah for the Jews, Athene for the Greeks, Attis for the people of Phrygia, and others, who determined the natural characteristics of the races over whom they presided. The traditional pagan myths were to be interpreted as allegories relating to the single great drama of creation.

It would, however, be a mistake to think of Julian's conversion as a radical break with the religion of his early upbringing. The Christian Logos had been displaced in his mind by the more visibly comprehensible sun. One will remember how Sun-god and Logos had shared Constantine's allegiance for more than a decade, while the idea of Christus-Helios was familiar to Christians in both halves of the Empire; Julian, moreover, uses the current theological language of the day *Ousia* and *Hypostasis* to describe Helios which the Christians employed regarding the Logos. To many of Julian's contemporaries, such as Basil of Caesarea and the young Augustine, Neo-Platonism was the bridge that led the inquiring mind from paganism or Manichaean dualism to Christianity. Julian went across the bridge but in the opposite direction. Above all, he feared and hated Constantius. His romantic mind looked back to a golden past. The Homeric legends were his bible. Constantine he regarded not as "the great" but as a criminal revolutionary[4] who destroyed traditional religious values in order to salve a loaded conscience, a tyrant with the mind of a banker.[5] He despised Christianity, he told the ex-bishop of Sirmium, Photinus, as the worship of "a new-fangled Galilean god," and Christians as "superstitious atheists."[6] For these two things, he wrote, elsewhere, "are the essence of their theology, to hiss at demons and to make the sign of the Cross on their foreheads."[7] But at the same time, he admired Christian social teaching and practice, and sought to make the pagan priesthood imitate them.

Meantime, his brother's career had ended in disaster. Sent to govern Syria, he had indulged in an orgy of cruelty and despotism. In the autumn of 354 Constantius ordered him to Milan and after a brief inquiry had him executed. In this case the Emperor may have had some reason, but it raised yet another barrier between him and Julian. He too was now in danger. He was accused of having met Gallus secretly at Constantinople, but the intervention of the Empress Eusebia saved him from harm. In July 355 he was allowed to go to Athens.

He was now a secret but avowed pagan, living in an environment where intellectuals who came thither from all parts of the Empire were evenly divided on matters of religion. Among his fellow students were two young men from Cappadocia, Basil and Gregory of Nazianze. The latter became one of Julian's bitterest critics and has left an unflattering description of him as an unstable visionary. He had, he says, "an air of wildness and unsteadiness, a wandering eye, an uneven gait, a nervous glance, an unreasoning and very loud laugh, and an abrupt and irregular manner of speech which betrayed a mind ill at ease with itself."[8] All this may well have been true: the strain of the double life he was forced to lead must have been severe. For a brief moment the representatives of the pagan and Christian heirs to the classical heritage met at the center of the classical world.

In the autumn of the same year Constantius summoned Julian once more to Milan. On 6 November he created him Caesar and married him to his sister Helena. On 1 December he was on his way to Gaul with orders to govern the great prefecture which comprised Britain, Gaul and Spain, and to defend the Rhine frontiers.

The situation which confronted him was disastrous. Hordes of Franks in the north and Alemanni in the south had crossed the Rhine, and established themselves on a strip of territory thirty miles deep. The cities of Cologne and Strasbourg and more than forty other towns and forts had fallen. The whole of Gaul was threatened with conquest. But Julian showed himself equal to the crisis. Though continually thwarted by his subordinates, he retook Cologne in the autumn of 356, and utterly defeated the Alemanni at Strasbourg in August 357, sending their king a captive to Constantius. In five years of campaigning, Gaul was cleared of the Germanic tribes, the war had been carried into their own country, and 20,000 Gallic prisoners liberated.

These were great victories which gave the Roman West a half-century's respite, and incidentally, afforded the opportunity for Christianity to conquer Gaul. Unfortunately, matters were going badly on Rome's Eastern frontier. On 6 October 359 the Persians took Amida on the Tigris, the hinge of Rome's northeastern defenses and the key to Armenia. Constantius thought of Julian's victorious troops. But these were Celts, and they had been fighting to defend their own homes against the invader. Now they were ordered to march 1500 miles east to strange lands and a torrid climate. They protested, and in February 360 mutinied, forcing Julian to assume the title of Augustus. The Roman world was faced with the prospect of another civil war.

Julian, however, temporized. From his headquarters in Paris he warned his cousin that "neither persuasion nor force will persuade any of the Gauls to serve in distant foreign parts. Their province has suffered continuous disturbance and cruel disaster. Their youth is almost exhausted" (*Letter* 17, ed. Bidez). Negotiations followed. Julian hesitated to avow himself openly a pagan. On 6 January 361 he attended the Epiphany celebrations at Vienne.[9] It was not until July that he began to march eastward. He reached Nish in October and thence he addressed the senates of Rome, Athens and Corinth justifying his conduct toward Constantius and proclaiming his intention of restoring the religion of Hellenism. His choice of audience proved the conservative and even antiquarian support he was seeking.

Meantime, Constantius, temporarily relieved of anxieties on the Persian frontier, was in Cilicia in southern Asia Minor. There he caught a fever and died on 3 November after designating Julian his successor. The new Emperor entered Constantinople on 11 December and had his rival's remains interred with impressive solemnity.

The first thing Julian did was to reform life at court. The crowds of parasites and eunuchs disappeared. Cooks, barbers, chamberlains and the rest were sent packing, so too, was the secret police, many of whose officials paid for their tyranny with their lives. For the first and last time in the later Empire the Emperor became an approachable Head of State, and not an Oriental demi-god. The Senate House rather than the Palace witnessed the reception of foreign envoys and the transaction of public business. Julian's ideal was an Empire governed by philosophers, under whom administrators and military commanders served on the model of Plato's Republic.[10] Thus, the semi-Arian bishops who had dominated Constantius were replaced by Neo-Platonist scholars. Like others before him Julian chose Alexander the Great as his example. He could have learned for once from his more cautious and practical predecessor.

But religion was the main issue of the reign. The early months of 362 saw the nearest approach to toleration in the Western world for centuries.

Paganism indeed became once more the religion of the Empire. The temples in the capital and in other cities were opened and the *labarum* removed from the standards, but the philosophic court was not exclusively pagan. We have a letter addressed to the Anomoean leader, Aetius (*Letter* 15), recalling their old friendship and inviting him to court. Julian's own public policy is summed up in an important letter to the people of Bostra, the capital of the province of Arabia, on 1 August 362. There, Christians and pagans were evenly balanced and there had been riots.

> Men should be taught and persuaded by reason, not by blows, invectives and corporal punishments. I therefore again and again admonish those who embrace the true religion in no respect to injure or insult the Galileans, neither by attacks nor reproaches. We should rather pity them than hate those who in the most important concerns act ill. For as piety is the greatest of all blessings, impiety certainly is the greatest of evils. Such is their fate who turn from the immortal gods to dead men and their relics. With those who are thus unhappy we condole, but them who are freed and delivered by the gods we congratulate (*Letter* 41).

Even so, the Emperor did not conceal his hostility toward Christianity. It is not easy to dismiss out of hand the Christian claims that after victory over the Persians he intended to turn against them.

The Church was weakened by means other than persecution. During February 362 Julian ordered the recall of all ecclesiastics who had been exiled by Constantius. They were, he said, free to observe their own beliefs without opposition. In one sense this was an act of toleration, but in another it was a formidable means of sowing dissension in the ranks of the Christians. This was clear to contemporaries. As Julian's friend and admirer, the historian Ammianus Marcellinus, noted, "On this he took a firm stand to the end that as this freedom increased their dissension, he might afterward have no fear of a united populace, knowing as he did from experience that no wild beasts are such enemies to mankind as are most Christians in their deadly hatred of one another."[11] The results were not quite what Julian expected. In Africa indeed, the return of the Donatist leaders caused the complete collapse of the Catholic ascendancy established by Constans in 347. The arrival of the embittered Lucifer of Calgiari at Antioch and his ordination of Paulinus was to cause a schism there which was to last nearly forty years. On the whole, Christians drew together in face of the common peril. In Alexandria, the mob had already removed Athanasius's rival George on 24 December 361, and Athanasius entered the city in triumph on the following 21 February. It was not long before he was making his leadership felt again.

Meantime, Julian's efforts at economic and social reform were stripping the Church of the privileges heaped on it by Constantius. He planned to make the cities administrative and commercial centers as they had been in the time of the Antonines. It was a vain hope, because already the real power lay with the great landowners, and this process was not to be reversed. Julian indeed realized that if they were to flourish again, the towns must have wider sources of income and that income could not always be derived from the laboring poor. Therefore, privileges which gave the Church a large measure of immunity from taxation and free use of the State posting and transport system were abolished. Temple property which had been alienated must be restored—a harsh measure, as the process had gone on for nearly fifty years. The special tax (*aurum coronarium*) payable by traders was mitigated. A system of justices on circuit in country areas was instituted. Julian's concern for the provincials, if impractical, was real and even his critic Gregory of Nazianze admits his popularity in Christian Asia Minor.[12]

The one measure which gave Christians a just cause of complaint concerned education. On 17 June 362 Julian ordered that all professors and schoolmasters must, before teaching, obtain a license from the city council countersigned by himself.[13] There was nothing in this about Christians, though obviously the latter would not receive licenses. Six months later Julian forbade Christians to teach the liberal arts, i.e., to take any part in the higher education of youth. He aimed indirectly at preventing the Christian young obtaining an education in the Classics. This measure shocked Julian's friends and it was not effective.[14] Some Christian teachers gave up. Others turned to composing religious works on the model of the Classics. Among these were the two brothers who were Christians from Laodicea in Syria, named Apollinaris, of whom we shall hear more. Even the pagan hold on higher education proved a wasting asset. In the decade or so after Julian's death the process of harmonization between

Gospel and Classics begun in Alexandria by Clement and Origen in the previous century had been carried further by Basil and the two Gregories. Neo-Platonism, found inadequate in its pagan setting, was gradually absorbed into the theology of the Greek-speaking Church. In a few decades the educated upper classes of Asia Minor had been almost completely won over to Christianity.

This feverish activity was accompanied by a great effort to put new life into paganism. In the East, it was a hopeless task. There were, it is true, still some islands of paganism centered round some of the big traditional shrines. Gaza and Ascalon in Palestine, Arethusa and Emesa in Syria, Bostra in Arabia are named as cities where there were still sizable pagan populations. There were also a number of highly educated men of pagan sympathies on whom Julian could call to staff his administration and high-priestly appointments. But the heart had gone out of the old religion. We hear of priests reduced to beggary, of ruined and deserted temples, and of priestly families being quietly absorbed into the dominant Christian environment. Julian himself was convinced that in the province of Asia (western Asia Minor) at least, everything had to be started afresh.

Two of his letters deserve careful study. In one, addressed to his friend Theodorus, whom he had appointed high priest of Asia (*Letter* 89a and b, Bidez), he analyzes the weaknesses of "Hellenism." Social misery had driven men to despair of the gods. The priests were apathetic. "We are in such a state of apathy about religious matters that we have forgotten the customs of our forefathers." They lacked organization, and had not bothered to develop a coherent defense of venerating the image of the gods. In his letter to the high-priest of Galatia (*Letter* 22), he admitted that "the Hellenic religion does not yet prosper as I desire," and points to the basic cause of the Christian triumph. "Why do we not observe that it is their benevolence to strangers, their care for the graves of the dead, and the pretended holiness of their lives that have done most to increase atheism (Christianity)?" The Christian social and ascetic ideal was converting the masses to the Faith.

Julian's remedial measures resembled those of the Emperor Maximin during the Great Persecution. He ordered the establishment of hostels for strangers and put outside an annual subsidy of 30,000 *modii* of corn for distribution to the poor in the province, by the pagan priesthood.[15] There was to be an ordered hierarchy of priests. Provincial high-priests were to supervise archpriests in the cities down through successive grades of country priest and shrine keeper. The life of the priest was to be set apart from the people. His conduct and even his reading was carefully regulated. His dress and bearing must fit his office. The pleasures of the circus, and the company of actresses and jockeys were forbidden, so too, the reading of erotic or Epicurean (by this time, tantamount to "atheistic") literature. The new theology was to be based on Plato and Aristotle, on the Pythagoreans, and Stoics—only those philosophers "who had chosen the gods as guides."[16] Julian went on to recommend attention to works of charity, the public recital of offices, and the singing of hymns. "Love for God and love of his fellow men" without regard for social status were to be the qualifications of the new priesthood. It was all a century too late. When in July 362 the Emperor sought to do sacrifice in the grove of Daphne near Antioch, all the high-priest could produce for the occasion was one of his own geese.[17]

Meanwhile, Julian was preparing his counterattack on Persia. His legislation and letters give us a day-to-day record of his moves from the time he left his capital on 12 May 362 until his death thirteen months later. He made Antioch his headquarters, but almost at once found himself at odds with the inhabitants. The presence of an army wrought havoc in the local supply situation. Prices rose to phenomenal heights. Emotional and sentimental, Julian blamed "black marketeers." He tried to smother the market by bringing in supplies from afar. He merely enriched the merchants who cornered these. Besides, there was the question of religion. Nothing illustrates better the religious revolution which had taken place in the first half of the fourth century than the situation in Antioch. Pleasure-loving, licentious and disorderly, Antioch was also a Christian city. Julian himself wrote,[18] "I have, however, annoyed many of you. I may say almost all, the Senate, the wealthy citizens, the common people. The latter indeed, since they have chosen atheism, hate me for the most part, or rather all of them hate me, because they see that I adhere to the ordinances of the sacred rites which our forefathers observed." The bones of St. Babylas martyred under Decius in 250 were held in greater veneration than the shrine of Daphne. This "had first been abandoned by its guardians and then destroyed by the atheists."[19] The people of Antioch disliked Julian as an antiquarian prig. They mocked his beard, made fun of his obvious distaste of horse racing and entertainments. He replied in kind. His satire entitled *The Beard Hater* shows the streak of irresponsibility and levity which was his weakness. In language fitter for a pamphleteer than the ruler of the Roman world he tells his critics "I put up with the lice that scamper about in it as though it were a thicket for wild beasts."[20] He contrasts bitterly the straw pallet on which he slept, and the luxury of the Antiochenes.[21]

As a final disappointment in this period, his policy of conciliating the

Jews and rebuilding the Temple at Jerusalem failed. Earthquakes brought the work to an unceremonious end.

Julian quit Antioch on 5 March 363. The first stages of his campaign against Persia were extraordinarily successful. In three months he had conquered the whole of the Persian province of Mesopotamia between the Euphrates and Tigris. He had equaled the feats of his great predecessors the Emperors Trajan and Galerius against a far more capable adversary. But he overreached himself; the coordinating attack on Persia from Armenia did not materialize and on 26 June he was killed while beating off a Persian counterattack. His successor, a brawny Christian officer called Jovian, extricated the Roman army at the cost of a disadvantageous peace.

Thus ended one of the most astonishing careers of the ancient world. Few men have tried to crowd so much into so short a space of time. He was a leader and an administrator who showed a clearer grasp of the ills of the Mediterranean world than any of his contemporaries. But he was also an unstable romantic who refused to face up to the religious and military realities of his day. The Roman and Christian worlds needed men of action and Julian was one.

In both halves of the Empire the brief reign left its mark on the history of the Church. The check to Christianity was only temporary, except in Gaul and Britain where between 360-80 paganism enjoyed an astonishing final phase of activity. In Britain the failure of urban Christianity to take root had a permanent influence on the island's history. The main effects, however, were upon the struggles over doctrine.

In the East, the return of Athanasius combined with the disorganization of the previously all-powerful court episcopate turned the scales in favor of the Nicene party. At a council held by Athanasius in Alexandria, probably during August 362, twenty-one bishops representing Origenists as well as conservative Nicenes, agreed on a policy of conciliation. The Nicene Faith must be professed, and "the Arian heresy" condemned, but a real effort was made to bridge differences arising from the different uses of the term Hypostasis. The Origenist use of "three hypostases" meaning "personal subsistence" in the Trinity was accepted, but so also was the Nicene use of "one hypostasis" meaning "essential nature," intended to safeguard the consubstantial nature of the Trinity. It was rather more than agreement to differ, though as it turned out the difference of usage was to worsen relations between the East and West in the next decade. A new source of dispute, too, was introduced by the requirement to accept the consubstantiality of the Holy Spirit. Moreover, in the great See of Antioch, the personal rivalry between the Origenist

(New-Nicene) Meletius[22] and the intrusive "Old Nicene" Paulinus supported by the West was to be a source of friction for another generation.

The council, however, was a triumph for Athanasius. He was the only churchman whom Julian feared,[23] and when he baptized some pagan ladies in Alexandria, the Emperor again sent him on his travels. This was in October 362. The Bishop's famous comment "It is but a little cloud and it will soon pass"[24] has become the world's verdict on Julian's reign.

In the West, the effects of Julian's policy were more lasting. In Africa, Catholicism had maintained itself on the unsound basis of imperial favor alone. Now this was removed. The Donatist leaders came back to Africa in triumph. A Catholic contemporary, Optatus of Milevis, leaves what may well be an eyewitness account of their homecoming. It was like Athanasius in Alexandria only more violent and more terrible for their enemies. They returned "frenzied in anger, tearing asunder the limbs of the Church, subtle in deceit, horrible in slaughterings."[25] Donatism swept through Numidia and Mauretania like a forest fire. Catholic churches were demolished, their bishops deposed, their sacraments thrown to the dogs. It was communal fury as our own day has known it. Catholicism in Africa did not become a serious force again until the time of Augustine thirty years later.

FURTHER READING

Athanasiadi-Fowden, P., *Julian and Hellenism. An Intellectual Biography*, Oxford University Press 1981

Bidez, J. *La Vie de l'Empereur Julien*, Paris 1930

— , *L'Empereur Julien, Oeuvres complètes*, Bude, Paris 1924

Bowersock, G.W., *Julian the Apostate*, Duckworth 1978

Cochrane, C.N., *Christianity and Classical Culture*, Oxford University Press 1939, ch.7

Frend, W.H.C., *The Rise of Christianity*, Darton, Longman and Todd and Fortress Press 1984, ch.17

Glover, T.R., *Life and Letters in the Fourth Century*, Cambridge University Press 1901, ch 3

Labriolle, P.de, *La Réaction paienne*, Paris 1934, 369-429

The story of Julian's reign is told by Ammianus Marcellinus, Books 20-25, Loeb Classical Library, Heinemann 1939.

Julian's works are available in the Loeb Classical Library, translated by W.C.Wright, Heinemann 1913-23 (3 vols). Except where noted, this edition has been used.

15

The Triumph of Orthodoxy
363–82

With the death of Julian the pagan reaction came to an end. On 16 September 363 a decree was posted in Alexandria that "only the Highest God and Christ were to be honoured, and that the people were to meet together in the churches for worship."[1] All its former privileges were restored to the Church, and magical practices, though probably not the heathen cults, once more forbidden. Though his reign lasted only eight months (he died of charcoal poisoning in Bithynia on 17 February 364), Jovian's rule was marked by events which led to the decisions of the second Ecumenical Council at Constantinople seventeen years later.

In the first place, Jovian himself accepted the Creed of Nicaea, and he did not hide his preference for clergy who did likewise. Semi-Arian bishops who met him at Edessa received a poor reception, as did Athanasius's opponents, but the great man himself was allowed to accompany the Emperor back to Antioch and sent off in triumph to Alexandria, which he reached on 14 Febraury 364. But there was another group who gained this short-lived emperor's favor. We have seen how Athanasius's council at Alexandria in the summer of 362 left a loophole for an Origenist interpretation of the *Homoousios* formula. This loophole was now seized upon by the Syrian bishops and their allies. Toward the end of 363 a synod of twenty-five bishops met at Antioch, at which the new Bishop Meletius was present. They acknowledged formally the Creed of Nicaea, but with the important gloss, "the Son is born of the essence of the Father *and in respect of essence is like Him*." This was an attempt to interpret the Nicene term in an Origenist manner. The Rubicon had, however, been crossed, though the problem of exact interpretation remained. Alexandria supported by Rome and the West was to cling to the conservative position, while the East generally was to accept the interpretation agreed by Meletius and his friends. In 363 Athanasius and Meletius met in Antioch but they could not agree. These were the issues which underlie much that appears as trivial personal politics in this period. The Ecumenical Council was to crown the Eastern point of view.

The sudden death of Jovian left the Empire without a head for ten days. Then, on 26 February 364, the troops elected the forty-three-year-old Commander of the imperial guard, Valentinian, and a month later he raised his brother Valens to be his colleague. Valentinian was also a Christian and a Nicene. He was a Westerner, and the center of authority shifted once more from Constantinople to Milan where he set up his headquarters. He was first and foremost a soldier, who made what was to be the final effort to stabilize the Western frontiers. The signal stations he had built on the Yorkshire and Cumberland coast are a reminder of his efforts. But he was cruel and bloodthirsty, and harsh as an administrator, the very opposite of Julian. His religious policy, however, was one of toleration toward paganism, and noninterference in the affairs of the Church. The statement for which he is remembered, spoken to a group of semi-Arian ecclesiastics, sums up his position: "I am a layman and should not interfere in such matters (details of the Faith). Let the priests, whose concern these things are, assemble where they please."[2] His brother, Valens, however, was to be baptized by the semi-Arian Eudoxius at Constantinople in 367 and favored the latter's standpoint. He was inferior in many ways to Valentinian, though his administration and diplomacy reveal him as by no means the nonentity that he is often painted. Though bad generalship cost him his life at the battle of Adrianople (9 August 378), in the early part of his reign he had stood up to and overcome a revolt by Julian's generals led by Procopius, largely thanks to the loyalty which he inspired (365–6). To the complications of the differences between the "old" and the "new" Nicenes was added the further difficulty of an emperor who sympathized with neither, and preferred with dogged loyalty the now dying cause of the creed of Ariminum.

In this outline we can pass rapidly over the events of the next few years. In the West clergy and people rallied to the creed of Nicaea, and such trouble as occurred came mainly from firebrands like Lucifer, Bishop of Caligari, who would accept no reconciliation with former opponents. Already during the interregnum caused by Julian's usurpation in February 360, a council had met in Paris and repudiated the creed of Ariminum. With the accession of Valentinian, progress continued in the same direction until, except for the Balkan provinces where it had become something of a "national" Christianity, and the bishopric of Milan until the accession of Ambrose in 373, Arianism had almost vanished from the scene.

It was only a side issue in the one major dispute in the West during

Valentinian's reign. In Rome, Bishop Liberius died on 22 September 366, and the succession was bitterly contested. His old rival, Felix, had died in December of 365, but now both parties had their candidates. The majority elected Damasus (366–84), a deacon who had formerly supported Felix, but the irreconcilables who felt that Liberius had been too forgiving to Felix's partisans after the events of 355–7, chose the presbyter Ursinus, and he was promptly consecrated by the Bishop of Tibur. A series of horrible riots followed, which culminated on 26 October 366 with the massacre of Ursinus's supporters in their basilica on the Esquiline. 137 people were said to have lost their lives. What contemporaries thought of Damasus's motives is given by Ammianus Marcellinus. In a passage which testifies to the wealth and luxury already credited to the Roman See, he says:

> I do not deny that those who are desirous of such a thing [the bishopric] ought to struggle with the exercise of all their strength to gain what they seek; for when they attain it they will be so free from care that they are enriched from the offerings of matrons, side seated in carriages, wearing clothing chosen with care, and serve banquets so lavish that their entertainments outdo the tables of kings. These men might be truly happy if they would disregard the greatness of the city behind which they hide their faults, and live after the manner of some provincial bishops, whose moderation in food and drink, and plain apparel also commend them to the Eternal Deity and to his true servants as pure and reverent men (xxvii. 3. 14, tr. Rolfe).

Damasus indeed was not a man to inspire "pure and reverent men." His nickname "the ear-scratcher of matrons," from his ability to attract legacies from rich widows, is not to his advantage.[3] To judge from his clergy, eloquently described by Jerome, his example was poor.[4] It took him twelve years to live down the events of his election, and it was only in 378 that he was formally cleared of a charge of murder. To this extent, the influence of the Roman See was weakened in the intricate negotiations with the Eastern bishops, which were to occupy so much of the decade which preceded the second Ecumenical Council.

Meantime in the East, Valens was attempting to continue the policy of Constantius. Faced with rival claimants for every major See, he decided to favor those who accepted the decisions of the last councils of Constantius's reign, those of Ariminum and Seleucia. This meant in many cases exile for the members of the "new" Nicene party as well as Athanasians. In the spring of 365 Valens issued an order for the expulsion of all bishops, who having been expelled by Constantius were recalled by Julian; and this resulted in yet another brief period of exile for Athanasius (365–6).

But the current of Christian opinion was now against a dictated religion from the court. The Arian party, mainly composed of bishops from near the capital, emerged as such, and it was quite evident that there could be little agreement between them and those who had formed the majority during the reign of Constantius. More and more of the Origenist clergy were prepared to accept the Nicene statement. Already in 359 both Hilary of Poitiers and Athanasius had sensed the change of opinion among the Origenist bishops of Syria and Asia Minor. The obvious unorthodoxy of the creed of Sirmium had frightened them and they were prepared to examine anew the formula of Nicaea. The synod of Antioch in 363 had pointed the way. A delegation journeyed to Rome in 365 to seek the support of Valentinian and Liberius. On their return in 367 preparations were made for a synod to be held at Tarsus where the acceptance of the Nicene Faith would be announced. This was vetoed by Valens. The time, however, for the complete reconciliation of the Origenists with Nicaea—on their own terms—was not far off. That it was brought about within the next decade was due to a remarkable group of men from the vast inland province of Asia Minor, Cappadocia, which had previously been a stronghold of Semi-Arianism. They were Basil, Bishop of Caesarea (died 379), and his brother Gregory, Bishop of Nyssa (died 394), and his friends Gregory of Nazianze (died circa 390) and Amphilochius of Iconium (died circa 385).

At the same time, two other problems were beginning to make their impact felt, namely the deity of the Holy Spirit, and the nature of Christ. The first problem has already been mentioned in connection with Athanasius's synod at Alexandria in 362. Athanasius himself in his *Letters to Serapion*, Bishop of Thmuis in the Delta, defends the full deity of the Holy Spirit, which in his mind followed as a corollary to the full deity of the Son. On the other hand, there were many, like the followers of Macedonius, Constantius's Bishop of Constantinople (died 362) who were prepared to accept the Nicene formula but would not regard the Spirit as other than a "creature," i.e., of the same nature as an angel. Among the leaders of this group was Eustathius of Sebaste in eastern Cappadocia. To illustrate how complicated personal positions had become, Eustathius had been on the embassy to Rome in 365-7, was a devoted ascetic, and at this time the friend and mentor of Basil.

The second controversy, which is associated with the name of Apollinaris, was to have more far-reaching results for the Church. Apollinaris was Bishop of Laodicea in Syria, and had already established himself as a fervent Nicene, and a brilliant and resourceful opponent of Julian's pagan revival. He was regarded quite rightly as the best theologian of the day after Athanasius, and Basil of Caesarea was one out of many of the younger generation of Christians who had consulted him. But Apollinaris was becoming interested in the problem of Christology presented by the acceptance of the Nicene doctrine. If Christ was consubstantial with God, what was his own nature? How were the human and divine natures related? Was not Christ's human soul replaced by the divine Logos? How else could he be considered consubstantial with God? Athanasius himself had seen this difficulty and in a letter to Epictetus, Bishop of Corinth, he had stressed the humanity as well as the divinity of the Lord. But the logical mind of Apollinaris saw difficulties, and by 370 he was already beginning to teach the one, divine, nature of Christ, and to oppose clergy who disagreed with him.

It was this maze of doctrinal and personal questions, affecting the relations between the great Sees, and between Eastern and Western Christendom, that confronted Basil and his friends. Basil himself had been born of a wealthy Christian family, the converts perhaps of the Apostle of Cappadocia, Gregory the Wonderworker. But Christianity meant to them the sublimation and not the rejection of pagan, principally Platonic, values, and Basil and his friend Gregory of Nazianze had gone to the largely pagan University of Athens. Here, as we have seen, they met Julian. Returned to Cappadocia in 356-7, Basil had first embarked on a lawyer's career, but then, prevailed upon by his sister Macrina, had turned to asceticism. His contribution to the Rule of the ascetic life we shall be considering later. He spent six years, 358-64, off and on in a retreat on the banks of the River Iris, but his acceptance of Orders marked him out for an episcopal career. He eventually became Bishop of Neo-Caesarea, the provincial capital, in 370. He was not an easy character. He was vain and touchy, excessively conscious of his position, and he was plagued with ill-health. He tried to do far too much, incessantly writing, quarreling and administering, but when he died on 1 January 379 he had laid down the main lines in theology and monastic life that the Eastern Orthodox Church was to follow for centuries to come.

As bishop and teacher, his chief contribution was the definition of the *Homoousios* in a form acceptable to the great majority of Eastern bishops. His approach to doctrinal problems differed from that of Athanasius. The latter had tended to envisage salvation in physical terms of salvation from death and destruction through the overthrow of demonic powers. These, as he shows in his *Life of Antony*, were stark realities to him, as they were to nearly every other Egyptian of the age. "The river of fire" which the soul must cross plays the same terrible role in Egyptian Christianity as it did in the Book of the Dead. Heaven could only be won by a soul infused with divine power through Christ, and to possess that divine power Christ must be fully God. But demonology has little or no part in Basil's thought. Instead, we find (as in Origen) the spiritual aim of raising the human soul stage by stage toward the divine goodness, which was God. Blessedness, to Basil, as later to Augustine, was the soul's rest in God. Evil was represented not so much by demonic powers as by the simple lack of goodness. To this Christian Platonism was added Biblical imagery. Man, "made in the image of God," had the means of increasing the intensity of his likeness through the saving work of Jesus Christ. And it stands to reason that if Christ was "unlike God" (*an-homoios*) or a part of "creation" he could not be the means of accomplishing the union of man and his creator. Christ, therefore, was always "with the Father" and of "the same essence as He."

This brought Basil to the acceptance of Nicaea, but, like the great majority of his colleagues he was determined to avoid Sabellianism, which he regarded as simply Jewish monotheism in disguise.[5] He did this by making a final, clear division between the terms *ousia* and *hypostasis*. The *ousia* was the essence of the Godhead shared by the Holy Trinity, the *hypostasis* the identifying quality, such as "sonship" or "sanctification" applicable to its members.[6] The fact was that *Homoousios*, for all its disadvantages, guaranteed the full deity of the Son, and to go back on it would merely invite return to the controversies of the previous 150 years. Instinctively Basil and his friends thought of God as Father, Son and Holy Spirit, and knowing that they were one, tried to express these realities in human language. The favorite analogy used by them of three individuals, each sharing a common humanity but each possessing different personalities, may not convince today. But to an era which thought in general categories, and had no idea of human evolution, their arguments were telling. Moreover, the Cappadocians were careful to guard against Tritheism—at least so far as words would let them. The Son "was begotten," and the Spirit "proceeded," but together they made up the entire Godhead. Beyond this central mystery lay creation and the visible world.

Thus the old and the new Nicenes start from opposite ends in discussing the divine mysteries and agreement could never be easy. It is, however, pleasant to record that Basil and Athanasius were personally on good terms until the death of the latter on 2 May 373. The continued, if somewhat desultory pressure exerted by Valens against Catholicism of all forms prevented their underlying differences from emerging into the open.

Unfortunately, this pressure ultimately strained relations between East and West and left an indelible mark on the canons of the second Ecumenical Council. As early as 371 Basil had come to the conclusion that the best means of restraining Valens was through his brother, who might be expected to act, if the Western bishops could be persuaded to make representations to him on behalf of their persecuted brethren. Basil wrote to Athanasius with the aim of killing two birds with one stone. First, Athanasius was the obvious intermediary between East and West, and secondly, he alone had the authority to clear up confusion which reigned in the See of Antioch, and persuade Paulinus to retire in favor of Meletius. In Basil's mind Antioch was the Mother-Church of the East, and perhaps of Christendom. Continual division there among the Catholics was a scandal which must be ended before Arianism could be crushed.

Basil did not live to see the victory of his cause. Rome obstinately clung to Paulinus, and when Valens was killed at Adrianople on 9 August 378 he was ailing fast. It was left for Meletius of Antioch to prepare the way for the second Ecumenical Council and reconciliation with the West. This he did through a council of 153 bishops which he held in Antioch in the autumn of 379. Meanwhile Gregory of Nazianze was initiating a religious revolution in the capital. Constantinople had been an Arian city for forty years. Successively, Macedonius, Eudoxius, and now Demophilus had occupied the church of the Twelve Apostles. All had been sensible and reasonable men, but had accepted the doctrinal views of the court, and therefore had maintained the Creed of Ariminum. The Nicene party was not strong, but now, after the death of Valens, they sent a delegation to Cappadocia to invite Gregory to minister to their needs. Gregory was already Bishop of the posting station of Sasima—a one-horse show if ever there was one, as he describes it—and he agreed to come.[7] But Peter of Alexandria had other ideas. He too had returned to his See, and sent his own candidate, an outrageous philosophical quack called Maximus, to take over Constantinople. Gregory found he had a rival, but his own position was weak because translations were forbidden under Canon fifteen of Nicaea. And Damasus, true to his pro-Alexandrian policy, backed Maximus, invoking Canon fifteen against him.

At this time, Constantinople was in a ferment. How deeply these seemingly abstruse theological issues affected the public is eloquently portrayed by Gregory of Nyssa, Basil's brother, in—of all places—one of his doctrinal sermons. He describes his own experiences, "If in this city you ask anyone for change, he will discuss with you whether the Son is begotten or unbegotten. If you ask about the quality of bread, you will receive the answer that 'the Father is greater, the Son is less.' If you suggest that a bath is desirable, you will be told that 'there was nothing before the Son was created.' "[8]

The perpetual flurry of ecclesiastical politics must not obscure the deadly peril in which the Roman Empire stood. Valens was dead and the Roman army shattered by the Goths. There was no emperor in the East. The command in the West was being exercised by a youth of twenty-one, Gratian, son of Valentinian I, who, however, had the good sense to summon from Spain one of the few able generals of Roman provincial birth in the service of the Empire. Theodosius obeyed. On 19 January 379, Gratian proclaimed him Emperor. His father had also distinguished himself, but only three years before had been judicially murdered at Carthage. It says much for the younger Theodosius that we hear of no acts of vengeance against his father's enemies. He had other work. In fact, the Gothic victors of Adrianople proved unexpectedly easy to drive back, and by 17 November 380 Theodosius's successes were being proclaimed in the capital. But the religious situation remained intractable.

Theodosius was a Spaniard, and therefore almost automatically Nicene. He knew nothing of conditions in the East, but he had a clear aim in mind, that of imposing religious unity on all his subjects. The Catholic Faith as proclaimed at Nicaea was to be the symbol of that unity. His first edict on religion shows a strong Western bias. On 28 February 380 from his military headquarters at Thessalonica (Salonica) he ordered the people of Constantinople to accept the doctrines upheld by Damasus of Rome and Peter of Alexandria as orthodox, and none other.[9] Then, in the late summer he became ill, and allowed himself to be baptized by the Bishop Acholius who had been installed by Damasus. He did not enter his capital until 24 November.[10] Next day he summoned Bishop Demophilus and offered him the choice of accepting Nicaea or deposition. To his honor he chose the latter course, and thereupon Theodosius placed Gregory on the episcopal throne of the Church of the Twelve Apostles.[11] On 10 January 381 he set the crown on this stage of his policy by an edict which again proclaimed the orthodoxy of the Nicene Faith alone, and forbade heretics of any color to assemble.[12] But this time, the "undivided substance" of the creed of Nicaea was rendered correctly by the Greek term *ousia* and Peter and Damasus were not mentioned.

This was really the death blow to Arianism. Its leaders survived, sometimes in vigorous obscurity, for a few more years. In 383 a fruitless conference between Theodosius and themselves ended with the Emperor throwing their various declarations of faith into the fire. But outside the frontiers of the Empire the Visigoths were already being converted to the Creed of Ariminum by one of the greatest missionary bishops of all time, the saintly Ulfilas.

In the capital the problems and rivalries consequent on the Nicene victory awaited settlement. Theodosius summoned a general council to meet during May 381. In fact arrivals were confined to the East, and at first included no bishops from Egypt where Bishop Peter had died on 14 February. 150 bishops assembled under the presidency of Meletius of Antioch. As a preliminary, a vain attempt was made to gain the adhesion of the powerful group of "Macedonians," but even a sermon by Gregory failed to persuade them that the Holy Spirit was not inferior to the Father and the Son.[13] They departed, to be numbered among the heretics, but the problems which they raised have never been solved satisfactorily. The council then acknowledged Gregory as Bishop of Constantinople and declared invalid the election of the Egyptian candidate Maximus. On matters of doctrine all were agreed. It looked as though the policy of Basil would succeed, when Meletius died suddenly at the end of May. At the same time the new Bishop of Alexandria, Timothy, and Acholius of Thessalonica arrived "like a breath of the rough winds of the West" as Gregory calls them. The pro-Western cause was not to be condemned unheard.

The council became convulsed with conflicts. Gregory himself would have preferred that Paulinus should be allowed to succeed Meletius at Antioch, but the anti-Western spirit ran too high. In addition, Timothy made clear that Damasus refused to recognize his position as Bishop of Constantinople. Pulled this way and that, beset by forces which would know no compromise, he resigned.

In fact, the Western party gained no advantage. An agreeable old magistrate called Nectarius was chosen bishop and he was far from willing to bow to Egyptian threats. The Canons which the Council published condemned all heresies, including Arianism, semi-Arianism and Apollinarianism, and then, with a hit at the Alexandrians, forbade interference by one ecclesiastical province in the affairs of another. Added to this, the third Canon declared, "however, the Bishop of Constantinople has the primacy of honor after the Bishop of Rome, because Constantinople is new Rome,"—a disastrous check to the ambition of Alexandria which was to haunt ecclesiastical politics for the next seventy years. Canon four repudiated Maximus and all ordinations carried out by him. The Council broke up on 9 July and the Emperor confirmed its decrees on the 30th. Soon after a successor to Meletius was found at Antioch in the person of the priest Flavian. Paulinus was again passed over.

All this was to mean that the West and its supporters had suffered a serious and far-reaching setback. A council that met at Aquileia in September under the presidency of St. Ambrose inflicted final defeat on the Arians in the Balkan provinces. Next year, however, nothing that Damasus could do at Rome could win recognition for Paulinus, nor the revocation of the third Canon of Constantinople. The schism at Antioch was the sign that East and West were going their separate ways. Petrine claims were no substitute for theological learning. The councils of 381-2 mark the end of Arianism in the Roman Empire. The Catholic Faith was the State religion but in the East the Emperor's will alone was to be decisive.

FURTHER READING

Campenhausen, H.von, *The Fathers of the Greek Church*, Random House 1959 and A.&C.Black 1963

Hardy, E.R. (ed.), *The Christology of the Later Fathers*, Library of Christian Classics 5, SCM Press and Westminster Press 1954

Raven, C.E., *Apollinarianism*, Cambridge University Press 1924

Swete, H.B., *The Holy Spirit in the Early Church*, Macmillan 1912

Wand, J.W.C., *Doctors and Councils*, Faith Press 1962 (has a useful sketch of St Basil)

For Basil's letters see R.J.De Ferrari, *St Basil's Letters* (4 vols.), Loeb Classical Library, Heinemann 1972-80

16

Ambrose of Milan and Theodosius
381–95

Theodosius had opened his reign in the East with a blast against all the opponents of Nicene truth. Though he was to modify his views in favor of the Eastern interpretation of the Nicene formulas, he never wavered in his conviction that this creed was not only the true faith, but the integrating force which would bind the entire Roman world together. In 380 he had been prepared to use the full power of the State to force Gregory of Nazianze and orthodoxy on the people of Constantinople. In the West, Ambrose of Milan was to provide him with a complete partner both in methods and ideas.

Ambrose is one of those rare historical characters whose claim to fame rests on a single incident, the result perhaps of two or three hours of concentrated thought and dictation, but which was to affect profoundly relationships between Church and State in the Western world for generations to come. Without the Thessalonican massacre and its sequel, it is less certain that his reputation as saint and statesman would have long survived his death.

He was born in 339, the son of Aurelius Ambrosius, the head of one of the few longstanding Christian families of senatorial rank in Rome who had risen to be praetorian prefect of the Gauls. He died, however, soon afterward leaving the young Ambrose and his brother in the care of his mother and elder sister. It was a strongly religious household, typified perhaps by the occasion in January 353 when his sister Marcellina received the veil from Pope Liberius and solemnly dedicated her life to virginity. Ambrose's house became the earliest of those Roman patrician palaces devoted to Christian piety and learning, such as were to flourish under the leadership of Jerome and Pelagius a generation later. There is some evidence that Ambrose did not take kindly to learning except to Greek in which he was to make a significant contribution. Years later he was to stigmatize the Arians for "leaving the Apostle to follow Aristotle,"[1] and in a work devoted to expounding the meaning of the seven days of creation, he could state that "Moses in the Holy Scriptures described the things which bear on our eternal hope. But he did not think it his duty to tell us how much of the air was occupied by the shadow of the earth when the sun leaves us at the close of day to illuminate the lower part of the heavens . . . These matters do not concern us."[2] This was a pity, for this attitude of mind, and the superstitions which accompanied it, retarded the growth of the spirit of scientific inquiry in the West for nearly a thousand years.

In due course Ambrose followed his father into an administrative career, and at the age of thirty-four found himself Governor of the important province of Aemilia-Liguria in which the city of Milan stood. This had been one of the headquarters of the Imperial Government in the West since the time of Constantine. It seems that even at this stage he was no stranger to ecclesiastical affairs, for he was already acquainted with the works of Josephus and either before or shortly after his episcopate compiled a Latin condensation of the *Antiquities*.[3] His presence in the cathedral of Milan at the time of the episcopal election following the death of the Semi-Arian Bishop Auxentius in 373, may not have been solely concerned with keeping order. He must have been known as a strong Nicene. There is no reason to doubt that he was acclaimed Bishop by popular favor. Having passed from neophyte through the various ecclesiastical grades in eight days he was consecrated Bishop on 7 December 373. His episcopate lasted until his death on 6 April 397. In these years Ambrose was confronted with four main tasks; first to extinguish the remains of Arianism in the West; secondly, to assert the rights of the Church over against the State, thirdly, to overthrow the remaining power of the pagan aristocracy, and finally, to condemn the various theological opinions which were challenging his own ascetic view of the Christian life. If one adds his zeal for propagating asceticism in the West, his application to Biblical exegesis of Neo-Platonic categories, and his molding of the Christian liturgy and hymnody in the direction of congregational singing, one has the picture of a busy and purposeful life.

Arianism in the West, in the form of support for the creed of Ariminum, was declining fast, but so long as Valentinian I lived, Ambrose was denied the opportunity of destroying the remnants. The Emperor, preoccupied with an able offensive-defensive campaign on the Danube, was staunchly determined to uphold a policy of toleration for all religions, only excluding the Manichaeans. As the admiring pagan historian Ammianus wrote, "He tolerated all the various cults, and never troubled anyone."[4] When he died on 17 November 375 Ambrose uttered no regrets. Even at this stage in his career zeal in defense of religious orthodoxy counted for more than statecraft. Nor was he more successful in attempting to influence the young Emperor Gratian. The latter became ruler of the Gallic, Italian, and African provinces, while his half brother, Valentinian II, was proclaimed Emperor of Sirmium in Illyricum.[5] Ambrose contented himself with establishing a convent in Bologna, disseminating the ascetic ideal throughout his diocese and studying the works of Philo, Origen, and Basil. He was the first senior bishop in the West to acquaint himself with the intricacies of Greek, Jewish and Christian thought. It was not until the autumn of 378 that his chance for action came. Then, in a sermon on the true Faith he pointed out how the "Arian provinces" of the Empire were being devastated by the Goths, while those under the protection of Gratian were safe.[6] The vacillating Emperor (Valens) had received his deserts. This backed by an armory of Scriptural texts upholding orthodoxy was a powerful argument which would carry conviction in due course. Meantime, however, Gratian, a kindly but immature youth of nineteen,[7] had explicitly continued his father's religious policy by granting toleration to all except the Manicheans, who were a permanent bugbear, Photinians and Eunomians, that is the extremists at each end of the orthodox-Arian spectrum.[8]

In the summer of 379 Ambrose met the Emperor at Milan, and gained there an ascendancy over Gratian's mind which lasted until the latter's death four years later. A general antiheretical law was the first result,[9] and the second was that in January 380 Gratian wrote to Ambrose asking him to send him his sermon "on the Faith"[10] and to come to Trier and instruct him personally in it. Further triumphs followed. In the autumn of 380 he had been instrumental in securing the election of a Catholic cleric to succeed the semi-Arian Geminius in the capital of Illyricum, Sirmium. His methods and his views, however, made him exceedingly unpopular with the Empress Justina, the mother of Valentinian II, who had her court there. The insult was not forgotten. Meantime, in September 381 Ambrose browbeat two of the remaining Arian leaders into an avowal of heresy and secured their deposition. When he returned to Milan he had achieved a position in the councils of the State which not even Hosius had been able to claim. This situation could have lasted a generation, for when Gratian was treacherously murdered at Lyon on 25 August 383, he was still only twenty-five.

The arrival of Justina with her son to establish their headquarters at Milan could have spelt disaster for Ambrose. That it did not was due to three main reasons. First, the Church in the West was still at heart anti-imperial. The tradition of Hosius, Liberius, Hilary, to say nothing of

Donatus, to give loyalty in proportion to the ruler's doctrinal orthodoxy was by no means dead. The "two Swords" theory of the relationship between Church and State was held with conviction, and Ambrose was determined that the Church's sword should be the sharper. Secondly, as the dispute with Justina showed, he could rely on public opinion, particularly when this had been impressed by miraculous happenings and the court was largely Gothic. Thirdly, Gratian's supplanter in the Prefecture of the Gauls, the Roman general in command of the troops on Hadrian's Wall, Magnus Maximus, was avowedly Nicene, and constantly threatened to intervene in Italy against the "heretical court" of Justina. The latter was compelled to use Ambrose as mediator with Maximus and protector of her son.

Justina indeed was one of the few liberal-minded women Sicily was to produce for many a day, and the picture of her court at Milan which may be derived from Book v. of Augustine's *Confessions* suggests that religious toleration was a fact there. In 385 Augustine was appointed court rhetorician on the nomination of the pagan Prefect of Rome, Symmachus, but due also to the influence of his Manichaean friends. Between Ambrose and the intellectually vigorous and far from ascetic Empress, conflict could hardly be delayed.

At first, however, all went well. The court at Milan was inclined to support Ambrose over the Altar of Victory in 384, and recognized a debt of gratitude to him for an embassy he undertook late in the previous year to Magnus Maximus at Trier. As a result, Maximus had promised not to attack Italy. There was, however, by now a considerable Arian colony in Milan made up of the original adherents of Bishop Auxentius, reinforced by groups from Pannonia and now by the Gothic soldiers attached to the court of Justina and Valentinian II. These found a leader in a disciple and biographer of Ulfilas, a Danubian prelate also named Auxentius. Early in 385 the court asked for a basilica for Auxentius's use, and named the Portian Basilica which was outside the walls of Milan (and therefore relatively inconspicuous). Ambrose refused, supported by his congregation, and on 9 April a memorable interview took place between him and high officials of the court.[11] The latter declared that in asking for the basilica the Emperor had acted within his rights, "as he had supreme power over all things." To this Ambrose replied that "if he required of what was my own, my estate, my money or the like, I would not refuse it, although all my property really belonged to the poor, but that sacred things were not subject to the power of the Emperor."[12] Valentinian himself was told "not to exact himself, that if he wished to maintain his authority he should submit himself to God."[13] Under this barrage the court gave way. The superiority of the Church over the State in ecclesiastical matters had been conceded.

Justina, however, was not yet defeated. In January 386 an imperial law was published which extended official religious toleration to adherents to the creed of Ariminum.[14] On the strength of this Ambrose was again requested to give up one of the Milanese churches for Auxentius's use. He refused, describing the edict as "this bloody law"—though without much reason.[15] He defied the Government. The Emperor, he declared, was within the Church and not above it.[16] He was then ordered to leave Milan. Again he refused, and remained instead within the precincts of his church. There he had to be left, and soon it appeared that heaven had come to his aid. Digging in the precincts of the basilica of SS. Felix and Nabor he unearthed two large skeletons whose bones were covered with red ochre. He may have chanced on Palaeolithic burials, but for him and the faithful masses these were the bones of the soldier-martyrs Gervasíus and Protasius. Miracles were performed, a blind man healed, God had spoken. Justina was discomfited.[17]

There was little more she could do. The threat of invasion from Magnus Maximus was growing, and the latter was claiming to be the true protector of Catholic orthodoxy in the West. In 385 he had been as good as his word, for he had allowed the tactless Encratite enthusiast Priscillian to be trapped on charges of indecency and witchcraft and executed.[18] Priscillian was the first Christian to lose his life on account of heresy. The West, including Ambrose, was shocked; Priscillian's accusers, two gluttonous and foul-mouthed Spanish bishops, were eventually deprived of their Sees, and the court of Milan gained a respite. But Ambrose was its only hope of survival. Justina was compelled to use him on another embassy to Maximus of Trier (spring 387), and with this, all hope of further resistance to Ambrose disappeared.

Ambrose's mission failed. It might even be suspected that he did not do his best. In the event, Maximus invaded Italy a few months later, and Justina fled with her son to Thessalonica to put themselves under the protection of Theodosius. The latter put his loyalty to the house of Valentinian before his affinity with the orthodoxy of Maximus and in a swift and decisive campaign defeated and killed the usurper at Aquileia on 28 July 388. Valentinian was now under the firm control of both the episcopal and imperial champions of orthodoxy.

Theodosius remained in Italy until 391. In the previous years what Professor King calls "the juggernaut of Theodosian policy" went grinding on its way.[19] All types of Arians had been declared heretical, and soon the "Macedonians," defective in their doctrine of the Holy Spirit, were added to the list. Interestingly enough, Novatianists and Luciferians were spared. Theodosius, it seems, shared the Western leaning toward puritanism. One other incident might have warned the observant of an uncertain streak in his character. In January 387 social and economic distress had overflowed in Antioch, when a special demand for money had been made on the occasion of the tenth and fifth anniversary of Theodosius's and his son Arcadius's rule respectively. The imperial images had been defaced and pulled down. Then the Antiochenes desisted, terrified at what they had done. The Emperor's wrath was about to descend, and the sword, the beasts and the stake awaited the guilty. Theodosius, however, allowed himself to be begged off by a combination of monastic and episcopal pleading.[20] Three years later the people of Thessalonica had cause to rue the lack of success of the monastic movement in the West.

Valentinian II was sent to Trier nominally to rule the Gallic provinces, and Theodosius took the remainder of the West under his personal control. In a few months he had his first clash with Ambrose.[21] At Callinicum on the Euphrates frontier a mob had rioted, and at the instigation of their bishop pillaged a synagogue, while in the same area monks had demolished a chapel belonging to the Valentinian sect of Gnostics. Theodosius ordered the bishop to rebuild the synagogue, and those guilty of riot to be punished. Ambrose intervened. In a long letter to his sister he told how he preached before the Emperor. Jews and pagans, he argued, had been guilty of similar acts in Julian's reign, yet no one had punished them. Why should heresy and infidelity be favored now? And Ambrose made it plain that unless all penalties were withdrawn against the monks he would not celebrate the Eucharist. Theodosius, like Justina before him, capitulated.

This was ecclesiastical tyranny pushed to preposterous lengths. Ambrose had claimed for the Church the right of veto over the acknowledged duties of the state. Religion came before public order and the way had been cleared for intervention by any clergy in secular affairs if they thought that their interests might be affected. A year and a half later, however, he had right on his side, and this time he used his authority wisely. The people of Thessalonica had been guilty of sedition and murdered one of Theodosius's senior officers. The Emperor with refinement of cruelty had the citizens invited to the circus, and when they were there sent in the soldiers to massacre them. In three hours, some 7,000 people, men, women and children had lost their lives.

This terrible deed would have been shocking in any context. This time, however, Ambrose did not rant. In mid-September 390 he sent a secret letter which rightly has been applauded as a masterpiece of firmness and devastating tact. Three paragraphs may be quoted.

[§ 4] Suffer me, gracious Emperor. You have a zeal for the faith, I own it, you have the fear of God, I confess it; but you have a vehemence of temper, which if soothed may readily be changed into compassion, but if inflamed becomes so violent that you can scarcely restrain it. If no one will allay it, let no one at least inflame it. To yourself I would willingly trust, for you are wont to exercise self-control, and by your love of mercy to conquer this violence of your nature.

[§ 12] I advise, I entreat, I exhort, I admonish; for I am grieved that you who were an example of singular piety, who stood so high for clemency, who would not suffer even single offenders to be put in jeopardy, should not mourn over the death of so many innocent persons. Successful as you have been in battle, and great in other respects, yet mercy was ever the crown of your actions. The devil has envied you your chief excellence: overcome him, while you still have the means. Add not sin to sin by acting in a manner which has injured so many.

[§ 13] For my part, debtor as I am to your clemency in all other things; grateful as I must ever be for this clemency, which I have found superior to that of many Emperors and equalled only by one, though I have no ground for charging you with contumacy, I have still reason for apprehension: if you purpose being present, I dare not offer the Sacrifice. That which may not be done when the blood of one innocent person has been shed, may it be done where many have been slain? I believe not (tr. B. J. Kidd).

The foundations of the road to Canossa were laid in 390. The germ of Gregory VII's claim to depose rulers for misgovernment can be traced to this act. But a vital principle in Christian society had been gained. Above the will of the ruler, and reason of State, stood some form of Christian moral order. From now on, no arbitrary destruction of human life by a State could pass unchallenged. In this one act of calculated heroism years of browbeating, pedantry and arrogance were expunged. The West had produced a great ecclesiastical statesman.

Between the two crises Theodosius had been in Rome, and there witnessed the submission to the Christian Faith of more than 600 members of the Roman aristocracy. Here too, the victory proved to be final. Paganism had been dying slowly. By 390 the majority of the provincial middle classes had probably become as completely Christian (to judge from Jerome's parents) as their forebears had been pagan. In the countryside, the last strongholds of the old religions in the Celtic West were being whittled away by the missionary efforts of men such as Martin of Tours in Northern Gaul, or Theodore of Valais in the Swiss valleys. In the provinces even, there was some demand for antipagan legislation, like that voiced by the Sicilian, Firmicus Maternus, circa 345.[22] In Rome, however, the pagan aristocracy had for the most part held firm to the old religion. As in the great days of the Empire, theirs was a cult of antiquity rather than a creed; a veneration for forms and customs which had preserved the Roman State, and whose disappearance they feared would endanger its survival. They would have agreed with Julian in regarding Christianity as a revolutionary force,[23] and in the person of Quintus Aurelius Symmachus, they found a powerful advocate.

In the last years of his reign Gratian had pursued an antipagan policy. At its outset, he had refused the traditional title of Pontifex Maximus. In 381, under Ambrose's influence he issued an instruction to his praetorian prefect forbidding sacrifices.[24] Next year, he ordered the removal of the Statue of Victory, the age-old symbol of Roman religion and Roman might, from the Senate House. At the same time, he instructed that the funds hitherto allocated by the State for the maintenance of the heathen sacrifices and ceremonies in Rome should be confiscated. A protest by the majority of the Senate was brushed aside. After Gratian's murder, however, the pagan party took heart. Famine and discontent in Rome, together with the appointment of Symmachus as prefect of the city, gave them their chance, and in the summer of 384 Symmachus presented a petition on behalf of the Senate at Valentinian's court.[25] The appeal for the restoration of the Statue of Victory was the aristocracy's final appeal to the glory that was Rome's. After pointing to the prosperity of the Roman State under the patronage of the old gods and the value of maintaining ancestral religious customs, Symmachus ended with an historic plea for religious toleration. "We plead then, for a respite for the gods of our fathers, the gods of our native land. It is right to believe that that which all men worship is The One. We look on the same stars: the same heaven is above us all; the same universe surrounds us. What matters it by what method each of us reaches the truth? We cannot by a single road arrive at so great a secret" (tr. Homes Dudden, *St. Ambrose, His Life and Times*, 262, slightly altered).

Few nobler words in the cause of man's right to seek God in his own way have been spoken. The final plea on behalf of the religion which had inspired the founding of the Roman Republic and Empire was its most memorable. Ambrose, however, rose to the situation. Using every artifice of traditional eloquence combined with Christian apologetic he implored Valentinian not to be misled by bad advisers, to remember that the pagans had persecuted the Church even as late as the reign of Julian, and to bear in mind that tradition and custom were not the characteristics of the natural world. There must be change and improvement, change from pagan error to Christianity. Had he stopped there, the debate would have been remembered as one of the classics of the ancient world. But Ambrose could not resist the bullying tactics that he had used against the Arians at Aquileia. He threatened. It was an "affair of religion." He spoke "as a bishop." If Valentinian were to accept the pagan petition, Christ would not accept his gifts.[26] The menace of excommunication together with an appeal to the memory of his dead brother, Gratian, carried the day. The petition was dismissed. Ambrose had gained an ignoble but decisive victory over the old religion. The position of Christianity as the religion of the Latin West was assured. The surrender of the pagan aristocracy to Theodosius in 389 was merely the aftermath of victory.

Ambrose's final years were mainly concerned with controverting and condemning opinions which had won support as a reaction against the increasingly asectic tendency among the leadership of the Western Church. In 391 he organized a large council at Capua which made a final effort to salvage the Western position at Antioch, but it was a waste of time, for the East recognized Flavian as bishop and continued to do so. More to Ambrose's liking was the condemnation of Bonosus, an Illyrian bishop, guilty of believing that the Virgin Mary after giving birth to Jesus, bore several more children in wedlock with Joseph. Two years later he convened a small council of bishops of Upper Italy to support a papal condemnation of Jerome's adversary Jovinian. The latter, having become disgusted with monasticism, taught that all baptized persons, whether married, widows or virgins, had equal respect in regard to their marital state and differed only in respect of their works, and that abstinence was no more pleasing to God than partaking of food with thankfulness. In his emphasis on works, Jovinian was preparing the way for Pelagius. Meantime, he united Pope Siricius, Jerome and Ambrose in unwonted unanimity. He was condemned by all three.

Ambrose survived the last civil war of Theodosius's reign, the usurpation after the murder of Valentinian II in 392 of the pro-pagan Eugenius. He saw his friend win his final victory on the River Frigidus in September 394 and thereby give the deathblow to pagan hopes. Within a few months Theodosius had died on 19 January 395, and Ambrose survived him a bare two years. In nearly a quarter of a century of episcopal government he had taken the Church of Milan to the peak of authority. Not the Pope but he had overthrown Arianism and paganism in the West and had assured the superiority of Church over State throughout the European Middle Ages. His scriptural exegesis, expounded week after week in his sermons in his basilica, had had a decisive effect in ending Augustine's hesitation whether or not to rejoin the Catholic Church. His hymns, if not his translations from Greek to Latin, became part of the

Church's permanent heritage. He was not, however, a wholly attractive character; there was something both of the tyrant and the obscurantist in him, but given the need for a man who combined the qualities of bishop and statesman on the eve of the fall of the Western Empire, no better could have been found than Ambrose of Milan.

FURTHER READING

Boissier, G., *La Fin du Paganisme*, Paris 1891

Campenhausen, H.von, *The Fathers of the Latin Church*, A.& C.Black 1964, US edition *Men who Shaped the Western Church*, Harper and Row 1965

Dudden, F.Homes, *St Ambrose, His Life, His Times*, Oxford University Press 1935

Glover, T.R., *Life and Letters in the Fourth Century*, Cambridge University Press 1901

Greenslade, S.L., *Church and State from Constantine to Theodosius*, SCM Press 1954

King, N.Q., *The Emperor Theodosius and the Establishment of Christianity*, SCM Press 1961

Piganiol, A., *L'Empire chrétien*, Paris 1947

17

Asceticism and the Monastic Movement in the Fourth Century

The fourth century was the age of Christian asceticism. The era of the martyrs had come and gone. There remained, however, martyrdom in intention, the fight against demons on the desert frontiers "by other means," by celibacy, poverty, self-abasement and rejection of the outside world. It was Ambrose who gave episcopal guidance to the movement in the West and provided the same moderating influence on the individualist zeal of the ascetics as Basil had done in the East.

The origins of the ascetic movement go back beyond Christianity itself. From the Quietist groups of Jews who betook themselves to the caves during the Maccabean wars, and refused to fight even to save their lives on the Sabbath,[1] to the Covenanters of Qumran and the Essenes and Therapeutae described by Philo there are strong connecting links. Of the latter, Philo tells us that they spent their lives "pursuing solitude" and that their ultimate aim was "the vision of the Existent to soar above the run of their senses, earnestly desiring things heavenly."[2] No wonder the historian Eusebius saw in these Jewish monks the forerunners of the Christian ascetics of his own day.[3]

In addition, the Eastern tradition of theology had always held "philosophy," meaning a life devoted to contemplation and asceticism, in high respect. The pagan philosopher accepted solitude, a strictly continent life and often a vegetarian diet. In the fifth century the historian Sozomen could still write of the monks as "practicing philosophy" (*Eccles. Hist.* vi. 24) just as Philo had described the Therapeutae. The asceticism practiced by well-to-do Christian households in the towns in the fourth and fifth centuries would seem to owe much to these ideas.

Before the victory of the Church it was taken for granted that the ascetic life was the mark of the true Christian. It was the "whole yoke of the Lord" in the words of the writer of the *Didache*.[4] Later, in the mid-second century it inspired the Encratite movement which was flourishing among the greater Churches of the Eastern Mediterranean.[5] It was regarded as a principal means of gaining the gifts of the Spirit and formed an essential part in the confessor's struggle with the Devil in the amphitheater.

This rigorous interpretation of the Christian message had to face two challenges. First, it was to some extent associated at this time with apocalyptic, and as the Montanist controversy showed, the spiritual claims of the prophet and martyr clashed with those of the bishop and clergy. Secondly, some elements of asceticism also became associated in parts of the East with the exaggerated disdain of the flesh taught by Gnostic heretics as Carpocrates. Already, about 200, Clement of Alexandria was replying that the "true Gnostic" could advance toward communion with the divine by progressive elevation of the soul without undergoing martyrdom.[6] This argument was reinforced by Origen. All his life Origen desired to die a martyr's death but his teaching led to different conclusions. The Christian should lay hold of life, and by using his free will to subdue his bodily passions defeat the Devil and rise toward God. Martyrdom could be the martyrdom of the spirit rather than of the body. Origen's way of life was that of an ascetic teacher, sleeping on the ground, going about barefoot, contenting himself with one garment only, and drinking no wine.[7] Quite rightly, his ideals have been regarded as an inspiration to the monastic movement, and his works were read eagerly in the monastic settlements.[8] Indeed, disputes among Egyptian mon. over his view of universal salvation were the occasion of his formal condemnation as a heretic in 399.

In the latter part of the third century other developments combined to replace the martyr by the ascetic as the highest example of the Christian way of life. First, the Church was attaining a recognized place in the Empire, and so the chances of dying a martyr's death were diminishing. In the Great Persecution it seems clear that except in Egypt and perhaps Numidia, not many died unless they deliberately provoked the authorities. The increase in the numbers of Christians, too, induced a less self-sacrificing spirit. Moreover, as we have already seen, a further impulse to go out into the desert was provided by the crushing weight of taxation which drove many a smallholder to abandon his farm and flee. In Antony's community "there was heard neither the evil-doer, nor him who had been wronged (by the magistrates) nor the reproaches of the tax-gatherer."[9] Finally, the last decade of the century witnessed the missionary activity within the Roman Empire of the new ascetic creed of Manichaeism—a challenge to the orthodox Christian to do better. But, the true aim of the monk still remained the spiritual imitation of martyrdom. This was never better expressed than in a seventh-century romance, the *Book of Barlaam and Joasaph*, "Monasticism arose from men's desire to become martyrs in intention" (chap. 12, 103). They were the new "friends of Christ," and "athletes" against the Devil.

These factors, together with the Egyptian climate, the nearness of the desert to the narrow strip of cultivable land flanking the Nile, and the presence of caravan routes whence hermits would draw supplies, made Egypt the obvious starting point for the monastic movement. The first steps may have been taken as early as the time of the Decian persecution when many Christians fled from the towns and villages into the desert. Some stayed there. Eusebius regards these as the first Christian hermits.[10] Even so, it is with Antony (251–356) that the story of Christian monasticism begins.

Despite his Greek name, Antony was a Copt, speaking nothing but Coptic.[11] He was the son of a well-to-do farmer from a large village on the upper Nile, south of Memphis. His parents were Christians. The story of his life is told by Athanasius who may have met him as early as 318 and held him in the deepest respect. His parents died in about the year 270. He placed his young sister in a community of virgins, and meditated on how to serve God. In this frame of mind he entered the village church, and then, to continue in the words of Athanasius (*Life*, 2), "It happened that the Gospel was being read, and he heard the Lord saying to the rich man 'If thou wouldst be perfect, go and sell that thou hast and give to the poor, and come follow me and thou shalt have treasure in heaven.'" Antony immediately went out and sold his farm for the benefit of the needy, keeping a small sum for the maintenance of his sister. He placed himself under the direction of an old man who was already a hermit and practiced asceticism alone near the edge of the village. His life now consisted of manual work, prayer, and memorizing the Bible. Temptations to return to ordinary secular life were severe. He describes how the Devil "tried to lead him away from the discipline, whispering to him the remembrance of his wealth, care for his sister and the claims of kindred" (*Life*, 5). Then, the Devil took "the shape of a woman and imitated all her acts to beguile Antony" (ibid.). But Antony held fast. He migrated to a cemetery on a mountainside, and later, in about 285, he crossed the Nile where he found an ancient fort which was to be his abode for twenty years. He was assaulted by temptations again. His cell "was filled with the forms of lions, bulls, bears, leopards, serpents and scorpions. He was struck down with bodily pains" (*Life*, 9). Another apparition admitted that he was Satan, and reproached Antony for troubling him (*Life*, 41), but all fled at the sign of the Cross.

By this time he was beginning to attract disciples, and by the outbreak of the Great Persecution the "desert was becoming full of monks." He went down to Alexandria, for "he longed to suffer martyrdom but not being willing to give himself up, he ministered to the confessors in the mines and prisons" (*Life*, 46). This is an interesting passage, because it shows, first, that martyrdom was reserved at this stage for those who literally demanded it and, secondly, that Antony himself did not regard the martyr's lot as the sole means of attaining Paradise.

After the Persecution he again retired, this time to a mountain in the eastern desert near the Red Sea. He now began to make his influence felt against the enemies of Athanasius with his followers throwing his weight alike against Arians, Meletians, Manichaeans and pagans. In 337–8 he came down to Alexandria to denounce the Arians with tremendous effect (*Life*, 68–70). He had become renowned as a prophet and seer. He could deal on equal terms with officials who were favoring Arianism and at the same time would give homely advice to those in difficulty; he cheered doubters and inspired many to follow his example. His affection for Athanasius never wavered. On his deathbed in January 356 at the ripe old age of 105, he bequeathed to him his most prized possessions—his old sheepskin tunic and the mantle on which he slept.

His monasticism was primarily individual and was based purely on his own understanding of the Bible. The asceticism which he taught was rigorous. "He kept vigil to such extent that he often continued the whole night without sleep. He ate once a day, after sunset, sometimes once in two days, and often even in four. His food was bread and salt and water only" (*Life*, 7). He told his monks "The Scriptures are enough for instruction" and armed with their power they could overthrow the demons (*Life*, 16). Basically, he was thinking in nonecclesiastical terms. It has been pointed out that his retirement proved that in his view the organized Church had become an impossible dwelling-place for anyone who wished to lead a truly Christian life.[12] The Bible, solitary prayer and fasting took precedence over the common life, public worship and ecclesiastical control. Though salvation in Paradise was his object, for most of his life he could never have received the Eucharist, and his monks were laymen. And yet, his friendship with Athanasius was to make his movement the most formidable weapon in the armory of the Church in Egypt.

Antony had many imitators, among whom was another Copt, a close friend named Amoun. In about 320 the latter had left his wife with whom he had been living for eighteen years in celibate union and went to the mountain of Nitria southwest of the Delta. Soon a vast settlement grew up. There were upwards of 5,000 monks, each living in a separate cell. Amoun and his wife visited each other twice yearly. At Nitria we begin to find evidence for a common way of life. The monks would assemble for services each Saturday and Sunday, and they were served by eight priests under the authority of the Bishop of Hermopolis. Similar developments took place at another center, Scete, west of Nitria. Nevertheless, there was no set discipline. Newcomers attached themselves to a "master" and learned asceticism from him. It was in these monasteries that prodigies of healing and fantastic competitions in spiritual perfection took place. Macarius of Alexandria, for instance, attempted to keep awake for twenty nights on end, to stand upright the whole of Lent, and to subsist on a diet of cabbage leaves.[13] Another monk, Pachom, we are told in Palladius's *Lausiac History*,[14] sought to be devoured by wild beasts but hyenas whose cave he invaded would not touch him.

This was the flight from the Hellenistic world carried to extreme lengths. With Packom (Pachomius) (290–345) we may discern the beginnings of a more ordered community asceticism which was to extend its influence throughout the Greek world, and ultimately provide a model for the monasteries in the West.

Pachomius was born of heathen parents and was originally a soldier in the army of Licinius. He experienced, however, the kindness and charity of Christians in the Thebaid when he was incarcerated with other recruits awaiting enrollment, and on his disbandment about 314, became a Christian himself. Almost at once he joined a solitary named Palaemon who had a hermit's cabin opposite Denderah on the right bank of the Nile in Upper Egypt. He felt himself, however, drawn strongly toward community life, and in response to a divine command established himself in the nearby village of Tabennese. "Stay here and build a monastery and many will come to you in order to be monks." He did so, and it was as the voice said. By the time he died in 345 there were nine monasteries and two nunneries with several thousand adherents forming part of his "Order."

The important step which Pachomius took was to transform the loose association of groups of hermits into an organized community subject to definite discipline. As with Antony, the Bible formed the basis of the monk's learning. Each novice first learned by heart twenty psalms, and two Pauline Epistles or their equivalent. He then had to become literate in Coptic. Greek-speakers were few and far between. After this, he was allocated to one of the houses in the monastery, where he would find himself living as a member of a group of about twenty monks probably working at the same trade. He would be clothed in uniform dress, which included hood, mantle of goatskin, girdle and stick, and he would be under the discipline of his seniors. There would be a superior in each house responsible to the father of the monastery, who in turn would take his instructions from Pachomius himself. These monasteries were large and self-supporting settlements carrying on every form of trade and occupation, whose inmates numbered thousands. Palladius speaks of 1,400 at Pachomius's chief monastery.[15] Socially, they represent a transition which was taking place throughout the Mediterranean world from the predominance of the city state to that of the rural native community.

In these great monasteries extremes of asceticism were discouraged. Though Pachomius emphasized the value of work, most of the monks' time was spent in services and the study of the Bible. Each Easter and on 13 August a general assembly was held at which all attended in a single vast congregation. Pachomius, like Antony, was entirely loyal to Athanasius ever since the latter visited his monasteries at the beginning of his episcopate. Pachomius's monks welcomed him on his return from his second exile in 346, and in Julian's reign Tabennese provided him with a retreat.

In Egypt, the monastic movement flourished as nowhere else. Monasteries and nunneries grew up outside practically every town and village of any size. In Upper Egypt alone there were nearly 490 settlements with their attendant monasteries. The numbers of monks must have been enormous. The alliance between the patriarchate of Alexandria and the monks provides the clue to the strength of the position occupied by successive patriarchs of Alexandria from Athanasius to Dioscoros (328–454). In the first half of the fifth century there was no more formidable a figure in Christendom than Schnoudi (343–451), abbot of the White Monastery, and head of the Pachomian monks. His was the leadership that ensured that the Coptic Church was to go its own way after the condemnation of the Patriarch Dioscoros at Chalcedon in 451.

In Palestine and Syria the early years of the fourth century had already witnessed the popularity of ascetic forms of Christianity. Here there was no difference of view between Athanasians and Origenists. Indeed, it is from one of the latter, Eusebius of Emesa (*flor.* 330–50), that we derive the most interesting picture of asceticism as it was practiced within the walls of the homes of prominent citizens in the first half of the century. The dedicated virgin read the Bible, observed daily hours of prayer, kept to a Lenten diet and wore distinctive dress.

In Palestine, one of Antony's disciples, Hilarion (*flor.* 320), established the first group of anchorites near Gaza, but in Syria the monastic movement seems to have begun independently. In that province, asceticism, particularly in the form of strict sexual continence, had long had its upholders, and there too the movement was primarily inspired by native, Syriac-speaking Christians. As in Egypt the monks finally established Christianity as the dominant religion of the countryside. Their spirit was individualistic.[16] They preferred great settlements of separate cells to common life in a monastery. When Jerome came from Rome to the desert of Chalcis in northern Syria in 373, he complained that the desert had already become overcrowded. The monks' doctrines, too, were not easy to fit into ecclesiastical patterns and their temper was often anarchic.[17] Fanatically orthodox on dogmatic subjects, their morality was tinged with dualism. Abhorring the world, they saw no sense of working in it. From the safety of their cells, Jerome commented, they damned the world.[18] The behavior of many of them was far more like that of Indian fakirs than Christians. Not for nothing were the Syrian ascetic sects of Messalians (prayers) and sack-wearers equated in 381-3 with the Manichees, as devotees who were carrying asceticism beyond the bounds of Christian teaching.[19]

A different concept of the ascetic's vocation was to prevail ultimately in Asia Minor. Significantly, the condemnation of the Messalians and the other Syrian sects was inspired by two of the greatest names in the story of monasticism, St. Basil and his friend Amphilochius of Iconium. We have already discussed Basil's work in preparing the way for the second Ecumenical Council. Even more important was his part in organizing monasticism in his native province of Cappadocia. The *Rule of St. Basil* has remained the model on which monasticism in the Orthodox Church is formed down to the present day.

The background of Basil's upbringing had been the Christian asceticism of his mother and grandmother. From them he had learned the ideal of the contemplative life with which Origen had inspired his disciples. In 357, after leaving Athens at the age of twenty-seven or twenty-eight, Basil made a journey through Mesopotamia, Palestine, Lower Egypt and Syria to study monasticism there. He returned deeply impressed with what he had seen. "I admired," he wrote, "their [the monks'] continence in living, and their endurance in toil. I was amazed at their persistency in prayer and their triumphing over sleep. . . . They showed in very deed what it is to sojourn for a while in this life and to have one's citizenship and home in heaven. I prayed that I might imitate them" (*Letter* 223:2). At first he did so. He retired to the magnificent country of the Iris valley in eastern Cappadocia, and there, encouraged by Eustathius, Bishop of Sebaste, led the life of an anchorite. But already in 359 he had taken deacon's orders, and three years later he was priest. He was committed to the Church as an organization. Ultimately, the earlier influences in his life were to prevail. The ideal of a hermit gave way to that of common endeavor toward sanctity within an ecclesiastical framework. Man was a social and not a solitary animal. So, too, the iron discipline and drive for self-sufficiency of the Pachomian rule was replaced by ideals of brotherliness (*adelphotes*) and social service. Basil's *Rules* were deduced from the requirements of the Christian Platonism which dominated his life. The spirit was that of an ideal society to which the monk gradually made his ascent. It was Hellenic in outlook, profoundly different from its Coptic and Syrian counterparts.

For the details of Basil's monastic organization we are indebted to two documents known as the *Longer* and *Shorter Rule of St. Basil*,[20] and also to numerous passages in his *Letters*. His object, described by his brother Gregory of Nyssa, was a mean between the solitary life of the hermit and the household asceticism practiced by some of his contemporaries.[21] The fundamental aim was the common life. The monasteries were small, restricted to some thirty–forty members directed by a Superior. There was common dress and property, but no excesses of asceticism were permitted, and even private fasts were discouraged. We hear little of visions and prophesyings. Emphasis was laid equally on prayer and work. Prayers were said in six services during the day and two during nighttime, the object being to destroy evil desires and prevent sloth by an ever varying cycle of devotions. The Eucharist was celebrated four times a week in a church attached to the monastery. The *Rules* recognized full episcopal control over the affairs of the cloister. Monasteries were placed in towns as well as in the countryside. Thus, religious life was no longer to be regarded as flight from the world, and Basil himself was Bishop as well as monk. Work was done with the deliberate aim of serving the community. Schools for children and hospitals were established and staffed by monks. There was scope for the learned to study as well as for the craftsman and laborer. The fulfillment of these aims was to bring lasting benefit to the people of Asia Minor. They elevated the monastic ideal from personal to social service. It is not surprising that last survivals of Christianity in Asia Minor were monastic rather than episcopal.

In the West the monastic movement was still in its infancy as late as 380. In northwestern Europe a rougher climate, the deep-rooted character of Celtic paganism, and the failure of Christianity to penetrate far beyond the walls of city and camp combined to prevent its spread. In Africa popular enthusiasm was concentrated in the Circumcellion movement which had extended the concept of martyrdom to the struggle against social injustice in an apocalyptic setting. The Donatist extremists, Fasir and Axido, were self-styled "leaders of the saints."[22] The deep-seated *impatience populaire*[23] of Mediterranean Christianity was still expressed by poets and authors such as Commodian and Salvian of Marseille who identified the powers of evil with the Roman Government and looked forward to persecution, conflict and the End.

In contrast to the East, Western monasticism was originally aristocratic and middle-class in inspiration. Athanasius's stay in Rome in 341 accompanied by two monks had aroused the curiosity and respect of the Christian Roman nobility. Jerome's early career among the orthodox Christian provincialdom of northeast Italy in the 360s shows how earnest young Christians were tired of this sort of thing, and longed to get away to quasi-solitary and celibate existence on the rugged islands off the Adriatic coast. Even so, monasticism was not always popular. There exists a curious work, the "Discussions between Zacchaeus and Apollonius," recording a supposed dialogue between a pagan and a Christian ascetic in which the pagan asks, "Tell me what is that community or nest of monks and why are they the object of hatred even among Christians?"[24] To this, the Christian replied that monks like every other calling included unworthy elements. In Jerome's time in the 380s the pale face of a fasting woman would be stigmatized as that of a "miserable Manichaean nun."[25]

At this period Eastern asceticism was still being admired as something of a sensation. Rich heiresses like the Roman aristocrat Melania went out and visited Antony's hermitage at Pispir as tourists. Jerome's friend, Rufinus, went to Scete and Nitria and others went to Palestine. By 350 there was a regular pilgrim route from Bordeaux to Jerusalem with hospices on the way. The story of Etheria,[26] a noble and observant lady from northwestern Spain who traveled as far as the Thebaid and then via the Sinai desert first to Jerusalem and then to Constantinople, reads like a modern travelogue. She was determined to see everything from monastic cells to the rock which Moses struck. The ancient world was gradually being transformed into the Middle Ages with its pilgrimages, its monastic sagas and elaborate cult of saints. In northern Gaul the 370s were to see the first and brilliantly successful piece of monastic missionary enterprise in the West, that of Martin of Tours among Celts at a time when Christianity had been still an unknown faith to most of them.[27]

Jerome's career (345–420) fits into the current pattern of intellectual asceticism. His wanderings in the East early in his life, his curiosity and enthusiasm combined with ignorance of Eastern habits of mind and theological problems, represented a prevalent outlook among the new generation of aristocratic Roman Christians.

His salon, centered on the household of the rich matron Paula and her daughter Eustochion, on the Aventine was a real center of religious life and learning. When in 385, disappointed of succeeding Pope Damasus, the translator of the Vulgate sailed away to Palestine and his "cave" at Bethlehem he left an example of asceticism combined with scholarship which the Benedictines of the early Middle Ages were to take to heart. Even so, the center of his activity as a monk was the East. Another generation was to go by before John Cassian provided the Western provinces with a monastic rule which they could accept, and which was to prepare the way for the Benedictine Order.

FURTHER READING

Brown, P., *Society and the Holy in Late Antiquity*, Faber 1982

Budge, E.A.Wallis, *The Wit and Wisdom of the Christian Fathers of Egypt*, Oxford University Press 1934

Burkitt, F.C., *Early Eastern Christianity*, London 1904

Butler, Dom C., *The Lausiac History of Palladius*, Cambridge Texts and Studies 6, Cambridge University Press 1898-1904

Cavallera, F., *Saint Jérome, sa vie et son oeuvre*, Louvain 1922, Vol.1 (biography)

Chadwick, H., *Priscillian of Avila: The Occult and the Charismatic in the Early Church*, Clarendon Press 1976

Chadwick, O., *John Cassian*, Cambridge University Press [2]1968

Clarke,W.K.L., *St Basil the Great. A Study in Monasticism*, Cambridge University Press 1913

Duchesne, L., *The Early History of the Church*, John Murray 1901-22, Vol.2, ch.14

Kelly, J.N.D., *Jerome. His Life, Writings and Controversies*, Duckworth and Harper and Row 1975

Labriolle, P.de, 'Les Débuts du Monachisme', in A.Fliche and V.Martin (eds.), *Histoire de l'Eglise*, Vol.3, Part 3, ch.1 (with an excellent bibliography)

Lietzmann, H., *The Era of the Church Fathers*, Lutterworth Press 1951, ch.6

Morison, E.F., *St Basil and his Rule: A Study of Early Monasticism*, Oxford University Press 1912

Rousseau, P., *Ascetics, Authority and the Church in the Age of Jerome and Cassian*, Oxford University Press 1978

Rousseau, P., *Pachomius. The Making of a Community in Fourth-Century Egypt*, University of California Press 1985

Waddell, H., *The Desert Fathers*, Constable 1936

Wilkinson, J. (ed.), *Egeria's Travels*, SPCK 1971

18

St. Augustine of Hippo
354–430

It is impossible to do justice to Augustine in a single chapter. Only the salient points of his life can be considered, but the impression one would want to leave is of a great man whose mind was turned irrevocably toward God at an early age, but whose attempt to reconcile the three determining influences in his life, Manichaeism, Neo-Platonism and Christian orthodoxy, ultimately failed. That failure involved him in formulating a policy of religious repression against his opponents which contributed to the downfall of Christianity in North Africa and provided a justification for the Inquisition and the stake. It also left the Middle Ages with a theological legacy of arbitrary predestination, which sacrificed the vast majority of mankind to everlasting torment in the name of the righteousness of an inscrutable God, and prevented the acceptance of the alternative and more hopeful Greek contribution to Christian theology. Even so, Augustine remains a man of immense intellectual and moral stature. He bestrode the European Middle Ages and the Reformation and counter-Reformation alike; yet it has not been all gain. As one recent critic has pointed out, "Any author who numbers Gottsschalk, Calvin and Cornelius Jansen among his expositors is much to be pitied."[1]

In the first place, it is not easy to disentangle the lasting influences on his thought caused by his personal experiences from the theological tradition shared by both Donatists and Catholics in Africa. It was almost inevitable that in any controversy over divine grace, predestination would be most strongly represented by North Africa, regardless whether Augustine had experienced the scene in the Milan garden or not. Similarly, questions concerning the nature of the Church had been already debated in Africa for two centuries before Augustine opened his onslaught against the Donatists. Theological tradition and the *genius loci*, consisting of history and environment, have played a far greater role in religious questions than is often conceded. Augustinianism was no exception.

Augustine was born into a reasonably well-to-do family in the northern Numidian town of Thagaste on 13 November 354. He was a member of a Latin-speaking minority in a mainly Berber-speaking area. His father Patricius was a pagan, his mother Monica a Catholic Christian. Though except for a moment when he was drawn to the Academics he never seems to have considered accepting the paganism of his father, from him he inherited a love of the Latin classics, a bent toward the rhetorician's trade, and a provincial Roman patriotism which was later to prevent his driving the antiimperial arguments contained in the *De Civitate Dei* to their logical conclusion. From his mother came his religious and moral sense, and his lack of tolerance, but not his actual beliefs. It is only too evident that the anthropomorphism, the crude cult of saints, the *refrigerium* (refreshment of Paradise), and the Judaic fasts in which Monica indulged even at Milan in 385 were, if not the actual pretext for his revolt to Manichaeism, the permanent casualty of that phase of his career.

The boy grew up not particularly brilliant in his early years, disliking Greek, and with a jealous temperament which he was never completely to control. At sixteen he moved to Madaura on the boundary between the Numidian High Plains and the rugged mountainous area to the north, and then on to the university at Carthage. Here the testimony of a later opponent contradicts the lugubrious assertions of the *Confessions*. He may not have been a Christian, but he was regarded as a serious student and "friend of truth."[2] The fact that he took a mistress (who was faithful to him for the next thirteen years) must not blind us to his interest in philosophy and morality. His study of Cicero's *Hortensius* was one sign, another was his preoccupation with the problem of evil, and his decision circa 373 to join the Manichaeans.

The Manichaean religion was Persian in origin and dualist in outlook. All life was to be interpreted in the terms of a struggle between good and evil or light and darkness, and the spark of light within each one of us had to be purged from the evil body that encased it by the most rigorous moral practices. There was a streak of the revolutionary about the creed, for from Diocletian onward it had been proscribed by successive emperors and alone among the religious deviations of the period had never been tolerated. Yet it made converts, particularly among the intellectuals and also the Catholic clergy. In Africa the Manichaeans passed as Christians. They had absorbed the former Gnostic and perhaps Marcionite communities and based their teaching not only on the apocryphal lives of the Apostles, but on the dualist elements found in the Pauline Epistles. It is interesting, for instance, that in the debate which Augustine held with the Manichee Fortunatus in 392, it was Fortunatus who quoted the great Pauline passage on grace (Eph. 2:1–18) in toto, to prove that as grace was so obviously needed for salvation the world was necessarily evil.[3] Augustine did not intend to cease to be a Christian. He accepted Manichaean teaching as a higher and more rational form of Christianity than the old wives' tales on which he had been brought up. There is no doubt, judging by the influential people he persuaded to join the sect, that, except so far as chastity was required of him, he was a wholehearted and enthusiastic adherent.[4]

His nine or ten years as a Manichee, when he was aged between nineteen and twenty-nine, 373–83, occupied an impressionable period of his life, and there seems little doubt that once the full rigor of the Pelagian debate was joined after 413, he gradually returned to some of the theses he had adopted during that period. But that was not yet. His inquiring and exact mind began to see flaws in the Manichaean system. A discussion with the leading African Manichee of the age, Faustus of Milevis, led to further doubts, and though when he emigrated from Carthage to Rome in 383 he accepted the friendship and advice of the Manichees he was gradually moving into another orbit.

That orbit was Neo-Platonism. He disliked Rome where the students, though less boisterous than those of Carthage, had the disconcerting habit of failing to pay tuition fees. But he had now won a considerable reputation as an orator and early in 385 he was appointed to an official post in that capacity at the court of Valentinian II. Here he came into contact with Ambrose, but first, and more important, with certain books of the Platonists."[5] It is not certain which; they were probably Latin translations of Plotinus's *Enneads* and Porphyry's *On the Retreat of the Soul*, as Augustine seems to have accepted the position held by Porphyry that Christ was "a man of excellent wisdom" in every way worthy of honor, but that his disciples and successors were not.[6] However, he was beginning to take another look at the Christian Faith, and as he tells us, having rejected the idea of returning to Manichaeism he resolved to remain what he always had been nominally, a Catholic catechumen.[7] The sermons which Ambrose was preaching also began to interest him, for Ambrose's application of an allegorical interpretation of the Old Testament based on St. Basil's sermons now had a message for him. It was not necessary for a Christian to believe literally in all the crudities of the Old Testament. The whole Bible properly understood could be accepted as the word of God and the authoritative interpretation given by Ambrose impressed him. He became more pliable to the moral entreaties of his mother who had followed him to Milan. The mistress was put away in favor of the prospect of respectable matrimony. He still "aspired to honor, money, and marriage,"[8] and feared that complete acceptance of Catholicism would sound the knell of all secular ambitions. The successive crises from which Ambrose emerged triumphant during 385 and 386 left him cold. In the early summer of 386, he was a Platonist—and except for his catechumen's status not a Christian-Platonist.

In the ensuing months two factors had a profound influence on him. Platonism by teaching him that evil, if it is to exist at all, must be placed in the realm of nonbeing, had answered the problem with which he had been wrestling for thirteen years, and which Manichaeism had once seemed to solve. It had also brought out in him a sense of the spiritual reality of God and of the mystical nature of truth without, however, being able to quell the equally real demand of sin within him. As he explains in the *Confessions* there were in Platonism "no tears of confession," no surrender to God, no humility, and no call toward an imitation of Christ.[9] He was beginning to see that Christianity and Platonism could be harmonized, but how? He went to the elderly priest and friend of Ambrose, Simplicianus. The latter told him of the conversion of a Neo-Platonist philosopher named Victorinus in Rome a quarter of a century before.[10] He saw that pride could be overcome, but could his lusts be overcome also? To use his words, "On all sides Thou didst show me that Thy words are true, and I, convicted by the truth, had nothing at all to reply, but the drawling and drowsy words 'Presently; see, presently. Leave me alone a little while.'"[11] He might have gone on like this, but for Ponticianus's story of the conversion of two of his friends near Trier on reading the *Life of St. Anthony*.[12] This touched the ascetic-idealist and the philosopher in Augustine. Suddenly, he realized that the message was for him. A last spasm and the indecision passed. There was a child playing in the garden, repeating a jingle "Take and read, take and read." The passage his eyes lit upon was Romans 13:13–14, "Not in rioting and drunkenness, not in chambering and wantonness, not in strife and envying, but put ye on the Lord Jesus Christ, and make not provisions for the flesh to fulfill the lusts thereof."[13] He had made up his mind. It was August 386.

Augustine resigned his post of Public Orator and with his friend Alypius was baptized in Milan Cathedral at Easter 387. The next four years were spent in attempting to orient his basically philosophic view of religion into orthodox Christian channels, to organize an ascetic yet non-Manichaean form of collegiate life, and to persuade the friends he had won over into Manichaeism back to orthodoxy. The dialogues at Cassiciacum (the villa outside Milan where he spent the interval before baptism with his mistress's son, his brother, mother and friends) are anti-Manichaean in direction. Questions for debate included the destruction of the dualistic explanation of evil, the vindication of free will (which he was forced partially to retract later on) and man's responsibility for his sin. After his baptism he left with his mother and friends for Ostia. There Monica died, and Augustine returned to Africa in 388. He was determined not to accept Orders, but the monastery which he established with his friends at Thagaste proved to be too valuable to an ailing African Catholicism. Two more years were spent in anti-Manichaean writings, seeking to reconvert friends such as Romanianus and Honoratus whom he had influenced in his youth. In 391, however, he accepted ordination as presbyter at Hippo on the Numidian coast, where the Catholic Church was being ineffectively governed by Bishop Valerius. He was Greek-speaking. His congregation spoke Latin. A new era had dawned for Augustine.

Augustine had been converted while abroad in Italy by the combined influences of tales of religious conversion to an ascetic but philosophical form of Christianity, and the influence of St. Ambrose's neo-Platonizing sermons. It was a reasonable religion for one who had been a public orator and lecturer. Now, Augustine came into contact with an entirely different interpretation of Christianity which he was to battle with for the next quarter of a century. The Donatists had enjoyed a generation of almost complete control of North Africa. Under an able disciplinarian named Parmenian who was not an African but either a Gaul or Spaniard, the Donatist Church had flourished. In town and countryside it possessed numerous splendid churches; in Tyconius, until he was excommunicated for excessive moderation, it had a first-rate theologian, and as Augustine was to discover, also an enthusiastic and well-instructed laity. But the Church remained provincial. There was no salvation outside the bounds of the small body of its African elect, since the remainder of the world had accepted Caecilian. Separation of Church from State was carried beyond a point tolerable to Western Christians in the Theodosian era. Persecution and martyrdom were expected as the mark of the Church of the Spirit, and behind the arguments of the Donatist lawyers and theologians lay the seething fanaticism of the Numidian countryside.[14]

With this religion Augustine had little sympathy. However it might be ultimately restricted, the Church must be universal in extent representing all classes and peoples. Its sacraments, originating in Christ its maker, must be valid *per se* independently of the personal worth of any minister. Thus in a famous sentence Augustine wrote in 399, "The untroubled globe of the world judges those men not to be good who in some particular part of the world separate themselves from the whole world."[15] They were merely guilty on a large scale of the sins of Dathan, Korah and Abiram; the sin of schism was lack of charity in its grossest form. But in using this text beloved of Cyprian, Augustine was taking a risk, for behind the theological issues of the Donatist controversy stood the majestic figure of Cyprian, and the Donatists were nothing if they were not his followers. Augustine attempted to overcome the difficulty first by paying elaborate homage to "the excellent grace" and "humility" of Cyprian, pointing out that not even in the baptismal controversy did he break communion with Stephen, but then going on to indicate the fallibility of his doctrine of the sacraments and by implication his doctrine of the Church. It was not too effective.

When the Donatist, Petilian of Constantine, claimed in regard to baptism, that "what we look for is the conscience of the giver, giving in holiness, to cleanse that of the recipient,"[16] Augustine replied that Christ only, the high-priest without sin, was the sole dispenser of sacramental grace. Christ's sanctity could not be corrupted by unworthy ministers and therefore the validity of the sacrament was unaffected by the character of the individual dispenser. But its effect on the recipient depended on the latter's spiritual standing. Without charity, by which Augustine meant communion with the Catholic Church, it "profiteth him nothing." Augustine agreed with Cyprian that there was "no salvation outside the Church," but his concept of the Church was wider. In its visible form it contained tares as well as wheat, vessels of dishonor as well as of honor, and fishes of every kind in its net. The moment of separation would be the Last Day, not the times of Donatus.

These were the arguments repeated incessantly over twenty years of discussion with Donatist leaders and congregations, down to the moment when he forced them into a conference at Carthage presided over by his friend the Imperial Commissioner Marcellinus in May 411, and had them condemned. Events had played into his hands. Parmenian and his Catholic rival Genethlius had both died in 391-2, and the Catholics had this time made the wiser choice as successor. Augustine who became Bishop of Hippo after Valerius's death in 396 found in Aurelius the Catholic Bishop of Carthage an ideal partner. The latter had the gift of organization, and year after year councils of Catholic bishops met in Carthage to legislate, administer and discuss the affairs of the Church. Augustine provided the brains and literary talent, continuously writing, discussing and controverting. The Donatists in contrast had elected a violent character named Primian to the See of Carthage. Schism had broken out in their ranks, and though the Primianists had gained the upper hand the

203

cohesion and confidence of the Church had been shaken. Why, asked Augustine, did the Primianists accept the schismatic Maximinianists back into their fold while refusing Catholic overtures to unity? Moreover, politically the Donatists had been unwise, supporting the revolt of the Kabylie chieftain Gildo in 397-8. When this failed they found they had left themselves open both to prosecution under the imperial laws against heresy and to the suspicion of disloyalty.

Augustine was quick to follow up these advantages. Though it would be a mistake to think that up to this time he had never considered invoking the antiheretical laws and the authority of local magistrates against his opponents he had preferred debate as a means of converting Donatists as he had the Manichaeans.[17] But after Gildo's failure his tone changed. To the readers of his three books *Against the Letter of Parmenian*, he affirmed that if rulers were justified in legislating against poisoners and other criminals, they were also justified in legislating against heretics.[18] In 399 he was favored also by an important judgment which deprived a Donatist bishop of a legacy on the grounds that a heretic could not benefit under a will.[19] The all-out attack on Donatism, fully supported by the State, followed as a matter of course. The Donatist rejection of a demand for a conference in September 403 followed by Circumcellion attacks on Catholic clergy and property resulted in Augustine supporting an appeal to the imperial court at Ravenna for the enforcement of antiheretical laws against the Donatists. The Edicts of Unity followed in 405, practically banning the sect. From then on, Augustine fully supported the forceful suppression of his Donatist rival. It may be that, as he argued in a letter to Vincentius, an old fellow student who had become bishop of a Donatist splinter group in Cartenna, he had changed his mind under the pressure of his colleagues.[20] A close study of the evidence, however, does not suggest that there was more than a change of emphasis. But now the Lucan text, "Compel them to come in," was invoked to justify the use of force with the gravest consequences for the future of Christian brotherhood and toleration.[21]

Augustine did not succeed in destroying Donatism. The Conference at Carthage in 411 brought about a massive confrontation of the two interpretations of the Christian social message and two theologies of the Church. The final, ceremonial condemnation of Donatism in January 412 indeed prevented the movement from becoming to North Africa what the Coptic Church was to become to Egypt. Islam found less resistance. The Christian world had to mourn the permanent loss of North Africa and learn by the hardest of lessons that religious persecution and the will of Christ are incompatible.

One of Augustine's arguments against accepting the fact of Donatism had been that religious liberty was merely "liberty to err." Man left to his own devices without the threat of Church and State coercion was bound to make the wrong choice.[22] His doctrine of the Church was already preparing the way for a determinist doctrine of grace. It was leading him to use arguments which he had specifically rejected thirteen years before.

Although the long period between 396 and 411 had been taken up largely with the Donatist controversy other theological problems had continued to occupy his mind. He had reread the Pauline Epistles circa 395-6, and the long prayer to God poured out in the *Confessions* (circa 397) reflects his continued deep concern with the problems of evil and human salvation. Though he now accepted the fact that the fall of man had not been due to some uncontrollable catastrophe but to human disobedience, his belief in his own providential deliverance from a life of desperate wickedness forbade him to assert that man possessed in himself the means even of the smallest step toward righteousness unassisted by God. As early as 397 he had written to his old friend Simplicianus in Milan that "without Grace it is impossible to resist concupiscence."[23] Years later in the *Revisions* he looked back on this particular work and recorded how he had pondered long over the problems of free will and Grace and that Grace had prevailed.[24] In the same letter he had also stated his view that man was part of a *massa peccati*, and that only a limited number were predestined to salvation. African theological tradition had always maintained that sin had been passed on seminally by Adam and this view combined with a doctrine of the Church based on the salvation of an elect had rendered predestination an acceptable belief. Whatever his personal experiences it is doubtful whether as an African bishop Augustine could have represented any other view. He had made up his mind more than a decade before Pelagius appeared on the scene.

Pelagius himself, whether the son of a Roman civil servant in Britain or not, had been in Rome for a long time.[25] Like his contemporary, Jerome, his influence had been strong among the younger generation of the Roman aristocracy, who were turning from paganism to Christianity. In contrast, however, to Jerome, Pelagius's message was one of active Christian witness against wealth and injustice, and his demand on his followers was to stay in this world and reform it. He preferred the term "Christian" to that of "monk"; and he believed that man through the free will with which God had provided him and through God's law, could carry out Christ's commands as laid down in the New Testament, and thereby live a virtuous life. Pelagius admitted neither Original sin nor Original fall. Man's sin was his own. Adam had set a bad example but his fault did not infect the human race. It merely led it astray.[26] He was against fatalism and his angry reaction when he heard, circa 405, a bishop quoting the passage from Augustine's *Confessions*, Bk. X. *Da quod iubes, et iube quod vis* (Give what thou commandest and command what Thou wilt)[27] is what one would expect from an active reformer. Moreover, to Pelagius, as to most Latins outside Africa, *gratia* (Grace) was synonymous with bribery and to suggest that this quality was necessary to salvation was blasphemy. God's aid was imperative to strengthen man's resolve to do good but not his "Grace."

It is not possible to follow out the details of the conflict between the two interpretations of man's relation to God.[28] It is not surprising, however, that when Celestius, Pelagius's disciple, arrived in Africa after the sack of Rome by Alaric in 410 and sought admission to the ranks of the Catholic clergy in Carthage his request was refused by Aurelius without Augustine's intervention. Augustine himself was drawn into the controversy by questions put to him by his friend Count Marcellinus who had presided over the recent conference at Carthage with the Donatists. In reply he wrote the classic work *On the Spirit and the Letter*, in which he pointed out that the "letter which killeth" was the Mosaic law which laid down what man ought to do, but gave him no strength to do it, and the "Spirit which giveth life" was the Holy Spirit through whom the will was lifted up and enabled to obey the law of God.

Had Augustine stopped there his contributions to the problem of free will and Grace would have been significant enough. It would also have been in full harmony with the African tradition which emphasized the perpetual role of the Spirit in the individual and the Church. But his worst enemy was his own love of controversy, and his refusal to concede the least virtue or success to opponents. Baited first by Celestius and then by his own clever, persistent and equally argumentative ex-pupil, Julian of Eclanum, he gradually elaborated the inhuman system of mankind's condemnation in the face of the inscrutable justice of God that is associated with his name. By his persistent mistranslation of Romans 5:12 ("in whom" instead of "*on account of* whom all die") original sin became literally transmitted to the human race, and Adam's sin exaggerated beyond recognition. His Manichaean period, and perhaps his frustrated desire for a normal family life, forced, *concupiscentia* into an obsessive role in his later years. All children were procreated in their parents' lust.[29] Unregenerate humanity was capable not of virtue but of "splendid vices" because the root of its existence was tainted. In his final, tedious and unfinished work against Julian, mankind was represented as a mass of sin waited upon by death, incapable of raising itself by its own effort.[30] That the Incarnation had removed the gulf between God and man was small comfort, for only a few would benefit. Here was fatalism unrelieved. The young radical who had once found his answers with the outlawed Manichees had become the crusted old pessimist driven back to Manichaeism by the logic of his argument. As Julian told him, as "a leopard could not change his spots or an Ethiopian his skin, so nor could he, Augustine, change his Manichaeism."[31] It was a mercy that the Vandals and malaria put an end to the debate on 28 August 430.

These last decades of Augustine's life, however, were not exclusively occupied with the Pelagians. Two great works were written in this period, the fifteen books of the *De Trinitate* and the twenty-two books of the *De Civitate Dei*. In the first one glimpses the full maturity of Augustine's mind, and what it might have contributed but for the arrival of Pelagius and Celestius in Africa. Here was a doctrine of the Trinity free from the metaphysical conundrums which had beset the East since Nicaea, the divine quality of love raised to be the binding force between the three persons, and from the Trinity descending to mankind as the creative force of forgiveness by which God recreates his own image in each sinner.[32] Here Augustine was inspiring a tradition of Western thought which has lasted until today.

The *De Civitate*, begun in 411 and finished in 426, was also inspired by a letter from Marcellinus. Were the fall of Rome and other disasters due to Theodosius's establishment of the Christian Church? Was this the vengeance of the neglected gods of Rome? In answering these questions Augustine not only crowned the long tradition of Christian apologetic, but expounded a scheme of Church-State relations which rid educated Western thought of the mirage of apocalypticism. Already in the 370s Tyconius had shown that the traditional two cities of Jerusalem and Babylon must be regarded allegorically. They were not empire and Church set over against each other, but two societies peopled by individuals according to whether their wills were directed toward Christ or toward the Devil. Augustine took up this definition, changing Tyconius' "will" to "love," and transformed the cities into ideal states, even though these were reflected in earthly governments according to the purpose of their existence. Thus the State, too, could be a reflection of divine purpose, lower indeed than the Church, for the discipline the State enforced on its inhabitants was the result of Original Sin, but sharing with the Church in forwarding God's purposes. The good emperor might still be he who served the Church best, but the Christian empire which he now ruled had some of the qualities of the divine monarchy in so far as it was Christian.[33]

These were great works, by a man who, whatever his faults, had sought to direct his mind exclusively toward God. "Why do we hesitate," he had once asked his friends, "to give up all wordly ambition and devote ourselves wholly to the search for God and the happy life?"[34] This was an influence dominating European thought far beyond the Reformation, the ideal of the only Latin theologian in the patristic period to equal the learning and insights of Origen, Athanasius, and the Cappadocian Fathers. Like these he displays the tremendous energy and resource of the early Christian mind, a mind ever restless until it gained its rest in God.

FURTHER READING

A few salient works from among the enormous library dedicated to St Augustine:

Baynes, N.H., *The Political Aspects of St Augustine's* De civitate Dei, Historical Association Pamphlet 104, London 1936

Bonner, G., *St Augustine of Hippo, Life and Controveries*, SCM Press 1963, Canterbury Press ²1989

Brown, P., *Augustine of Hippo*, Faber and University of California Press 1967

Brown, P., *Religion and Society in the Age of Saint Augustine*, Faber and Harper and Row 1972

Burnaby, J., *Amor Dei*, Hodder 1947

Chadwick, H., *Augustine*, Oxford University Press 1986

Courcelle, P., *Recherches sur les 'Confessions' de Saint Augustin*, Paris 1950

Courcelle, P., *Les 'Confessions' de Saint Augustine dans la tradition littéraire*, Paris 1963

Evans, R.F., *One and Holy*, SPCK 1972

Evans, G.R., *Augustine on Evil*, Cambridge University Press 1982

Ferguson, J., *Pelagius: A Historical and Theological Study*, Cambridge University Press 1956

Markus, R.A., *Saeculum: History and Society in the Theology of St Augustine*, Cambridge University Press 1970

O'Meara, J., *The Young Augustine*, Longmans 1954

Pagels, E., *Adam, Eve and the Serpent*, New York 1988

Willis, G.G., *St Augustine and the Donatist Controversy*, SPCK 1950

Various authors, *A Monument to St Augustine*, Sheed and Ward 1931

On Manichaeism, see S.Lieu, *Manichaeism*, Manchester University Press 1988

19

The Conflicts
of Eastern Christendom
381–431

An invitation had been sent to Augustine to attend the Council of Ephesus, but he had been dead many months when the Council opened in June 431. This Council, perhaps the most tempestuous that ever assembled in the name of the whole Church, marked an important step in the longstanding rivalry between the Sees of Alexandria and Constantinople. Perhaps more important than that, it marked a stage in the conflict between the two rival concepts of our Lord, that of Antioch emphasizing his humanity, redeeming mankind by his divine example, and that of Alexandria emphasizing a divinity saving man from the consequences of sin by manifesting in his life the full essence of the divine nature. In the third century the Origenists of Alexandria had gained a victory over Paul of Samosata. A century and a half later Theophilus and Cyril, uncle and nephew, successive patriarchs of Alexandria, John Chrysostom and Nestorius their victims at Constantinople, were the main characters in the tangled story.

The third Canon of the Council of Constantinople had decreed that "However, the bishop of Constantinople is to have honorary preeminence after the bishop of Rome, because Constantinople is New Rome." It looks almost as though this had been set down as a gloss on the previous Canon which forbade bishops to interfere in the affairs of other "dioceses" (i.e., the larger divisions of the Empire), and that the word "however," with which the Canon begins, was intended as a safeguard for the position of the bishop of the new capital of the Roman world. This provision coupled, however, with the failure of the ill-conceived attempt by Peter of Alexandria to foist Maximus the Cynic on the throne of Constantinople was regarded as an affront to Alexandria, while in stressing the civic claims of Constantinople to precedence it had offended the Roman See as well. The alliance between the two aggrieved parties was to be of great importance in the next fifty years.

While the amiable Nectarius lived nothing could be done, but after his death in 397, the opponents of Constantinople found their chance to act. Theodosius had left the Empire divided between his two sons, Arcadius (395–408) the elder ruling the East, and Honorius (395–423) the West. Both were incompetent, and power was vested in the hands of their chief ministers, a situation which gave full scope for intrigue. After much debate the choice as Nectarius's successor fell on the famous presbyter of Antioch, John Chrysostom (circa 345–405). The latter was a great preacher; he had distinguished himself by keeping up the spirits of the people of Antioch by his sermons during the affair of the Statues in 387. He was a champion of social reform, and a hater of Jews and heretics. However, he talked incessantly—the twelve volumes of his works in the Migne *Patrologia Greco-Latina* testify to the fact—and he lacked tact. Tact was needed at Constantinople. Theophilus of Alexandria having failed to get his own nominee elected instead of John bided his time. He did not have long to wait. In Nectarius's last years Church discipline had quietly gone to sleep, and very soon the new archbishop undertook a purge of unworthy clergy and denounced an equally unworthy public morality. Both acts were to cost him dearly. Nor were references to Jezebel appreciated at court, where the Empress Eudoxia may well have had on her conscience the murder of Eutropius, who had been Arcadius's chief minister up to 398 and had been her benefactor.

In the event, trouble arose in an unexpected way. Toward the end of 401 there arrived in Constantinople a number of Egyptian monks from the Nitrian mountains who claimed that they had been persecuted by Theophilus as Origenists. The campaign against "Origenism" which was uniting Theophilus and Jerome in a heresy hunt was under way.[1] John was perhaps unwise to give the monks shelter and so add the Patriarch of Alexandria to the tale of his opponents.

The monks meantime had made an impression at the imperial court, and it had been agreed that the accusations against them should be examined by the Praetorian Prefects, and also that Theophilus should himself be summoned to answer for his conduct before John. Theophilus took his cue. He would certainly come to the capital, but there he would brand his opponent as a heretic and turn the tables on him. Though his attempt to use Epiphanius of Salamis, a veteran heresy hunter, to charge John with Origenism failed, he arrived full of confidence knowing that John had enemies in high places, and that others at court were susceptible to well-placed gifts. In the background were the sailors of the Egyptian corn-fleet, ready to lend a strong right arm if needed.

Theophilus avoided John, made contact with his enemies, and in the early 'summer of 402 transferred himself across the Bosporus to a villa called the Oak, which had once belonged to Theodosius's minister, Rufinus. There, supported by twenty-eight Egyptian bishops and half a dozen others he defied John. The latter had forty bishops with him on the Constantinople side of the Bosphorus. However, he felt a scruple about crossing to Chalcedon which was technically in the Diocese of Asia and therefore outside his own territory, to preside over a court to hear a complaint against Theophilus. This was a fatal mistake and not easily comprehensible, since John had spent the early months of 401 in Asia settling the affairs of the Church of Ephesus the capital of the diocese of Asia. From now on the initiative lay with his enemies. Theophilus who had no scruples proceeded to bring countercharges against John, summoned him to appear and when he refused had a sentence of deposition pronounced against him by his Council. By including some of John's less tactful utterances concerning the Empress among the charges, he won over court support for his case though not for the sentence. John was to be exiled from Constantinople, but not deposed.

His work done, Theophilus departed. He had damaged his opponent's position severely, but he had not yet won a complete victory. This was to be the work of a jealous and outraged court. Meantime, the populace of the capital remained true to their bishop, and for a short time John was able to return. "My Church," he commented, "has remained faithful to me; our modern Pharaoh has desired to take it from me as he of old had taken Sara. But once more Sara has remained pure: the adulterers are put in confusion."[2] Within two months trouble had broken out again. A statue of the Empress was inaugurated in front of St. Sophia amid boisterous scenes. Once more the "Golden Tongue" wagged too much. Once more, John denounced Eudoxia in Biblical terms; it was as Herodias this time. The breach became irreparable, and finally on 9 June 404 the Emperor Arcadius signed an order for banishment. This time it was enforced.

John's career ended in failure. He died on his way on foot to yet harsher quarters in 407. When one compares his fate with that of Ambrose his failure becomes the more significant. Both men were vigorous and ascetic pastors. Both denounced evil, and both were prepared to defy the imperial court. Behind Ambrose, however, was the long tradition of Western opposition to the Empire whereas John knew only subservience. "The emperor," he wrote in 387, "is without a Peer upon earth, for he is the head and crown of everything in this world."[3] Though he might protest the superiority of the priestly over the imperial status,[4] when put to the test his attitude was submissive. Ambrose could defy an imperial order, and command an emperor. John when similarly pressed could do neither. Ambrose remained in Milan, John departed to exile and death. No two careers illustrate more clearly the difference in the position of an Eastern and a Western bishop, and the difference between Church-State relations in the two halves of the Roman Empire.

John's death was followed by a long lull in the relations between Constantinople and Alexandria. Theophilus was content with his success and left well alone. He died in 412, and was succeeded by his able and unscrupulous nephew Cyril. For the time being the affairs of Alexandria kept Cyril busy. The murder of the philosopher Hypatia in 415 in which he may have been involved was a grave scandal. His relations, however, with the patriarch at Constantinople, Atticus (406–25), were cordial enough, for Atticus had been among John Chrysostom's opponents. But after the death of Atticus's short-lived successor at the end of 427 matters began to change.

Once again there was a disputed election. For months interested parties wrangled, until the court decided that it would have to look for a new archbishop outside the ranks of the clergy of the capital. The choice fell on Nestorius, a presbyter and the superior of a monastery outside Antioch. He was enthroned on 10 April 428.

Theophilus had not been able to press seriously a charge of heresy against John, and had confined his complaints to matters of discipline. From the turn of the fifth century onward, however, both Antioch and Alexandria had been evolving schools of theology which held contrasting ideas concerning the nature of Christ, and now once more a representative of Antioch was ensconced as patriarch of Constantinople.

The theological problem was extremely complicated. It will be remembered that Apollinaris of Laodicea had attempted to establish that the human and divine element of Jesus' nature were united, but united in such a way that the human element was partly sacrificed. There were not two persons or natures, but only the divine nature, which possessed, however, human aptitudes corresponding to the functions of the body and soul in a man. "One is the Incarnate Nature of the Divine Word," the watchword both of Apollinaris and Cyril. This was too much like Gnosticism and Modalism for the Eastern bishops to accept, but it did strike deep responsive chords in popular piety in Egypt, Asia, and not least in the West. How was Jesus Christ God? How could the man-god, consubstantial with God, be regarded as having been born, suffering and dying? There is little doubt that the great majority of the Egyptian and Asian Christians simply thought that in some way the Word of God died on the Cross and had been resurrected for man's salvation. Indeed, in an age when the physical terrors of the world beyond were a dominating fact in men's lives, and the Eucharist of Christ's body and blood regarded as an antidote to the corruption of death, these ideas seemed reasonable enough.

In Alexandria, there is reason to believe now from the discovery of the text of Didymus the Blind's *Commentary on the Psalms* written circa 390, that the question of Christ's nature was already being discussed a generation before Nestorius appeared on the scene.[5] Cyril's views also had been quite consistent. In his Paschal homily for 421 he had attacked those "who divide the One Christ." The Word "was made flesh but not transformed into flesh."[6] How this came about was incomprehensible, but it was necessary to believe that by the union the Word made the flesh to be "his one temple." The connection between this metaphysic and human salvation was evident enough. As Professor Henry Chadwick has pointed out, throughout Cyril's exegetical and polemical writings was the theme that "in the Eucharist we receive the flesh of Christ, the selfsame body that he took from Mary." The body of life which we receive was like a "life-giving seal" within us making us deathless and incorruptible.[7] Many of Cyril's ideas were taken directly from Apollinarian writings circulating under the names of orthodox leaders such as Athanasius and Pope Julius but this made no difference. He spoke for the native Christian of his own province and Asia against a background of longstanding Modalist tradition, and he could be sure of the support of Rome.

The Antiochene view was more difficult to justify. It had been elaborated in opposition to Apollinarianism near the turn of the fifth century by Diodore of Tarsus (died 394) and his pupil Theodore of Mopsuestia (in Cilicia). Their views were grounded in the New Testament from which they derived a clear perception of the human nature of the Lord. Jesus Christ really went through the normal experiences which man must live. He was a true man. But his sonship to God meant that God dwelt in him to a unique degree, indissolubly united with him, and enabling him to offer a perfect pattern of virtue and redemption to humanity. But despite all, the Antiochenes thought of Christ "in two Persons" or "*hypostases*" (individualities) whose union must be conceived more as a conjunction of opposites (i.e., God and man) brought about by a harmonization of wills, rather than a union of essences as taught by the Alexandrians. Their beliefs were recognizably akin to those of Paul of Samosata, and this was not lost on their opponents. In the last resort the Antiochene Christ redeemed through his baptism and self-sacrifice on the Cross, "drawing all men unto him," the Alexandrian through the death-destroying power of the divine elements in the Eucharist.

Theodore of Mopsuestia had died in 428 in the peace of the Church and at the height of his reputation as a scholar and bishop. Indeed, but for the personality of Nestorius the two systems might have continued to be held without conflict in Egypt and Syria respectively. Nestorius, however, was as tactless and headstrong as John Chrysostom had been. No sooner had he been enthroned than he started a drive against heretics in the capital. This may have been correct in theory, but those whom he struck, the Arians, the Novatianists and Macedonians, were respected groups in Constantinople and capable of making trouble for the new archbishop. Moreover, when one of the Arian churches was being burned down, the flames spread to neighboring houses in the poorer quarter of the city. Nestorius was an enemy of the poor it was said.[8] Then, had he known it, the debate on the expression "Mother of God" had been going on a long time. In the early centuries, the martyrs had been regarded as the mediators between God and the faithful at the Day of Judgment. Now, with the ending of persecutions, the Virgin Mary had been accepted more and more in that role.[9] If Christ was God, was she not his mother, and able to intercede with him as he sat in judgment? "Mother of God" was an expression which came easily to pious lips. Nestorius objected. It seemed absurd to him. The Virgin was the mother of Jesus Christ, not of the divine Word. "Let no one call Mary *Theotokos*: for Mary was but a woman, and it is impossible that God should be born of a woman," declared his representative, the Syrian priest, Anastasius.[10] The most he would allow was that she was *Christotokos* (bearer of Christ) not *Theotokos* (bearer of God). Feelings were roused. The monks and the crowd were stirred. Already the name of the monk Eutyches was being heard in the capital as the representative of true religion.

Nestorius, however, had the favor of the court, unlike John Chrysostom, and could still have avoided trouble but for two further errors. First, he gave shelter to prominent Pelagians including Julian of Eclanum who had been deposed from their bishoprics some years before by the Pope and had emigrated to the Eastern capital. The patronage may not have been accidental, for looked at logically there was a connection between the Antiochene doctrine of Christ and the Pelagian doctrine of man. Both stressed the part played by the will in the divine scheme of sanctification and redemption, and of the role of Jesus Christ as the pattern and example for man to follow.[11] This was the aspect of Nestorianism which aroused the ire of Pope Celestine (422–32) and placed him firmly on Cyril's side.

Meantime, Nestorius was playing into the latter's hands by a second piece of folly, namely interesting himself on behalf of some Alexandrian clergy whom Cyril had deprived. Cyril's reaction when he heard that Nestorius was opening proceedings on their behalf was characteristic. Councils sometimes had different results from those expected by the people who summoned them. If Nestorius thought he was going to try him he would soon find the roles reversed—especially if he could prove Nestorius to be an heretic.[12] The years 429 and 430 were spent in the maneuverings of the rival parties. Cyril first of all sought to attack Nestorius indirectly by means of a lengthy defense of the title of *Theotokos* addressed nominally to his own monkish dissidents at Nitria, but made sure that a copy reached Constantinople. Nestorius replied. He also sent Nestorius a long and not altogether discourteous letter setting out his views, namely that Jesus was "One Christ and Lord, not as worshipping a man conjointly with the Word . . . but as worshipping one and the same person."[13] Then came Nestorius's intervention on behalf of the rebellious Alexandrine clergy in the capital, to which Cyril made a masterly reply. Pope Celestine was already angered at Nestorius's attitude toward the Pelagian refugees, and from his agent in the capital, Marius Mercator,[14] had received alarming accounts of Nestorius's doctrines. Thus, when a letter from Cyril complete with a Latin translation arrived toward the middle of 430 requesting in deferential terms his assistance in defending the East against Nestorius's unsound opinions he was only too willing to comply. A council held in Rome in August 430 declared Nestorius's teaching impossible, the various excommunications pronounced by him void, and demanded that he must either mend his ways or resign. Cyril was commissioned to act as Celestine's representative to see that this sentence was carried out.

A less wise sentence designed to exacerbate an already strained situation would be difficult to imagine. Celestine had shown neither theological nor worldly wisdom. This was left to Theodosius II and his court who rebuked Cyril for stirring up trouble and informed him that a council would now be called to discuss the questions at issue and that he himself must be present. This letter was dated 19 November 430. Meantime, Cyril fortified by Papal authority had given his enthusiasm free rein. While affecting to keep on reasonably good terms with Bishop John of Antioch he was busy winning over Juvenal of Jerusalem, a cunning and ambitious prelate who aimed at carving out a separate territorial patriarchate for himself at the expense of Antioch. Secure in his alliances, on 6 December he wrote to Nestorius acquainting him of Celestine's sentence and inviting him either to anathematize twelve doctrinal propositions or resign.[15]

The Twelve Anathemas showed how far Cyril's ambitions were leading him. The comparative care of the "dogmatic letter" of the previous February was abandoned, and the Christian world was presented with an exaggeration of Alexandrian theology which Cyril now claimed was the theology of the Church universal. Asserting that the Word of God was "hypostatically united with flesh and is one Christ in His own flesh," he invited the condemnation of any definition that made him two persons or two "Hypostases," and also attacked those who claimed that the Scriptures contained some texts as applying to the manhood and others to the divinity of Christ. In so doing, Cyril was condemning both the Antiochenes and the Western view later to be embodied in the Tome of Leo. Celestine, however, was his ally, and as events were to show, Cyril could brush aside the opposition of the Antiochenes. Nestorius meantime had found sympathy with the latter and his own counter-anathemas against Cyril did not show him to be unorthodox.

The test was to come. The council was summoned to meet at Ephesus for Whitsun 431. The onus now lay on Cyril to justify his anathemas which to many appeared to be Apollinarian inspiration. Moreover, having accepted a general council convoked by the Emperor he could no longer fall back on his previous claim to be the Pope's executor against Nestorius. This change of position, however, did not deter him. He had other means of enforcing his will. The Egyptian fleet included fifty bishops, to which were added a motley concourse of lesser clergy, fanatic and untutored monks, including the famous archimandrite Schnoudi of the White Monastery, strong-arm men called *parabolani*,[16] who acted as Cyril's bodyguard, and Egyptian sailors. He arrived at Ephesus in good time, and there he found a staunch ally in Memnon, Bishop of the city. Ephesus was jealous of its independence of Constantinople, but behind this lay the long tradition of Modalism among the Asiatic Christians which found Cyril's doctrines in entire sympathy with their own. The people of Ephesus were to turn the scale in Cyril's favor. To complete the tale of Cyril's allies were fifteen bishops who accompanied Juvenal of Jerusalem. Against this army Nestorius could only count on the Macedonian and other local bishops and clergy, the powerful contingent of Syrians under John of Antioch, and the scrupulous fairness of the imperial commissioner, Count Candidian.

John of Antioch had taken the land route to Ephesus, and as is not unusual in such cases the caravan proceeded more slowly than planned. This factor gave Cyril his chance. Claiming to represent Pope Celestine and as senior prelate present apart from Nestorius, he summoned the council to meet at twenty-four hours' notice on 22 June. Despite the protests of no less than ninety-eight bishops and of Count Candidian, he persisted. Next day 158 bishops met in the Church of the Virgin at Ephesus, Nestorius refused to attend, his theology was condemned as being in conflict with the Creed of Nicaea, and by evening he had been declared deposed as "the new Judas"—the same phrase Cyril had once used against John Chrysostom.

There were scenes of enthusiasm in Ephesus, the crowds demonstrating day and night in favor of Cyril,[17] but four days later on 26 June, John of Antioch arrived and forthwith "without taking off his cloak" held a council in his lodgings at which forty-three bishops were present. Cyril and Memnon of Ephesus were declared deposed for their disorderly proceedings and heterodoxy. Count Candidian had given his approbation to John's council, but riots continued in the city. On 29 June Theodosius II sent a rescript forbidding the protagonists to leave Ephesus and announcing the dispatch of another Imperial Commissioner. Meantime, however, the Papal Legates had landed at Ephesus and their weight was thrown into Cyril's scale. Cyril proceeded to set aside the decisions of John's council (10 and 11 July) and rewarded his supporters such as Juvenal of Jerusalem, though not to the extent anticipated by the latter.[18] Meantime, the wealth of the See of Alexandria was being used to good effect at court, and when at last the Emperor bestirred himself to end the undignified wrangles, those around him had been well primed with Cyril's case. In September he received the deputies of both sides at Chalcedon, and ordered the restoration of Cyril and Memnon. The term *Theotokos* the starting point of the controversy was accepted as orthodox. Cyril's Twelve Anathemas were not condemned and Nestorius returned to his old monastery of Euprepius near Antioch.

Cyril had won. Nestorius had fallen but few were deceived by his methods. One of the most influential monastic leaders Isidore of Pelusium wrote frankly, "A number of those who have been at Ephesus represent you as a man burning to avenge a personal injury, not to seek in right teaching the glory of Jesus Christ. He is, they say, the nephew of Theophilus."[19] Even in Egypt it was now regarded as discreditable to have removed John "the Saint, the Friend of God."

Whether because he realized the weakness of his position or because he wanted to divide the Syrians, Cyril set about healing the breach with John. The "formula of Union," however, which was agreed in 433 through the intermediary of Paul of Emesa was far from being another victory. John of Antioch accepted Nestorius's deposition, the term *Theotokos* and the "union of the two natures" in Christ, rather than their "conjunction." But Cyril was obliged to accept the concept of "the two natures," and not even their "unconfused union" could make this palatable to the more intransigent of the Egyptian clergy.[20] The seeds had been sown for the Monophysite schism of twenty years later.

FURTHER READING

The best account of this long and turgid period is still to be found in L.Duchesne, 'The Downfall of Nestorius', in *The Early History of the Christian Church*, John Murray 1901-1922, Vol.3, 219-71

Baynes, N.H., 'Alexandria and Constantinople. A Study in Ecclesiastical Diplomacy', in *Byzantine Studies and Other Essays*, Athlone Press 1955

Bethune-Baker, J.H., *Nestorius and his Teaching*, Cambridge University Press 1908

Chadwick, H., 'Eucharist and Christology in the Nestorian Controversy', *Journal of Theological Studies* NS 2, 1951, 145-64

Driver, G.R. and Hodgson, L., *The Bazaar of Heracleides*, London 1925 (Nestorius' account of his own position, written from exile)

Grant, R.M., *Early Christianity and Society*, Harper and Row 1977

Greer, R.A., *Theodore of Mopsuestia: Exegete and Theologian*, Faith Press 1961

Grillmeier, A., *Christ in Christian Tradition*, Mowbrays [2]1975

Loofs, F., *Nestorius*, Cambridge University Press 1914

Sellers, R.V., *Two Ancient Christologies*, SPCK 1940

For the documents, especially Cyril's Letters and the Formula of Union, see T.H.Bindley, *The Oecumenical Documents of the Faith*, Methuen 1950, 97-156

20

The Development of the
Papacy from Damasus to Celestine
378–440

At Ephesus Pope Celestine had played an important, if not a decisive role in the downfall of Nestorius. Without papal backing Cyril would have been unable to assume the presidency of the council where at least nominally he shared with his opponent the position of defendant. Moreover, the arrival of the papal legates early in July 431 had much the same effect on the situation as that of Blücher at Waterloo. They transformed a hard-fought success into a decisive victory. In this short chapter we trace how the See of Rome had gained influence in the previous half-century, and how the rest of Christendom regarded its ever-increasing claims.

Damasus (366–84) was under no illusions about the dignity of his position as the heir to St. Peter. While his attempts to intervene in the affairs of the Church of Antioch were being politely rebuffed, two important steps were taken near the end of his long reign to consolidate the authority of the Roman See in the West. First, toward the end of 378 during the interregnum between the death of Valens and Gratian's summons of Theodosius, Damasus held an important meeting of his suffragan bishops and the Roman presbyters. For the previous twelve years charges of murder arising out of the riots which accompanied his election had hung over him. He had faced trial before Valentinian I. Now the council formally pronounced him guiltless, and in order to prevent their bishop being subject to ordinary civil jurisdiction in the future, petitioned Gratian for his exemption from this jurisdiction. In addition, it asked for the formalization of the Pope's right to hear the appeal of a bishop over the head of his metropolitan, and finally, for the cooperation of the civil power in carrying out a papal sentence against a suffragan bishop. Partly this was due simply to the need of maintaining discipline among the latter, but partly it was the natural result of the vacuum in the supreme authority over Church affairs in the West. There, what the Emperor decided was not necessarily a canon, and though Gratian avoided granting the judicial immunities asked on behalf of the Roman bishop, his appellate jurisdiction so far as his suffragans were concerned was recognized.

Four years later, in 382, an even more important council was summoned perhaps in reply to the canons of the second Ecumenical Council. At this, Damasus seems to have claimed formally the possession of "a primacy over all other churches in virtue not of conciliar decisions, but of the Lord's promise to St. Peter, i.e., the *Tu es Petrus*. For its foundation both he and St. Paul were together responsible."[1] The precedence of the other great Sees was determined by their connection with Peter— and Constantinople had none.

Damasus died in December 384 having reinforced the position of the Roman See in the West by the momentous step of initiating the translation of the Hebrew Scriptures into Latin and entrusting the work to Jerome. The Vulgate was to become one of the pillars of the Roman primacy. His successor Siricius (384–99) consolidated the ground won in the previous six years. In his pontificate we find the Pope not only hearing appeals, but beginning to take the initiative in settling disputes. "We dare not keep silence when scandal arises," he wrote, "for the Prophet says 'Lift up your voice like a trumpet.' "[2] In a letter to the Gallic clergy he instructed, "Therefore let the offenders put the matter right in synod, and remove those on whom the [clerical] status has unfittingly been conferred; else let us be informed of their names that we may know from whom we must withhold communion."[3]

As Jalland points out, the old language of "appeal" had given way to a new phraseology of "menace."[4] In other writings of this period the papacy was already beginning to speak to its suffragans in terms reminiscent of an imperial edict. The authority of Peter was outstaying the feeble authority of the Emperor. The reigns of Innocent I (402–17) and Boniface I (418–22) provide other instances of the same language. The crises of the Church in the East were judged less on their merits than according to which of the contestants appeared to be in agreement with the "tradition of Peter." In fact, this proved to be more often Alexandria where "Mark, Peter's disciple and evangelist" had taught, than Constantinople which could boast no such claims. Thus, the formula of Union between Alexandria and Antioch was greeted by Xystus III (432–40) in what might be termed in lesser men an egotistical spirit. "You have learnt," he wrote of John of Antioch, "by the outcome of this affair what it means to be like-minded with us. The blessed Apostle Peter had handed down in his successors that which he received. Who could wish to be parted from the doctrine of that Apostle whom the Master Himself instructed first before the rest."[5] The authority of Peter confronted that of the Emperor, and it is noticeable that by this time it is no longer the joint apostleship and martyrdom of Peter and Paul that is being invoked, but that of the chief of the Apostles only. It was but a short step from the claims of the popes of the early fifth century to the sonorous assertions of Leo.

The Papacy had laid claim sporadically to the primacy of Christendom in earlier centuries, but these claims had either been denied or ignored by those to whom they had been addressed. The same was by and large to be true in the first half of the fifth century. With the Eastern provinces the test came over the allegiance of the bishops in Eastern Illyricum. This was the prefecture which Theodosius formed after being called to be Emperor in order to defend the Danube against the Visigoths, and consisted of what today is most of Jugoslavia, Albania and Greece, with the city of Thessalonica (Salonica) as its principal administrative and ecclesiastical center. In 381 Bishop Acholius had been Damasus's trusted agent and his dependence on the See of Rome was an accepted fact. Pope Siricius took this as a basis for delegating powers as "vicar" to Acholius's successor. This arrangement was not, however, accepted in Constantinople, and the Patriarch Atticus, John Chrysostom's successor, set himself against papal control of the episcopate of the prefecture. In this he had the full backing of the court until in 421 Theodosius II issued an instruction that disputes arising among the churches of the Illyrian prefecture were to be referred to Constantinople on the grounds that the city enjoyed "the privileges of ancient Rome."[6] Pope Boniface protested, but the assertion that the claims of the See of Rome rested on the Dominical commission contained in Matthew 16:18 fell on deaf ears. In subsequent years papal influence on this important cultural and linguistic bridge between East and West declined still further. The Latin "vicariate" of Thessalonica disappeared in all but name.

In Africa the attitude of both Donatists and Catholics toward the Roman See was ambivalent. The Donatists, to be sure, made the point of always maintaining contact with the See of the Apostles. Their objective in sending one of their leaders, Victor of Garba, to Rome in 314, was to see a bishop there who was unspotted by the crime of *traditio,* and with whom therefore they might remain in communion. A regular succession of bishops followed Victor in opposition to the popes for another century. Moreover, in no Western country was the cult of the Apostles so assiduously observed as in North Africa, and most of these *memoriae Apostolorum* (shrines in honor of the Apostles) appear to be Donatist.[7] Yet with all their emphasis on contact with the See of Rome, there is no indication that the individual holders were credited with jurisdictional rights. At the Conference of Carthage in 411, the Donatist Bishop of Rome, Felix, signed the memorandum of his Church embodying their case against the Catholics, after the Bishop of Carthage and Primate of Numidia.[8] Respect for Rome was due to respect for Peter and Paul as martyrs, the pillars of their own "evangelical" Church of the Martyrs.

The Catholics were more positive, Optatus of Milevis regarding Siricius as the ally of his Church, and the successor of Peter the "head of all the Apostles." But for them, too, it was a question of precedence, of Rome symbolizing the Church as a whole without regard to her jurisdictional and appellate claims. For Augustine, too, rejected the idea that "the power of the keys" had been entrusted to Peter alone. His primacy was simply a matter of personal privilege and not an office. Similarly, he never reproached the Donatists for not being in communion with Rome, but with lack of communion with the apostolic Sees as a whole. His view of Church government was that less important questions should be settled by provincial councils, greater matters at general councils.[9] When in 401 an African council concerned with the feasibility of ordaining former Donatists to the priesthood considered that further advice must be sought, a letter was sent jointly to Rome and Milan.[10] Pelagius's condemnation by Rome merely confirmed previous African decisions against him. Like some other obiter dicta, the famous *Roma locuta est causa finita est* was a fine sentence, but only the last three words were said by Augustine!

The African Church, whether Donatist or Catholic, was jealous of its independence. Between 417 and 423 Roman attempts to interfere in African doctrinal and disciplinary decisions were repulsed. The short pontificate of Zosimus (March 417–December 418) was a chapter of accidents for the papacy which illustrates clearly the gulf which separated papal claims from the current practice of the African Church.

What Augustine had really said in his Sermon was, "In regard to this matter (the excommunication of Pelagius and Celestius) two councils have been referred to the Apostolic See: the replies have arrived. The case is ended, may the same be equally true of the error."[11] He was mistaken. Pope Innocent's letters were dated 27 January 417. Within two months he was dead. His successor, Zosimus, whatever his background may have been,[21] was entirely untrained in theology. It was not long before both Pelagius and Celestius had found support among the Roman clergy (including it appears the future Pope Xystus) and a Roman council was manifesting its joy at the orthodoxy of their statements. Naturally, the Africans were furious. The Bishop of Carthage, Aurelius, remonstrated, secured from Zosimus an undertaking not to come to any final decision without consultation with the African bishops, and summoning an impressive council of 214 bishops on 1 May 418 reaffirmed the African view of Original sin and the need for Grace. Harassed also by an order from Ravenna banning Celestius from Rome as a fomentor of disorders Zosimus surrendered.[13] Pelagius and Celestius were soon on their way East once more.

The disciplinary questions were even more grotesque. Zosimus seems to have accepted the appeal of a worthless cleric named Apiarius against his bishop out of something akin to spite, sending the man back to Carthage accompanied by no less than three papal legates, the strength usually reserved for a papal representation at an ecumenical council. They got nowhere. Aurelius's council of 407 had banned appeals overseas by African clergy and was not impressed by quotations from canons claimed to be Nicene but which in fact were Sardican. All they knew was that the Donatists were in the habit of quoting Sardica at them to prove their communion with Eastern Christendom. Meantime, Zosimus died on 27 December 418, a schism had broken out in Rome, and the legates were left to kick their heels in Carthage. Eventually, Apiarius confessed to crimes of such a degree that excommunication was the only course. The legates retired discomfited. This time it fell to the Africans to rebuke the pride of the Roman See. "Do not send clerics of your own, at anyone's request," they wrote, "to execute orders of your own, lest the billowy pride of the world appears to penetrate the Church of Christ."[14] Basil of Caesarea had not been the only one to complain of Rome on this score. In another case a young priest of Augustine's who had been made a bishop of a former Donatist center behaved in a manner such as to warrant his removal. Like Apiarius he appealed to Rome, and now Rome used the threat of the secular arm to enforce his restoration.[15] This time Augustine threatened to resign his See if such a thing happened, and once again the papacy (in this case, Pope Boniface I, 418–22) climbed down.

Such was the practical implementation of the papal claims. In both East and West the decision of a council rather than the fiat of the Pope was the supreme instance of Church government. Against the Africans led by men like Augustine and Aurelius the popes were powerless. In the East they were confronted by a theory of Church government which had a place for episcopal authority, but none for Roman Primacy. "Since when do the Orientals accept dictates from the West?" the question addressed to Pope Julius still had its relevance. Even at this stage divergent theories of Church government were beginning to emerge, the conciliar, the imperial, and the papal, represented by Africa, Constantinople and Rome respectively. The issues between them remain to be settled.

FURTHER READING

Dvornik, F., *Byzantium and the Roman Primacy*, Fordham University Press 1979
Jalland, T.G., *The Church and the Papacy*, SPCK 1944, ch.2
Kidd, B.J., *The Roman Primacy*, SPCK 1936

21

Leo and Chalcedon
440–61

Pope Xystus III died in August 440 and was succeeded by Leo I. The
latter was an Italian from Volterra in Tuscany, and from an early age
had shown his interest in theological questions. He evidently rose rapidly
in the hierarchy of the Roman Church, for by 430 he was already a senior
deacon and the authority to whom the organizer of monasticism in southern Gaul, John Cassian, addressed a tract against Nestorius. When Xystus
was elected Leo remained his theological adviser and appears to have
used his influence to prevent any weakness being shown toward the
remaining members of the Pelagian party, including Augustine's old opponent, Julian of Eclanum. He was on a mission in Gaul when he was recalled to succeed Xystus. This was the man, able administrator, experienced cleric and rigidly orthodox who was to become Bishop of Rome
for twenty-one years.[1]

If there was one guiding principle in his work it was to safeguard and
uphold the privileges of his See. These he regarded as a sacred trust to
be jealously guarded above all else. What his predecessors had claimed
in response to different situations he systematized and formulated in
terms which have persisted down to our own day. For him Peter had
been "the Rock" on which the Church was founded, and the ever-living
guide of its fortunes. His successors were merely his temporary personal
representatives, but while they held their office the leadership of the
Church throughout the world was theirs. Theirs alike were the initiative,
the executive power and the ultimate decision on matters of doctrine. All
bishops held their authority merely as participants in the responsibility
given once and for all by the Lord to Peter.[2]

Two statements made in Leo's early years as bishop illustrate his view.
Thus he writes, "Moreover, because our care extends throughout all the
Churches since the Lord demands this of us, who entrusted to the most
blessed Apostle Peter the primacy of apostolic honor in reward for his

faith, establishing the universal Church on his firmness as a foundation, we share the duty of responsibility with those who are joined to us in love with the whole fraternity."³ Again, to justify his intervention in the affairs of the churches in Sicily and to uphold his right to overrule a local ecclesiastical custom, he asserts that he was bound to do so "to avoid the danger of sloth: lest the profession of the Chief Apostle, by which he bore witness that he was a lover of the Lord, be not found in us."⁴ It was the same sense of authority that led him into conflict with Hilary of Arles in 445 whom he stripped of metropolitan authority over the bishops even in the province in which Arles stood, on flimsy grounds. Moreover, the Western Emperor Valentinian III (425–55) instructed the military commander in Gaul, the famous Aetius, that "the primacy of the Apostolic See as appropriate to St. Peter" must be observed.⁵ Fortified by this authority, and undisputed master of the Church in the Western provinces, Leo was prepared to intervene with full force in the crisis which was now brewing in the East.

Cyril of Alexandria had died in June 444, and his successor the archdeacon Dioscoros was altogether a man of lesser caliber. Just as the arrival of the limited and violent Primian provoked a crisis in the Donatist Church in Africa, so the election of the equally turbulent Dioscoros was to have a similar result in Alexandria. Basically the problems at issue in the next few years were a continuation of those debated at Ephesus in 431, and some even of the participants in that drama were still alive. Theodosius II was in his mid-forties, Eutyches the monk of Constantinople was now a venerable archimandrite, and Nestorius, the hated Nestorius, in exile in the Kharga oasis in the Nubian desert.

Dioscoros has been justly termed one of the "violent men" in the history of the early Church.⁶ To his arch-opponent Leo he was "the Egyptian plunderer" and "preacher of the Devil's errors," but to Palestinians and Egyptians, even to so reasonable a man as Severus of Antioch (467–538) he was "an apostolic preacher and true martyr," the man who had "refused to bow the knee to Baal in the assembly of schism" (i.e., the Council of Chalcedon). The evidence shows that he was overwhelmingly ambitious and that he was harsh and cruel in his methods like previous Alexandrian patriarchs. He meant to blot out "Nestorianism" forever and in the process to humble the rival Sees of Antioch and Constantinople. But what marked him off from Cyril was his supreme self-confidence in the power of Alexandria alone. His excommunication of Leo on the eve of Chalcedon without any sort of formal synod was an act of breathtaking audacity which only complete success in the ensuing meeting could have justified. In the event, the tables were turned against him, and he trod the same path of deposition and exile that he had prepared for his opponents. It is doubtful whether he was a heretic in the sense of Apollinarianism. His declaration "no man shall say that the holy flesh which Our Lord took from the Virgin Mary by the operation of the Holy Spirit, in a manner which he himself knows was different from or foreign to our body," would appear to fall within the terms of the formula of Re-union.[7] Jesus Christ was constituted "out of two natures," Godhead and manhood, and each element remained a reality in the subsequent union. The real problem which confronted Dioscoros as well as his predecessors was how to avoid the purely Docetic theology of Manichaeism which was a formidable threat in Egypt and at the same time uphold the traditional popular and monastic theology. It was only a hair's breadth that divided the theologies of Cyril and Dioscoros at the grand climax of Chalcedon, but Cyril had been the cleverer man.

Meantime, Christendom had been turned upside down. Unlike Cyril, Dioscoros had directed his first attack against Antioch. In this great ecclesiastical territory which included the bishoprics on Rome's Euphrates frontier, as well as Syria, the decade which followed the signature of the formula of Re-union had been extremely fruitful. Bishop John of Antioch had been succeeded by his vigorous nephew Domnus, the city of Edessa where there was a celebrated Christian school had as its bishop Ibas, a Syriac scholar and disciple of Theodore and Diodore, and in Theodoret, Bishop of Cyrrhus, the Antiochenes had a leader who combined great pastoral gifts with historical learning and theological insight. Unfortunately for them, the balance of influence in Constantinople had been shifting in a direction favorable to Alexandrian theology. In the Ephesus crisis, Theodosius II had supported Nestorius as long as he could, but since 441 the influence of his strong-willed sister, Pulcheria, had been replaced by that of the eunuch and Grand Chamberlain, Chrysaphius. Their favorite theologian was the archimandrite Eutyches. Eutyches was a crafty and experienced theologian who concealed a litigious mind under a cloak of monastic humility. In 431 he had been anti-Nestorian, and had gradually moved to a position where he not only accepted the Anathemas of Cyril, that is the "natural union" and the one nature of the incarnate Word, but seems to have denied, what Cyril tried to avoid doing, that the humanity of Christ was like our humanity.

The results of such a doctrine, as Theodoret of Cyrrhus at once realized, would have been to deprive humanity of solidarity with Jesus Christ. His resurrection would have been that of a God and therefore no pattern for the resurrection of mankind. Similarly, his life and ministry would have had no bearing on man's salvation. A divine messenger from another world was the Manichaean but not the Christian Christ. None the less, secure in imperial favor Eutyches had flourished, until Flavian who had become Patriarch of Constantinople in 446 began to examine various statements attributed to him.

Meantime, Dioscoros had begun his attack on the Antiochenes, and on 16 February 448 Theodosius signed an order proscribing the works of Porphyry (the anti-Christian writer of the third century), and Nestorius, and all works not in conformity with the Faith set forth at Nicaea and Ephesus and interpreted by Cyril of blessed memory.[8] Dioscoros's agents meantime unleashed popular agitation against Ibas and Theodoret in their own dioceses.

Such was the position in the autumn of 448 when Flavian at last began his formal examination of the propositions upheld by Eutyches.[9] The Patriarch was essentially a moderate and would have let sleeping dogs lie, but confronted by an accusation leveled against Eutyches by a fanatic for the middle of the road, Eusebius of Dorylaeum, he was obliged to take action. In doing so, he found himself the victim of a craftily laid trap. Eutyches eventually presented himself for examination on 22 November 448, assured of the support of Chrysaphius and other powerful members of the court. Some of the latter, for reasons which remain obscure, seem to have been determined to play the Alexandrian game against their own Patriarch. While the latter showed himself anxious to get from Eutyches an avowal that Jesus' humanity was our humanity and not some incomprehensible divine humanity embodied in his one nature, the Patrician Florentius, who took a leading part in the discussion, insisted on finding out what Eutyches in fact believed. He knew that his rejection of the two natures would assure his condemnation, but equally surely his appeal to a higher court which Dioscoros and the Alexandrians would dominate would be successful. Once more, Alexandria would turn the tables on Constantinople.

This is what happened. "Two natures before the union, only one after it." What did Eutyches mean by that? Surely the opposite was true, for after the Incarnation there must be both divine and human nature. Eutyches was prepared to say what Flavian wanted him to say, but not to condemn "his Fathers," i.e., the Alexandrians. He was therefore deposed and excommunicated. With considerable rapidity however, Theodosius and the court decided that the issue must be settled by a council, which was to be convened at Ephesus on 1 August 449. Leo received his summons by about 12 May, and during the next month he composed an extremely important document in the form of a letter to Flavian. This was the famous *Tome* of Leo.[10] For the first time a bishop of Rome, knowing only Latin, had ventured into theological disputes whose terminology was exclusively Greek.

The *Tome* was an able document, the product of a clear mind which knew the tradition of the West and was prepared to state it authoritatively. Leo, like Flavian, stood on the firm ground of the formula of Re-union, and rejected the views of Eutyches and his Alexandrian supporters. He affirmed on the basis of Scripture and Creed the reality of the two natures but avoided the obvious mistakes of the Nestorians. "The property or distinctive character then of each nature and substance remaining entire, and coalescing into one person, humility was assumed by majesty, weakness by might, eternity by mortality . . . Very God therefore was born in the entire and perfect nature of very man, whole in his own nature, whole in ours." Each nature in union with the other performed the actions which were proper to it. "To hunger, thirst and to sleep were manifestly human, but the satisfaction of the five thousand with five loaves and walking on the sea were manifestly divine." In Jesus neither true manhood nor true Godhead could exist without the other. This *communicatio idiomatum* prevented Leo accepting the Nestorian notion of dividing Christ into "two Sons," by "making his flesh one thing and his Godhead another." It also enabled him to condemn Eutyches, and in a characteristic piece of Leonine prose he expressed surprise that "his so absurd and so perverse a profession (two natures before the union, and one after) met with no rebuke from the judges, and that a sentence so extremely foolish and blasphemous was allowed to pass without notice as though nothing offensive had been heard."[11] It was a masterly expression of the Roman view.

Leo, however, was far from the scene of action, and meantime Eutyches was speeding his triumphal way to Ephesus. There, 130 bishops were assembling, but the vast majority were favorable to Dioscoros and Eutyches. Dioscoros, too, had his army of monks and *parabolani* at hand and they were assisted by other monks from the Syrian desert who hated Ibas and Theodoret. Antioch was never able to present the same united front as the Pharaoh of Alexandria. In addition, the Roman delegation had been weakened by the death of one of the legates en route, and the Bishop of Puteoli arrived supported by two Roman clerics only. Flavian was also there, but as in the past, the Patriarch of Constantinople had no large contingent of suffragans on whom he could rely.

The meeting which opened on 8 August in the Cathedral Church of Ephesus was marked by scenes incredible in themselves and unparalleled in the history of the early Church.[12] Dioscoros presided, and saw to it that only documents favorable to his own cause were read. The *Tome* was not among these. In vain the legates protested. The imperial letters had precedence. They must be read first. The imperial court wanted Eutyches rehabilitated and this was speedily done. Shouts of rage began to echo against those who adhered to the two natures. "Burn him alive. Cut him in two this man who divides the Christ," they shouted at Eusebius of Dorylaeum. At the mention of Ibas's name, there were cries of "Satan and his son to the fire, both together." Hysterical anger mounted against Flavian and the legates. Dioscoros maintained that the two natures infringed the Creed of Nicaea and demanded that all present should state their view and attach their signature whether or not Eusebius and Flavian should be deposed accordingly. Wild scenes followed. "Where are the Counts?" cried Dioscoros. The imperial commissioners came in. Reluctant bishops were forced to sign their assent to Flavian's deposition amid the urging of soldiers and the vociferations of monks. The Roman deacon, Hilary, shouted "*Contradicitur*" and disappeared. Flavian was less fortunate. He was shamefully manhandled by Egyptian clerics and died shortly afterward. In the end, not only he, but Domnus of Antioch, Ibas of Edessa, Theodoret of Cyrrhus and all suspected of "Nestorianism" had been deposed. The Faith of Dioscoros and Eutyches had been proclaimed the Faith of Christendom.

For the moment Leo had met his match. Against an alliance of the imperial court and the See of Alexandria he was powerless. He could only fulminate against the *Latrocinium* (Council of Robbers) from a distance. Permanent schism between East and West became a serious possibility, when the wheel of fate turned once more. On 28 July 450 Theodosius II died as the result of a fall from his horse.

The new regime, that of Pulcheria and the elderly soldier-statesman Marcian who ruled from 450-7, was much more favorable to Leo. It was realized that matters could not be left as they were, and in the summer of 451 the joint rulers summoned a council to be truly representative at least of Eastern Christendom and to meet at Chalcedon in October of that year.

The result was the largest gathering of bishops ever held. As many as 520 were present. Even so all were Easterners except the four papal legates. This time, however, they had the whip hand, for it was decided that they had the right to speak first in the debate. Chrysaphius meantime had fallen, and the officers of the new regime were loyal to the views of Pulcheria and Marcian. They drew up the agenda and drafted the motions which the assembly should decide. Dioscoros was to be given a taste of his own medicine.

He was not yet beaten. The Council met on 8 October in the church of St. Euphemia across the Bosporus from Constantinople. The imperial officers were seated before the chancel in front of the altar and the bishops seated on their right and left. Paschasinus, Bishop of Libybaeum and papal legate, sat in the place of honor on the left supported by Anatolius the new patriarch of the capital. On the right were Dioscoros, Juvenal of Jerusalem and the bishops of Illyricum. This time Dioscoros was not to have his own way. Though catcalls of "Jew," "insulter of Christ," and "fighter against God" greeted Theodoret of Cyrrhus when he entered, they were quickly quelled. Dioscoros was ordered to be seated in the midst of the assembly as an accused person, and pressure began to mount against his supporters. The Acts of Second Ephesus were read. Bishops blushed with shame when in the cold language of the text they heard how they had lent themselves to a travesty. Some protested their innocence; others asked for pardon. Then came Flavian's doctrinal statement in which he had condemned Eutyches at the synod of the clergy of the capital in November 448. Bishops were asked whether they thought it orthodox. Psychological pressure now prevailed. Juvenal of Jerusalem and his fifteen Palestinian bishops "crossed the floor of the House" and took up their positions on the left with the legates. They were followed by lesser fry: even four of the Egyptian bishops joined them. Dioscoros, to his credit, refused to yield. He remained "the valiant Dioscoros." His bearing on this occasion ensured that Egypt would go its own way.

By evening he and five other bishops had been deposed and Eutyches once more condemned. The next four sessions of the Council between 10th and 22nd October were occupied by consideration of a definitive symbol of Faith. The *Tome* of Leo was read and received with acclamation, but it seems evident that this was not accepted by the bishops without modification. There were objections to the phrase "in two natures," and the Council went into committee to draft its own definition. This, unfortunately, has been lost, but it is evident that there were great heartsearchings whether the phrase "out of two natures" would not be more appropriate. This time the legates objected and ultimately the Chalcedonian definition was compiled which stated that after the Incarnation Christ was in two natures without mixture, change, division or separation.[13] Even so, over 150 bishops found it convenient to be absent when signatures were being appended, and only 350 signed.

So far, all had gone well for Leo. Dioscoros and his followers were on their way into exile, the acts of the Latrocinium had been annulled and the *Tome*, or something very like it, accepted as the definition of the Faith of Christendom. In the ensuing sessions which dealt with administrative matters he was to suffer a serious check. Not merely was the ambitious and unscrupulous Juvenal rewarded by Jerusalem being elevated into a fifth Patriarchate, but the Council clearly intended to rid Constantinople of all fear of yet another attack by the Pharaohs of Egypt. By Canon 28 not only were the decisions in favor of Constantinople as New Rome ratified, but its patriarchal jurisdiction extended into Thrace on the one hand, and Asia and Pontus in Asia Minor on the other. The legates were not deceived by the primacy of honor accorded to Rome. They protested loud and long. The Council, however, had decided, and the decision of the Council was superior to the wishes even of the Bishop of Rome.[14]

So ended Chalcedon. The Church was still the Church of the great patriarchates, maintaining an equilibrium in respect of each other, whose differences could be solved not by the edict of one against the other but by a council inspired and directed if no longer presided over by the Emperor. It was a system of Church government opposed to that of the papacy, but one which like its rival has stood the test of time. From Chalcedon the way led to Constance, and thence to the Reformation, and perhaps one might assert, to the World Council of Churches. What then of the doctrinal issues? At least the survivors of earlier encounters believed that a lasting peace had been achieved. In the final weeks of his life Nestorius in his desert exile in Upper Egypt heard rumors of the flight of Dioscoros to avoid deposition and exile. It is the last entry in the *Bazaar of Heracleides* as he called his Memoirs. We do not know whether or not he knew the results of Chalcedon before he died, but he realized that his ideas were in essentials those of Flavian and Leo. "My dearest desire is that God should be blessed in heaven and upon earth. As for Nestorius let him remain anathema."

If then Nestorius came to agree with Leo's *Tome* and, at the same time Cyril was orthodox, had not the whole dispute been unnecessary, the classic example of theological hairsplitting that has disgusted later ages? The answer is, not quite so. On the one hand, the twenty years of controversy had shown that the nature of Christ the redeemer and savior could not be expressed adequately in current philosophical terms. *Physis, prosopon, henosis, synapheia* only led to even greater complications. The old question put by the Neo-Platonist Celsus, how God could come into contact with the material world and yet remain undefiled, was never adequately answered and indeed could not be answered in terms of a philosophy which was not also a soteriology. Cyril and Nestorius represented the alternative positions. Was the compromise of Chalcedon a better solution?

The *Tome* of Leo had been received with acclamation. But was the answer really as simple as Leo supposed? Was it sufficient merely to tell the Greek Fathers to read their Bibles, and after assessing various incidents in Jesus' life, to decide which belonged to his manhood and which to his Godhead, and then by the formula of the *communicatio idiomatum* bridge the two resultant natures into one perfect God and perfect man. It was an able concept, far abler than any previous Western Christology, but in the last resort it robbed Jesus Christ of his individuality as a human being. He became man but not a man. Hence the selection of texts to put on one side or the other of the ledger, as appertaining to manhood and Godhead, was always arbitrary. This Cyril had seen, for to him all the acts of the Savior must be those of a unitary person, God-in-Christ.

The formula "a single Person in two Natures" may have satisfied the exhausted bishops at Chalcedon, but like other ingenious formulas of reunion it was soon to run up against the fanaticism of popular religion. A generation ago, the Conference of Carthage had given the deathblow to Donatism only to witness African Catholicism and Romano-African civilization go down before the bands of Circumcellions. These cared not a whit for formulas that denied their Biblicism and craving for rough-hewn social justice. Now much the same was to happen in Egypt and Palestine. The populace led by the monks rejected Chalcedon. In Jerusalem events akin to a revolution greeted the turncoat Juvenal, and despite the fact that he eventually regained possession of his See, the newly formed Patriarchate of Jerusalem was not to be safe for some years for Orthodoxy. In Egypt the situation was more serious. The tragedy of Proterius, who after having been left behind in Alexandria as Dioscoros's trusted agent, found himself "Chalcedonian" Patriarch of Alexandria, and was savagely murdered by the mob in 457, was warning enough as to the depths of Monophysite religious feeling among the Egyptian masses. To them it seemed that the hated Nestorius had had his revenge. Leo the "dyophysite" was the instigator, anathematizing Nestorius, while canonizing his opinions. Moreover, they had already begun to associate the "Chalcedonian" bishop as the "Imperialist," while the Monophysite bishop was the "true successor" of Cyril.[15] Such were the bitter feelings with which the Monophysite Schism opened. Like Donatism in the West it represented an outlook of religious protest which no formula however cunningly devised could suppress.

Chalcedon, then, ends an epoch. The religious unity of the Eastern Christian world had been sundered. The first attempt by the papacy to secure religious uniformity throughout Christendom had failed. Other tasks occupied Leo's remaining years. These lay mainly in the West, in the famous successful mission that turned Attila back from his invasion of Italy in 452, in upholding the fragments of central authority after the murder of Valentinian III and Gaiseric's sack of Rome in 455, and the destruction of the Manichees in the city of Rome. In what must have seemed the twilight of Latin Christianity he remained serene. Undoubtedly the papacy was providing a rallying point for all who wished to maintain the Latinity of the West. To this extent Leo can be called "the real founder of the medieval papacy." He died on 10 November 461.

FURTHER READING

Bright, W., *The Age of the Fathers*, London 1905, Vol.2

Frend, W.H.C., *The Rise of the Monophysite Movement*, Cambridge University Press [2]1979

Jalland, T.G., *The Life and Times of Saint Leo*, SPCK 1941

Sellers, R.V., *The Council of Chalcedon*, SPCK 1953

Woodward, E.L., *Christianity and Nationalism in the Later Roman Empire*, London 1916

There is useful material in T.G.Jalland, *The Church and the Papacy*, and B.J.Kidd, *The Roman Primacy* (p.224 above).

The documents of the crisis of 449-51 are to be found in T.H.Bindley, *The Oecumenical Documents of the Faith*, SPCK 1950, 168, and in J.Stevenson, *Creeds, Council and Controversies*, revised by W.H.C.Frend, SPCK [2]1989, sections 23-26.

22

Church and People
from Constantine to Leo

We began this outline story by pointing out how by the middle of the fourth century Christianity had become a great popular movement throughout the Mediterranean lands of the Roman Empire. In this final chapter we shall be inquiring how this movement was organized and administered, the sort of men who took office, the careers they were offered, the liturgy they served, and the part played by the laity in the life of the Church.

Constantine's aim had been a magnificently endowed Church served by a clergy drawn from the necessitous (but not too necessitous) classes, a nice balance between wealth and poverty as befitting the "ministers of the supreme God." His object was set out in a directive addressed to Bassus, the Praetorian Prefect of the West in 320 or 326.[1] Clergy should be "persons of slender fortunes," but also people who were not held bound by compulsory municipal services which were the mark of the provincial middle classes. It was an aim impossible to fulfill, for from the period of Diocletian onward provincial society had tended to become increasingly stratified into a compulsory caste system in which peasant, artisan, tradesman, teacher and landowner became fixed into immovable patterns for the benefit of the imperial administrator and tax gatherer. The Church, and to some extent the central administration, provided the only practicable outlets, and once the Church began to acquire a privileged status, the pressure to enter its ministry became irresistible. From 320-6 onward successive emperors sought to prevent decurions (i.e., the town councilors who were responsible for collecting the quota of taxes from their area) on the one hand, and land workers on the other, from finding refuge in Church office. No series of laws in the Theodosian Code show more clearly the dilemma of the authorities when confronted by their duty toward the State on the one hand, and on the other toward the divine power who safeguarded the State.

In the event, the senior clergy of the fourth and fifth centuries represented an extraordinarily varied collection of human experience. At one end of the scale was Ambrose of Milan, a member of an aristocratic Roman household and protégé of Anicius Probus, the richest man in the Roman Empire. At the other was an African bishop like Samsucius, an illiterate who had risen from the rural population. In between came a very fair cross section of the provincial middle classes. Augustine's father had been a decurion, and so Augustine himself would have been liable to recall to the city council of Thagaste. His friend Alypius had also come from the same but slightly wealthier background, and he had managed to migrate to the civil service before entering on Orders. Jerome's parents too were members of the middle classes, and so were those of Basil and his friends in Asia Minor. Petilian of Constantine, the Donatist leader, had been a lawyer, Martin of Tours a soldier, and Epiphanius of Salamis the son of a Jewish farmer in Palestine. Irenaeus of Berytus "the twice-married," who was deposed at the second Council of Ephesus, had been a senior imperial official and had, so to speak, retired into Orders and become a bishop. Synesius of Cyrene, a Platonist philosopher, found himself drafted into the same calling late in life, and Nectarius, patriarch of Constantinople, moved from the Senate to the patriarchate in 381. The Church of the classic age of the Fathers was recruiting its ministry from a varied field which included many of the best minds of the Empire.

The position which the Church occupied in society was an enviable one. Already in 313 Constantine had freed orthodox clergy from obligations to contribute to municipal levies. Though this may have been intended as a relief to clerics "of slender means," it not only put a financial premium on orthodoxy as we have seen, but set a precedent for a long series of grants and privileges in favor of the Church. One of the most important of these was in 321 when the Emperor permitted the Church complete freedom of accepting bequests, and Christians freedom to bequeath to the Church.[2] In addition to this, it became the custom among Christian families to leave a certain proportion of their goods to the Church as a sort of guarantee against the worst in the next world. Basil of Caesarea intimated that the Church should receive the equivalent of a first-born's portion.[3] These measures enabled the Church to amass very considerable wealth during the fourth and fifth centuries. For Rome this was the reality behind the "Donation of Constantine." In Africa, Augustine administered an income belonging to the Church of Hippo amounting to twenty times as much as his father's, that is more than 6000 gold *solidi*.[4] The Church of Ravenna had approximately double this income, while Alexandria, benefiting from not only offerings but from an unofficial linen tax paid by the faithful nominally toward the upkeep of vestments, could disburse up to 1500 lbs. in gold in bribes and still find more in the treasury.[5] Perhaps it was not surprising that in circa 432 Possidius, Augustine's biographer, commenting on the swift success of the Vandals lamented that "the Church was hated because of its lands"[6] and that half a century later the Vandal King Huneric (477–84) regarded Afro-Roman nobles and Catholic priests as more or less synonymous.

Wealth from bequests and grants apart, the Church had gained numerous privileges under Constantine and his sons. The alleviation of an obvious hardship in the form of an obligation to billet soldiers in 343,[7] was followed in 349 by the exemption of clergy and their children from all fiscal burdens in respect of their city.[8] Soon after, the Church was actually granted a share in the general taxes in kind (the *annona*) paid by the provincials,[9] and equated with state officials for the purpose of using the public posting services, which they practically wore out.[10] At Ariminum, though a petition for exemption from all taxation was refused, the Church was to be exempted from all new taxes.[11]

The end of Constantius's reign marked the climax of the alliance in material terms between Church and State. Under Julian most of the privileges were rescinded, and were not renewed by Valentinian I. But sufficient were restored under Theodosius I and his successors for the connection between Church and State to remain close. In Africa, Augustine depended on the great landowners like Celer and Pammachius for the success of his anti-Donatist campaign, and indeed the Donatists were the only force in the West who remained rootedly independent of the State. They retained to the last a theory of social justice grounded on a theology of the Holy Spirit which justified forceful measures against wrong and oppression. Elsewhere the Church seldom took action against oppressors of the poor unless heresy was suspected as well as evil. As Salvian of Marseilles pointed out, in the face of appalling misgovernment, the clergy either said nothing or their words were no more effective than silence.[12] In the East, though the connection between court and Empire was theoretically more binding, the clergy gained a reputation for being just men, generous to the poor and leaders of their communities. Whereas the African Circumcellions were beyond the pale of recognition, the monks who were often equally clamorous in the cause of justice were respected and much heeded members of society.

The clergy too, despite the continuous recruiting of older men from the professions, was tending toward a career and a caste. This was partly due to the ever-increasing complication and proliferation of Church services, and the need therefore of clergy long specialized in the minutiae of the liturgy.

To the traditional Sunday nocturnal vigil and morning "station," each concluded by the Eucharistic liturgy, were now being added Matins, and in St. Basil's monasteries, the offices of Terce, Sext, Nones and Vespers, spaced out so that the religious life became a daily round of work, rest and prayer. The pilgrim Etheria has left a fascinating account of the Vigil and Eucharist on a Sunday in Jerusalem circa 390: "But on the seventh day," she writes, "that is on the Lord's Day, the whole multitude assembles before cockcrow in as great numbers as the place can hold, as at Easter, in the basilica which is near the Anastasis, but outside the doors, where lights are hanging for the purpose. And for fear they should not be there at cockcrow they come beforehand and sit down there. Hymns as well as antiphons are said, and prayers are made between the several hymns and antiphons . . . and as he comes out all approach to his hand."[13]

Such scenes were being reenacted all over the Mediterranean world. It marks a point of transition between the ancient world and the Middle Ages. Other tendencies recognizable in the third century continued to lead in the same direction. As the Church expanded in wealth and numbers, offices and auxiliary duties multiplied. Clerics in a variety of minor Orders were needed. The Bishop of a large See was now a great officer of State, paid 720 *solidi* a year like a provincial governor, and expected as Gregory of Nazianze complained during his short tenure of the See of Constantinople (380-1) "to rival the consuls, the generals, the governors, the most illustrious commanders," to eat well and to dress splendidly.[14] But the work was incessant. He baptized, absolved, preached and excommunicated. He had a host of pastoral duties. He was an administrator, judge, debater, defender of the Faith against rebels and heretics, and sometimes an ambassador and imperial counselor. Ideally the holder of such a position must be one who had already served a long apprenticeship in the Church. In circa 390 Pope Siricius had tried to lay down a sort of *curriculum vitae* for clergy. One started at six as a *lector*, one then proceeded to subdeacon, and after not less than three years as deacon, advanced to the presbyterate. At the age of about forty one could expect to be bishop.[15] Though exceptions were many, the clerical career had become designed to rank *pari passu* with the grades of the imperial civil service, just as the bishoprics were becoming coterminous with civil boundaries. There were two swords: and it was not made easy for the layman of mature years to change to clerical status and scale the heights of a clerical career.

Indeed, the tendency through the fourth and fifth centuries was to diminish the number of church offices which laymen could hold. The African *seniores* remained, in both Catholic and Donatist churches, the outstanding example of the continued employment of laymen as assessors, treasurers and judicial counselors of churches.[16] In some churches in Africa and Italy there were *defensores ecclesiae,* lawyers who were prepared to defend their particular church's interests in the courts. But this was an unusual development, and soon even bailiffs on the estates formed by the papacy and other great Sees would have to be in deacon's orders. So far as the liturgy was concerned, until Ambrose introduced antiphonal singing by the congregation, Church music had been in the hands of professional chanters. The congregation was barred from the altar precincts, and left in no doubt that the days when the Church was where "two or three had gathered together" in the name of Christ had gone forever.

Yet the period between Constantine and Leo can reasonably be called the "age of the laity." It was not merely the enormous interest in theological affairs taken by laymen in this period—an interest which marked a corresponding lack of interest in technical and scientific matters—but the considerable contribution laymen made to the life and thought of the Church. This was the long Indian summer of the ancient world, when standards of education among the wealthy and middle classes were still high, and pessimism had not yet driven the intelligent and sensitive into the refuge of the monastery.

The Emperor, of course, was a layman, and two at least in this period, Constantine in his later years, and Theodosius II were skilled theologians. Their existence was a guarantee against the complete clericalization of the Church. Theodosius II ensured that some order was kept in the bear garden of ecclesiastical politics that was the feature of the period of Nestorius, Cyril and Dioscorus. Ibas was spared from being cut in two for dividing the nature of Christ and Nestorius remitted to oasis-exile instead of to the mercies of Cyril's monks. The great officials of the court were also active theologians. The role of Count Candidian at First Ephesus or the Grand Chamberlain Chrysaphius at the "Robber synod" of Second Ephesus will be remembered, while Augustine's friend, Count Marcellinus, apart from steering the Catholics through the Conference of Carthage in 411, was the first to draw Augustine's attention to the teaching of Pelagius. He himself addressed a number of pertinent questions to him on the subject of Grace and free will.[17]

Further down the social scale the role of the laity was equally varied and important. Two of the most important historians of the Church in the late fourth and early fifth century, Socrates and Sozomen, were civil servants in Constantinople. The father of Biblical exegesis in the West, Tyconius, was a layman in the Donatist Church, and the reliance which that Church placed on instructed lay theologians may be judged from the career of the grammarian Cresconius (circa 400–10) against whose arguments Augustine had to deploy four lengthy tomes. In the Pelagian controversy, the keenest mind on the Pelagian side was that of the lawyer Celestius. The importance, too, of the Christian households in the lives of men such as Augustine and Basil should not be underestimated. A revealing passage from Libanius shows the influence of lay-women in maintaining the hold of Christianity on those who in their hearts would have preferred to return to traditional paganism. "When men are out of doors they listen to your plea," he wrote to Julian, "for the only right course and they come to the altars. But when a man gets home, his wife and her tears and the night plead otherwise and they draw him away from the altars"[18]—an interesting picture not completely without application in our own day.

Finally, the layman contributed enormously to the missionary effort of the Church. The Christianization, both of the kingdoms of Axum (northern Ethiopia) in the mid-fourth century and Ireland in the first half of the fifth century, was due to the work of individuals who had originally beer made captive by the barbarians and then, having gained their masters' trust, converted them. The Christian merchant in this period was the propagator of his Faith as the Moslem merchant has been in more recent centuries.

The Church of the laity, however, was not destined to survive into the Middle Ages. Already by the first quarter of the fifth century the comparative optimism of the era of Theodosius had faded. "The fifth century is a melancholy century," wrote Duchesne.[19] Increasing fear of the approaching End killed independent lay theological thought. The future lay with the cleric and the monk. In every field, military, administrative and religious, the ancient world was shading into the Middle Ages. Within a few years of Leo's death Church and people in the West faced an exclusively barbarian world.

FURTHER READING

Frend, W.H.C, 'The Layman in the Church in the Later Roman Empire', in S.Neill and H.-R.Weber (eds.), *The Layman in the Church*, SCM Press 1961, ch.2

Jones, A.H.M., *The Later Roman Empire 284-602*, University of Oklahoma Press and Blackwell 1964, chs. 22,23

Macmullen, Ramsay, *Christianizing the Roman Empire*, Yale University Press 1986

A Bibliography of
General Works on Church History

Bright, W., *The Age of the Fathers*, London 1903 (two vols.)

Brown, P. *The World of Late Antiquity*, Harcourt, Brace Jovanovich and Thames and Hudson, 1971

Campenhausen, H.von, *Ecclesiastical Authority and Spiritual Power in the Church of the First Three Centuries*, Stanford University Press and A.&C. Black 1969

Carrington, P., *The Early Christian Church*, Cambridge University Press 1957 (two volumes)

Daniélou, J., and Marrou, H.I., *The Christian Centuries*, Darton, Longman and Todd 1964, Vol.1 (many inaccuracies)

Duchesne, L., *The Early History of the Church*, John Murray 1901-22 (3 vols.)

Fliche, A. and Martin, V. (eds.),*Histoire de l'Eglise*

  1. J.Lebreton and J.Zeiller, *L'eglise primitive*, Paris 1934

  2. J.Lebreton and J.Zeiller, *De la fin du IIe siècle à la paix constantinienne*, Paris 1935

  3. J.R.Palanque, G.Bardy and P.de Labriolle, *De la paix constantinienne à la mort de Théodose*, Paris 1936

  4. P.de Labriolle, G.Bardy, L.Bréhier and G.de Plinval, *De la mort de Théodose à l'election de Grégoire le Grand*, Paris 1948

Grant, R.M., *Augustus to Constantine: The Thrust of the Christian Movement into the Roman World*, Harper and Row 1970

Grant, R.M., *Early Christianity and Society*, Collins 1978

Kelly, J.N.D., *Early Christian Doctrines*, Longmans [5]1978

Kidd, B.J., *A History of the Church to A.D.461*, Oxford University Press 1922 (2 vols.)

Lietzmann, H., *A History of the Early Church*, Lutterworth Press 1936-51 (four vols.)

Markus, R.A., *Christianity in the Roman World*, Thames and Hudson 1974 and Scribners 1975

Momigliano, A. (ed.), *The Conflict between Paganism and Christianity in the Fourth Century*, Oxford University Press 1963

Simon, M., *La Civilisation de l'Antiquité et le Christianisme*, Paris 1972 (fine illustrations)

DOCUMENTS

Bindley, T.H. (ed.), *The Oecumenical Documents of the Faith*, revised W.Green, Methuen [4]1950

Meer, F.van der, and Mohrmann, C., *Atlas of the Early Chrisitan World*, Nelson 1958

Chronological Guide:
Events Relevant to
Church History to 461

30/3	The Crucifixion.
35	St. Stephen's martyrdom and conversion of St. Paul.
47–9	St. Paul's first missionary journey.
49	The Council of Jerusalem.
49–62	St. Paul's letters to the Churches.
50–8	Further Pauline missionary journeys.
60	St. Paul in Rome.
63(?)	St. Peter's mission to Rome (?).
64	The great fire at Rome and the Neronian persecution. Deaths of SS. Peter and Paul (?)
66–73	The first Jewish war.
70	The fall of Jerusalem to Titus.
70–90	Pastoral and Catholic Epistles.
81	Accession of Domitian to imperial throne.
95	Action by Domitian against aristocratic Christians in Rome, followed by a persecution in Asia.
circa 95	The Revelation of St. John the Divine and Johannine letters.
96	Murder of Domitian, September; succeeded by Nerva and relaxation of measures against Christians and Jews.
98	Death of Nerva and the accession of Trajan as Emperor.
circa 100	*1 Clement*.
circa 107	Ignatius's Seven Letters.
108	Polycarp's letter to the Philippians.
112–13	Pliny in Bithynia.
115	The Jewish Revolt in Mesopotamia, Cyrenaica, Egypt and Cyprus.
117	Hadrian succeeds Trajan as Emperor.
124	Hadrian's rescript to Minucius Fundanus, governor of Asia, concerning the Christians.
132–5	The second Jewish war.
138	Antoninus Pius, Emperor.
133–60	Activities of Basilides and Valentinus at Alexandria.
circa 150	Valentinus in Rome.
144	Marcion expelled from the Roman community.
150	Justin Martyr's *First Apology*.
154–5	Polycarp in Rome. His discussion on the date of Easter with Bishop Anicetus.

243

161	Death of Antoninus Pius: succeeded by Marcus Aurelius.
165	Execution of Justin Martyr at Rome.
circa 165	Martyrdom on Polycarp at Smyrna.
circa 165	Lucian of Samosata's satire on "The Death of Peregrinus."
166–75	Germanic barbarian threat to Roman frontiers.
172	Outbreak of the Montanist movement in Phrygia.
175–7	More martyrdoms in Asia Minor. *Apology* of Melito of Sardes.
177	*Apology* of Athenagoras.
177	Martyrdoms at Lyons, 1 August.
circa 178	Celsus writes against the Christians.
circa 178	Irenaeus becomes Bishop of Lyons.
180	Death of Marcus Aurelius and accession of his son Commodus.
circa 180	Founding of the Catechetical School at Alexandria by Pantaenus.
180	Martyrdom of the Scillitans in North Africa. First appearance of the North African Church.
183	Execution of Apollonius at Rome.
circa 185	Irenaeus's five books *Against the Heresies*.
186	Birth of Origen.
189	Victor, the first Latin-speaking Bishop of Rome.
189	Election of Demetrius as Bishop of Alexandria. Rules forty-three years.
190	Serapion, Bishop of Antioch.
192	Murder of Commodus 31 December. Period of uncertainty and civil war until Septimius Severus becomes sole Emperor in 197. Severan dynasty lasts until 235.
190–200	Clement of Alexandria.
circa 195	The Easter Controversy in Rome.
197	Tertullian writes his *Apology*.
200–10	The Monarchian controversies in Rome.
202–3	Persecution aimed at Christian proselytes. Death of Leonides at Alexandria. Origen head of Catechetical School. Martyrdom of Perpetua and Felicitas at Carthage.
207	Tertullian becomes a Montanist.
212	The Constitutio Antoniniana confers Roman citizenship on nearly all free men in the Empire.
213	Tertullian's *Adversus Praxean*.
circa 215	The salon of Julia Domna.
217	The Roman bishop's edict relaxing some aspects of Church discipline. Controversy with Hippolytus of Rome and Tertullian.
circa 218	Origen visits Rome.
222–35	Reign of Alexander Severus. Period of security and toleration for the Church.
220–9	Origen's first period of literary activity. Beginning of the Hexapla, the *De Principiis* and *Commentary on John*.
229–31	Origen leaves Alexandria, is ordained to the priesthood in Palestine. His breach with Demetrius and exile to Caesarea.
232	Origen visits Julia Mammaea at Antioch.
232	Construction of the Christian Church at Dura-Europos.
235	Revolution by Maximin Thrax overthrows Severan dynasty.
235	Persecution directed against the Christian leaders. Origen writes the *Exhortation to Martyrdom*.

238–49	Reigns of the Gordians and Philip provide another period of peace for the Church.
242	Mani begins his preaching in Persia.
243	Beginning of the missionary activity of Gregory the Wonderworker in Cappadocia and Pontus.
circa 245	Conversion of Cyprian of Carthage.
circa 245	Novatian's *De Trinitate*.
247	Secular games celebrate 1,000 years of Rome.
248	Anti-Christian riot in Alexandria.
248	Cyprian becomes Bishop of Carthage.
249	Decius becomes Emperor.
249–50	General persecution against the Christians.
251	Cyprian's *De Unitate Ecclesiae Catholicae* against the Novatianists in Rome. Holds council in Cathage (April) to deal with the problem of the lapsed. Death of Decius (June).
253/4	Death of Origen at Tyre.
255–6	The Baptismal Controversy in Carthage. Cyprian's Seventh Council, 1 September 256.
257	Persecution by Valerian. Attack on clergy and corporate life of the Church, followed by (August 258) the executions of Christian leaders such as Bishop Xystus of Rome and Cyprian of Carthage.
259–64	Dionysius of Alexandria controverts Chiliasts and Sabellians. Controversy between Dionysius of Rome and Dionysius of Alexandria.
260	Capture and death of Valerian at the hands of the Persians.
260/1	Gallienus's rescript of toleration.
268	Condemnation of Paul of Samosata.
270–5	Reign of Aurelian. Restoration of the frontiers of the Empire.
270–300	Steady conquest of rural Egypt, Syria and North Africa by Christianity.
284	Accession of Diocletian as Augustus, 17 September.
286	Diocletian chooses Maximian as co-Augustus, 1 April.
292	Galerius and Constantius, Caesars.
296–7	Galerius's Persian campaign.
298	Beginning of repressive measures against the Christians.
303	Beginning of the Great Persecution, 23 February.
304	The "Fourth Edict" of Persecution.
305	Diocletian and Maximian abdicate, 1 May. Cessation of persecution in the West.
309(?)	Council of Elvira.
311	Death of Galerius, 5 May.
312	Constantine's victory at the Milvin Bridge, 28 October, ends the era of persecution.
313	"The Edict of Milan," February. Proclaimed in Nicomedia by Licinius, 13 June.
313	Constantine intervenes in the dispute between Caecilian and his opponents.
314	The Council of Arles, 1 August.
316	Caecilian declared innocent of charges brought by Donatus and his colleagues against him, November.
318	Beginnings of the Arian controversy.

324	Constantine defeats Licinius at Chrysopolis, 18 September, and becomes sole ruler of the Roman world.
325	The Council of Nicaea, May–June.
326	The judicial murders of Crispus and Fausta.
328	Athanasius elected Bishop of Alexandria, June.
330	Constantinople becomes Constantine's capital.
335	The Council of Tyre. Condemnation of Athanasius, August.
335	Council of Jerusalem, September. Exile of Athanasius to Trier, October.
337	Death of Constantine, 22 May.
339	Death of Eusebius of Caesarea.
340	Constans defeats Constantine II and becomes sole ruler of the West.
341	The Dedication Council at Antioch.
342 or 343	The Council of Serdica.
346	Death of Pachomius. Athanasius returns from second exile.
350–3	Civil war in Empire from which Constantius II emerges as supreme ruler of Roman world.
355	Death of Donatus of Carthage in exile.
356	Death of Antony. Athanasius again exiled.
357–9	Synods of Sirmium.
359–60	Synods of Ariminum-Seleucia.
361–3	Reign of Julian. Pagan reaction. Return of Athanasius. Donatist triumph in Africa.
364	Valentinian I Emperor in the West. Valens Emperor in the East.
366–84	Pontificate of Damasus I.
370	Basil becomes Bishop of Neo-Caesarea (dies 379).
373	Death of Athanasius: Ambrose becomes Bishop of Milan, 7 December.
375	Beginnings of the Apollinarian controversy.
378	Battle of Adrianople and death of Valens, 9 August.
379	Theodosius Emperor in the East, January.
380	Edict of Theodosius against Arianism, 28 February. Council of Saragossa condemns Priscillianism.
381	Second Ecumenical Council, summer. Council of Aquileia, September. Condemnation of the Western Arians.
383	Death of Ulfilas, evangelizer of the Goths.
384	Altar of Victory controversy.
circa 385	Jerome leaves Italy for Bethlehem.
386–7	Conversion and baptism of St. Augustine at Milan.
388	Civil war resulting in victory of Theodosius over Magnus Maximus, 28 July.
390	The Massacre of Thessalonica. Ambrose's intervention.
391	Death of Parmenian Donatist Bishop of Carthage and his Catholic rival Genethlius.
392	Theodosius's antiheretical law.
395	Death of Theodosius, 17 January. Arcadius Emperor in the East; Honorius in the West. Augustine Bishop of Hippo.
396–7	Augustine's *Confessions*.
397	Death of Ambrose, 6 April.
398	Gildo's revolt in Africa. Crushed, end July. John Chrysostom becomes Bishop of Constantinople, 26 February.

403–4	Theophilus of Alexandria's intervention in Constantinople. Synod of the Oak. Exile of John Chrysostom, 20 June.
408	Death of Arcadius, 1 May. Accession of Theodosius II as Emperor in the East. Murder of Stilicho, Honorius's chief minister.
410	Sack of Rome by Alaric, 24 August.
411	Conference of Carthage. Condemnation of the Donatists, May–June. Pelagius and Celestius in North Africa. Augustine begins the *De Civitate Dei.*
413	Augustine's *De Spiritu et Littera.* Beginning of the Pelagian controversy.
415	Synod of Jerusalem: Augustine's *De Trinitate.*
417–18	Fiasco of Pope Zosimus's pontificate.
418 and 419	Important Catholic councils at Carthage. Pelagius condemned.
418	Visigothic occupation of Aquitaine.
423	Death of Honorius, 15 August.
426–9	Rivalry between Count Boniface and Aetius. Boniface appeals to the Vandals for help.
428	Nestorius elected Patriarch of Constantinople, 10 April.
429	Vandals invade Africa, May.
430	Death of St. Augustine, 28 August, during the siege of Hippo.
431	Council of Ephesus. Deposition of Nestorius.
432	Patrick's mission to Ireland begins.
433	Formula of Union between Cyril of Alexandria and John of Antioch.
439	Fall of Carthage to the Vandals, 19 October.
440	Leo becomes Pope, 29 September.
444	Death of Cyril; succeeded by Dioscoros.
448	Eutyches the archimandrite condemned at Constantinople, November.
449	Second Council of Ephesus (the "Robber Council"), August.
450	Death of Theodosius II, 28 July.
451	Council of Chalcedon, October. Dioscoros condemned. Beginning of the Monophysite Schism.
451–3	Huns menace Western Europe.
455	Fall of Rome to Gaiseric.
457	Murder of Proterius, Chalcedonian Patriarch of Alexandria, 28 March.
461	Death of Pope Leo.

Notes

INTRODUCTION

1. Tacitus, *Histories*, v. 9, "Sub Tiberio quies."

CHAPTER ONE

1. *O.G.I.*, 458, lines 40–52.

2. *Fasti*, i. 609, "Sancta vocant augusta patres."

3. *Dio Cassius* (ed. and tr. E. Cary), liii, 16. 8.

4. L. R. Taylor, *The Divinity of the Roman Emperor*, New York, 1931, 193.

5. F. de Visscher, *Les édits d' Auguste découverts à Cyrène*, Louvain, 1940, p. 76.

6. Aristides of Smyrna, *Panegyric on Rome* (Oratio xxvi, 70 ed. B. Keil, Berlin, 1898, ii, 111).

7. *Adversus Haereses*, IV. 30. 3.

8. See my article, "A Note on the Influence of Greek Immigrants on the Spread of Christianity in the West," *Mullus (Festschrift Th. Klauser)*, Bonn, 1964, 125–30.

9. R. E. M. Wheeler, *Rome Beyond the Imperial Frontiers*, London, 1954, 145 ff. The first-century Roman trading post at Arikamedu just south of Pondicherry.

10. See M. P. Charlesworth's summary, *The Roman Empire*, Home University Library, 1951, ch. vii.

11. In 79, observing the eruption of Vesuvius.

12. Seneca, *De Consolatione, ad Marciam* (ed. J. W. Basore), 18. 3.

13. Wis. 2:6–9; 1 Cor. 15:32.

14. One example of such a grave memorial may be cited, *CIL*, vi. 3, 17958a (Rome, translation from J. M. C. Toynbee and J. Ward Perkins, *The Shrine of St. Peter*, London, 1956, 58.) "Tibur is my native place, Flavius Agricola my name. Yes, I'm the one you see reclining here, just as I did all the years of life fate granted me, taking good care of my little self and never going short of wine. Primitiva, my darling wife, passed away before me, a Flavian too, chaste worshipper of Isis, attentive to my needs and graced with every beauty. Thirty blissful years we spent together; for my comfort, she left me the fruit of her body, Aurelius Primitivus, to tend my house (or tomb?) with dutiful affection; and so, herself released from care she has a dwelling-place for me for aye. Friends who read this, do my bidding. Mix the wine, drink deep, wreathed with flowers, and do not refuse to pretty girls the sweets of love. When death comes, earth and fire devour everything." Probably second century A.D., and an excel-

lent summary of a religious outlook which combined family affection, optimistic materialism and adhesion to the mystery religion of Isis.

15. For instance, *Justin, 1 Apol.*, 14, and Athenagoras, *Plea Regarding Christians*, 11 and 12.

16. Tertullian, *Apol.*, 32. 1.

17. Rabbi Haninah, *The Wisdom of the Fathers* (ed. J. Goldin, Yale University Press, 1955), iii. 2. "Do thou pray for the welfare of the empire, for were it not for the fear it inspires, every man would swallow his neighbour alive." (Mid-first century A.D.)

18. Polybius, vi. 56. 6. See F. Walbank's *Commentary on Polybius*, Oxford, 1957, 1. 741–2.

19. Celsus, cited by Origen, *Contra Celsum* (ed. H. Chadwick), viii. 67. See M. P. Charlesworth, "Providentia and Aeternitas," *Harvard Theological Review*, 29, 1936, 107–22.

20. *Papyrus Giessen*, 40 (preamble). See S. N. Miller, *Cambridge Ancient History*, xii, 45.

21. *Meditations*, iv. 22.

22. Ibid., iv. 19.

23. Ibid., vi. 22.

24. Ibid., vi. 33.

25. *Dialogue with Trypho* (ed. A. Lukyn Williams), 2. 3.

26. Apuleius, *Metamorphoses*, xi, 23. Cited from A. D. Nock, *Conversion*, Oxford, 1933, 145.

27. Livy, XXXIX, 8–18.

28. Ibid., XXXIX, 16. 6.

CHAPTER TWO

1. Cited from A. H. Silver, *A History of Messianic Expectations in Israel*, New York, 1927, 28.

2. Hecataeus of Abdera, cited from S. Reinach's *Textes d'auteurs Grecs et Romains relatifs au Judaisme*, Paris, 1895, 19.

3. 1 Mac. 8:11.

4. The case is argued cogently by A. Dupont-Sommer in his *Aperçus préliminaires sur les Manuscripts de la Mer Morte*, Paris, 1950, 105–17 and accepted in F. M. Cross's brilliant study, *The Ancient Library of Qumrân*, London, 1958.

5. Qumran document, I.Q.S. v. 9 (ed. Dupont-Sommer, *Essene Writings from Qumrân*, 83).

6. Ibid.

7. F. M. Cross, op. cit., 147.

8. Ibid.

9. Josephus, *Antiquities* (ed. R. Marcus, Loeb Library) xii. 4. 150.

10. Josephus, *Wars* (ed. H. St. J. Thackeray), vii. 3. 45.

11. Philo, *In Flaccum* (ed. F. H. Colson, Loeb Library), 43 and 55, see H. I. Bell, *The Jews and Christians in Egypt*, Oxford, 1924, 10–11.

12. *In Flaccum* 46.

13. Acts 13:50.

14. Acts 19:31.

15. See W. M. Ramsay, *Cities and Bishoprics of Phrygia*, Oxford, 1895, chap. xv.

16. Cicero, *Pro Flacco*, 28. 67–8.

17. See E. Kitzinger, "A Survey of the Town of Stobi," *Dumbarton Oaks Papers*, iii, 1946, 141 pp.

18. Origen, *Letter of Africanus*, 9, written circa A.D. 240.

19. Eusebius, *H.E.*, v. 16. 10.

20. Josephus, *Wars*, vii. 3. 45.

21. Josephus, *Against Apion*, II, 28. 210.

22. See E. M. Smallwood, ed. Philo, *Legatio*, Introduction, 14 ff.

23. Josephus, *Wars*, II. 20. 560 (Damascus), II. 18. 466 (Scythopolis) III (Ascalon).

24. Valerius Maximus, 1. 3. 2. See E. N. Lane, "Sabazius and the Jews in Valerius Maximus: a re-examination," *Journal of Roman Studies*, LXIX, 1979, 35–39.

25. Cited by Josephus, *Antiquities*, xiv. 10.

26. Ibid., xiv. 10. 225–7.

27. Ibid., xiv. 10. 213–16. The name of the Roman official is uncertain.

28. *Pro Flacco*, 28. 69.

29. Horace, *Satires*, 1. 9, 67–72.

30. Josephus, *Antiquities*, xviii. 3. 5; cf. Tacitus, *Annales*, ii. 85.

31. See Philo, account, *Legatio* (ed. Smallwood), 299–305, and Josephus, *Antiquities*, xviii. 3. 55.

32. See Miss Smallwood's account of events in her edition of Philo, *Legatio* (Leiden, 1961), 14–19.

33. The story of the events is told by Philo in *In Flaccum*, 25 ff.

34. H. I. Bell, loc. cit., 1 ff.

35. H. I. Bell, loc. cit., 29.

CHAPTER THREE

1. *Legatio*, 299–302.

2. Th. Gaster, *The Scriptures of the Dead Sea Sect*, London. 1957, 27. Cites other examples.

3. *Manual of Discipline*, vi. 25 (Gaster, 61).

4. Acts 5:1–11.

5. See W. Telfer, *The Office of a Bishop*, London, 1961, ch. i, for a recent and balanced account of James.

6. A. Harnack, *Kirchenverfassung*, Berlin, 1910, 26.

7. Epiphanius, *Panarion*, xxx. 16. 7 and lxxviii. 17; Eusebius. *H. E.*, ii. 23. 4.

8. *The Gospel of Thomas* (ed. Grant and Freedman), Logion 11.

9. Mt. 16:18.

10. See W. M. Ramsay's essay on "Paul and Thecla," in *The Church in the Roman Empire Before 170*, London, 1906, ch. xvi.

11. Irenaeus, *Adversus Haereses*, v. 24. 2.

12. Suetonius, *Life of Claudius*, 25. 4.

13. *Wars*, vii. 3. 51.

14. *1 Clement*, 5.

15. *Sibyll*, ii. 678.

16. *Life of Nero*, 16. 2. "Punishment was inflicted on the Christians, a class of men given to a new (revolutionary) and malevolent superstition."

17. A. N. Sherwin White, "The Early Persecutions and Roman Law Again," *Journal of Theological Studies*, N.S. iii, 1952, 194–209, and his notable *Roman Society and Roman Law in the New Testament*, Oxford, 1963.

18. *Apologeticus* 5.

19. On this question in particular, G. E. M. de Ste Croix, "Why were the early Christians persecuted?" *Past and Present*, 26, 1963, 6–38. (A very valuable contribution.)

20. Josephus, *Antiquities*, xx. 9. 1, Eusebius, *H.E.*, ii. 23.

21. Eusebius, *H.E.*, iii. 5. 3.

22. Josephus, *Wars*, vii. 9.

CHAPTER FOUR

1. See W. M. Ramsay, *Cities and Bishoprics in Phrygia*, ii, 657 ff.

2. Above, p. 00.

3. Justin, *Dialogue with Trypho* (ed. A. Lukyn Williams), 8.

4. *Letter to Diognetus* (ed. Kirsopp Lake, *The Apostolic Fathers*, ii. Loeb Edition), 4. 6.

5. Ignatius, *To the Magnesians* (ed. Kirsopp Lake, *The Apostolic Fathers*, i, 166 ff.), 10. 3.

6. Ibid., 8. 1.

7. *Epistle of Barnabas* (ed. Kirsopp Lake, *The Apostolic Fathers*, i, 337 ff.) 4 ff., specially 13 and 14.

8. See T. C. Skeat and H. I. Bell, *Fragments of an Unknown Gospel* (London, British Museum, 1935), 16–41.

9. Rev. 2:11 and 3:9.

10. A. Fliche and V. Martin, *Histoire de l'Église*, Paris, 1948, i. 268.

11. A. Fliche and V. Martin, op. cit., i. 266–9.

12. See H. Lietzmann, *The Beginnings of the Christian Church* (Eng. to 1934), ch. 8.

13. A. A. T. Ehrhardt, *The Apostolic Succession*, London, 1953.

14. For instance, *Didaché* (ed. Kirsopp Lake, *The Apostolic Fathers*, i. 305 ff.), 15. 2.

15. See *Gospel of Thomas*, Logion 11; cf. with Matt. 16:18.

16. See W. Telfer's judicious survey, *The Office of a Bishop*, London, 1962, ch. 2, "Presbyter-bishops."

17. In the seven genuine letters of Ignatius the word *episcopos* (*episcopein*) occurs no less than fifty-five times.

18. It is later than the letters of Ignatius as one of Polycarp's purposes in writing to Philippi was to send the congregation there copies of these letters (ed. Kirsopp Lake, *The Apostolic Fathers*, i. 280 ff.), 13.

19. Polycarp, *Letter to the Philippians*, 10. 2.

20. Tacitus, *Histories*, v. 5.

21. *Satire*, viii. 96–104.

22. Dio Cassius, lxvii. 14.

23. Ibid., xviii. 1. 2.

24. Pliny, *Letter*, x. 96. 1.

25. Melito of Sardis, cited by Eusebius, *H.E.*, iv. 26.

26. *Letter to the Philippians*, 12. 3.

27. Pliny, *Letters*, x. 96. 3.

28. Pliny, *Letters*, x. 97.

29. *Letter to the Philippians*, 12. 3.

30. Pliny, *Letters*, x. 33.

31. Lucian, *On the Death of Peregrinus* (ed. Harmon, Loeb Library), 11.

32. Origen, *Contra Celsum*, 1. 1.

33. Dio Cassius, lxviii. 32. See also a useful and well documented account by A. Fuks, "The Jewish Revolt of 115–17," *Journal of Roman Studies*, li. 1961, 98–104.

34. Text of the rescript to be found in J. Stevenson, *A New Eusebius*, 16–17.

35. Published by Y. Yadin in *Illustrated London News*, Archaeological Section, 4 and 11 Nov. 1961.

36. Dio Cassius, lxix. 13–14.

37. 2 Pet. 3:4.

CHAPTER FIVE

1. *Didaché*, 8.

2. *Contra Celsum*, iii. 12 (Eng. tr., H. Chadwick).

3. R. M. Grant, *Gnosticism and Early Christianity*, Columbia-Oxford, 1959, 33 ff.

4. *Letter to Rheginos*, cited from F. L. Cross (ed.), *The Jung Codex*, 55.

5. Cited by Clement of Alexandria, *Excerpts from Theodotus*, 78. Compare with the *Gospel of Truth*, cited in F. L. Cross (ed.), *The Jung Codex*, 30.

6. Cited from Epiphanius, *Panarion*, 26.

7. Tertullian, *Against the Valentinians*, 5.

8. Irenaeus, *Adv. Haer.*, 1. 26. 1.

9. Cited from F. L. Cross, op. cit., 51–2.

10. Ibid., 59.

11. An English translation can be found in R. M. Grant (ed.), *A Gnostic Anthology*, London, 1961, 184.

12. As Grant points out, *Gnosticism and Early Christianity*, 53, perhaps connected with the twenty-nine days in a lunar month.

13. Ignatius, *To the Smyrnaeans*, 6.

14. *The Apocalypse of the Great Seth*, cited from H. C. Puech, "Les nouveaux écrits gnostiques découverts en Haut-Egypte," *Coptic Studies in Honour of W. E. Crum*, Boston, 1950, 108.

15. For instance, the followers of Basilides were described as asserting that there was no harm in eating things offered to idols, or in lightheartedly denying the faith in times of persecution. Agrippa Castor, cited in Eusebius, *H.E.*, iv. 7. 7.

16. See my article, "The Gnostic Origins of the Assumption Legend," *The Modern Churchman*, 43, 1953, 23–8.

17. See A. Harnack's account of Marcion, *History of Dogma* (Eng. tr. N. Buchanan, London, 1905), v. 1. 267–86.

18. *O.G.I.*, 608.

19. Cited by Eusebius, *H.E.*, v. 13. 7.

CHAPTER SIX

1. Recorded by Justin, *Dialogue with Trypho* (ed. A. Lukyn Williams), but in its present form written up about a quarter of a century after the event.

2. Mentioned by Celsus in Origen, *Contra Celsum*, iv. 52.

3. Eusebius, *H.E.*, v. 20. 4.

4. Ibid., iv. 15.

5. This would seem to be the meaning of the "new decrees" indignantly referred to by Melito of Sardis in the fragment of his *Apology* preserved by Eusebius, *H.E.*, iv. 26. 5 and 6.

6. I am accepting a revised date of Polycarp's martyrdom, based on Eusebius's chronology rather than the traditional 155–6.

7. Eusebius, *H.E.*, iv. 15. 5.

8. Eusebius, *H.E.*, iv. 15. 26 and 41. Here the Eusebian account of Polycarp's martyrdom is accepted as an early record, probably earlier and more reliable than that preserved in the *Acta Martyrum* printed in K. Lake (ed.), *The Apostolic Fathers* (Loeb Library), ii. 312–45.

9. Eusebius, *H.E.*, v. 1–3. A letter sent by the superiors of the churches of Lyons and Vienne to fellow Christians in Asia and Phrygia.

10. See the brilliant reconstruction of events by J. H. Oliver and R. E. A. Palmer, "Minutes of an Act of the Roman Senate," *Hesperia* 24, 1955, 320–49.

11. Where any of the accused spoke in Latin it was specially noted.

12. Eusebius, *H.E.*, v. 1. 14–15.

13. Ibid., v. 1. 47. See A. N. Sherwin-White's comments in *The New Testament and Roman Law*, pp. 69–70.

14. Lucian, *On the Death of Peregrinus* (ed. Harmon, the Loeb Library), 11–16.

15. The best English edition is that of H. Chadwick, *Origen, "Contra Celsum,"* Cambridge, 1953, which I have used for quotations in the text.

16. *Contra Celsum*, i. 1.

17. Ibid., viii. 67.

18. Ibid., viii. 73.

19. Ibid., iv. 23.

20. Ibid., iv. 56; cf. iv. 99.

21. Ibid., iv. 2. 3.

22. Ibid., ii. 63. cf. ii. 35.

23. Ibid., iv. 11, cf. vii. 22.

24. Ibid, iv. 23.

25. Ibid., iii. 55. Also iii. 50.

26. For instance, *The Letter to Diognetus* (ed. K. Lake, *The Apostolic Fathers*, ii, Loeb ed.), 2 and 3.

27. Athenagoras, *A Plea on Behalf of the Christians*, 31; compare with Minucius Felix. *Octavius*, 21. 3.

28. *Letter to Diognetus*, 6. 1.

29. *i Apol.*, 16; Also *Dialogue*, 110, 3–4.

30. Athenagoras, *Plea*, 11.

31. *i Apol.*, 23.

32. Ibid., 46, and *ii Apol.*, 13.

33. Too little is known about Irenaeus's career to make a biography possible, but J. A. Robinson's introduction to the *Demonstration* (S.P.C.K., 1920) has an interesting review and reconstruction of the known events of his life.

34. *Against the Heresies*, 1. 10. (This text is translated by C. C. Richardson among the extracts from this work contained in vol. i of the Library of Christian Classics.)

35. Eusebius, *H.E.*, iv. 22. 1–3.

36. See W. M. Ramsay, *Cities and Bishoprics*, ii. 722–3.

37. *Adv. Haer.*, iv. 26. 2, and also, iii. 3. 4.

38. *Adv. Haer.*, iii. 3. 4.

39. *H.E.*, v. 6. 1.

40. *Dialogue with Trypho*, 100.

41. *Adv. Haer.*, v. 19. 1; and also *Demonstration*, 32–4.

42. Ibid., iii. 18. 1.

43. Ibid., iv. 36. 3, 38. 1.

44. Ibid., iii. 38. 1.

45. Ibid., iii. 18. 6.

46. Eusebius, *H.E.*, v. 3. 4.

47. The Anonymous anti-Montanist writer, cited by Eusebius, *H.E.*, v. 17. 2.

48. Ibid., v. 16.

49. Ibid., v. 16. 17.

50. As shown on Montanist inscriptions from the Tembris valley in northern Phrygia in the late-3rd century. See W. M. Calder, "Philadelphia and Montanism," *Bull. of John Rylands Library*, 7, 1923, 309 ff.

51. *Adv., Haer.* iii. 11. 9 and iv. 33. 6.

52. Ibid., v. 28–32.

53. Tertullian, *De Monogamia*, 14.5 (ed. V. Buhlart, *C.S.E.L.*, LXXXVI, p. 73).

CHAPTER SEVEN

1. Text in J. Stevenson, *A New Eusebius*, pp. 144–7.

2. J. N. D. Kelly, *The Early Christian Creeds*, London, 1950, ch. ii and iii.

3. *i Apol.*, 61–2. Compare Hippolytus, *Apostolic Tradition*, 21 and 22 (Eng. text J. Stevenson, *A New Eusebius*, 155–6).

4. Taken from J. N. D. Kelly, *Early Christian Creeds*, 82. The words in brackets are not found in all MSS.

5. Eusebius, *H.E.*, vi. 12. 2–6.

6. At the end of the second century, Eusebius, *H.E.*, v. 28.

7. *Adv. Haer.*, iii. 3. 2.

8. J. M. C. Toynbee and J. Ward-Perkins, *The Shrine of St. Peter*, London, 1956, 159.

9. *H.E.*, v. 21. 1.

10. Eusebius, *H.E.*, v. 23–5.

11. Recorded in the Letter of the Council of Nicaea to the Egyptian Church, Socrates, *Hist. Eccl.*, 1. 9. 12.

12. Hippolytus, *Against Noetus*, 1 (see J. Stevenson, op. cit., 159).

13. See a useful summary of Sabellius's views and their danger to orthodoxy in Basil's *Letter*, 210 (ed. de Ferrari, Loeb Library).

14. Eusebius, *H.E.*, v. 28. 3–6.

15. His followers put up a statue to his memory which shows him as a venerable figure seated on a throne with a catalog of his works on the side. Not all these can be identified and there are surprising differences in style among those officially attributed to him. See P. Nautin's views on Hippolytus-Josephus in *Lettres et écrivains chrétiens*, ch. 9 and 10.

16. Hippolytus, *Philosophumena*, ix. 12. 16.

17. *Philosophumena*, ix. 12. 20–6.

18. *De Spectaculis*, 2.

19. *Apol.*, 39.

20. *De Oratione*, 29.

21. Ed. J. A. Robinson, *Cambridge Texts and Studies*, i. 1891.

22. *Passio Perpetuae*, 5.

23. Ibid., 14.

24. *De Spectaculis*, 25.

25. Tertullian, *De Praescriptione*, 44.

26. *De Carne Christi*, 5.

27. Ibid.

28. *Adv. Nationes*, ii. 1.

29. *De Praescriptione*, 7.

30. *Apol.*, 32. 1.

31. *Apol.*, 39.

32. *Apol.*, 50. 14.

33. *De Baptismo*, 5 and 15.

34. *De Pudicitia*, 18.

35. *Adv. Praxean*, 3 and 7.

36. *Protrept.*, 1.

37. *Stromates*, 1. 7. 3.

38. Ibid., 1. 5. 28.

39. Ibid., vi. 13.
40. Ibid., vi. 9. 71.

CHAPTER EIGHT

1. His name, "Child of Horus," suggests an Egyptian background.

2. See, for instance, Justin, i *Apol.* 29 and Hippolytus, *Philos.*, ix. 12. 11 (the eunuch-presbyter, Hyacinthus).

3. Eusebius, *H.E.*, vi. 19. 7.

4. Werner Jaeger, *Early Christianity and Greek Paideia*, Harvard, 1962, 68.

5. Eusebius, *H.E.*, vi. 19. 7.

6. Cited from the *Dialogue with Heracleides* (Eng. tr. J. E. L. Oulton and H. Chadwick, *Alexandrian Christianity*, SCM Press, 1954, 439).

7. Eusebius, *H.E.*, vi. 19. 16–19.

8. Ibid., vi. 23. 4.

9. Ibid., *H.E.*, vi. 23. 4.

10. *Comment. on St. John's Gospel*, vi. 2. 8–12.

11. Eusebius, *H.E.*, vi. 23–4.

12. Ibid., 36. 3.

13. Ibid., vi. 28.

14. His *Address to Origen* has been edited by W. Metcalfe and published in S.P.C.K. Translations of Christian Classics, London, 1920. Also, Eusebius, *H.E.*, vi. 30.

15. *Address*, 15.

16. Ibid., 7.

17. Ibid., 15.

18. Eusebius, *H.E.*, vi. 33.

19. Eusebius, *H.E.*, vi. 39. 5.

20. *Dialogue with Heracleides*, 446–8.

21. H. Lietzmann, *The Founding of the Universal Church* (Eng. tr. B. L. Woolf, London, 1950), 316.

22. Eusebius, *H.E.*, vi. 25. 12.

23. Eusebius, *H.E.*, vii. 25.

24. *Contra Celsum*, vii. 18.

25. *De Principiis*, iv. 2. 4.

26. *Comment on John*, x. 4. Other examples, *De Principiis*, iv. 3. 1. See R. M. Grant, *Earliest Lives of Jesus*, London, 1961. ch. 3.

27. *Contra Celsum*, v. 23.

28. *De Principiis*, 1, Preface, 2–7 and 10.

29. *Homily on Jeremiah*, ix. 4.

30. *Dialogue with Heracleides*, 438 (ed. and tr. H. Chadwick), and *Contra Celsum*, v. 39 and vi. 61.

31. *De Principiis*, 1. 8. 1 (tr. G. W. Butterworth, *Origen on First Principles*, 67).

32. *Dialogue with Heracleides*, 454. See also H. Leitzmann, op. cit., 314.

33. For this view see W. Jaeger, *Early Christianity and Greek Paideia*, 65–7.

34. *Contra Celsum*, ii. 30.

35. Ibid., viii. 73.

CHAPTER NINE

1. Origen, *Homily on Jeremiah*, xii. 8, and *Comment. on Matthew*, xv. 26.

2. *Adv. Nationes*, ii. 1, also *Ad Scapulam*, 2.

3. *H.E.*, vi. 36. 1.

4. Kephalaion, 154. See H. C. Puech's excellent brief account of Manichaeism *Le Manchéisme*, Paris, 1949, 63.

5. *Homily on Genesis*, x. 1. See J. Daniélou, *Origène*, Paris, 1948, 54–6.

6. *De Lapsis*, 5 and 6.

7. The best short account of Dura and its cultural and religious life is that of M. Rostovtzeff, *Dura Europos and Its Art*, Oxford, 1939.

8. *C.I.L.*, viii. 10570. See Tenney Frank's exhaustive article "The Inscriptions of the Imperial Domains of Africa," *American Journal of Philology*, 47, 1926, 55–73 and 153–70.

9. *Contra Celsum*, ii. 79.

10. Described by Bishop Dionysius to Bishop Fabius of Antioch, quoted by Eusebius, *H.E.*, vi. 41. 1–10.

11. Cyprian, *Letter* 55. 9.

12. Texts given by J. R. Knipfing, *Harvard Theological Review*, 16, 1923, 363 ff.

13. Quoted by Eusebius, *H.E.*, vi. 41. 11.

14. *De Lapsis*, 8.

15. Cyprian, *Letter* 59, 10.

16. Described in the *Acts of Pionius*, ch. 15.

17. *De Viris Illustribus*, 53.

18. Cyprian's *Letter to Donatus* written circa 245 after his conversion.

19. *Letter* 11.

20. See E. W. Benson's *Cyprian, his Life, his Times, his Work*, London, 1897, 79 ff. (Still the best account of this period.)

21. *Letter* 23.

22. Cyprian, *Letter* 27.

23. Defiance of the bishop was comparable with the sin of Korah, *Letter* 3.

24. *On the Unity of the Catholic Church*, 6.

25. *Letter* 55, 6 and 17.

26. Also *Letter* 55.

27. Cyprian, *Letter* 67.

28. *Letter* 67. 4.

29. Cited in Cyprian's *Letter* 73, 14.

30. Cyprian, *Letters* 69–74.

31. Firmilian of Cappadocia to Cyprian, published as *Letter* 75 among Cyprian's *Letters* (= *Letter* 75, para. 25).

32. Statement by Bishop Successus of Germanicana (published in Ante-Nicene Library, *The Writings of Cyprian*, ii. 200–1).

33. *Letter* 52. and compare *Letter* 62 (ransom and relief).

34. *Letters* 34, 4, and 1.

35. Eusebius, *H.E.*, vii. 10. 2–9.

36. Eusebius, *H.E.*, vii. 10. 6–9.

37. The text of neither edict has survived. The general tenor can be pieced together from Dionysius's letter to Bishop Herammon (ap. Eusebius, *H.E.*, vii. 10) and Cyprian, *Letters* 77–81.

38. See the *Acta Proconsularia of* Cyprian (Hartel, *C.S.E.L.*, iii. 3, cx–cx, iv), English translation reproduced in J. Stevenson, *A New Eusebius*, 260–3.

39. Eusebius, *H.E.*, vii. 13.

CHAPTER TEN

1. Eusebius, *H.E.*, vii. 15.

2. Ibid., viii. 1. 4 and 9. 7.

3. Ibid., vii. 30. 20. 21. Lactantius. *De Mortibus Persecutorum* (ed. Moreau), 6. 2.

4. See F. Oertel, chapter *C.A.H.* xii, "The Economic Life of the Empire," p. 266 ff.

5. Cyprian, *Ad Demetrianum*, 4.

6. Pap. Oxyrhynchus, xxi. 1477. Also *O.G.I.* 519 (244–7)

7. Eusebius, *H.E.*, vii. 31. See F. C. Burkitt's brief but succinct account in *C.A.H.* xii, 504–14, as well as his *The Religion of the Manichees*, Cambridge, 1925.

8. *C.I.L.*, viii. 20435.

9. Ibid., 20478.

10. Gregory of Nyssa, "Life of Gregory Thaumaturgus," *P.G.* 46, col. 945.

11. Published by W. M. Calder, "Philadelphia and Montanism" (*Bulletin of John Rylands Library*, vii. 1923), 309 ff.

12. *Monumenta antiqua Minoris Asiae*, vii. 305.

13. Alexander of Lycopolis, *De Placitis Manichaeorum*, *P.G.* 18, 411.

14. Athanasius, *Life of St. Antony*, 46.

15. Council of Elvira (ed. Hefele-Leclercq), Canons 2 and 3.

16. *Apol.*, 39.

17. Council of Nicaea, Canon 6. Their privileges were referred to as "ancient custom," for the special status of Jerusalem, Canon 7.

18. Optatus of Milevis, *De Schismate Donatistarum* 1. 17.

19. Eusebius, *H.E.*, vi. 43.

20. Ibid., vii. 25.

21. Optatus of Milevis, op. cit., 1. 16.

22. Eusebius, *H.E.*, vii. 6. The ecclesiastical jargon used by the Cyrenaicans is given by Epiphanius of Salamis, *Panarion*, chap. 57.

23. Dionysius of Rome's letter of the Church of Alexandria, cited by Athanasius, "On the Decrees of the Council of Nicaea," 26 (See J. Stevenson, op. cit., 268–9 for Eng. tr.).

24. See J. F. Bethune-Baker's chapter on the correspondence of the two Dionysii in his *Early History of Christian Doctrine*, ch. viii.

25. Eusebius, *H.E.*, vii. 30. 6–16, for an hostile description of Paul.

26. The salient facts relating to Paul's beliefs will be found in J. Stevenson, op. cit., 277–9.

27. See G. L. Prestige's explanation in *God in Patristic Thought*, 202.

28. *H.E.*, viii. 1. 7.

CHAPTER ELEVEN

1. The English text is given in J. Stevenson, op. cit., 282–3. The date is almost certainly 297.

2. For a summary of his attack, see P. de Labriolle, *La Réaction païenne*, 223 ff.

3. The tradition recorded by Eusebius, *Life of Constantine* ii. 50; Lactantius, *On the Deaths of the Persecutors*, 11. 8 is not so specific.

4. Lactantius, op. cit., 12–13 (ed. J. Moreau, Lactance, *De la Mort des Pérsecuteurs*, Sources Chrétiennes, 39) Eusebius, *H.E.*, viii. 4–5.

5. Lactantius comments on the surprise and indignation which greeted the appointments, op. cit., 19.

6. Augustine, *Letter* 88. 2.

7. *Acta Sanctae Crispinae* (ed. Knopf and Krüger), 110.

8. *Acta Saturnini*, 16 (*P.L.* viii, col. 701).

9. See A. H. M. Jones's account of Constantine at this period, *Constantine and the Conversion of Europe*, London 1948, 58.

10. *Panegyrici Latini* 6 (7) 21. 3–6 (Eng. tr. J. Stevenson, op. cit. 297–8).

11. *C.I.L.*, iii, 13132 (Stevenson, 297). Maximin was senior Augustus at this period.

12. *H.E.*, viii. 10.

13. Lactantius, *De Mortibus*, 46.

14. Text, Lactantius, *De Mortibus*, 48, 2–12. Eng. tr., J. Stevenson, op. cit., 300–2.

15. These points are made by Lactantius, *Divine Institutes*, v. 22.

CHAPTER TWELVE

1. *Acta Saturnini* 17, *P.L.* viii. 700–1.

2. Augustine, *Breviculus Collationis cum Donatistis* iii. 13–25, *P.L.* xliii. 638.

3. The record of events is preserved in a document known as the *Gesta apud Zenophilum*, printed as Appendix i of Optatus of Milevis *C.S.E.L.* 26, 186 ff.).

4. Cf. Augustine, *Contra Cresconium*, iii. 27. 30 (*P.L.* xliii. col. 510).

5. Optatus, *De Schismate Donatistarum*, 1. 17.

6. Ibid., 1. 19.

7. The whole incident is related by Anulinus in his report to Constantine, which is reproduced by Augustine, *Letter* 88. 2. Also, for the text of the petition, Optatus, *De Schismate*, 1. 22.

8. Cf. Augustine, *Contra Cresconium*, iii. 56. 62 (*P.L.* xliii. 529).

9. Optatus of Milevis, *De Schismate*, iii. 3. See my description, *The Donatist Church*, 165.

10. Augustine, *Contra Epistolam Parmeniani*, ii. 2. 5. "Si verba dant Christo, cor autem Donato."

11. Optatus, *De Schismate*, 1. 23. This of course would mean that nearly all the Donatist appointments became invalid.

12. Cited by Eusebius, *H.E.*, x. 5. 21–2.

13. Council of Arles, Canon 9. Text in J. Stevenson, *A New Eusebius*, 321–5.

14. The letter *Aeterna et religiosa* to be found in App. iv of Optatus of Milevis, *De Schismate* (Ziwsa, 208–10). Rejected by me, *The Donatist Church*, 152–3, but accepted by H. Chadwick, *Journal Eccl. Hist.* v, 1954, 104.

15. *Acta Purgationis Felicis* = Optatus of Milevis, App. ii, Eng. tr., J. Stevenson, op. cit., 325–6.

16. Constantine's letter to the Donatist bishops—App. vi in Optatus, op. cit.

17. For the details and chronology of this stage of the dispute, see N. H. Baynes's Constantine the Great and the Christian Church (*Proceedings of the British Academy*, xv, 1929) 15–16.

18. Letter to Domitius Celsus, preserved in Optatus of Milevis, App. vii (Ziwsa, 210–11).

19. Augustine, *Contra Cresonium*, iii. 71. 82.

20. Augustine, *Letter* 105. 9. "Legem contra partem Donati dedit severissimam." The text has not survived.

21. Indicated in an interesting document, *Sermo de Passione Donati*, *P.L.* viii. 752–8. Imperial money and gifts had been used amply to undermine the faithful.

22. *Gesta apud Zenophilum*, Ziwsa, 185–97.

23. The question was the interminable issue of rebaptism. Donatus was obliged to accept a more liberal interpretation of Cyprian's doctrine from colleagues intent on uniting all Africa under the Donatist flag. Augustine, *Letter* 93. 43.

24. The story is told in Epiphanius of Salamis *Panarion*, written circa 375. Epiphanius was, however, well briefed on the affair by Egyptian bishops.

25. Text to be found in M. J. Routh, *Reliquiae Sacrae* (Oxford, 1815) iii. 321–43.

26. Letter of Peter of Alexandria to his flock 306–11. Text in M. J. Routh, op. cit., iv. 84. Eng. tr., J. Stevenson, op. cit., 293.

27. Sozomen, *Hist. Eccl.*, 1. 15. 2

28. See Dr. H. S. Carpenter's interesting "Popular Christianity and the Theologians in the Early Centuries," *J.T.S.*, N.S. xiv, 1963, 294–311.

29. There had been Manichaean missionaries in Egypt since the 270s.

30. See articles by M. F. Wiles, "In Defence of Arius," *J.T.S.*, N. S. xiii, 1962, 339–47 and G. C. Stead, "The Platonism of Arius," *J.T.S.*, N.S. xv, 1964, 16–31.

31. Athanasius, *On the Synods of Ariminum and Selevcia*, 16. Eng. text, J. Stevenson, op. cit., 346–7

32. Athanasius, *Speech Against the Arians*, 1. 5 (*P.G.* xxvi, 21 C). For other extracts of Arius's *Thalia* emphasizing the subordination of the Son of the Father, see J. Stevenson, op. cit. 350–2.

33. Eusebius, *H.E.*, x. 8. 10–15, and *Life of Constantine*, 1. 51 and 53.

34. *Codex Theod.*, ii. 8. 1.

35. Published by J. M. C. Toynbee and J. Ward-Perkins, *The Shrine of St. Peter*, Pl. 32.

36. Eusebius, *Life of Constantine*, ii. 56.

37. Ibid., ii. 64–72 (Eng. tr. J. Stevenson, op. cit., 352–4).

38. For the text see J. Stevenson, op. cit., 354–9. Discussion, see J. N. D. Kelly, *Early Christian Creeds*, 210–11.

39. Socrates, *H.E.*, 1. 23.

40. See J. N. D. Kelly's reconstruction of events, op. cit., p. 211–30.

41. Constantine's responsibility seems clear from Eusebius of Caesarea's account of the proceedings, Socrates *H.E.*, 1. 8. 1–11 in para. 4.

42. See W. Bright's *Canons of the First Four General Councils*, 2nd ed., pp. ix–xv and 1–89, and J. Stevenson's analysis, op. cit., 358–64.

CHAPTER THIRTEEN

1. Socrates, *Hist. Eccl.*, 1. 9.

2. Athanasius, *Defence Against the Arians*, 6.

3. See E. R. Hardy, *Christian Egypt*, 53. On the Meletian document of this period, H. I. Bell, *Jews and Christians in Egypt*, Part ii.

4. Socrates, *Hist. Eccl.*, 1. 29.

5. Zosimus, *Historia Nova*, ii. 29. Also Julian, *De Caesaribus*, 336 (ed. W. C. Wright, 412).

6. Eusebius, *Life of Constantine*, iv. 8.

7. For some of the privileges granted by Constantius to the Church, Sozomen, *Hist. Eccl.*, v. 5.

8. Athanasius, *Defence Against the Arians*, 87.

9. Eusebius, *Theophania*, iv. 7.

10. Julius, *Letter to the Antiochenes, P.L.*, viii. 879–906, specially chaps. ix–xiii.

11. Ibid. chap. xiv.

12. See J. N. D. Kelly, *Creeds*, 263–74.

13. On this council, Kelly, op. cit., 275 ff., and H. Hess, *The Canons of the Council of Serdica*, Oxford, 1958.

14. The point recognized by the historian Socrates a century later. Of the situation after Serdica, he wrote, "From that time therefore the Western Church

was severed from the Eastern, and the boundary of communion between them was the mountain called Soticis which divides the Thracians from the Illyrians." (*Hist. Eccl.*, ii. 22, representing the situation, circa A.D. 440).

15. Details H. M. Gwatkin, *Studies of Arianism*, 130; Kelly, op. cit., 280–2.

16. Athanasius, *History of the Arians*, ii. 44; see S. L. Greenslade, *Church and State from Constantine to Theodosius*, London, 1954, 45.

17. Hilary of Poitiers, *On the Synods*, 10. Eng. tr. of text J. N. D. Kelly, op. cit., 285–6.

18. Hilary, *On the Synods*, 10, *P.L.*, x, 486.

19. Jerome, *Chronicle* for the year 352.

20. Athanasius, *Defence Against the Arians*, 89.

21. Sozomen, *Hist. Eccl.* iv. 17. 1.

22. Kelly, op. cit., 288–9.

CHAPTER FOURTEEN

1. Julian, *Beard-Hater (Misopogon)* (ed. W. C. Wright), 353B; also 352C.

2. *Letter* 38.

3. See T. R. Glover, *Life and Letters*, 52. For his admiration of Libanius, *Letter* 53.

4. Ammianus Marcellinus (ed. J. C. Rolfe), xxi. 10. 8.

5. Julian, *The Caesars* (ed. W. C. Wright), 335–6.

6. Julian, *Letter to Photinus*, No. 55.

7. *Letter* 19 (Wright, p. 53).

8. Gregory of Nazianze, *Oratio*, v. 23 (*P.G.* xxxv, 692B and C). Compare Socrates, *Hist. Eccl.*, iii. 23. 18.

9. Ammianus Marcellinus, xxi. 2. 4–5.

10. Ammianus Marcellinus, xxii, 3–4.

11. Ammianus Marcellinus, xxii, 5. 4.

12. *Oratio*, iv. 75 (*P.G.* xxxv, *P.G.* 600C).

13. *Codex Theod.*, xiii. 3. 5.

14. Ammianus Marcellinus, xxii. 10. 7.

15. *Letter* 22. Also Gregory of Nazianze, *Oratio iii against Julian* regarding Julian's social program in Asia.

16. *Letter* 22.

17. Julian, *The Beard-Hater*, 362C.

18. Ibid., 357C and D.

19. Ibid., 346B.

20. Ibid., 338C.

21. Ibid., 340B.

22. In 360 Meletius had been translated to Antioch. His opening sermon had proved too Nicene for Constantius's liking and he was exiled. He was also to be exiled by Valens, but even this did not make him orthodox enough for the Paulinist diehards.

23. *Letter* 47 to the Alexandrians. Also 46 to Ecdicius the Prefect of Egypt.

24. Sozomen, *Hist. Eccl.*, v. 15.

25. Optatus, *On the Donatist Schism*, ii. 17.

CHAPTER FIFTEEN

1. *Historia Acephala* (Eng. tr. Library of Nicene Fathers, Athanasius p. 496), 12. This is an Alexandrian work dated to about 367–8.

2. Sozomen, *Hist. Eccl.*, vi. 6. 2.

3. Cf. *Codex Theod.*, xvi. 2. 20 addressed to Damasus forbidding priests in Rome to visit houses of widows and orphans in search of bequests.

4. *Letter* 22. 16.

5. *Letter* 210 (ed. de Ferrari, iii. 201), "Sabellianism is Judaism which is being imported under the appearance of Christianity into the preaching of the Gospel."

6. *Letter* 236, to Amphilochius.

7. Gregory of Nazianze, *Poem concerning His Life,* 439–46, *P.G.* 37, 1059.

8. Gregory of Nyssa, *On the Deity of the Son and the Holy Spirit, P.G.* 46, col. 557.

9. *Codex Theod.,* xvi. 1. 2.

10. Socrates, *H.E.,* v. 6. 6.

11. Socrates, *H.E.,* v. 7, Sozomen, *H.E.,* vii. 5. See also the Arian historian Philostorgius, ix. 19.

12. *Codex Theod.,* xvi. 5 .6. For this period, see in particular, N. Q. King, *Theodosius and the Establishment of Christianity,* London, 1961, 28–36.

13. Socrates, *H.E.,* v. 8.

CHAPTER SIXTEEN

1. *Expositio in Ps.* 118, 22. 10, *P.L.* xv, 1514D.

2. *In Hexaem,* vi. 2. 7–8, *P.L.* xiv. 244–5.

3. See F. Homes Dudden, *St. Ambrose, His Life, His Times,* Oxford, 1936, 113 n. 5.

4. Ammianus Marcellinus, xxx. 9. 5.

5. Valentinian II was at this time aged four. His mother, Justina, was Valentinian I's second wife.

6. *De Fide,* ii. 139–42 (*P.L.* xvi. 588–90).

7. Ammianus Marcellinus, xxxi. 10. 8.

8. *Codex Theod.,* xvi. 5. 5. Socrates, *H.E.,* v. 2.

9. Ibid., xvi. 5. 5.

10. See also Ambrose, *De Fide,* Prologue, *P.L.* xvi. 527–30. Gratian's letter is prefixed to Ambrose's Letters. Translated by Homes Dudden, *St. Ambrose,* 192.

11. Ambrose, *Letter* 20. To be found in Kidd, *Documents Illustrative of the History of the Church,* ii, 135–43.

12. Ibid., para. 8.

13. Ibid., 19.

14. *Sermo contra Auxentium,* 16, 22, 24.

15. Ibid., 24.

16. Ibid., 35, 36.

17. See Homes Dudden. op. cit., ch. 2, xii.

18. Sulpicius Severus, *Chronicon-* ii. 50.

19. N. Q. King, op. cit., 54.

20. Account of Homes Dudden, op. cit., 356.

21. Ambrose, *Letter* 41; Kidd, *Documents,* 145–6.

22. His work is entitled "On the Falsehood of Profane Religions," and published by K. Ziegler, Teubner, Leipzig, 1907.

23. Ammianus Marcellinus, xxi. 10. 8.

24. *Codex Theod.,* xvi. 10. 12.

25. See T. R. Glover's description of Symmachus, *Life and Letters in the Fourth Century,* ch. vii, and C. N. Cochrane, *Christianity and Classical Culture,* 349–50.

26. *Letter* 17.

CHAPTER SEVENTEEN

1. 1 Mac. 2:33–8.

2. Philo, *On the Contemplative Life* (ed. Colson), ii. 11–12.

3. *H.E.*, ii. 17. 3.

4. *Didaché*, 6. 2.

5. See Eusebius, *H.E.*, iv. 21 (Correspondence of Dionysius of Corinth).

6. *Stromata*, iv. 11, and following.

7. Eusebius, *H.E.*, vi. 3. 9.

8. Palladius, *Lausiac History* (ed. and tr. W. K. Lowther Clarke, London. 1918) xi.

9. Athanasius, *Life of Anthony*, 44.

10. *Commentary on Psalm*, 83, 4, *P.G.* xxiii. 1008C.

11. Palladius, *Lausiac History*, xxi. 15.

12. Duchesne, *Early History of the Church*, ii. 390. "The hermit was a living criticism of ecclesiastical society."

13. Palladius, *Lausiac History*, xviii. 1 (Macarius of Alexandria).

14. Ibid., xxiii.

15. Ibid., xviii, also xxxii for some details of the Rule.

16. See Sozomen, *Hist. Eccl.*, vi. 33 and 34.

17. Jerome, *Letters* 16 and 17.

18. Jerome, *Letter* 17, 2, "de cavernis cellularum damnamus orbem."

19. *Codex Theod.*, xvi. 5. 7–11 (A.D. 381–3).

20. Ed. and tr. W. K. Lowther Clarke, *St. Basil the Great: A study in Monasticism*, Cambridge, 1913, also E. Amand de Mendieta (Dom Amand), *L'ascète monastique de Saint Basile*, Maredsous, 1949.

21. *Funeral Oration in Honour of his Brother*, *P.G.* 46, 812–13.

22. Optatus of Milevis, *On the Donatist Schism*, iii. 4.

23. The phrase is J. P. Brisson's, *L'Autonomisme et christianisme dans l'Afrique romaine*, Paris, 1958, 325 ff.

24. "The Discussions between Zacchaeus and Apollonius," iii. 3. (*P.L.*, xx. 1151).

25. Jerome, *Letter* 22, 13 and 38.

26. Ed. and tr. M. L. McClure and C. L. Feltoe, London, 1919.

27. Sulpicius Severus, *Vita Sanct. Martini* 13, ed. Halm, *C.S.E.L.*, 1.

CHAPTER EIGHTEEN

1. Gerald Bonner, *St. Augustine of Hippo: Life and Controversies*, SCM Press, London, 1963, 312.

2. Vincentius of Cartenna, quoted by Augustine, *Letter* 93. 6.

3. *Contra Fortunatum*, 16, *P.L.*, xlii. 118–19.

4. I have suggested this in an article, "The Gnostic and Manichaean Tradition in Roman North Africa," *Journ. Ecc. Hist.* iv. 1953, 13–26.

5. *Confessions*, vii. 9. 13. For this phase in Augustine's career, see P. Courcelle, "Les 'Confessions' de Saint Augustin dans la tradition littéraire," Paris, 1963, chap. i.

6. *Conf.*, vii. 19. 25.

7. *Conf.*, v. 13. 25.

8. *Conf.*, vi. 6. 9.

9. *Conf.*, vii. 9. 14.

10. *Conf.*, viii. 2.

11. *Conf.*, viii. 5. 12.

12. *Conf.*, viii. 6, 15.

13. *Conf.*, viii. 12. 29.

14. Details, see the author's *Donatist Church*, 172 ff. and 261 ff.

15. *Contra Ep. Parmeniani*, iii. 4, 24, *P.L.* xliii. 101.

16. Cited by Augustine, *Against the Letters of Petilian*, ii. 3. 6 and iii. 8. 9.

17. For instance, *Letters* 43 and 44.

18. *Contra Ep. Parmeniani*, 1. 10. 16, *P.L.*, xliii. 45.

19. Ibid., i. 12. 19. *P.L.* xliii, 48.

20. *Letter* 93. 5. 17.

21. *Letter* 93. 2. 5 and 173. 1; See P. R. L. Brown, "Religious Coercion in the later Roman Empire: The Case of North Africa"; *History*, xlviii, 1963, 283–305.

22. *Letter* 105. 16. For the Donatist pleas for toleration, see *Against the Letters of Petilian*, ii. 80. 177.

23. *On Various Questions*, to Simplicianus 1. 120 (*P.L.* xl. 107).

24. *Revisions*, ii. 1.

25. For Pelagius's early career see G. de Plinval's study, *Pélage*, Fribourg, 1945, 57 ff.

26. For a summary of Pelagius's and Celestius's main tenets and for the course of the controversy, see L. Duchesne, *The Early History of the Church*, iii, ch. vi, and Plinval, op. cit.

27. *Confessions*, x. 29. 40.

28. See G. Bonner, op. cit., ch. 8 and 9; and John Ferguson, *Pelagius*, Cambridge, 1956.

29. *On Marriage and Concupiscence*, ii. 15.

30. *Unfinished Work Against Julian of Eclanum*, 1. 9.

31. Ibid., iv. 46.

32. See J. Burnaby's chapter "The Order of Love" in *Amor Dei*, London, 1938, 113–79.

33. See N. H. Baynes, "The Political Aspects of St. Augustine's *De Civitate Dei*" (Historical Association Pamphlet, 104) 1936 (reprinted, 1949).

34. *Confessions*, vi. 19.

CHAPTER NINETEEN

1. For Jerome's vindictive ire against "Origenism," see his *Adversus Ioannem hereticum*, ch. 7. (*P.L.* xxiii. 360: Eng. tr. Kidd, *Documents* ii, 185–6.)

2. See Socrates, *H.E.* vi. 16 and Sozomen, *H.E.* viii. 18, for an account of the crisis.

3. *Homily on the Statues*, ii. 2.

4. Ibid., ii. 3.

5. See L. Gesché's full and illuminating account in the *Revue d'Histoire Ecclésiastique*, liv. 2, 1959, 385–425.

6. Cyril, *Paschal Homily*, viii, *P.G.* lxxvii. 568–72.

7. H. Chadwick, "Eucharist and Christology in the Nestorian Controversy," *Journ. Theol. Studies*, N.S. ii. 1951, 145–64, 153.

8. See Socrates, *H.E.*, vii. 29.

9. For some interesting examples of the Virgin replacing the martyrs in their intercessory role, see A. Grabar, *Martyrium*, Paris, 1946, 20–1.

10. Socrates, *H.E.*, vii. 32.

11. Bishop Gore's famous aphorism, "The Nestorian Christ was a fitting Saviour for Pelagian man," if unfair was not completely devoid of truth (*Church Quarterly Review* of 1883).

12. Cyril, *Letter* 10.

13. February 430, Cyril, Letter 4. (Eng. tr. Kidd, Documents ii. 251–5). This *Letter* was received with acclamation at the Council of Ephesus.

14. A friend of Augustine, a theologically minded merchant who had settled in the Eastern capital.

15. See T. H. Bindley, *Ecumenical Documents of the Faith* (ed. F. W. Green, London, 1950), 108 ff.

16. In theory, these men were "hospital attendants" in minor orders.

17. Cyril, *Letter* 24 (*P.G.* lxxvii. 137B).

18. Juvenal was permitted to consecrate bishops in the provinces of Arabia and Phoenicia, but gained no territorial patriarchate.

19. *Letter* 310 (*P.G.* lxxviii. 361).

20. Text in T. H. Bindley, *The Ecumenical Documents of the Faith*, 141-4.

CHAPTER TWENTY

1. T. G. Jalland, *The Church and the Papacy*, 256.

2. Letter to Himerius of Tarraco; Siricius, *Letter* 1. 6.

3. *Canons of a Roman Council to the Gallic Bishops* vi. *P.L.* xiii, 1193–4.

4. Op. cit., 269.

5. Jalland, op. cit., 300–1.

6. *Codex Theod.*, xvi. 2. 45.

7. My article, "The *Memoriae Apostolorum* in Roman North Africa," *Journal of Roman Studies* xxx, 1940, 31–49.

8. To be found in *P.L.* xi. 1321 (*Gesta Collationis Carthaginensis*, 1. 157).

9. Augustine, *De Baptismo contra Donatistas*, vii. 53. 102, *P.L.* xliii. 242–3. "Peter" to Augustine represents "the Church" and not Rome; see ibid., 54, 103 (*P.L.* xliii, 244).

10. To be found in *P.L.* xi. 1195–7.

11. *Sermon*, 131. 10.

12. He was said to have been a Greek-speaker. His father's name is, however, recorded as Abraham. Perhaps another indication of the close links between Jew and Christian at Rome in the early Church.

13. See the excellent account of events in L. Duchesne, op. cit., iii. 161–73.

14. The document *Optaremus*, précis in B. J. Kidd's *The Roman Primacy*, 103–5.

15. Augustine, *Letter* 209, and also *Letter* 20, bibliography in C.S.E.L., n. 3. 87, 1981.

CHAPTER TWENTY-ONE

1. I am indebted in the following outline mainly to T. G. Jalland's two works, *The Life and Times of Leo the Great*, London, 1941; and *The Church and the Papacy*, 301 ff.

2. *Sermon*, iii, 2–3 (P.L. liv. 146); cf. *Sermon*, v. 4.

3. *Sermon*, v. 2. (*P.L.* liv. 153).

4. *Letter* xvi. Preface (*P.L.* liv. 696A).

5. Valentinian III, Novel 17 directed against Hilary of Arles.

6. See R. V. Sellers, *The Council of Chalcedon*, London, 1953, 30.

7. Cited from R. V. Sellers, op. cit., 31.

8. *Codex Justinianus*, 1. 1. 3.

9. Sellers, op. cit., 56 ff. I am inclined now to a less jaundiced view of Florentius.

10. Text in T. H. Bindley, *Documents*, 168–73.

11. *Tome*, Bindley, op. cit., 173.

12. For the events, L. Duchesne, *The Early History of the Church*, iii, 286–94; and Sellers, op. cit., 78–88.

13. Bindley, op. cit., 193, lines 115–25.

14. See B. J. Kidd, *The Roman Primacy*, 147.

15. See E. L. Woodward, *Christianity and Nationalism in the Later Roman Empire*, London, 1916, 45. For the slow development of the actual schism see W. H. L. Frend, *The Monophysite Movement*, 2d ed., Cambridge, 1979. (Chapters 4 and 5.)

CHAPTER TWENTY-TWO

1. *Codex Theod.*, xvi, 2. 6.

2. *Codex Theod.*, xvi. 2. 4.

3. Basil of Caesarea, *Sermon to the Wealthy*, P.G. 31, 299.

4. *Letter* 126. For further facts and figures, A. H. M. Jones, *The Later Roman Empire*, Oxford, 1964, 895-910, and vol. iii (notes, 301-2).

5. See the list given in J. B. Bury, *History of the Later Roman Empire*, i, 354, n. 2.

6. Possidius, *Life of St. Augustine*, 23.

7. *Codex Theod.*, xvi. 2. 8.

8. *Codex Theod.*, xvi. 2. 9.

9. Sozomen, *Hist. Eccl.*, v. 5.

10. Ammianus Marcellinus, xxi. 16. 18.

11. *Codex Theod.*, xvi. 2. 15.

12. *On the Government of God*, v. 5.

13. *The Pilgrimage of Etheria* (ed. M. C. McClure and C. L. Feltoe), 49.

14. Gregory of Nazianze, Farewell Sermon to the people of Constantinople (*Sermon*, 42, 24, *P.G.* xxxvi, 486).

15. Siricius, *Letter* 1. 9–10, *P.L.* xiii. 1142–3.

16. Described in my article, "The Layman in the Church of the Roman Empire," (chap. ii, pp. 64–5, in *The Layman in Christian History*, ed. S. Neill and H. R. Weber, London, 1963).

17. Augustine, *Revisions* ii. 33 and 37.

18. Libanius, *Letter* 1057. Cited from B. J. Kidd, *Documents*, ii. 131.

19. *The Early History of the Church*, vol. iii, Preface.

Index